# Iraq since the Gulf War

## Prospects for Democracy

Edited by Fran Hazelton
for CARDRI

Zed Books Ltd

London & New Jersey

*Iraq since the Gulf War* was first published by
Zed Books Ltd, 7 Cynthia Street, London N1 9JF, UK, and
165 First Avenue, Atlantic Highlands, New Jersey 07716, USA,
in 1994.

Copyright © Fran Hazelton, 1994.

Cover designed by Andrew Corbett.
Typeset by Ray Davies.
Map by Jenny Ridley.
Printed and bound in the United Kingdom
by Biddles Ltd, Guildford and King's Lynn.

A catalogue record for this book
is available from the British Library.

US CIP data is available from the Library of Congress.

ISBN 1 85649 231 1 Hb
ISBN 1 85649 232 X Pb

# Contents

Preface                                                              vii
List of Contributors                                                 viii
**Introduction** *Fran Hazelton*                                     1

**1. Cultural Totalitarianism** *Fatima Mohsen*                      7
    Culture and politics                          7
    Saddam Husain                                 11
    Ba'thist cultural policy                      13

**2. State Terror and the Degradation of Politics** *Isam al-Khafaji*   20
    The terror network                            20
    Cousins and comrades                          23
    Uncle Saddam                                  24
    Incorporation and coercion                    26
    Divide and rule in Kurdistan                  27
    Legacy of despotism                           27
    Life after Saddam?                            
                                                                     30
**3. Ba'thist Ideology and Practice** *Zuhair al-Jaza'iri*           32
    Ideological crisis in Arab nationalism        32
    Iraqi Ba'thism                                33
    Theory and practice                           34
    Consolidating power                           35
    Pan-Arab issues                               37
    Turning point                                 38
    Patriotic Front – Ba'thization                40
    Saddam Husain                                 42
    The Leader-Symbol                             46
    Voluntarism                                   47

**4. Saddam as Hero** *Kamil Abdullah*                               52
    Voluntarist politics                          53
    Kuwait                                        53
    The Iraqi state                               53
    Political violence                            54
    The nihilistic tendency                       55

## Contents

Legitimacy · 56
The man in the street · 56
Ridicule · 58
National identity · 58
Ideological crisis · 59

5. Women: Honour, Shame and Dictatorship *Suha Omar* · 60
Women's rights strengthen the state · 61
Nuclear families · 62
Pressure at work · 63
Decrees against women · 63
Increasing the birth-rate · 64
The General Federation of Iraqi Women (GFIW) · 65
Official rape · 66
Women in Iraqi Kurdistan · 66
After the Gulf War · 68
Conclusions · 69

6. Economic Devastation, Underdevelopment and Outlook
*Abbas Alnasrawi* · 72
Impact of the Iran-Iraq war on the Iraqi economy · 72
Economic crisis and the failure of privatization policies · 74
Oil, Iraq's economic crisis and the invasion of Kuwait · 76
Economic consequences of the invasion · 77
Estimated human and economic destruction · 79
Impact on personal income and cost of living · 81
Iraq's economic prospects · 82
Oil revenue · 82
Foreign debt · 83
United Nations sanctions · 84
Conclusion · 86
Tables · 87

7. Why the Intifada Failed *Faleh 'Abd al-Jabbar* · 97
The Iran-Iraq war and the opposition · 98
Seeds of the Gulf War · 100
The exhaustion of Iraqi patriotism · 100
Exhaustion of the Army · 102
Regime fantasies, opposition blindnesss · 104
The people rise up · 105
An approximate record · 107
Disastrous slogans · 108
A different landscape · 109
The uprising that wasn't · 111

All silenced 112
Changes and prospect 114

**8. The Kurdish Parliament** *Falaq al-Din Kakai MP* 118
Free and fair elections 118
The parliament 122
Coalition 123
Council of Ministers' programme 124
Head of the national liberation movement 127
Federation 129

**9. Suppression and Survival of Iraqi Shi'is**
*Hussein al-Shahristani* 134
Najaf and Karbala' 134
Marsh Arabs 135
Surviving in the cities 136
Security forces 138
Democracy in post-Saddam Iraq 139

**10. Destruction of the Southern Marshes** *Hamid al-Bayati* 141
The Marsh Arabs 141
The *intifada* 142
Canal-building: drainage projects 143
Human rights abuses 144
Refugees 145
Oil 146
Conclusion 146

**11. Human Rights, Sanctions and Sovereignty** *Laith Kubba* 147

**12. The Opposition** *Rend Rahim Francke* 153
Survey of the opposition 155
Islamists 156
Arab Nationalists 161
Kurds 164
Communists 167
Democrats 169
Efforts at unification 171
Facing the future 175

**13. Attitudes to the West, Arabs and Fellow Iraqis** *Ayad Rahim* 178
Iraqi Attitudes to the United States and the West 178
Unfriendly neighbours 182
Kuwait 184

## Contents

Iraqis Inside 184
Iraqis Outside 187
All Iraqis 188

**14. Intolerance and Identity** *Kanan Makiya ('Samir al-Khalil')* 194
Intolerance 194
Identity 200

**15. Charter 91** *Arif Alwan* 205
Charter 91 – the Text 206

**16. Federalism** *Ali Allawi* 211
The nature of Iraq 213
Kurdish view 214
Islamist view 215
Liberal democracy 215
Visions for the future 217
Federalism – the problems 218
International responses 220
Conclusion 221

**17. The Rule of Law** *Ahmad Chalabi* 223
The Iraqi regime and Iraqi society 224
The legal system corrupted 225
Competing universalist ideologies 226
Totalitarianism and terror 226
International law flouted 227
United Nations 228
Iraqi National Congress (INC) 229
International support 230
Conclusion 231

**18. Playing by the Rules** *Dlawer Ala'Aldeen* 232
Kurdish safe haven 233
Southern Iraq 235
The opposition and the future political system 236
The Kurdish federal state as a model for Iraq 241
Conclusion 243

Chronology 244
Further Reading 253
Index 254

# Preface

*Iraq Since the Gulf War* is CARDRI's second book. Eight years have passed since publication of CARDRI's first book, *Saddam's Iraq*, but the terror regime it analysed and exposed is still in place, and continues to be the major obstacle to progress in Iraq and the region. For the first time this book makes available in English the views and ideas of opposition Iraqis, scattered across three continents, who have thought long and hard about the regime that continues to ruin their country; how the get rid of it; and how to salvage a stable future for their fellow citizens. These views and ideas need to be heeded by all who seek to prevent a tragedy even greater than that which has already befallen modern Iraq.

Ann Clwyd MP,
Chairperson of CARDRI
(Committee Against Repression and for Democratic Rights in Iraq)

# Contributors

KAMIL ABDULLAH is a postgraduate philosophy student in Belgium. He has published many articles in the Arabic press on the problems of social thought.

DR DLAWER ALA'ALDEEN is an acdemic medical microbiologist and secretary of the Kurdish Scientific and Medical Association. During the exodus of the Kurds in 1991 he undertook relief operations for the Save the Children Fund and Christian Aid. He is a member of the British Working Party on Chemical and Biological Weapons and author of *Death Clouds: Saddam Hussein's Chemical War Against the Kurds* (London 1991)

ALI ALLAWI is a development and investment banker who has been opposed to the Ba'th regime since 1968. Politically independent and a member of the general assembly of the Iraqi National Congress (INC), he lives in London.

ABBAS ALNASRAWI is professor of economics at the University of Vermont, Burlington, USA.

ARIF ALWAN is a satirical playwright, storyteller and political writer with strong anti-militarist views. He fled Iraq in the early 1970s in protest against curbs on self-expression and lived in Lebanon, Morocco and Italy before seeking political asylum in Britain.

DR HAMID AL-BAYATI is the UK representative of the Supreme Council for the Islamic Revolution in Iraq (SCIRI).

DR AHMAD CHALABI is president of the executive council of the Iraqi National Congress (INC). He spends much of his time at the INC headquarters in Iraqi Kurdistan.

REND RAHIM FRANCKE is co-founder and director of the Washington-based Iraq Foundation, a non-profit organization dedicated to democratic principles and practices in Iraq. She lectures and writes on Iraq and is a member of the general assembly of the INC.

FALEH 'ABD AL-JABBAR is a political journalist and academic specialist on modern Islamic thought. His publications include the Arabic translation of *Das Capital Vol 1-3* by Karl Marx (Progress Publishers, Beirut 1985-1989), and, in Arabic, three books on fundamentalism in the Arab world and *Nationalism and Myths in Arab Political Thought* (Saqi Books, London 1993). He left Iraq in the late 1970s and lived in Beirut, Damascus, Algiers, Prague and Kurdistan before settling as a political refugee in London.

ZUHAIR AL-JAZA'IRI is a novelist and short-story writer who has also published books on fascism. His work focuses on individual responses to Ba'th ideology and he was one of the first to identify the central role of fear in the Saddam Husain regime. Since 1979 he has lived in Beirut, Damascus, Kurdistan and Budapest. He is now settled in London as a political refugee.

FALAQ AL-DIN KAKAI is a member of the Kurdish Parliament elected in May 1992 and of the KDP politbureau. He is a prolific writer in Kurdish and Arabic. Throughout the 1980s he was a clandestine broadcaster and journalist for the Kurdish guerrilla movement. He lives in Iraqi Kurdistan, in Salah al-Din, a mountain resort close to the city of Arbil where the Parliament meets.

ISAM AL-KHAFAJI is an economist who has translated many works on economics into Arabic. He has published two books on the state and capitalist development in Iraq and edits the magazine *Jadal* (Debate) which is published in Nicosia. He left Iraq in the late 1970s and lived in Beirut and Damascus before settling in Holland.

DR LAITH KUBBA is a founder-member of the INC and broadcast widely in the US and UK as a spokesman for the Iraqi opposition following the Gulf War. He is director of public relations at the al-Khoei Foundation in London and well-known as a contributor to debates on Iraqi issues.

KANAN MAKIYA ('SAMIR AL-KHALIL') is the author of *Republic of Fear* (Berkeley and London 1989, 1990), a powerful analysis of the Iraqi regime which sold 150,000 copies after Saddam Husain invaded Kuwait. His book *The Monument* (London 1991) deals with the aesthetics of power and kitsch exemplified by the Victory Arch built in Baghdad after the Iran-Iraq war. *Cruelty and Silence* (London 1993) confronts the rhetoric of Arab and pro-Arab intellectuals with the realities of political cruelty in the Middle East, particularly Iraq. He is a fellow of the Centre for Middle Eastern Studies at Harvard University.

DR FATIMA MOHSEN is a journalist and critic who writes in the Arab press on literature, films, fine art and women's issues. After escaping from Ba'thist security police in 1979 she fled through Kurdistan and Iran to live in Budapest and Damascus before settling in London.

DR SUHA OMAR gained her doctorate in sociology from a university in the UK, where she now lives and works.

AYAD RAHIM is a journalist and the research co-ordinator of the Iraq Research and Documentation Project at the Centre for Middle Eastern Studies at Harvard University.

DR HUSSEIN AL-SHAHRISTANI was senior advisor on nuclear affairs to the Iraqi government until 1979 when he protested against Saddam Husain's tyranny and efforts to redirect the nuclear programme to military uses. He was tortured, sentenced to life imprisonment and spent ten years in solitary confinement. After freeing himself in February 1991 he established a human rights monitoring group and now, based in Tehran, maintains contacts with victims and witnesses of human rights abuses and directs humanitarian relief projects.

FRAN HAZELTON (editor) studied politics, philosophy and economics at St Hugh's College, Oxford, and the modern middle east at the School of Oriental and African Studies, London University. Formerly secretary of the Committee Against Repression and for Democratic Rights in Iraq (CARDRI) and editor of *Saddam's Iraq* (Zed Books, London 1986,1989), she was an observer at the Kurdish elections (May 1992) and a guest at Iraqi opposition conferences in Beirut (March 1991), Vienna (June 1992) and Salah al-Din (October 1992).

Translation, research and general support were provided by Saadi Abdul-Latif, Salem Ali, Rosemary Bechler, Kate Clark, Mary Cooper, Karen Dabrowska, Ben Griffith, Kate Hudson, Faleh 'Abd al-Jabbar, Ghanim Jawad, Mary Joannou, Susan Norris, Don Redding, Colleen Rogers, Gareth Smyth, Teresa Thornhill and Michael Wood. Special thanks to Marion Farouk-Sluglett and Peter Sluglett.

ANN CLWYD MP for Cynon Valley, is Shadow Employment Minister in the UK. Previously Shadow Secretary of State for National Heritage (1992-3), for Wales (September-November 1992) and for Overseas Development (1989-92), she is also a former Member of the European Parliament. Her interest in Foreign Affairs, and particularly Iraq, started while she was a journalist working for the BBC and the *Guardian*. She has chaired CARDRI since 1984.

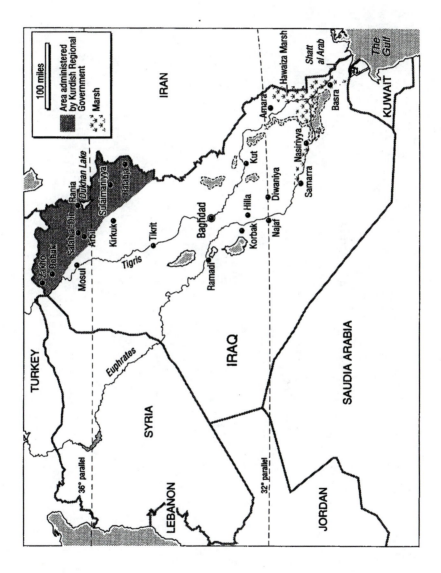

# Introduction

*Fran Hazelton*

Under Iraqi law it is a capital offence to criticize President Saddam Husain or suggest any alternative to his Ba'thist regime, which is precisely what is done by the authors of this book, all of whom are Iraqis. They write from a variety of perspectives in defiance of the campaign to control Iraqi intellectual life which the regime has ruthlessly and relentlessly conducted for more than two decades. For some of the authors their defiance has entailed imprisonment and torture.

In Iraq, intellectuals must actively praise and support Saddam Husain to secure success. They risk their lives if they make any overt attempt at free and independent thought. Those in exile persevere with oppositional writings and activities to protect their culture and support those inside who are resisting repression. The mechanics of that repression were exposed in unprecedented detail by documents seized from government buildings during the March 1991 *intifada* which followed the Gulf War. The terror network protecting the Saddam Husain dictatorship relies to a large extent on kinship and regional patterns of personal loyalty, and the republic of Iraq has lapsed into family rule. The population will find it very difficult to develop alternative state structures because many years of terror and repression have deeply impoverished their political culture.

That impoverishment is starkly illustrated by the degeneration of Ba'thism from a theory of Arab renaissance to quasi-religious one-man rule. Ba'thism developed in the 1940s with an abstract, voluntarist and mythical ethos, but incorporating constitutional and democratic principles. These were, however, never applied by Ba'thists when they staged coups d'etat, including the Iraqi Ba'thists who seized power in July 1968. This group sidelined Ba'thist commitment to Arab unity in favour of building up an Iraqi party and emphasising its leading role over the state and society. Party decisions were made equivalent to state decisions and as the state became controlled by the party, the party was controlled by its security organs, which were controlled by Saddam Husain. He took over the presidency in 1979 with a security cordon around him of close male relatives connected by ties of blood and marriage. Ba'th Party membership reached a million but there was no longer equality between members, and the party was subordinated to the leader-symbol. All citizens were deemed to be Ba'thists and the leader-symbol was said to be necessary not only for Iraq but for the Arab nation and the whole Third World.

Iraqis were said to be 'homogenous socially and psychologically', a
single 'body' in which – by the triumph of will over practical reality –
Saddam Husain became the 'mind', making decisions to be implemented
by the 'muscles'. The imposition upon a subdued population of this
voluntarism and irrationality – in which the leader symbolized naked
power and ruthless determination – created a tragic society devoid of
spontaneity. Such totalitarianism can disintegrate into tribal, ethnic or
religious allegiances, and the futility of Saddam Husain's notion of collective identity has been clearly demonstrated by the disastrous effects of
his 'heroic' adventures.

Concentration of power in the hands of one family, charismatic leadership and total disregard for democratic aspirations characterise the states
of the Arabian peninsular and Iraq alike, despite the latter's supposed
modernity. The status of Iraqi women has been much vaunted as evidence
of Iraq's modernity, but dishonouring women to attack social cohesion has
been a crucial tactic employed by the Ba'thist regime to secure political
control. In a democratic Iraq, women will have to overcome the oppression
of both distorted modernity and distorted Islam. At present their main
burden is feeding their families, because of the drastic pauperization which
has occurred in Iraq since the Gulf War.

That pauperization came on top of the economic decline which followed the 1970s boom. Iraq lost over 100 per cent of its GNP for each of
the eight years of the Iran-Iraq war. Despite a postwar privatization
programme, there were multiple economic crises of heavy foreign debt,
inflation, unemployment and conflict over oil prices. International sanctions imposed in December 1990 cut off 90 per cent of Iraq's imports and
97 per cent of its exports, leading to further disruption of the economy and
hardship for the people. The devastation of the Gulf War bombing reduced
a highly urbanized and mechanized society to a pre-industrial age and it
will take Iraq decades to recover its past rates of economic growth.

The economic crisis which followed the Iran-Iraq war precipitated the
invasion of Kuwait, which in turn precipitated the Gulf War. Iraq's defeat
in the Gulf War then precipitated the March 1991 *intifada* which was
phenomenally successful for two weeks before it was bloodily crushed. It
failed partly because the US, particularly in its bombing of retreating Iraqi
troops at the Mutla Pass, relieved Saddam Husain of the rebellious parts
of his army while preserving his loyal divisions. The slogans raised in the
south calling for Shi'i rule – which made people fearful of Iranian
domination – consolidated support for the regime, as did indiscriminate
killing of Ba'thists.

The mass exodus of Iraqi Kurds fleeing from Saddam Husain's vengeance across the border into Iran and Turkey created such a refugee problem
that the international community was moved to establish a 'safe haven' in
northern Iraq. When the Baghdad administration withdrew from three

Kurdish provinces, and negotiations between the regime and Kurdish leaders broke down, the Iraqi Kurdistan Front (IKF) assumed control of the area and called elections. The Kurdish parliament, elected in May 1992, is a fragile flower of democracy in a very hostile environment but it is a model for what could be achieved in Iraq as a whole.

In southern Iraq, where the people are predominantly Shi'i Arabs, repression has intensified since the Gulf War. Democracy is widely identified with the Western states, which are felt to have abandoned Iraqis to their fate under Saddam Husain. Many demand *hurriyya*, or freedom, as well as self-determination and respect for Islamic ideals of justice, equality and fraternity. The regime's draining of the marshes and flooding of agricultural land are human and ecological disasters aimed at securing political control and exploiting oil supplies.

Saddam Husain's troops in the marshes were ordered to 'withdraw all foodstuffs, ban the sale of fish and prohibit transport to and from the area'. This internal embargo, like that imposed on the Kurdish-administered area of northern Iraq, is added to the international sanctions which have been in force since August 1990. Maintainance of international sanctions on Iraq as a whole, without implentation of measures to bring down the Saddam Husain regime, does not make sense politically to the people of Iraq or to their relatives and friends abroad. If sanctions are to be maintained they should be accompanied by the imposition of UN human rights monitors throughout Iraq, the exemption of the Kurdish-administered area in the north and the no-fly zone in the south, the indictment of Saddam Husain for war crimes and crimes against humanity, and support for the Iraqi opposition in its attempt to overthrow the dictatorship.

The Iraqi opposition – mostly in exile – which was able to emerge from clandestinity after Saddam Husain invaded Kuwait in August 1990, consists of five main currents: Islamists, Arab nationalists, Kurds, communists and independent democrats. They all agree that the overthrow of Saddam Husain is a precondition for change and endorse the territorial integrity of Iraq. They all accept the principle of democratic elections and constitutional government and also the need for a special status for the Kurds based on a degree of self-government. Attempts at unification began with the Beirut conference in March 1991, and in June 1992 the Vienna conference inaugurated the Iraqi National Congress (INC), which now has headquarters in Iraqi Kurdistan.

The Gulf War and its aftermath deeply affected the attitudes of Iraqis to the West, to the Arab world and to each other. Most are enraged and disappointed by Palestinian sympathies for Saddam Husain, and by the antagonism and ignorance shown by western leftists, Muslims and other Arabs towards the plight of Iraqis and their recent history. Iraqis living in Iraq are desperate and cynical, aware that nobody in in the world – not the West, not the UN and certainly not Arabs – has come to their aid. It is possible for an Iraqi observer from the leftist, anti-imperialist tradition to conclude that the US army would probably be welcomed by the overwhelming majority of people in Baghdad and the rest of Iraq, if it saved them from Saddam.

The distinctive position of dissident Iraqis within the Arab intelligentsia is their condemnation of silence in the face of Middle Eastern cruelty, particularly that of Saddam Husain. They consider that breaking this silence is a moral obligation upon every Arab, more important even than the 'struggle against Israel'. They argue that silence in the face of cruelty arises from a way of looking at the world – almost always entered into with the best of intentions – which is morally bankrupt. That moral bankruptcy is the principal cause of a deep cultural malaise in the Arab world.

This understanding prompted the launch of Charter 91 by Iraqis anxious to find a mode of government which will end the vicious cycle of violence in their country. Charter 91 states that people have rights for no reason other than that they exist as individual human beings. Freedom from fear is the essential prerequisite for realizing the inherent dignity of the human person. Rebuilding civil society means elevating the principle of toleration into a new public norm soaring above all ideologies. Representative parliamentary democracy is the rule in the republic of toleration. The notion that strength resides in large standing armies and up-to-date weapons of destruction has proved bankrupt.

Federalism is a key concept for those considering the future of Iraq. All Iraq's communities, it is argued, would benefit from the dismantling of the centralized state and a devolution of power to regional units that reflect the ethnic and cultural make-up of the population. The design of a successful federal system in Iraq must, however, take into account the very serious concerns of neighbouring countries about how such a system would affect their own stability and security.

Contemporary Iraq is threatened by Sunni-Shi'i sectarianism and Arab-Kurdish bitterness. It is divided into two incompatible political systems – the fragile parliamentary democracy in three provinces of Iraqi Kurdistan and the Baghdad-based dictatorship controlling the rest of the country. The international community is involved through the imposition of two no-fly zones and sanctions. It should pursue the application of international law to Iraq, particularly in respect of Security Council Resolution (SCR) 688, and support the INC in its attempt to establish both the rule of law and a democratic political system through the removal of Saddam Husain.

Before this can happen there has to be an improvement in mutual understanding between the international community and Iraqi opposition leaders. The US administration has yet to show that it recognizes the difference between Iraqi Shi'ism and Iranian Shi'ism, and the very complex nature of their relations. The Iraqi Shi'i organizations have underestimated the power and danger of an unrivalled superpower. The Kurdish parliamentary system demonstrates the possibility and desirability of non-sectarian politics in Iraq. Despite the difficulties, democracy is the only strategic alternative to instability and war.

CHAPTER ONE

# Cultural Totalitarianism[1]

*Fatima Mohsen*

Since its foundation, modern Iraq has generally lacked stable democratic institutions within civil society. In the cultural sphere, independent publishing houses, distribution networks, newspapers, art galleries, theatres and film companies have always been thin on the ground. Whenever such cultural institutions emerged, in embryonic form, they were subject to state censorship of varying severity according to the prevalent political climate. The British-installed monarchy (1921-58) did not have a strong policy on state control of culture, but neither did it have a commitment to state education as being essential for the cultural development of the Iraqi people as a whole.

The concept of mass culture found in the socialist regimes of Eastern Europe, in which the masses were seen as an object whose consciousness could and should be manipulated by the state, was adopted by the successive regimes of republican Iraq after 1958. All these regimes came to power through coups d'état, and none of them lasted long enough to develop a thoroughgoing cultural policy until the Ba'th regime of 1968, which has survived for more than two decades.

The commodification of cultural production did not take place gradually in Iraq, as it did in some European countries, but was precipitated by the enormous increase in world oil prices in 1973, soon after the nationalization of Iraqi oil. Colossal revenue from oil then became available to the state, some of which was directed to funding the arts. But the state itself came to be identified with the personality of one man after Saddam Husain took over as president in 1979. This chapter examines the historical development of cultural policy in Iraq, and shows how both brutality and bribery have been used by the Saddam Husain regime to secure totalitarian control of Iraqi intellectual life.

## Culture and politics

The link in Iraq between culture and politics was firmly established in the 1940s and 1950s. This was a time of flowering cultural activity in many parts of the Arab world, and an interest in innovative modes of expression affected all the arts. The majority of literary and artistic figures in Iraq were sympathetic to the active Marxist or nationalist political groups in the opposition. Intellectuals had some freedom in which to manoeuvre and could participate, if they so chose, in moulding an oppositional mass consciousness. Influential daily newspapers were edited by intellectuals like the great Arab poet Muhammad Mahdi al-Jawahiri, by the president of the Democratic Party, Kamil Chadirchi, and by others of a high cultural calibre such as Husain al-Rahhal, Fahmi al-Mudarris and Ibrahim Salih Shukr. However, the government used various methods to hamper the growth of an independent cultural movement, isolating intellectuals from the public sphere by interfering with the circulation of books, prohibiting cultural imports and imposing censorship and detention. Many literary figures, among them the prominent poets Badr Shakir al-Sayyab, 'Abd al-Wahhab al-Bayati and later Sa'di Yusuf, were arrested or exiled and, some intellectuals, including Sha'ib Tu'ma Farman the distinguished novelist, lost their citizenship.

The revolutionary government of July 1958, presided over by General 'Abd al-Karim Qasim, had a programme of land reform and opposition to British rule and the multinational oil companies which won it the support of Iraqi intellectuals. But the honeymoon was shortlived. Glorification of the leader began, and the traditions of cultural hegemony and containment were quickly re-established, with publishing houses and the media becoming instruments of state propaganda. The harshest attack came in February 1963 when the Ba'thist coup overthrew Qasim, and hundreds of intellectuals were imprisoned, executed or forced into exile, their organizations banned or destroyed.

The Ba'thists were superseded by General 'Arif's regime, in which the prime minister was a liberal intellectual, 'Abd al-Rahman al-Bazzaz. Despite the government's weakness and corruption, a cultural detente prevailed between the military and the intelligensia. Some writers remained in prison and those in exile were sceptical. But there were signs of an independent cultural movement. From 1965 a number of newspapers and magazines were launched calling for democracy, freedom of expression and a normal political and cultural life.

1967, the year of Arab defeat by Israel in the June war, saw all Arab culture enter a phase of despair and revision. Polemical rejection of accepted ideas resulted in a rapprochement in which heterogeneous cultural elements came together, dedicated to innovation and modernity in art and literature. This development enhanced the position of the Left, particularly the Marxist Left, but was also a sympathetic response to the student revolution in Europe. In Iraq there was a radical literary and artistic upsurge in 1968 in which quasi-religious dogmas were abandoned and the subservience of literature to politics was widely denounced.

The second Ba'thist regime, which came to power in July 1968, sought to please intellectuals by inviting Iraqi writers in exile to return home and build a new cultural movement. But it met resistance from intellectuals who vividly remembered the bloodshed of the first Ba'thist regime (February-November 1963), in which many of their colleagues had perished. Even those who subscribed to Ba'thist ideology wanted to break with the Ba'thist past which was, for them, criminal.

As a gesture of goodwill, the Iraqi government hosted the Seventh Congress of Arab Writers in 1969. In his speech to the congress, 'Abdullah Sallum al-Samarai, the minister for culture and information, said: 'The exiled writers have returned home, political prisoners have been set free and all channels for writing and publication are now open before them. The revolution of 17 July 1968 does not boast about what it has achieved in the fields of literature, culture and art because it takes its inspiration in everything it does from its firm and basic belief in freedom and openness.'[2] However, under the subsequent minister of culture and information, Salah 'Umar al-'Ali, lists were drawn up of writers and artists who had sources of income other than their creative work.[3] The view that financially independent and politically non-aligned intellectuals posed a threat to the regime, which should be contained by their appointment to state-run cultural agencies, met with opposition within the Ba'th Party but eventually won the upper hand. The defeat of the Ba'thist faction calling for openness by those advocating an 'iron fist' policy was a portent of the coming one-party and, subsequently, one-man rule in Iraq.

The late 1960s and early 1970s were years of great tension in Iraqi cultural life. In 1966, young poets and writers founded *al-Kalima* (the Word), a literary magazine which was printed in the holy city of Najaf to escape state censorship, from which religious houses were exempt. The editor-in-chief, Hamid Matba'i, was summoned to Baghdad to be appointed to one of the state-run journals, and *al-Kalima* ceased publication. Instead, the Ministry of Culture and Information launched *Sha'r 1969* (Poetry 1969), a literary magazine which reflected a wide range of dissident ideas from the new Marxism to Existentialism. Only four issues were published before it was closed down by the authorities after Muhammad Sa'id al-Sahhaf, then director-general of radio and television, personally threatened Fadhil 'Azzawi, its assistant editor. The precarious political alliance that came into being in 1972 between the ruling Ba'thists, who could muster little literary weight, and the Iraqi Communist Party (ICP), whose intellectual weight was considerable, had its impact on cultural policy. The ICP was granted the right to publish weekly, daily and monthly papers and the Kurdish Democratic Party (KDP) was also allowed to publish an independent daily, *Taakhi*. Carried away in the euphoria induced by minor concessions and marginal liberties gained after many years of repression, the ICP agreed to share the leadership of the writers', journalists' and artists' unions with the Ba'thists, and in practice to play second fiddle to them.

The ICP, which did not question, let alone resist, the increasingly savage policing of literary activity by the Ba'thist regime, must clearly bear its share of responsibility for the development of totalitarian state control of cultural life in Iraq. The publications of the ICP remained silent when writers were detained and tortured, when academics and civil servants were summarily dismissed from their posts and when radio and television stations were offically declared military establishments in which all political activity was prohibited. Communist attitudes helped both to reinforce the prevalent belief among non-aligned intellectuals that resistance to the status quo was futile and to secure the legitimacy of the Ba'thist state in the cultural sphere.

What may appear to be a period of literary and artistic achievement because of the increased volume of cultural output (for example, more publications and theatrical productions generously sponsored by the state) was, in fact, an era in which the pillars of totalitarian culture were firmly laid in place. The generous funding of artistic endeavours and the formal affirmation of democracy, freedom and socialism were all within predetermined limits set by the state. Measures to subordinate cultural activities to the official political line and to empty the former of their creative essence and aspiration started at this time, leading to a shallow political culture in which genuine creativity was stifled.

In addition, the Ba'th Party took practical steps to consolidate its influence in the writers', journalists' and artists' unions, taking full advantage of their 'open affiliation' policy, whereby all employees of the state-run cultural agencies – clerical and security staff, cleaners and administrators – were eligible to join. The Journalists' Union increased its membership from 400 in 1976 to over 1,000 in 1977. In 1978 it jumped to 2,000 after many security personnel were given short courses in journalism. The Artists' Union (mainly musicians) and the Fine Arts Society received hundreds of new requests for affiliation from 'artists' with dubious credentials.

The Kurdish Writers' Union (KWU) met with a harsher fate. In Kurdistan it proved to be too difficult to conjure up an army of supporters from among the Kurds and Turcomans. The KWU resisted attempts at containment throughout the 1970s but its literary activities were subjected to tight police surveillance. The censorship department even sent letters to the KWU specifying that words like 'revolution', 'armed struggle', 'rebellion' and 'peace' should not be used because of their subversive potential.

In 1977, in accordance with the principle of one-party rule unanimously endorsed by the 7th Congress of the Ba'th Party in 1972, Saddam Husain, then vice-president, convened a meeting of Ba'th Party cadres in the media and embarked on a programme of purging all journals and cultural agencies of non-Ba'thist employees, above all those affiliated to other parties. Tariq 'Aziz, then minister for culture and information, stated: 'Our cultural and information agencies are not hotels open for guests of different political forces.'

In the space of a few months many literary figures found themselves consigned to lowly positions in isolated educational establishments and far-flung customs posts. The distinguished poet Sa'adi Yusuf was ordered to work in the library of the irrigation ministry and the well-known writer Ali al-Shawk was sent to teach in a secondary school. Most prominent writers disappeared from leading journals and were replaced by hastily gathered nonentities. The offices of *Taakhi*, the Kurdish daily, witnessed the strangest of coups led by security personnel. One morning they stormed the *Taakhi* premises, dismissed some fifty journalists and installed in their place a team of editors and reporters they had brought with them. The familiar journal appeared the next day under a new title, *The Iraq Newspaper*.

In 1979 the security and intelligence services were given a free hand to manipulate cultural life as they wished. The premises housing ICP publications, the last remaining non-Ba'thist media, were occupied without warning and those working there were arrested. After this attack more than two hundred poets, storytellers, musicians, theatre directors, filmmakers and painters were arrested and tortured with electric shocks, with the *khuzuk* (a wedge driven into the anus) or with the *falaqa* (a cable or bar used to beat the soles of the feet). Both men and women were raped. Many writers and artists were executed, died under torture or were poisoned with thallium (a lethal rat-poison favoured by the Ba'thist regime). There followed an exodus into exile of more than seven hundred Iraqi intellectuals, some of whom were killed by the regime's police outside the country.

## Saddam Husain

Throughout all the tragic events which Iraq has experienced since 1979, Iraqi writers and artists inside and outside the country have been unable to express themselves freely. Individual creative activity and intellectual dialogue have been crushed. Instead a 'mass culture' has been created which serves purely as a means of Ba'th Party control over the hearts and minds of the Iraqi people. The Ba'thist regime has a cultural code of its own: Ba'thist literature, Ba'thist aesthetics and a Ba'thist notion of history centred on the role of the absolute leader as a saviour with whom the destiny of the nation is identified. The veneration of the leader requires endless songs of praise and a continual display of his image on TV screens, on the front pages of newspapers and magazines, on posters and as statues throughout the country. His ideas and political slogans, however absurd, have to be extolled. The literary critic Tarrad al-Kubaisi, for example, has claimed that Saddam Husain is not only a great leader but also a great philosopher, a modern Pindar.

In his early speeches Saddam Husain argued that the role of artists was to remould themselves and transform the heterogeneous masses into a homogeneous entity. But the establishment of his personality cult, and the subjugation of Iraqi cultural life to it, were not achieved easily or quickly. During the first two years of Ba'thist rule (1968-70) Saddam Husain had to hire Lebanese journalists to depict him as the strong man of Iraq. He could not find a single Iraqi to do this, since the majority considered themselves to be free and independent individuals to whom the practice of complimenting political leaders was alien.

Being Iraq's strong man meant being the incarnation of all that was desirable in the traditional tribal ethos: strength, aggression, alertness and readiness to confront danger. 'Once when I was very young,' Saddam Husain told students at a training camp, 'around 13 or 14, I could not sleep for three successive summers because of the bullet belts around my body, as well as the revolver and rifle I carried in my hands so that when the call came I would be ready. I want the enemies to lose hope when they catch sight of us.'[4] Presenting himself to the Arab press as a keen man with a strong personality, piercing eyes and a handsome face, he boasted of his past heroic deeds, particularly his role as a teenager in the assassination attempt against General Qasim in 1959. These tales were to become major themes for many novels, plays, TV dramas and poems, as well as theoretical articles seeking to justify the legitimacy of political assassination as a means of teaching enemies a lesson.

In the mid-1970s, fifty or so writers and journalists were summoned to hear Saddam Husain narrate his autobiography; some were then selected for a series of special meetings in which further details were given. A literary competition was then announced for the best novel on the General Qasim assassination attempt. For two months two writers – 'Adil 'Abd al-Jabbar and 'Abd al-Amir Mu'alla – raced against the clock to win the prize. It went to 'Abd al-Amir Mu'alla, and an Egyptian filmmaker, Tawfiq Salih, was invited to direct the film of the novel, for which a budget of 13 million Iraqi dinars (then the equivalent of $39 million) was allocated. To play himself Saddam Husain chose Saddam Kamil, a young man from his home town of Tikrit, who was banned from ever playing any other part and went on to became Saddam Husain's son-in-law and one of the prominent officers in his special protection apparatus. In the course of making the film – entitled *The Long Days* – Tawfiq Salih tried to add a love scene but 'Abd al-Amir Mu'alla, fearful of displeasing Saddam Husain, begged him not to.

'Adil 'Abd al-Jabbar went on to write a total of three novels and dozens of short stories about Saddam Husain. The Egyptian writer Amir Iskander, a former leftist, received huge sums and a life salary for a glossy book published in Paris that depicted Saddam Husain as a 'thinker and fighter'. 'Abd al-Razzaq 'Abd al-Wahid published dozens of poems hailing Saddam Husain as a legendary character. Tarrad al-Kubaisi, Basim Jamil Hammudi, Sulaiman Bakri and others wrote about the 'leader-symbol', who is half-man, half-god. Hasan 'Alawi, who later became a dissident in exile, published a series of essays, entitled *The Quality of Genius in Saddam Husain*, analysing how the then vice-president, known to be a fighting and killing man, managed his party work and also possessed unprecedented theoretical creativity.

When, in 1979, the ailing President Ahmad Hasan al-Bakr was ousted and Saddam Husain assumed the presidency, a herd of writers and journalists, among them Sahib Yasin, 'Abd al-Jabbar Muhsin, Sabah Salman and many others, hastened to publish similar essays and articles. The hall of the presidential palace became a waiting room for Iraqi and non-Iraqi poets, novelists and biographers. They were warned by members of Saddam Husain's entourage that their leader had magical, magnetic eyes that read thoughts and penetrated souls but they remained, undeterred, to sell the desired merchandise for the desired fortune. In the edification and glorification of Saddam Husain a set of clumsy idioms and phrases were injected into Iraqi cultural life. They include 'The Mind of the Revolution', 'The Man', 'The Necessity', 'Miraculous', 'Modern Hammurabi', 'President Nebuchadnezzar' and 'The Architect of the Mind'.

## Ba'thist cultural policy

Cultural policy in Iraq since 1968 has been implemented by five ministers for culture and information chosen not for their knowledge or intellectual refinement but for their loyalty to the regime. The first three – 'Abdullah Sallum al-Samarra'i, Salah 'Umar al-'Ali and Shafiq al-Kamali – held office before terror and violence became extreme in the late 1970s. They were nevertheless suspected by Saddam Husain of being liable to promote independent opinions and views within the Ba'th Party. Sallum al-Samarra'i and Salah 'Umar al-'Ali survived continuous purges and both were sent abroad soon after being relieved of their posts. Shafiq Kamali, a prominent Ba'thist poet, was appointed and dismissed several times but remained in Iraq and was eventually executed with his son, the many poems he had written to Saddam Husain's glory failing to save his neck. As Salah 'Umar al-'Ali has confirmed, Shafiq al-Kamali was obsessed by the idea that he would be killed on Saddam Husain's orders because he had not voted for him in a clandestine party election held in the 1960s. The fourth minister of culture and information was Tariq 'Aziz. According to Salah 'Umar al-'Ali, Tariq 'Aziz's greatest expectation was to be appointed as cultural attaché at the Iraqi embassy in Moscow. When he was given the whole ministry instead he took it as an unforgettable favour and he left the post with even greater loyalty and submissiveness to Saddam Husain. The fifth minister for culture and information was Latif Nisayyif al-Jasim who was appointed in 1979 and remained in office throughout the Iran-Iraq war and the Gulf War.

Latif Nisayyif al-Jasim, who became known to television viewers throughout the world in the Gulf War, was a leading figure during a critical phase in the development of Iraq's terror state. His style was characterized by quick decision-making, with bold, self-confident initiatives rooted in deep hatred of and contempt for culture and cultured people. He did not display the intellectual pretension, arrogance and conceit of his master, Saddam Husain, but presented himself as a simpleton with whom the man-in-the-street could identify, boasting of his naïvety. This was perhaps the secret of his long survival in a highly sensitive post where not only ministers but also their whole entourage were liable to be dismissed in cabinet reshuffles.

On 16 April 1981, al-Jasim despatched a large number of writers and journalists to the Iran-Iraq war zone in three groups. Those who dared to object were subject to harsh penalties and the well-known short-story-teller Muwaffaq Khudayyir died of a heart attack en route. This action was taken, al-Jasim told the *al-Watan al-'Arabi* magazine, 'to teach intellectuals how to write under gunfire' so that they would 'pay with poetry, prose and stories the price of being exempted from military service.' He regularly met writers, wearing his military uniform, but as the war progressed and some of them remained inactive, he issued a directive under the rubric 'Loyalty to Qadissiya' (a reference to a seventh-century battle between Arabs and Persians). 'We should detect the slightest opposition to the "Loyalty to Qadissiya" directive,' he threatened on 30 April 1989, 'and draw attention to it. We cannot understand why some have kept silent for the past eight years of the Iraq-Iran war. Our memory holds some names of those in our society who have been waiting, like snakes hiding in their holes, for the right moment to show their teeth and tongues while we hear their breath.'[5]

Since 1980, when the Iraqi Writers' Union and the Kurdish Writers' Union were abolished by a decree of the Revolutionary Command Council (RCC),[6] writers had been organized in a professional association whose appointments, budgets and activities were administered by the Ministry of Culture. Throughout the 1980s the Ministry of Culture spent lavishly on festivals and congresses, on paying poets and writers, and on the purchase of journals published abroad. At the same time it was at its most barbaric in oppressing intellectuals.

Hundreds of Arab writers were hosted in Iraq but Iraqi writers were allowed to leave the country only on official visits. In 1986 alone more than forty cultural festivals were held, the main purpose being to show guests the achievements of the Ba'thist revolution and receive telegrams of support for Saddam Husain. He attended many of these festivals, presenting each poet with a gun in accordance with tribal tradition and listening until dawn to popular poems written in colloquial Iraqi dialect. Originally such popular poetry was prohibited by the Ba'th Party on the grounds that it encouraged regionalism and weakened the classical Arabic language which was essential to pan-Arab national unity. But it proved to be an important means of mobilizing the masses for war. It upheld backward, tribal values and appealed to those for whom the language of the cultured was inaccessible, particularly the rural population living in the mud-hut villages and marshlands of southern Iraq and the shanty-town dwellers of Baghdad. These were the communities which provided the foot-soldiers and sergeants of the Iraqi army, the cannon-fodder for the Iran-Iraq war. In return for thousands of Iraqi dinars from the state, 'Abd al-Razzaq 'Abd al-Wahid began writing *rajiz* poems, a Bedouin form usually used in tribal wars, and revived the old violent language.

At the same time official linguistic terms were developed and aggressively propagated through the media and literature to integrate intellectuals into the militarized state. They included words and phrases such as 'mobilization', 'the mighty Iraqi power', 'the blood melted in the heat of Iraqi victory' and 'Iraq is the conscience of the Arab nation and the builder of its glory'. These were not mere slogans but new figures of speech, a jargon of war which enabled Iraqi state intellectuals to extend their influence in an Arabic-speaking world fearful of Iranian expansionism. This was explained by 'Abd al-Razzaq 'Abd al-Wahid in an interview published in the Sa'udi magazine, *Yamama*, in March 1986.

> Before the revolution we had a fighting language but it was wounded, its vocabulary was defeated, the meaning of traditional victory was absent. Pride was missing in the language. Hence words expressed some sort of a hopeless fighting spirit, sometimes suicidal. An arrogant, colourful, victorious language is present now. Blood, bullets, the names of weapons, cannons, armoured vehicles. With such words we live daily. I remember that one of the military commanders told me: 'You made us love our weapons because you made them into people, you made them living humans.' This means that language is so elastic that it can humanise iron and fire.

In literature only one theme was officially sanctioned: the 'actual victory'. Deviation from this could cost a writer's life. More novels were published in Iraq in the 1980s than in the previous half-century, according to official figures. The Ministry of Culture and Information printed twenty-six in 1983 alone, partly as a result of the 'Stories Under Flames of Fire' literary competition which it organized. Writers were told by Minister for Culture Latif Nisayyif al-Jasim to depict the 'new Iraqi man', using as models of human heroism the real-life father who killed his son,

or brother who killed his brother, or woman who informed the security
police about her husband – in each case because they had deserted from
the army.

The function of literature, according to the state intellectual Sulaimen
Bakri, was to glorify martyrdom, making life inferior to death. 'Characters
in novels,' he wrote, 'realize the dangers of war but take part in it in defence
of sublime ideals. That is why they boldly move to face the enemy and
look at war as an unavoidable reality that has to be lived for the sake of
the homeland.' A typical character is formed on the basis of ethical
uniformity imposed from without. In the collection *The Songs of Trees* by
the late storyteller Muwaffaq Khudayyir, the story 'Words' describes how
the writer meets a great revolutionary leader who with his magical,
objective and historical words could change the weakness of the hero of
the story into productive energy. 'Revolution starts with challenging the
self, eradicating its negative and weak aspects', as Bakri put it.[7]

The realistic school in literature was attacked as being critical of
society. Those who tried to renew literary language and those who wrote
fantasy were also attacked. The minister for culture condemned them as
being surrealists harbouring a plotting spirit that should be eliminated.
Basim Jamil Hammudi, a state writer, boasted that 'the revolution could,
with its achievements, put an end to the dialectic of generations, the
dialectic of estrangement and the non-serious accretions to literature,
because each socio-political era has its own literary structure on the level
of creativity.'

Despite all the crushing methods used to control Iraqi writers, a counter-
literature has rejected the official point of view in different ways. In 1988
a special issue of the Baghdad review *Aqlam* published thirty-four short
stories. The relation between state and citizen was tackled as a theme, and
a sense was conveyed of the feelings of persecution and the weight of the
ordeal which had befallen Iraq.

The experience of writers is shared by intellectuals in other fields,
including literary criticism, fine arts and historical research. The 'military
victory literature' or 'battles literature' pumped out by state-run printing
houses in the 1980s was generally accepted uncritically, although one of
Iraq's most important critics, 'Abd al-Jabbar 'Abbas al-Basri, gave up his
career to avoid the embarrassment of writing about such work. Theatre
critics have cited Saddam Husain as an authority on the deterioration of
Iraqi theatre.

He has similarly been deferred to in painting and sculpture, the most
famous example being 'The Arch of Victory' which was realized by two
of Iraq's best sculptors, the late Khalid Rahhal and Ghani Hikmet.[8] The
colourful fine art of Iraq has now been reduced to having a mere 'official
function'. It has been forced into the zone of cold neutrality versus life, in
which there is no room for the artist's aesthetic taste, which has to be

lowered to the level of the inferior, backward taste of the leader. The art of military mobilization has drastically changed the status of the artist, who in the past could seek to develop the artistic sensibility of the public. Jawad Salim's 'Freedom Monument', for example, was not widely popular but won critical acclaim from intellectuals and the middle class in general. Today, the posters and statues of Saddam Husain throughout Iraq impose an artistic uniformity as well as acting as propaganda for the state and its head. The best and most rebellious fine artists had to go to the presidential palace to paint portraits of Michel 'Aflaq, the founder of Ba'thism, or make sketches of ideas that occurred to Saddam Husain. As with literature, hundreds of new artists appeared who bought themselves a good career by organizing an exhibition containing portraits of the president, some of them created not with paint but with blood.

The Ba'thist redefinition of the national past, in which literature and art have played their part, inevitably meant rewriting history. 'We take from the past what is good for us and leave the unwanted,' in the words of Saddam Husain. Dr Fawzi Rashid, an archeologist, dug back thousands of years to discover that the enmity between Arabs and Persians was deep-rooted and therefore the *Qadissiya* (the Iran-Iraq war) was only a historical continuation. 'The enemy' remained constant as an emotive article of faith to cement the social fabric and justify the totalitarian, militaristic state. Those who looked at history differently risked being imprisoned, as happened to the theatre group that tried to put on a play about the revolution of the Qarmatis, members of an Islamic sect who seized Basra and built their own state in Bahrain during the Abbasid era.

The distortion of history certainly served the war effort and helped contaminate literature and language. As 'the enemy', Iranians were not seen as humans and only the worst names were used for them. Nawaf Abul Haija, a Palestinian novelist living in Iraq, was exceptional in describing Iranian soldiers realistically. In general they were presented as cowards: cruel, desperate and unable to fight. Extreme paranoiac cruelty imbued some literary language, which dwelt on death with lurid descriptions of rotting corpses and skeletons. By contrast, the poets Ja'far Alaq, Sami Mahdi and Hamid Sa'id romanticized war. For them, because just wars are sublime and beautiful, fallen soldiers are not dead but living heroes who visit our houses at any time, decorated with roses. They are happy and have left behind no orphans or widows, no destruction.

When the Iran-Iraq war ended there was even greater glorification of Saddam Husain. A poem by 'Abd al-Razzaq 'Abd al-Wahid, for example, spoke of his son as his successor:

> What we could not perceive of your great secret
> We see now, oh Great Lord,
> In the eyes of your Great Son.

A host of Arab writers, including the Kuwaiti princess Su'ad al-Sabah, joined in the chorus of praise, minimizing Saddam Husain's crimes against his own people and maximizing his role in containing the Iranian threat. After his invasion of Kuwait many others who had previously championed democratic rights in Iraq switched to supporting him in his 'duel' with the USA.

During the Gulf War (2 August 1990 to summer 1991) a controversy raged among Arab intellectuals in which dissident Iraqis found themselves in a minority in their condemnation of Saddam Husain. They rejected his mystical mottoes and understood the tragedy precipitated by his actions. In Iraq, literary magazines were able to seize unscrutinized moments of expression, mainly concentrating on purely cultural and spiritual matters, and a few voices were clearly heard opposing the status quo. This was despite threats from the minister for culture, who wailed:

> Some are still writing in a surrealist style. I mean that they do not commit themselves to a definite position and whoever is reluctant to commit himself to a clear position, a question mark will be raised against what he writes. Surrealism is good for canvas but not in writing, where things should be clearly named. As for those who twist and move in a roundabout way, they are sick people and they must be kept under watchful eyes in order to analyse them to see how far this sickness goes.[9]

There is no doubt that Iraq's cultural development has been savaged by the political success of Saddam Husain's Ba'thist regime. The citizen is deprived by the power of the state security apparatus of honour, liberty, prosperity, dignity and integrity, as these realities have been hijacked by political jargon and no longer exist in daily life. Similarly, real knowledge has been eradicated, as culture is moulded not to serve people but to control them, dominating their minds with the notion of the absolute, omnipresent, omnipotent leader. A new generation of intellectuals has been created to work in culture as a department of state. These are the 'state intellectuals' who devote their energies into supporting the 'machine of state' which is merciless towards opposition or dissent.

The transformation of Iraq's intelligentsia into a body of functionaries operating within the propaganda and information bureaucracy was achieved by a combination of brutality and bribery. All employees in publishing houses or cultural departments, up to the highest levels, are under continuous surveillance by security officers. Intellectuals not integrated into the official establishment face continuous intimidation, threats of imprisonment and torture, and even physical elimination. For example, Abd al-Wahhab al-Daini, a prominent playwright, was sentenced to life imprisonment on the basis of a secretly tape-recorded conversation in which he criticized the government. Ahmad Khalaf, a storyteller, suffered a similar fate. The whereabouts of both are unknown.

Hand in hand with the ubiquitous violence is the possibility of earning unprecedented wealth, which has persisted for more than twenty years. In the past, Iraqi writers were poor but honest and respected. The low levels of economic development and literacy meant that the market for literary work was too small to sustain profitable careers. Saddam Husain's cultural policy, by contrast, has enabled those who use their creative talent in his praise to enjoy financial privileges denied to those reluctant to do so. Yosuf al-Sayigh, for example, was imprisoned, tortured and kept under house arrest for three years, but when he began to devote his poetry to the glorification of Saddam Husain he was appointed director of a theatre department and became a representative of Iraqi writers at all Arab festivals and conferences.

For many writers in Iraq, praising the ruler is now a practice unconnected with literature but necessary to secure a comfortable life. They may acknowledge to close friends that culture in Iraq is deteriorating, while claiming the opposite in their published work. Others allow the agonies and depression harboured deep in their souls to creep into their officially sanctioned texts. Some, a very small minority, avoid the 'duality' involved in being an officially sanctioned writer by accepting severe economic conditions and an overwhelming sense of insecurity. Those forced into exile have established cultural groups and persevere with their oppositional writings and activities to complement the hidden opposition inside Iraq.

## Notes

1. This chapter is based on articles published in *al-Hayyat*, April 1992.

2. Documents of the 7th Congress of Arab writers, Baghdad, 19-22 April 1969.

3. The drawing up of lists was confirmed by Salah 'Umar al-'Ali in an interview given in London, where he lives as a dissident in exile.

4. Speech entitled 'The Spirit of New Iraq' in Saddam Husain's *Collected Works*, vol. 4 (Baghdad), p. 229.

5. *Al-Jumihurriya*, 30 April 1989.

6. Decision no. 504. Act no. 70, 1980.

7. Sulaiman Bakri, 'The Novel in Time of War' in *Aqlam*, 4 April 1989.

8. The Arch of Victory is formed of two right fists modelled on Saddam Husain's, clutching two crossed swords. Each fist is mounted on a pedestal in which is rooted a net containing 2,500 Iranian helmets. See the study by Samir al-Khalil (Kanan Makiya), *The Monument*, (London, 1991).

9. *Al-Jumihurriya*, 30 April 1989.

CHAPTER TWO

# State Terror and the Degradation of Politics[1]

*Isam al-Khafaji*

The degradation of Iraqi politics and society under the Ba'th regime is a story that can now be pieced together from documents to which no one until the *intifada* of March 1991 dreamed of having access. Baghdad's brutal repression turned the *intifada* into another tragic episode. But one thing should be recognized: for several tumultuous weeks a terrorized population overcame its fear and attacked the state which it considered responsible for its humiliation and suffering. In the course of these events tens of thousands of invaluable documents were captured from the various Iraqi intelligence organizations.[2] These documents not only recount the sad and painful fate of untold numbers of Iraqis; they are also an excellent source for understanding how the Ba'th regime increasingly exacerbated cleavages in Iraqi society while simultaneously claiming to do the opposite in creating 'the new Iraq'. The risky and unstable equilibrium which guaranteed the regime's survival for more than two decades is now crumbling, with grave consequences for the future of the country.

## The terror network

During the past two decades the Ba'th regime has constructed a network of multiple intelligence apparatuses that pervades all aspects of Iraqi society. Besides Saddam Husain's *Jihaz al-Himaya al-Khas* (Special Protection Apparatus), the Ba'th Party and its mass organizations which all function as surveillance systems, the following organizations often compete with each other and overlap in their domains:

*Jihaz al-Mukhabarat al-Amma* (General Intelligence Apparatus) is mainly concerned with matters of 'foreign enemies', but an official ideology that considers most of the opposition to be foreign agents frees *al-Mukhabarat* to pursue virtually all domestic opponents of the regime.

*Al-Istikhbarat al-Askariya* (Military Intelligence) is responsible for detecting 'enemy' infiltration in the armed forces. Since military service is compulsory for all male adults, this agency too is sanctioned to target virtually all of the regime's domestic opponents. *Al-Istikhbarat* has almost unlimited authority in Iraqi Kurdistan under the pretext of combating *al-mukharribin* (saboteurs).

*Mudiriyat al-Amn al-Amma* (General Security Directorate) has wide authority to combat all manner of political and economic 'crimes.'

*Maktab al-Amn al-Qawmi* (Bureau of National Security) oversees and coordinates these apparatuses and reports directly to the president.

Corruption, competition for influence and authority, and a rigid hierarchy have rendered this system highly effective in achieving one of its major objectives: promoting a sense of helplessness among the population. Each of these apparatuses engages a vast network of informers. Recruitment of agents was institutionalized under the Ba'thist regime by the 1979 Law no. 83, decreed one month before the rise of Saddam Husain to the presidency. 'The Law of Securing the Trustworthy [*al-Mu'taman*] in Defending the Revolution' regulates such matters as agent function, recruitment, salary and rank.[3]

The *mu'taman* is not just an informer. And the term 'recruitment' is too mild to describe the mechanism through which *mu'tamanin* begin their careers, as the experience of Kifah illustrates. Kifah is a barely literate young woman from al-Mishkhab, a town south of Baghdad. As a *mu'tamana*, she was instructed to pose as a nurse and go to Kurdistan after the defeat of the March 1991 *intifada*. Her assignment was to gain the confidence of those who controlled the region, and then invite other agents to join her under the guise of health workers. Kifah had been told that the USA was the only armed presence in Kurdistan. When she found herself amidst armed Kurds, she panicked and simply surrendered. When I interviewed her in August 1991, she had already spent two months detained by the *peshmerga* (Kurdish guerrillas).

Kifah told me how she had been 'recruited'. In 1988, newly married, she was stopped by four *Mudiriyat al-Amn al-Amma* officers in a car, who told her to go with them to answer questions about her husband. She was taken instead to an orchard, where she was forced to drink alcohol and was raped by the four men. This was all videotaped. The agents threatened to send the video to her husband, who would most likely kill her when he saw it. Kifah felt she had no choice but to work for *al-Amn*. She began her career by 'recruiting' three friends through the same practice – pretending to take each of them to a house to visit a friend. Instead, *al-Amn* officers would be waiting.

Most *mu'tamanin* are members or ex-members of political organizations who fall victim to the combined pressure of threat and persuasion. Before release from prison, political detainees are forced to sign a *ta'hud* (pledge) not to join any organization other than the Ba'th Party, under penalty of death. An officer is assigned to keep in touch with each detainee after their release. Those who agree to work for *al-Amn* are instructed to continue working inside their original organizations and report to *al-Amn*. Thousands more *mu'tamanin* are recruited in similar fashion from among people who occupy positions in the state-run trade unions, city councils and even the rubber-stamp National Assembly.

Captured memos reveal how the Iraqi regime uses *mu'tamanin*. Responding to the Erbil Governorate's request for information about two men seeking approval to run for the National Assembly, a confidential telegram from *al-Amn* dated 6 September 1988 says: 'Secret investigations have shown that Mr. Mughdid Muhammad is politically independent. As for Mr. Mamend ... he was formerly a Communist and at present he is a Ba'thist [with the rank of] *nasseer* (supporter). He is a good and loyal element. We recommend that their candidature to the National Assembly be approved.' According to another memo, dated 15 July 1979, the 'good and loyal' Mr. Mamend was in fact 'a *mu'taman* in the field of the Communist Party, with a monthly salary of 50 dinars and under the code number 286.'

Political commitment to the cause is rarely an important criterion. The standard form issued by *al-Amn* to evaluate *mu'tamanin* consists of fifteen questions about the agent's economic situation and motivation for working as an informer. Many completed forms state explicitly that it is for money. Another question asks bluntly: 'Do we have any written proof to frame him in case he reneges on cooperating with us?'

Regular conferences of *al-Amn* officers evaluate the overall achievements of *mu'tamanin* through detailed surveys of each political organization in Iraq, including obscure ones such as the Wahhabi Islamists. The survey includes the number of agents who have infiltrated the organization, the organizational lines over which *al-Amn* has control, and the ranks of agents in the organization.

In 1977, when the Iraqi Communist Party (ICP) was formally allied to the Ba'th Party, with two ministers in the cabinet, the 'first conference for following-up the activities of the ICP' was held in the headquarters of *al-Amn*. The conference sent a letter to its directorate in Wasit marked 'top secret, to be opened personally'. The letter expresses 'thanks to Security Lieutenant Kamil Msayar ... and presents him with a watch for his good approach in the field of infiltrating [the ICP].'

Similarly, when the regime's relations were improving with the Patriotic Union of Kurdistan (the PUK, led by Jalal Talabani), a confidential report briefed *al-Amn* on a February 1984 meeting of the 'Comrade Directors' of Sulaimaniyya, Arbil and Dohuk. Point seven of the report reads: 'We explained to the participants that our increased *tashbik* [literally dovetailing, a frequently used term denoting infiltration] inside the PUK is not aimed against it; rather it is to preserve the safety of its march. ... This requires alertness and attention to gain a complete picture.'

## Cousins and comrades

The methods by which the Iraqi regime promotes a sense of duty and solidarity among the staffs of the terror systems include periodic conferences, gifts from senior officials and suggestions on how to improve performance. Directives and reports are normally replete with phrases aimed at enhancing an elite consciousness. The 1990 annual plan for *al-Amn* begins by citing Saddam Husain's description of agents as 'militant, loyal, pure, faithful and glorious'. A special information office (*idarat al-tablighat*) was set up at its Baghdad headquarters, whose main function seems to be advising officers of the eighteen branches on the personal and family occasions of their colleagues (births, marriages, deaths) so that they can send one another telegrams of congratulation or condolence.

Seniors and juniors in the system are aware of the existence of other, more cynical and arbitrary bases around which solidarities form. On the form that each *al-Amn* employee must fill out, half of the thirty-six questions relate to the employee's family. The key questions are: 'Have any of your relatives been sentenced in a case that relates to state security?' and 'Name any relatives who work in foreign companies or with foreigners.' Finally, the employee must sign under the following *ta'hud*: '(a) I pledge that none of my relatives has any relation with the traitors and conspirators [involved] in the last conspiracy [or with] the sectarian events, enemy parties, [or is of] Iranian origin … (b) In case such a relationship with those mentioned in article (a) above does exist, indicate who they are, how they relate to you and what were their sentences.' In Iraq, where conspiracies are discovered or invented as needs arise, few families escape having one of their sons involved in one plot or another, in one way or another.

*Al-Amn* staff in Erbil, the capital of Iraqi Kurdistan, were not part of the elite and had to report either to Kirkuk or to Baghdad. Furthermore, as Arabs serving in a Kurdish region they developed the sense of being an isolated occupation force. *Al-Amn* reports from Erbil show that many staff members considered an appointment there to be a sign of official displeasure. On the eve of the March 1991 *intifada,* the Erbil staff consisted of sixty-eight employees: nineteen officers and forty-nine non-commissioned officers (NCOs) and lower ranks. The nineteen officers had thirteen brothers and three uncles, cousins or brothers-in-law who were officers in General Intelligence (*al-Mukhabarat*), Military Intelligence (*al-Istikhbarat*), General Security (*al-Amn*), the Republican Guard or the Special Protection Apparatus (*Jihaz al-Himaya al-Khas*). Of the six officers who did not report having relatives in such distinguished posts, four were Shi'is from governorates south of Baghdad and one was the only Kurdish officer, who had joined *al-Amn* four years before the Ba'th Party came to power. The forty-nine NCOs and lower ranks had ten brothers and twenty-six other relatives in security apparatus posts.

While the intelligence organizations are not closed to men from non-privileged regions or families who have proved their loyalty to the party and the revolution, such posts are nevertheless concentrated in the hands of men from particular regions and families. Eleven of the nineteen officers and eighteen of the forty-nine lower-ranked men employed by *al-Amn* in Erbil came from the 'Sunni Arab triangle' – the region extending from Baghdad north to Mosul and west to the Syrian border. People from this region have a much higher chance of securing a job in the intelligence agencies, but they generally come from the lower classes. Those from towns, tribes or families that are better off, or have access to higher education, tend to shy away from such employment. Many of the Erbil staff came from the poorest towns north of Tikrit and south of Mosul, such as al-Sharqat and Baiji. At least sixteen of the nineteen officers joined as NCOs and later enrolled in the police or national security college. Those from the 'Sunni Arab triangle' formed less than 40 per cent of the lower ranking *al-Amn* employees in Erbil. Fifteen of the others came from Arab enclaves within Iraqi Kurdistan, a fact which encouraged a sense of serving a common cause against 'separatist Kurds'.

Employees with few job opportunities and much to lose tend to develop a sense of loyalty to the agency and solidarity with colleagues. This is especially true during a time of crisis such as the *intifada*. The absolute authority of such agents might have aroused envy in ordinary times, but envy gave way to hatred during the *intifada*, when it was too late for agents to distance themselves from the security apparatus. This might account for the ferocious resistance which rebels faced when they stormed the various intelligence headquarters during the *intifada*.

One leader of the rebels in Hilla was an army captain and full member of the Ba'th Party at the time of the *intifada*, but he nevertheless helped launch the revolt in his town in the name of the 'oppressed majority of Iraqis' – that is, the Shi'is. He admitted that no fewer than 70 percent of *al Amn* staff in Hilla were Shi'is, though not in command positions. In semi-class terminology, he proceeded to explain that these former paupers owed their present affluence to corruption rather than their talents or personal qualities. There is no single explanation for how the various sections of the security and intelligence organizations saw themselves, but Shi'i and Sunni alike linked their fates to the regime's survival.

## Uncle Saddam

The least known but most fearsome of the Ba'thist organs of repression, the *Jihaz al-Himaya al-Khas* (Special Protection Apparatus), illustrates how bribery, kinship and regional solidarities intersect to produce a cohesive organization. The *Jihaz* comprises Saddam's real praetorian guard. No records or documents about it have as yet come to light. The following description was compiled from the interrogation minutes and testimonies of nine *Jihaz* NCOs arrested by *peshmergas* after the *intifada*, and from personal interviews with two of them. None of the nine NCOs had finished high school when they were recruited. Yet their monthly salary at the beginning of their career was 400 Iraqi dinars, equivalent to that of a university professor.

The *Jihaz* is composed of thirteen battalions, each with 1,300-1,500 men from Tikrit, Baiji, al-Sharqat and small towns south and west of Mosul and around Baghdad. A typical *Jihaz* member is a young man in his mid-twenties, recruited from a poor town. After undergoing six months of harsh physical training, he spends two more months intensively studying the structures of the various opposition movements, assassination techniques, electronic inspection devices, use of explosives, protection of strategic sites (especially Saddam's numerous palaces) and recruiting collaborators. He is then assigned to one of the bureau's five departments. In early 1991, four of these departments were headed by Tikritis, the fifth by an officer from Baiji. Apart from the handsome salaries, members are provided with elegant apartments in the heavily guarded complex of Karradat Mariam in the vicinity of the presidential palace, or in the al-Radhwaniyya complex in the outskirts of Baghdad, close to Iraq's worst prisons.

The 'technical' department in the *Jihaz* is responsible for what Saddam considers important dissident cases. One *Jihazi* told me that he was in al-Radhwaniyya in April 1991, one month after the *intifada*. He said that there were then 62,000 prisoners awaiting interrogation, which was being carried out under the direct supervision of Saddam's younger son, Qusayy, and his son-in-law, Saddam Kamil Hassan.

The Jubur tribe has been one of the main pools for the recruitment of intelligence personnel, including the *Jihaz*. A Juburi NCO in the *Jihaz* told me how he, like many of his fellow tribesmen, had spent his childhood in al-Sharqat dreaming of Baghdad. He recalled his first visit there in 1987, how he felt when he saw a shower for the first time and the thrill of touching the 'soft flesh' of women in the Baghdad Sheraton. No brainwashing was needed to turn envy of the lavish lifestyle of 'soft' city dwellers, especially Baghdadis, into a sense of gratitude and devotion towards those who enabled the *Jihaz* recruits to conquer that alien city. And conquer it they did.

The creation of Saddam's praetorian guard owes much of its success to the fact that it does not rely on ideological indoctrination. Rather, it follows the path taken by Saddam Husain and most other influential personalities in the regime since they emerged from their impoverished home towns looking for someone to give them a humble job in Baghdad. A reliance on kinship and town solidarity inevitably develops, and a feeling of un-bounded loyalty to Saddam Husain by the *Jihaz* members which is best illustrated by the fact that they never use formal titles for him. Instead, he is *Ammi*, a word that means paternal uncle but is also used by servants to refer to their masters.

## Incorporation and coercion

Within the overall context of Iraq's social structure, practices such as these cast serious doubt on the type of analysis that emphasizes the secular, modernizing and integrating drive of the Iraqi regime, a popular approach among many American 'experts' during the Iran-Iraq war.[4] The present leadership did not invent the ethnic, religious, sectarian, regional and tribal cleavages in Iraqi society. But it has perpetuated and exacerbated these cleavages rather than worked to overcome them. The supporting actors (or victims) in Iraqi politics have not been individuals or citizens as such. Rather, they represent this sect or that tribe, this town or that region. This applies both to the way some are incorporated within the state system, and to the way others are excluded from it, or assigned subordinate roles.

Until recently, the official discourse tried to conceal the reinforcement of stratification along these lines. The 'revolution' was building the 'new Iraqi man'. Episodes such as the deportation of tens of thousands of Shi'is in the early 1980s were not acts of discrimination towards Iraqis: the victims were dismissed as non-Iraqis.[5] For those whom the regime considered 'authentic' Iraqis – Sunni Arabs – the basis for privilege was 'their closeness to the principles of the revolution and its leading party'; principles that could change according to circumstances.

In the mid 1970s, a decree by the Revolutionary Command Council (RCC) prohibited the use of family names that referred to the tribal or regional origin of their bearers. Official propaganda portrayed this as a step towards civic equality. Critics argued correctly that the aim was to hide the family, tribal and regional connections of those in power. In late 1979, four months after Saddam Husain became president, his press secretary wrote an article in *al-Thawra*, the Ba'th Party organ, entitled 'Kinship in the Revolutionary Society'. 'If the relative is the son of the Party and Revolution,' he asked cynically, 'would it harm the revolution-ary march when he is promoted?'[6] A few years later, a front-page obituary in all Iraqi papers carried the news of the death of Saddam Husain's mother. She was described as 'the mother of the militants' and the names and political positions of several of her sons were published, foremost among them being Saddam.

Just as positions of power are reserved for loyal families, the regime holds families of dissidents responsible for their 'crimes'. The special form prepared by *al-Amn* on 'the elements of the hostile parties' states the tribe of each 'element' and records the names of his/her brothers, sisters, uncles, aunts, nephews, nieces, cousins and friends.

## Divide and rule in Kurdistan

*Jash* (donkey) is the name used by Kurds for the National Defence Battalions established under the supervision of *al-Istikhbarat* (Military Intelligence) and *al-Amn* (Security Directorate). With the regime's destruction of the economic base of Kurdish society, many clans, particularly those involved in disputes with neighbouring clans over territory or water supplies, had no place to turn to but the state. They became mercenaries to secure the means of preserving and enhancing their authority. Thus many Zibaris, Hirkis, Sorchis and Doskis were turned into *jash* by their chiefs.

At the height of their strength, there were some 250 such battalions incorporating more than 100,000 men. The aim of the regime was to split and neutralize the Kurds, turning some into informers against their brothers. The chiefs would habitually report fictional military operations, or otherwise inflate their 'achievements' in order to keep their power base and funds. Some reports by *al-Istikhbarat* focus less on military performance and more on personal character – how interested is the chief in money, alcohol, sex and gambling? Does he cooperate with the security apparatuses? Does he or his clan have hostilities with other chiefs or clans? Does he have any relatives in senior positions in the state, or opposition parties?

In a confidential letter dated 19 August 1989, the officer responsible for *al-Mafariz al-Khassa* (special *jash* patrols organized by *al-Istikhbarat* for counter-guerrilla operations) lists twelve 'negative aspects' in the functioning of these patrols. One is that commanders are 'not committed to their work ... a commander is occupied with his private business, including trading in cars and running farms.' Another is that 'a very large number of fighters are engaged in private occupations and have never reported to their units. Their commanders know about them.'

## Legacy of despotism

More than three-and-a-half decades since the 1958 revolution overthrew the monarchy and ended the domination of tribal landowners in Iraqi politics, Iraq has relapsed into family rule under a republican guise. The most traumatizing aspect of this is that Iraqis have come to take it for granted that a social hierarchy runs along regional, tribal, sectarian and ethnic lines. Official discourse no longer tries to conceal this. It does not mean that Iraqis are content with the allocation of privilege within the

regime, nor that they acquiesce in the rule of Saddam's family, but they
have regressed to expressing themselves in terms of such identities.

The *intifada* demonstrated this. Not only did many of the key leaders
come from within the ruling establishment, but they tended to view the
cause they were fighting for in terms dictated by the regime itself. The
Hilla officer who identified his cause as that of the oppressed Shi'i
majority is typical. Though he bitterly denounced the fundamentalist Shi'i
organizations and the Iranians, he took his instructions during the *intifada*
from the Shi'i spiritual leader in Najaf. In Kurdistan, many *jash* chiefs
sided with the *intifada*, some out of a change of heart, others out of sheer
opportunism. In Dahok, it was the *jash* units which sparked the *intifada*.
Then *jash* chiefs of clans decided they should form a political party of their
own. 'Clans will have a word to say on the future of Kurdistan,' claimed
Husain al-Surchi, a multimillionaire who laid on a lavish banquet at his
palace near Shaqlawa in April 1991 for officers of the allied forces in the
region. He told his guests that he had been working as a 'little soldier'
under Saddam, but from then on would be a faithful ally to the West.

Perhaps the position of the Shaikh of Shammar is the best illustration
of how the regime's perspective is adopted even by those seeking to
overthrow it. The Shammar, one of the largest Sunni Arab tribes in Iraq,
was until recently a major power base for the regime. I met its sheikh in
January 1991, shortly after he left Iraq to live in exile. Reflecting on the
various alternatives to succeed the present regime, he concluded that 'our
brothers, the Samarra'i officers, are the only brave men who can take
power.' His solution, in other words, was a coup d'état that would elevate
a new Sunni clique, this time from Samarra, a rival Sunni Arab town to
Tikrit.

Iraqi politics after the *intifada* is a manifestation of the bitter harvest of
more than two decades of the present regime's strategy. A regime that has
just survived a humiliating defeat by foreign adversaries and a huge
popular revolt might be expected to relax its brutal practices, at least for
tactical reasons. Many observers expected that Saddam Husain would be
forced to introduce some new Shi'is, Kurds and Christians into government – as a façade, if nothing else. Instead power has been more tightly
consolidated. Two months after the *intifada* the Iraqi press began publi-
cizing preparations for a new Ba'th Party congress, whose aim was to
'draw plans for the coming stage'. For the first time there was talk of local
conferences to elect delegates to the congress. Then, on 15 September
1991, newspapers reported the happy results of the congress which had
taken place a few days before. The congress had 'decided to adopt the
speech of the Comrade Leader as its main document'.

The regional command of the Ba'th Party did experience a decisive
shift in its composition, but in the direction of greater sectarian and
regional imbalance. At the 9th Congress, in July 1982, the fifteen-strong

regional command consisted of eight Sunni Muslims, six Shi'i Muslims and one Christian. At the 10th Congress, in September 1991, the seven-teen-strong regional command consisted of thirteen Sunni Muslims, three Shi'i Muslims and one Christian. Similarly, the number of regional com-mand members from the 'Sunni Triangle' increased from five to twelve, those from Baghdad declined from four to one, and those from the fourteen other governorates declined from six to four. The process of institutional-izing regional and tribal stratification has come to its logical conclusion. In place of the old rhetoric of the 'party of all Iraqis, even of those who have not joined it', 'Iraq' itself has joined 'nation', 'party' and 'revolution' as yet another example of abstract Ba'thist jargon. Words like 'majority' and 'minority' are irrelevant when it comes to describing how Iraq is run.

*Al-Thawra* published three editorials in April 1991 to 'explain' the *intifada*, an episode known officially as 'the page of treachery and be-trayal'. The march of the 'revolution', we were told, has been a voluminous record of confrontation with foreign enemies of the 'nation'. The 'Iranian aggression' and the 'aggression of the 30' – the US-led attack – were mere chapters. When all these conspiracies failed, the 'enemy' mobilized its local agents for the most dangerous of all 'conspiracies'. Why was the conspiracy rooted in the south? In the words of the *al-Thawra* editorialist turned sociologist, probably Tariz 'Aziz, 'a certain sect [i.e., the Shi'i] has been historically under the influence of the Persians ... they have been taught to hate the Arab Nation.' As for the Iraqis in Nasiriyya and Samawa, known for their secularism, *al-Thawra* dismisses them as 'marsh people', so accustomed to breeding buffalo that they have become 'indistinguish-able from them'. When they migrate to big cities like Baghdad, they make their living through begging, prostitution and robbery, not out of poverty, but because of their intrinsic degraded nature. A true Arab, of course, cannot be so degraded. 'These are not Arabs. They were brought with their buffalo from India by Muhammad al-Qasim' (the Abbasid leader who conquered India in the ninth century).[7]

Emboldened by such racist discourse, the Iraqi press proceeded to announce the names and positions of members of Saddam's family when they were awarded medals for their 'heroic deeds during the mother of battles.' These included 'Ali Hasan al-Majid, Saddam's paternal cousin and minister of defence; Watban Ibrahim, a half-brother and interior minister; Sab'aui Ibrahim, Watban's brother and general director of *al-Amn*; Qusayy Saddam Husain, Saddam's younger son and head of *Jihaz*; and Abid Hasan al-Majid, his paternal cousin and assistant to the head of the *al-Mukhabarat*.[8] Others in the family whose titles were not specified but were also awarded medals included: Saddam's elder son 'Uday; Saddam Kamil Hasan, his son-in-law; and Arshad Yasin Rashid, his brother-in-law and aide-de-camp.

Iraqis living outside the 'Sunni Triangle' have been given a new chance to prove their loyalty to the revolution. During the year that followed the *intifada, Babil,* a new daily run by 'Uday Saddam Husain, began publishing full pages of statements of loyalty to 'Uday's father by tribal chiefs. For the government to address citizens through their chiefs had been unthinkable by Iraqis since the last days of the monarchy. Such is the degradation of Iraqi politics that interior minister Watban Ibrahim hailed the chiefs as 'the real, undepletable asset for the protection of Iraq'.[9]

## Life after Saddam?

A year after the *intifada,* Iraqis were looking more apprehensively at the future than at any time before. Restrictions on foreign travel were lifted for the first time in more than a decade, but people found no air flights between Iraq and the outside world. The vast majority of countries imposed formidable barriers to prevent Iraqis from entering. Jordan, the only neighbouring country with open borders with Iraq, was flooded with tens of thousands of Iraqis, many of whom had sold their possessions to migrate to any country that might accept them. In the north, on the Iraqi side of the Tigris river, hundreds of Kurds and Christian Assyrians assembled every week in the hope that a Syrian boat might bring them to a refugee camp near al-Hasaka, from which they could possibly find a safe haven in Europe or North America. Most of those deserting Iraq belong to the silent, unorganized majority of urban professionals, technocrats and university students 'fed up with ideologies' and wishing to live in peace. Most of them have been counting the days in hope that the dictatorship will end. The *intifada* aroused fears in many that post-Saddam Iraq might not be the place where their modest dreams could be fulfilled.

Iraqi opposition parties have adopted such principles as pluralism, the rule of law and respect for the will of the people. But such principles are far from democracy, even if the various parties' commitment to them was beyond question. Such principles are closely related to secular politics, which in Iraq have been associated in one way or another with the Left. With the Left at a low ebb, it is hardly surprising that secularists in the opposition find themselves, more than ever, as misfits. In February 1991, when opposition representatives held intensive meetings to prepare for a general congress of the Iraqi opposition, the draft of a legal paper was repealed because it began by stating the equality of all Iraqis irrespective of their sex, religion or race: according to the *shari‘a,* males are superior to females. One chief of an Arab tribe challenged the Kurds on their demand for autonomy: 'My territory is comparable to yours: so should I demand autonomy for my tribe?' A council of Iraqi tribes boasts that it has the backing of the USA and Sa‘udi Arabia. Whether the claims are true or not, it remains a fact that a democratic outcome would not be welcomed by most of the regional superpowers that can influence Iraqi politics.

Many in the West argue that it is precisely the atomization of Iraqi society that makes democracy a risky alternative to the present regime. They tend to forget that this atomization is, to a large extent, a direct consequence of the regime. And so the Iraqi nightmare continues. Twenty years of uninterrupted brutal dictatorship have left the political culture of the people of Iraq more impoverished than ever. As a result they are unlikely, in the foreseeable future, to be able to develop the radically different state structures required to replace the existing system.

## Notes

1. This is an edited version of an article which first appeared in the *Middle East Report* (MERIP), May-June 1992.

2. I would like to express my deep gratitude to all those brave and honest individuals, whose names cannot be mentioned here for obvious reasons, who enabled me to review thousands of files belonging to the various intellegence organizations in Kurdistan. I would also like to thank those who helped me in conducting dozens of interviews with participants in the *intifada*, prisoners and military deserters. Special thanks go to members the Interrogation Committee of the Kurdistan Front who allowed me to interview detained Iraqi intelligence agents.

3. Law no. 83 of 1979, ratified by Resolution 797 of the RCC 20 June 1979, published in *al-Waqai' al-Iraqiya* (The Official Gazette) No. 2740, 9 July 1979.

4. See, among others, Phebe Marr, *The Modern History of Iraq*, (Boulder: Westview Press, 1985) p. 281. For a more radical but similar approach, see Peter Gowan, 'The Gulf War, Iraq and Western Liberalism,' *New Left Review*, no. 187 (May-June 1991). Basing himself on some simply innaccurate facts or reading them superficially, Gowan adopts such subtitles as 'Ba'thism in the 1970s: State Building and Reform', (p. 61).

5. Not even officials took that claim seriously. See, e.g., Fadhil al-Barrak's interview with the weekly *Alf-Ba'* (17 June 1980). The then Director General of *al-Amn* confessed that any family who did not prove loyal to the revolution would be deported, even if it provided proof of its Iraqi identity.

6. *Al-Thawra*, 13 November 1979.

7. *Al-Thawra*, 1-3 April 1991.

8. All Iraqi papers, 12 January 1992.

9. All Iraqi papers, 1 January 1992.

CHAPTER THREE

# Ba'thist Ideology and Practice

*Zuhair al-Jaza'iri*

At the heart of the round city of Baghdad, near the presidential palace, is a large building with striking Arab and Islamic features. Sometimes illuminated to highlight its symbolic significance, this is the headquarters of the Baghdad-based Pan-Arab Command of the Arab Ba'th Socialist Party. In the 1970s it also housed the lavish offices of the founder of Ba'thism, Michel 'Aflaq, during his intermittent stays in Iraq. Official guests of Iraq paid their respects to him here and the Iraqi leadership visited him for consultations. He was given ceremonial precedence over President Hasan al-Bakr and the then vice-president, Saddam Husain. He was addressed as 'Master' (*al-'Ustadh*) to emphasize the subservience of students to their master, of 'the branch to the whole', of the state to the party, and of practice to theory. This façade of respectful protocol, however, had little to do with political reality.

## Ideological crisis in Arab nationalism

When the Ba'th Party seized power in Iraq in 1968 Ba'thism was in crisis. The Arab nationalist movement, of which the Ba'th Party is a component part, had been deeply affected by the military defeat in June 1967 of its living incarnation, Jamal 'Abd al-Nasir (Nasser). There had been radical critical revisions, and a series of splits in which breakaway groups adopted Marxism, an ideology vehemently opposed by Ba'thists. The metamorphosis affected some of the more active sections of the Arab nationalist movement, including the Popular Front for the Liberation of Palestine (George Habash), the Democratic Front for the Liberation of Palestine (Nayif Hawatmah), the Popular Front for the Liberation of the Occupied Gulf, the Organization of Lebanese Socialists (Muhsin Ibrahim), the Arab Socialist Action Party (Hashim 'Ali Muhsin) and the Arab Socialist Movement of Iraq.

As regards the Ba'thists themselves, the inner rules of the Ba'th Party state that 'the Ba'th Party is a single Arab party led by a single leadership, the Pan-Arab Command, and its division into regional organizations is due to the partition of the Arab nation into many states and the practical requirements of revolutionary struggle.' However, Ba'thists had been split since 1966, when the ruling Ba'th Party in Syria expelled from membership the philosopher and founder of Ba'thism, Michel 'Aflaq, accusing him of being right-wing, of submerging the party in obscurantist ideology and of conniving with Nasser to dissolve the party. The new leadership, headed by Salah Jadid, arrested some of the historic leadership, while others fled the country, including Michel 'Aflaq, who went to Iraq.

## Iraqi Ba'thism

In Iraq the Ba'th Party had previously been in power and exercised a reign of terror after the regime of 'Abd al-Karim Qasim was overthrown on 8 February 1963. Several months of confusion ensued with rival groups of Ba'thists and nationalists jockeying for power, in the course of which 'Ali Salih al-Sa'di came out on top. On 22 November 1963, in a second coup later referred to by Ba'thists as 'the November setback', the military Ba'thists – Ahmad Hasan al-Bakr, Salih Mahdi 'Ammash and Hardan al-Tikriti – prioritized military discipline over their civilian party comrades, formed an alliance with the Nasserites to oust al-Sa'di and share power with them under the leadership of 'Abd al-Salam 'Arif. Ahmad Hasan al-Bakr and Hardan al-Tikriti were appointed Vice-President and Minister of Defence but in the spring of 1964 'Arif engineered their resignations. The Nasserites had ousted the Ba'th.

From November 1963 to July 1968 the Ba'th Party in Iraq consisted of small, interconnected conspiritorial groups of like-minded friends and kinsmen. In 1964 al-Bakr and Hardan al-Tikriti were almost certainly responsible for the appointment of al-Bakr's relative, Saddam Husain, then aged twenty-seven, as principal full-time organiser of the non-military wing of the party. Their chances of regaining power increased in the volatile situation created by the accidental death of 'Abd al-Salam 'Arif in April 1966 and the succession of his brother 'Abd al-Rahman 'Arif, and by the change of leadership in Damascus that led to the formation of two separate Ba'th parties in Syria and Iraq.

On 17 July 1968 the 'Arif regime was overthrown in a bloodless coup carried out by Colonel 'Abd al-Razzaq al-Nayif, Director of Intelligence, and Colonel Ibrahim 'Abd al-Rahman al-Da'ud, commander of the Republican Guards, acting in conjunction with Ba'thist officers. The gentlemanly removal of 'Arif was, however, only a prelude to much more far-reaching developments which culminated in the emergence of the al-Bakr/Saddam Husain wing of the Ba'th as 'the government' thirteen days later. Ba'thist officers seized al-Nayif and forced him into exile in London where he was finally assassinated in 1978. Ibrahim 'Abd al-Rahman al-Da'ud never returned from Jordan, where he had gone to inspect Iraqi troops, leaving Hardan al-Tikriti in charge of armed forces in Iraq.

Such were the circumstances in which the Ba'thists seized power in Iraq in July 1968. It is questionable how far the Ba'th as a political party

were involved in the events of 17 July, but after 30 July they were to hold
on to power by any means.

## Theory and practice

The report of the 8th Regional Congress of the Iraqi Ba'th Party, held in
January 1974, noted in its third chapter the contradiction between Ba'thist
theory and practice when in power: 'In the 1960s, the party faced the
complex problems of ruling, while still adhering to the original fundamental ideological principles that had come into being and been developed
during the 1940s and 1950s.' Those principles offered no models of
society, let alone detailed programmes for practical application. Despite
the fact that the founders of the Ba'th Party – the Syrian Michel 'Aflaq,
Salah al-Din Bitar and Zaki al-'Arsuzi – had studied in France, their
writings did not reflect the influence of the charters and theories of the
French Revolution, such as those defining the relationship of the individual to the state; the division of legislative, executive and judicial powers;
and the nature of a representative state independent from the person of the
ruler.

Their attention had instead focused on the German nationalist movement, in which the petty German states had been united from above
through the alliance of the landed nobility and the military, rather than
through the rise of a powerful bourgeoisie interested in unification. They
were also attracted to German nationalist ideology, which laid more
emphasis on how to propagate the spiritual unity of the nation than on the
means of giving this unity a constitutional and executive form. One of the
old Ba'thists recalled that his generation of young Ba'thists was 'influenced by Nietzsche's *Thus Spoke Zarathustra*, Fichte's *Fourteen Letters
to the German Nation*, and Hitler's *Mein Kampf*. German spiritual nationalism was for us a response to the British and French colonial powers that
were occupying the Arab countries'.[1]

'Aflaq himself did not write a book to explain his ideas. His philosophy
was expressed in articles and ceremonial speeches imbued with a highly
abstract, voluntarist and mystical ethos. During the initial period, the
founders of Ba'thism were living in Syria under French mandate. In July
1945, members of the higher leadership of the party – Michel 'Aflaq, Salah
al-Din Bitar and Midhet al-Bitar – applied to the ministry of the interior
to start a legal 'Arab Ba'th Party'. With it they submitted both the party's
programme and its rules. The founding congress was held in Damascus
on 4 April 1947.

The 4th article of this constitution stated: 'The party strives to formulate
a constitution for the state that guarantees for Arab citizens absolute
equality before of the law', and that the state would 'safeguard the
freedoms of speech, publication, assembly, protest and the press ... and

allow the setting up of clubs, societies and parties'.[2] These constitutional principles were ignored at the first opportunity. The Ba'th Party leadership supported the three military coups which took place in Syria in 1949. It was the only party to support the first of the coups, which was staged by the commander of the Syrian army, Husni al-Za'im; it then supported the coup of Sami al-Hinnawi who displaced and killed Husni al-Za'im; and then that of Adib Shishakli on 20 December of the same year. This was despite the fact that the Ba'th Party was banned in both the first and second coups.

When the Ba'th seized power in Syria and Iraq in 1963, it radically changed its attitude towards parliamentary democracy as stipulated in its first constitution. The 6th Pan-Arab Congress held in Damascus in October the same year envisaged 'transcending parliamentarism as being one of the forms of feudal and bourgeois hegemony over the toiling masses'. It noted that 'interpreting democracy in an abstract and absolute manner as a multi-party system represents a bourgeois approach'. The Ba'th Party adopted the Stalinist concept of a 'popular democracy' which was concretely embodied in the one-party system. However, in its 7th Pan-Arab Congress, which was held in Damascus in February 1964 when the Iraqi Ba'th was out of power, it relinquished the one-party idea and declared its acceptance of the policy of the United Patriotic Front – in other words, sharing power with allies.

When the Iraqi Ba'th Party seized power again in 1968, it had no clear vision of the structure of the polity it sought to establish. Neither the classical dogmas nor the practice of the ideological leaders offered any guidance. Instead, the Ba'thists came to believe that their chief concern was the extent to which they could make use of existing reality to consolidate their power.

## Consolidating power

Their first preoccupation was a major domestic restructuring of power. After deposing 'Abd al-Razzaq al-Nayif and 'Abd al-Rahman al-Da'ud (who had been their partners in the coup of 17 July 1968), on 30 July 1968, the full membership of the Ba'th's Regional Command joined the Revolutionary Command Council (RCC). Only three members (Hammad Shihab al-Tikriti, Sa'dun Ghaidan, Hardan al-Tikriti) from outside the Regional Command remained in the RCC. A new government dominated by Ba'thists was formed. The party leadership integrated with the state bureaucracy as the party took hold of the leading decision-making centres of the state.

Military commanders loyal to al-Na'if had been removed and the civilian wing of the Ba'th now controlled the RCC and government. However, the coup of November 1963 had taught them that a military commander, even one without a popular or party base (such as 'Abd al-Salam 'Arif) could threaten their power as long as he occupied an appropriate position in the army with a loyal tribal following. Consequently, they carried out a gradual purge of the army and brought back into active service all retired Ba'thists, even reserve officers who had not completed their service.

Despite tight control over the RCC and the army, stability remained a source of deep concern for the political leadership. Saddam Husain was authorized to set up a shadowy security apparatus, on military lines but not under army control – a security organization free of the traditional police bureaucratic structures, with a unique, secretive character. The nucleus of this apparatus was set up before the Ba'th Party came to power. It was known as the *Jihaz Hanin*[3] and its task was 'to protect the party from sabotage'. After assuming power, it was renamed the 'Public Relations Bureau' and assumed responsibility for 'liquidating the reserves of counter-revolution'. These in practice turned out to be rival intelligence networks, pro-Nayif officers and former Ba'thist leaders reluctant to cooperate with the new regime, as well as Communist cadres and organizations. Any members of the *Jihaz Hanin* who displayed some hesitation in carrying out the orders were themselves killed. Assassinations were carried out carefully, so as to avoid the fierce reactions triggered by operations of the National Guards after the February 1963 coup.

Apart from securing hegemony over the state, the Ba'th Party also had to improve its image in the minds of those who had greeted its return to power with suspicion. As a sign of good will, political detainees who had been held during 'Arif's rule (1963-68) were released, and those expelled from the civil service on political grounds were re-employed. A dialogue with the Kurds was initiated, and in 1970 the 11 March Declaration on the the Kurdish Problem achieved a truce of sorts. On 15 November 1971, the draft of the 'National Action Charter' was issued calling on anti-imperialist and anti-reactionary forces to cooperate for the peaceful solution of the Kurdish problem on the basis of the 11 March Declaration, to agree on a programme for economic transformation with a socialist orientation, and to consolidate relations with the socialist bloc. The Kurdish Democratic Party (KDP) turned down the Ba'thist National Action Charter but the Iraqi Communist Party (ICP) saw in it a potential basis for further dialogue and cooperation. This led to the setting-up of the Patriotic Front in July 1973.

Concern over ways of consolidating power and other domestic problems diverted the Iraqi Ba'thists from their pan-Arab ends. They avoided their earlier ideological language, too reminiscent of the archaic formulae of the February 1963 coup. Instead, their leaders and cadres took to the streets in a series of public meetings under the slogan: 'You ask and the party answers', in order to explain their new policy and reply to the questions of the people. In one of these meetings, Saddam Husain appeared for the first time before a large audience in al-Kashafa stadium in late 1969 to tell them: 'Do not give us your confidence unconditionally.' Asked whether or not other parties would join the cabinet, he replied: 'We will not allow the person who rides on the mule behind us to lay his hand on the saddlebag.'

## Pan-Arab issues

Despite these domestic preoccupations, international relations remained a central concern, not as a matter of Pan-Arab rhetoric, but because of real events taking place in the Arab world. On the eastern borders, there was an Iranian army that numbered 200,000: double the size of the Iraqi army at the time and the biggest regional power in the Gulf. This expanding army constituted the basis of an Iranian sub-imperialism, apparently threatening the small Gulf states. In April 1969 Iran forced Iraq into sharing the Shatt al-'Arab waterway, and occupied the three Arab islands of the Great Tunb, the Lesser Tunb and Abu Musa in 1972. Iranian troops were also stationed in Oman under the pretext of protecting the Straits of Hormuz from guerrillas in Dhofar. Ba'thist propaganda stressed the Iranian threat to the Arab world, the coordination between Israel and Iran to occupy the Gulf, and the threat Iranian communities posed for the demographic balance of the Gulf countries. No concrete steps were taken, however, other than striking at internal Shi'i groupings and presenting them as Iranian agents.

Iraq had about twenty-five thousand troops in Jordan as part of what remained of the joint Arab Salah al-Din Forces. The Jordanian front was almost quiet, but questions were raised about Iraqi troops remaining idle when the Palestinian resistance movement along the Jordan valley carried out intensive operations across the river. In particular there was concern over the battles of Ghor al-Safi on 12 November 1969 and al-Karameh in 1970, in which Jordanian troops took part.

Following Nasser's acceptance of the Rogers' initiative in July 1970, the need for Pan-Arab solidarity intensified. It was during this period that 'Aflaq, who had been sentenced to death in Syria, paid his first visit to Iraq. Inside the Iraqi Ba'th, a trend developed demanding that Iraq's potential become involved in the Arab nation's battles, assuming that this would strengthen the party's Arab appeal and enable it to take the leading Arab role from Nasser. The Iraqi Ba'th encouraged demonstrations in Arab countries to protest against Nasser's 'compromise' and to demand the total liberation of Palestine. Iraq attempted to forge an Arab alliance against UN Resolution 242, a stand on the left of the Palestinian organizations themselves.

These slogans, however, were put to the test when the Jordanian regular army staged the 'Black September' operation in 1970. This military attack on the Palestinian resistance movement – widely regarded as 'the only sign of hope in the darkness of defeat' – appalled many in the Arab world. The Ba'th Party was seriously embarrassed. It had claimed Palestine as its central cause and had used the Palestinian flag as the party's banner, an equivalent to the official flag of state. Iraq had twenty-five thousand soldiers and one hundred tanks stationed in the areas where the fighting took place, but these units did not intervene despite pressure from the street and the Ba'th Party rank-and-file. They even opened up a path for the Jordanian army to outflank the Palestinian resistance as it withdrew northwards into Syria. This position created 'a dangerous situation and contradictory sentiments inside the party', as was later admitted at the 8th Regional Congress. The rank-and-file could not comprehend the obvious discrepancy between the public rhetoric in support of the Palestinians and what actually happened. A decree was issued by the RCC justifying non-intervention as necessary to prevent 'an American-Israeli intervention that would occupy new parts of the Arab world'. The leadership held urgent meetings with the rank-and-file to explain its stand. It retreated into ever more radical gestures, refusing to attend the Arab summit held in Cairo, and rejecting as 'a compromise' the Cairo Agreement which had been approved by the Palestinian resistance.

This policy of escaping into the politics of gesture was also apparent in the stand of the Ba'th Party leadership during the October 1973 War. Three days after the outbreak of the war, Iraq sent 500 tanks to the Syrian front, when the war was almost nearing its end. The Iraqi Ba'th Party used its rejection of UN Resolution 338 as a pretext to withdraw its forces as soon as the fighting stopped.

## Turning point

The 8th Regional Congress, held in January 1974, was an important turning point in the development of the Iraqi Ba'th Party. The Congress took place at the peak of the oil boom after the October War. In 1972, oil revenues were $575 million, in 1973 they suddenly jumped to $1,480 million, and by 1974 they were $5,700 million. The living standard of broad sectors of the Iraqi population improved, and a large class of big contractors emerged (nearly eight hundred millionaires at least, according to income tax data for 1980). Sub-contractors, traders and owners of construction factories were given huge amounts of financial credit (after changes in banking policy in 1974). The state was their main customer, having embarked upon so-called 'explosive development' plans. The biggest contractors had close family connections with the state leadership, an expression of the dependent relationship between this rising group and the state. They began to impose their interests on state policy, leading to an increasing schism between the official ideological discourse and current practice. The new class had no need for Arab markets: the state sufficed. It turned its back on any developmental effort in the Arab world, decried the catastrophic consequences of Black September and the October War and retreated further into isolationism, calling for avoidance of any national losses.

The 8th Party Congress Report strengthened particularistic tendencies in the policy of the Ba'th Party. Out of a total of 273 pages, 15 pages only were given over to pan-Arab issues (Palestine, the Gulf, Arab relations), while the rest were devoted to internal matters, in particular the issues of development and consolidating power. Although the report warned against attempts to give predominance to the pan-Arab over the domestic, or the domestic over the pan-Arab, it ended with the conclusion that fulfilling specifically Iraqi national tasks would create a solid base for pan-Arab struggle. The report's language, particularly in the fifth chapter (The Tasks of Socialist Transformation) reflects a clear Marxist, even Leninist influence: it contains analyses of feudal and semi-feudal relations in the countryside; the parasitic nature of the urban bourgeoisie; the development of productive state sectors; the bureaucratic state bourgeoisie; trade unionism; state farms and cooperatives. But the new classes that were being engendered by the state, and were gaining hegemony over it, were already reorganizing production in their own interests. New accounts of 'nationalist socialism' developed, and Saddam Husain started praising the role of the private sector in socialist construction.

Changes in the social base of the party soon translated into rapid turnover within the higher echelons of the regime. The leaders who had carried out the 'revolution' of 1968 gradually disappeared, and none of the members of the first RCC survived, apart from al-Bakr (Saddam was not a member of the first RCC). During the 8th Congress, three members were expelled and eight new members were added to the RCC,[4] whose task was defined as 'legislation, appointing the government and relieving it'.[5] The process of removing the military from the RCC was completed and the weight of the party civilian bureaucrats was enhanced. The merging of the party and the state intensified: more emphasis was laid on the leading role of the party in state and society. The report stated that 'the party's leadership of the state and society is a task that has urgent priority, and must never be approached lightly ... for it is a central condition of the survival and development of the revolution. It is a patriotic and national necessity as well as the duty of all our militants.'

## Patriotic Front – Ba'thization

The charter of the Patriotic Front established in July 1973 between the ruling Ba'th Party and other parties including the Iraqi Communist Party (ICP) stipulated that 'the Front embodies the joint leadership of the Iraqi people's struggle'. But the Ba'th Party began to proclaim the idea of itself as the 'leading party'. The RCC issued a decree that adopted the 8th Ba'th Party Congress Report as 'a law for the state and society'. With this decree, the decisions of the party became officially equivalent to state decisions for the first time. This was not merely a formal change, it was also implemented by exercising more pressure on the other political forces, particularly the ICP.

The process of purging and Ba'thization continued in the armed forces and the security apparatus. The Ba'th Party put pressure on the ICP to stop any political activity inside the armed forces; Communists and their supporters inside the army were threatened with the death penalty. The ICP gave directives to thousands of its members and supporters inside the army to dissolve their organizations and to sever their relations with the party during their military service. The Communist press was banned from the barracks, and the military were barred from reading Marxist literature, under threat of execution.

After the armed forces and the media, it was the turn of mass organizations, particularly student and youth organizations, to be purged. Saddam's slogan 'If we win over the youth, we win the future'[6] was transformed into a plan of action to prevent other political forces from maintaining a foothold in this field. There were Communist organizations dating back to the late 1940s. The General Union of Students in the Iraqi Republic (GUSIR) had been founded on 14 April 1948 as the first student organization in Iraq. In the first student elections during the rule of 'Abd al-Rahman 'Arif in 1967, the Communists had swept in with 80 per cent of the seats. An alliance of nationalist forces, which included the Ba'th Party, won less than 10 per cent of the seats. Before it was banned in 1975, the Communist-led union had 10,000 members in Baghdad alone.

A second more dangerous challenge came from Shi'i religious forces. Young people attending mosques heard a discourse different from that of the Ba'th Party, and regarded it as a sectarian leadership incapable of representing the Shi'i. In a speech delivered before an enlarged meeting of the official Union of Iraqi Youth, Saddam explained his plan as follows: 'While we work seriously to achieve our central slogan – "if we win the youth we win the future" – we should achieve other objectives, namely to eradicate the roots of other political movements.'[7]

A law prohibiting any activity outside the framework of the Patriotic Front was enacted. Violations carried the death penalty. This law was first applied to the Communists who were forced to dissolve their youth, student and women's organizations, transforming them into mere party branches.

The second part of the Ba'th Party's plan to win over the youth was to concentrate on the universities and schools. This target group included more than 4 million students, nearly a quarter of Iraq's population, and it was increasing at the rate of 14 per cent annually.[8] The curriculum, especially in human sciences (history, geography, political science) was rewritten. The Ba'th Party leadership specified the fundamental references for guidance in educational programmes as being: (1) The Report of the 8th Regional Congress of the Arab Ba'th Socialist Party; (2) The directives of the Leadership; (3) The Directives of the Council of the Republic's Presidium.[9]

The aim of this campaign was to educate a new generation from the nursery up; the first batch of which graduated in 1986. In the minds of this generation the state was identified with the Ba'th Party, the only party they had known. The indoctrination began with the 'Pioneers' (8-14 years old), who numbered 60,000 in 1975 – and continued in the youth organizations, in which adolescents underwent ideological and military programmes in summer labour camps.

Monopolizing and concentrating work among the country's youth was the first target of the Ba'th Party leadership throughout the second half of the 1970s. They banned any youth or student organizations set up by other parties, and exercised strict control over admittance to the principal universities and colleges, requiring party or other recommendations. In short, the rising generation was reserved for the Ba'th Party alone. From this generation 'supporters'[10] were chosen, the lowest and broadest rank in the party hierarchy. According to Saddam Husain's reply to the American researcher Christine Helms, these supporters do not have the right to see the Inner Party Norms until they become full members of the party.[11] The Inner Party Norms stipulate that the lower organs do not have the right to criticize the higher ones or the party as an institution; they can exercise criticism only at their own level.[12] The meetings of the lower party organs take the form of one-sided lectures, beginning with quotations from the leadership, then conveying to the rank-and-file central directives that are not open to discussion except in terms of the methods of implementation.

The process of centralization of power within the the party continued. The party's control over the army was exercised through the middle ranks first, then upwards to the higher ranks. The army's structure was changed from outside through the Party Military Bureau, which was parallel to the Defence Ministry. Official police organs were penetrated by the party's own secret security organ, which was later transformed into the 'public relations bureau', carrying out assassinations and terrorism against all elements and groups that constituted a danger to the party. This organ later turned into a monitoring apparatus which had the upper hand over the party, army and state. In 1977 the party was merged with the state by turning all members of the Regional Command into ministers and appointing them automatically as members of the RCC. The number of RCC members was increased from five to twenty-one, and decision-making inside it became concentrated in the hands of the president and his deputy. In practice, the party apparatus changed into a civilian militia for protecting the state, while control over the party itself became dominated by one part of the state: the security service.

## Saddam Husain

Saddam Husain managed to reach the top through backstage control of party institutions that operated in parallel to their state equivalents: the 'public relations bureau' rather than the security and intelligence services; the 'military bureau' rather than the Ministry of Defence; the 'culture and information bureau' rather than the Ministry of Culture and Information; the 'bureau of vocational organizations' rather than the party itself.

Ahmad Hasan Al-Bakr, although bearing such titles as 'the Leader', and then 'the Father Leader' eventually ceased to exercise real power in the state and the party. Saddam Husain emerged, first as second in command, then as the real power, and finally as the actual leader, depriving the party of any say in the matter. Finally, the contradiction was resolved by the massacre of 22 July 1979, in which Saddam Husain physically liquidated a third of the RCC members, about half of the Regional Command.

It was at this point that Saddam Husain began to explain a new fact: there is no absolute equality between Ba'thists, because there is in fact a single mountain peak that is Saddam Husain; the rest are slopes. Equality is possible on the slopes, but not between them and the mountain peak. The first step towards betrayal begins with the Ba'thist having a sense of injustice because his comrade is a mountain peak. Saddam said during the trial of some of his erstwhile colleagues: 'It is not my fault if they were slopes who sought equality with the peak.'[13] This idea of a chasm between the peak and the slopes was not confined to the emotive trial, but it soon became be established in other ways. The word *Sayyidi* (My Lord) came to replace 'Comrade' when speaking to the president. In this, the vice-presidents and the ordinary citizens were equal. The same distance was reproduced in arranging the seats around the meeting table: the vacant gap between the president's seat and that of his closest deputy ('Izzat al-Duri) is equivalent to at least three seats.

The party was deemed an inadequate defence against the dangers threatening the president. Saddam set up a security cordon around himself made up of close relatives. His half brother Barzan became the head of intelligence; his half-brother Sab'aui the head of his private office; his half-brother Watban the head of his deputy's office; his cousin Hassan al-Majid the director of security; his cousin Sa'dun Shakir the minister of interior; his brother-in-law 'Adnan Khairullah the minister of defence. This family regime was strengthened with a series of marriages that consolidated the positions of the grooms: Saddam's son 'Uday married the daughter of his deputy 'Izzat al-Duri. Husain Kamil advanced to the post of official in charge of palace security after marrying Saddam's daughter Hala; his brother Saddam Kamil married Saddam's second daughter Rana. In terms of security and confidence, kinship mattered far more than creed.

Saddam Husain, as Chairman of the RCC, Secretary of the Regional Command, President of the Republic, Prime Minister and Commander in Chief of the Armed Forces stands aloft above his closest deputies. None of them has any post exclusively to himself: each is in office only as a deputy of Saddam. At the 9th Regional Congress in 1982, Saddam's grip on the Regional Command was further strengthened. Six members were originally his own deputies, either in the RCC or the cabinet; six others were his advisers in various affairs; four were relatives; four were members of his security organization.

The subordination of the party to the leader was manifest in the wording of the report issued by the 9th Congress. The report of the 8th Congress had analysed the party's development with a realistically critical language that pinpointed successes and failures; leftist and rightist mistakes that cost dearly; hasty formulae; emotional and noisy methods; conceitedness; combining party and govermental posts, etc. The assessment spoke of the party as an entity that had its faults and merits. The preface to the 9th Congress Report, by contrast, begins with a clear division of the role of the party and that of Saddam Husain, 'a leader of special type who emerged and developed in unique circumstances'. He is credited with all the historic achievements of the Ba'th Party during fourteen years of its rule: 'playing the leading role in achieving the historic explosions; the creator of the Patriotic Front and its leader; the designer of the historic March Declaration; the actual leader of the process of oil nationalization; the first planner of the process of total development; the brain behind the strategy of nuclear research; and the guiding light in the field of culture and information'. The report divides the 'march of the revolution' into two phases: before and after Saddam Husain assumed the leading role. There is no mention of al-Bakr. His period of rule is referred to as being 'a constitutional situation with plenty of complications' – complications hampering the inevitable advance of Saddam to the leading position.

The 9th Congress report did not, however, long remain a theoretical guide for the state and society. It was published in daily papers on 26 January 1983, six months after the congress, but afterwards disappeared from circulation. Instead, Saddam's speeches became the ideological guide. Daily extracts were published on the front page of the newspapers, and Ba'thist authors quoted him as reference. The leader was approaching the people directly, speaking to both Ba'thists and the general public through the media. The party itself had become a mass party – that is, its membership reached one million: in 1980 one party member for every ten citizens. In several of the speeches of that period, Saddam concentrated on abolishing the distinction between the Ba'thist and the citizen. He developed the expression: 'faith in the line of the Ba'th and revolution', instead of 'affiliation to the Ba'th party'. He made the citizen's faith equivalent to actual membership, thus abolishing the ideological demarcation between the two. Streets, government offices and army camps were filled with banners emphasising this trend: 'The good citizen is a good Ba'thist!', 'The good soldier is a good Ba'thist!', 'Every citizen is a Ba'thist even if he has not affiliated!' In a speech delivered to soldiers at an advance army post, Saddam declared: 'the Ba'th Party of which you are members does not discriminate between outsiders and insiders, because there is no distinction between an organized and a non-organized Ba'thist, but only between those who have faith in our nation and those who do not.'[14]

Affiliation to the Ba'th Party no longer interrupted the vertical stratification of the state apparatus, because from 1981 directives stated that the Ba'thist should be accountable to his superiors in the state apparatus, contrary to what prevailed during the first half of the 1970s. The party was reduced to a body whose tasks centred on mobilizing citizens in processions and gatherings, and forming an armed militia to protect the regime. During the war with Iran, conscription into the militia (People's Army) was imposed on Ba'thists and citizens alike.

The role of provincial organizations was to enlist as many as possible to the war effort, hunting deserters and anti-war elements and executing them. The party no longer embodied the idea of the state and its course of action; it was no longer even an ideological mediator between the mind that thinks and the people who are supposed to assimilate this thought: it was rather transformed in practice into an extension of the military and security organs of the state.

Ba'thists and ordinary citizens alike became equal before the 'leader-symbol'. This title expressed more than additional adulation for Saddam Husain. It was stipulated in the articles of the new constitution in which the President is defined as 'the head of state, and the people's leader and symbol'.[15] The rise of a single individual at the expense of the collective leadership of the party, and at the expense of the state organs, altered Ba'thist theory. All the previous formulae for rule – 'parliamentary democracy', 'people's democracy', 'leadership of the patriotic front', 'the leading party' – disappeared, leaving only the formula of 'the leader – symbol and necessity'.

In order to build the prestige of the symbol, Saddam was surrounded with pseudo-religious ceremonies. Thus, the leader's visit to any town, village or school came to be regarded as an honour and blessed feast to be celebrated annually. In all the national celebrations, particularly the processions of torch-bearers, raising the picture of the leader and reciting his name has become a consistent ritual. Celebrations culminate in a pledge which often takes the form of a supplication addressed to the leader 'to march under his banner and to follow his example'. Such pledges are sometimes signed in blood. The annual celebrations of the leader's birthday on 28 April is a major event; celebration of the party's anniversary (7 April) has become an intermediate step, building up to the rituals around the birthday event. Virtually everybody is supposed to take part, beginning with each household lighting a candle in front of the leader's picture. The celebrations culminate on 28 April with a procession from all parts of Iraq towards the leader's hometown, Tikrit. Such celebrations did not stop during the war with Iran, nor after the disastrous defeat of Iraq by the allied forces.

Enormous pictures of the leader are to be found at the entrances of towns, institutions and schools. Everywhere, the wall-picture must present him as an example to be followed. At the entrance to the town of Najaf, for example, his picture shows him as a humble visitor holding the rails of the shrine. At the entrance to the offices of 'peasant unions', he is shown in peasant costumes holding a spade. At the entrance to universities, he wears academic robes. And at Babylon's historical ruins, his picture faces that of Nebuchadnezzar.

A third of the period of television transmission, lasting seven hours a day, is devoted to covering the activities of the leader and his speeches, repeated in full during the three news bulletins. The president's picture, three columns wide and ten inches long, appears in the middle of the front page of every daily paper, even when no news about him is reported. Two of his statements occupy the top of the first page. In an issue of *al-Thawra* picked at random, (1 August 1984), Saddam's name and his titles are repeated 147 times on the paper's eight pages. His photograph appears 27 times. The same issue contained news about the unveiling of five new wall-pictures of the president at the entrances of various towns and government buildings.

The daily paper *Iraq* published on 18 November 1984 carried a story highlighting the 'positive' effects that this repetition has had on the subconscious of a girl named Ghadah Jalal al-Din al-Rumi. She was hit by a car when crossing the road, and while receiving treatment under anaesthetic she repeated in her delerium the phrase 'Saddam ... Father Saddam'.[16]

All this propaganda aims at emphasising the overwhelming presence of a single leader in the collective and individual consciousness. Not surprisingly Saddam's pictures were the first target for the participants in the March *intifada* (1991), and the repairing of these pictures was the first task carried out by the troops after regaining control of the towns.

On the national level, it is stressed that the symbol is a purely Iraqi need which emanates from historical and demographic factors. Historically, this need starts from the fact that 'Iraq had for centuries (700 years) lived under foreign occupation and control. It came under many political, cultural and psychological influences'. Those influences hampered the development of the Iraqi national identity for a long time. This approach naturally ignores earlier manifestations of Iraqi nationalism, against both Ottoman and British occupation, and the united stand of Iraqis in welcoming King Faisal I as the first Arab monarch of Iraq. National consensus was further demonstrated in the massive uprisings against treaties with Britain in 1948 and 1953, and afterwards in the overwhelming support for the 14 July 1958 revolution. Yet the Central Report of the 9th Regional Congress of the Ba'th Party assumes that 'nationalism acquired its full dimension only after the 17-30 July 1968 revolution and under Saddam Husain's leadership'.[17]

## The Leader-Symbol

The fact that Iraq is a multi-ethnic and multi-religious state is invoked to show that 'the existence of a symbol is essential for safeguarding it from being torn apart'. Saddam may have been thinking of Stalin when replying to a Kuwaiti journalist who questioned him about the Iraqi media's emphasis on his personality. 'Iraq', he said, 'needs a symbol far more than Moscow does, because the state of development is new and the state of backwardness is deep, and because there are in Iraq various religions, sects and ethnicities. Saddam must therefore be shared by all of them'.[18] Saddam wears the white *kufiya* headband and the golden-laced mantle when he visits Tikrit, the red traditional Kurdish turban when visiting Kurdistan, the uniform of a field commander when inspecting the troops at the front lines, and a civilian suit when attending the seminars of technocrats.

Ba'thist propaganda turns him into a Sumerian, or a Babylonian or Islamic divine monarch. He is likened to Gilgamesh, based on the first verse of that ancient epic, 'Of him who found all things, I shall tell the land'; or to Nebuchadnezzar who built Babylon and its hanging gardens. During the war with Iran, he was likened to Sinharib who defeated the Elamites in the east, to the Abbassid Caliph Mu'tasim and to the early Islamic general Khaled bin al-Waleed.

The Ba'th Party found the stage ready for the emergence of such a hero. Since the departure of Nasser in 1970, the Arab world had suffered a leadership vacuum and faced a desperate need for a leader-symbol to unify all the aspirations of the Arab nation. The rise of Saddam coincided with

Sadat's visit to Jerusalem in 1976 and the signing of the Camp David accords. It was in Iraq that the Arab summit was held which decided to expel Egypt from the Arab League and to transfer its headquarters to Tunisia. The exclusion of Egypt was, for the Ba'th Party, a golden opportunity to occupy the leading position, for Saddam to play Nasser's role as the leader of the Arab nation.

The concept of a 'leader-symbol' was always present in the religious and nationalist discourse of the Ba'th and in the early theses of 'Aflaq (*Epoch of Heroism, Ba'th and Change, In the Anniversary of the Arab Prophet*). In these accounts, 'the leading nation with a historic mission' is living through a period of division and degradation that distanced it from its spiritual unity and its moral message to the world. The outlook is rooted in the traditional Islamic view of history, seen in terms of its golden era (the era of Muhammad's prophecy); the times that followed are regarded as periods of deterioration and degeneration.

In Ba'thist ideology, a leader called 'the historic leader' or 'the necessity-leader' emerges to carry the nation forward. 'In the crucial periods, through suffering and painful lessons of experience, something resembling a call ascends from the conscience of the nation to indicate things which are missed, to which those eligible among its sons respond and thus their life follows a clear path.'[19] The relationship of this promised leader with his society is one of aloofness rather than of interaction, and his emergence is the result of some sort of divine selection, similar to the selection by God of the Prophet who emerges from the solitude of the desert in order to put right the corrupt cities.

The Egyptian author Amir Iskandar draws on religious vision when he portrays the moment of Saddam Husain's birth in his chapter entitled 'A star shines from mud houses.'[20] The Arab world, before the birth of the 'star', is portrayed as a desert suffering from 'intellectual and creative emptiness ... a mystical solitude that awaits the miracle'. This idea presupposes that the masses were totally passive before the birth of the promised leader, doing nothing except await his arrival. 'Saddam was born in this difficult moment and amidst its pains. Perhaps, the historical coincidence between the moment of his birth and the coming into being of the Ba'th had a deeper significance than mere accident. The stage had been prepared, and the role had started to look for its actor. Saddam grew up and stood in the wings, eligible and ready to respond to history's call.'

## Voluntarism

Ba'thist voluntarism assigns to the leader the ability and responsibility for creating, or re-creating, his society rather than responding to factors of change that have already matured. The spiritual process of change comes before actual material change. It starts, according to 'Aflaq, with 'revolt against one's self' which takes the form of a moral suffering through which the leader renders himself free of his society's corruption. He then sharpens his will, in a manner similar to the solitary prophet in the desert. The second stage, 'the revolt against the society', begins. The history of society thereby becomes an extension of the conduct of the leader, 'who marks a historical stage and marks the people with his stamp'.[21]

The greatness of the people comes second to the greatness of the leader and is tested by their 'speedy and deep conformity with his standards'.[22] Although the Ba'th Party does not despise the masses in its public statements, it views them purely as objects. Saddam Husain illustrated this understanding in his conversation with Christine Helms. 'The leader can shape his people as he wishes, can make it negative or positive.'[23] In order for the leader to be able to do this, the masses should be prepared to accept this adaptation submissively – to be united as a single spirit.

The way the Iraqi Ba'th have viewed the masses has varied in accordance with two factors, first the social strata it relied on and secondly, the social nature of the people it addressed. In the report of the 8th Regional Congress, dealing with 'development and socialist construction', the Ba'th relied to a certain extent on Marxist social classifications such as: feudalism, semi-feudalism and rural bourgeoisie; big, parasitic bourgeoisie and bureaucratic bourgeoisie; poor peasants, workers, petty-bourgeoisie.[24]

However, with the development of the idea of the 'leading party', 'the party of the people' and the 'party of all Iraqis', the Ba'th reverted to the original premises by giving precedence to the spiritual unity of the people over their class contradictions. This conception appeared in the report of the 9th Congress: 'We start in these concepts from a thorough knowledge that Iraqis have become homogeneous, socially and psychologically, and closer together to a great extent.'[25] Here, the voluntarist approach negates any form of class or political struggle or the struggle between generations or individuals, and fuses everybody in the crucible of 'spiritual unity'. This imposed uniformity of the people leads to a more important identity between them and the government under a single and unifying symbol and leader.

The Ba'th Party 'methodology' is not drawn from any historical or economic approach, but rather from the science of mass psychology which allows the people to be dealt with as an organic being possessing a single body and spirit led by primitive instincts. By alternating fear and indoctrination from above, the leader can impose his will and re-create 'the new man of the revolution' in the leader's image. Ba'thist idealism holds that 'the spirit is the essence in everything, and the spiritual motive not only controls the object and the means but also creates them'.[26] This translates in practice into giving precedence to will and action over recognizing necessity. When history loses all rationale, it is seen as a negative field open to adventure. This method is backed by the confrontational Ba'thist apparatus with its gangster-like origins and the adventurous military wing inside the army. The alliance of the two and the policy of taking rivals by surprise with unrestricted adventurism gave rise to a series of successful or unsuccessful coups. The 8 February 1963 coup against 'Abd al-Karim Qasim succeeded. The 4 September 1964 coup attempt against 'Abd al-Salam 'Arif – based on storming the national assembly during a meeting of the leadership inside the building, with Saddam opening fire from his machine-gun to kill everybody – was discovered before being carried out.

Before 1968 two lines appeared inside the Ba'th. 'Excluding the idea of overthrowing the regime and embarking on a programme of prolonged negative popular struggle' was one. The other was 'the determination to overthrow the counter-revolutionary regime and regain revolutionary power.'[27] The latter, voluntarist tendency triumphed in the 17 July 1968 'gentlemanly' coup against 'Abd al-Rahman 'Arif and afterwards in the 30 July 'revolutionary' coup against the 'Al-Nayif/Da'ud bloc.

The Ba'th, and particularly Saddam Husain, regard acceptance of the status quo as weakness. He boasts about 'potency' (*al-iqtidar*) in most of his speeches. Since reality is material, it is capable of being subjugated by the power of the spiritual motive and the will. Saddam continuously warns Ba'thist cadres against being 'beseiged by events so that they are forced to do something they did not decide on their own, but which was imposed upon them by outside conditions or forces'.[28] He therefore puts emphasis on initiative (*al-mubada'a*), which means taking decisions before they are dictated by reality. Although a decision is a practical ruling on people and things, its formulation takes place through what Hitler called 'igniting ideas', inside a high head separated from the rest of the body by the neck. Decision-making should not await clarification as to the method of implementation. This is because the structure of the world to which the decision applies is not seen by the voluntarist mind as a separate entity. Rather it is something that exists only insofar as it is intuitively grasped as a fluid state receptive to the leader's decision once made.

Saddam presupposes a clear-cut division between the mind which thinks and the organs which execute. 'The idea matures in the head first and then arrives at action.'[29] From the top to the bottom, the decision goes ready-made from a thinking mind to other bodies who have been prepared by force of habit to play the role of the implementing muscles. Whenever the pressure of reality on the Ba'th increases from outside, it turns into an enemy or worse still a conspiracy. There can be no question of comprehending reality or responding to it. Instead the relationship turns into a war of wills. Hence the continuous bloody alternation of repression and war.

## Notes

1. Interview with author.
2. *The Socialist Arab Ba'th Party*, al-Tal'ia Press, Beirut.
3. Most of functionaries of this apparatus assumed high posts later on, some were assassinated at the hands of their fellows. For example, Samir al-Shaikhli became: director of Baghdad Prison, the capital's mayor, minister of higher education, member of the Regional Command, minister of interior. Sa'dun Shakir became: director of the Vocational Organizations, member of the Regional Command, member of the Revolutionary Command Council. Nadhem Kazzar became: director of security, member of the Party's Military Bureau. He was executed after leading an abortive coup in July 1973. Mohammed Fadhil, member of the Military Bureau, was killed after the coup attempt by Kazzar. Jabbar al-Kurdi turned into a contractor, then was assassinated at the hands of Saddam's bodyguard Sabah Mirza because the former refused to carry out new assignments in the apparatus.
4. The eight new members were: Na'im Haddad, Tayih 'Abd al-Karim, Muhammad Mahjub, 'Adnan al-Hamdani, Shanim 'Abd al-Jalil, Mahmud Yasin, Tahir al-'Ani.
5. Shihab was killed in the Nadhim Kazzar coup.
6. Saddam Husain: in a meeting with the General Union of Iraq Youth on 15 February 1976.
7. Ibid.
8. An interview with the minister of education 'Abd al-Qadir 'Izz al-Din, published in the Iraqi *al-Jumhouriyya* on 7 July 1990.
9. Ibid.
10. The Ba'th ranking begins from the bottom: supporters, 'ansar', members (in cells), members of group (to lead a district), division (to lead larger areas), members of a branch (to lead a province), then members of the Regional Command who number fifteen (to lead on the level of the country).
11. *al-Thawra*, 28 August 1983.
12. From the testimony of a former Ba'thist kept by the author.
13. The trial took place in an emergency meeting for the leading cadres of the party held after announcing the discovery of a plot planned by five members of the Revolution Command Council (Muhi al-Din Mashhadi, 'Adnan al-Hamdani, Ghanim 'Abd al-Jalil, Muhammad Mahjub, Muhammad 'Ayish). It took place after the execution of the accused. On the court bench sat a single judge, Saddam Husain, and there was a single accused, Muhi el-Dein Mashhadi, who made a full confession concerning the conspiracy and those participating in it. The rest of the participants were seized and taken away directly from the meeting hall to the firing-squad. The quotations are taken from a videotape of the trial that was leaked to the opposition abroad.
14. Saddam Husain, speech in the enlarged seminar devoted to discussing the working paper on the field of teaching and higher education, *al-Thawra*, 2 July 1981.
15. *Al-Thawra*, 30 July 1990.
16. After Saddam found out about the story of this girl, he decided to send her to London for treatment at his own expense. *Al-Yawm al-Sabi'*, 29 January 1990.

17. 'The Second Seminar on the Thought of Leader Saddam Husain', *al-Thawra*, 6 May 1984.

18. 'A meeting with the Kuwaiti press, at the end of the Arab summit in Fez (Morocco)', *al-Thawra*, 11 September, 1984.

19. Text attributed to 'Aflaq, published in 7th edition of *'Aflaq Arabyyah*, July 1989.

20. Amir Iskandar, *Saddam Husain: A Man and a Thinker*.

21. 'Aflaq, *In the Arab Mission*.

22. 'Aflaq, *Complete Works*, part 5, p. 316.

23. *Al-Thawra*, 28 August 1983.

24. *Political Report issued by the 8th Regional Congress of the Arab Ba'th Socialist Party – Iraqi region*, Arab Ba'th Socialist Party, January 1974, pp. 102-5.

25. *Central Report of the 9th Regional Congress of the Ba'th party*, Arab Ba'th Socialist Party, June 1982, p. 19.

26. *Shibli al-'Aysami*, Arab Ba'th Socialist Party, part II, p. 182.

27. *Political Report issued by the 8th Regional Congress of the Arab Ba'th Socialist Party – Iraqi region*, Arab Ba'th Socialist Party, January 1974, p.17.

28. Saddam Husain,: 'A debate of the paper on pluralism among the members of the Revolution Command Council and the Regional Command', *al-Yawm al-Sabi'* journal, Paris, 29 January 1989.

29. Ibid.

# CHAPTER FOUR

# Saddam as Hero[1]

## *Kamil Abdullah*

'Unhappy is the land in need of heroes', wrote Bertolt Brecht. Iraq is indeed an unhappy land in which Saddam Husain has arisen as a 'hero' for whom the invasion of Kuwait was a frivolous adventure, however disastrous the consequences for the people of Iraq and Kuwait. What is the meaning of the dictator's occupation of Kuwait?

It is not just that necessity creates men, but rather that men themselves create their necessity. We may differ in our estimates of the value of men, especially those who play the role of dictators. But differences between people cannot affect the actual role a dictator can play. The dictator's brutality, for example, may be seen in relation to his contribution to great causes like the protection of national identity or independence. Following his departure, the dictator's vestiges remain, as it were, a substitute for an unarticulated self-affirmation. 'Mankind,' wrote Karl Marx, 'inevitably sets itself only such tasks as it is able to solve, since closer examination will always show that the problem itself arises only when the material conditions for its solution are already present or at least in the course of formation.'[2] He was referring to the emergence of new relations of production and their connection with material conditions, but this idea also implies an attempt to comprehend the relationship between politics and its socio-historical context. The contemporary history of Iraq, however, and perhaps to a large extent the history of most developing societies, offers an example contradicting this Marxian idea.

The social forces which took it upon themselves to solve the tasks confronting their societies were not up to the national (or class or modernizing) tasks they faced. Not only did they fail to solve them but, worse still, they generated all kinds of complex side issues as solutions became difficult. These forces seemed to have acquired the power, but not the knowledge, to resolve these tasks. This knowledge is, in my view, nothing but a theoretical possibility of an open conversation between the logic of the will and that of reality. On the contrary, many examples from developing countries show a striking coincidence between the historical nature of the problems they faced and the 'non-historical' solutions they came up with. The voluntarism of the Ba'th Party is not something new. Throughout the ages politics has been linked to this tendency, which cuts across ideological differences and strategies.

## Voluntarist politics

Politics is always tempted to transcend the 'objective' sense of history even as it tries to affirm it. The imaginary starting point of voluntarist politics allows it to idealize a unified image of the people, in which tension and heterogeneity are denied. Thus, for example, Nazism combined the myth of racial purity with practical measures to abolish the existing centres of power and set up its own centralism with national and universal pretentions. The voluntarism of the Ba'th in Iraq proceded along similar lines: idealizing the Arab people to prepare the ground for the emergence of a Leviathan (an all-powerful state). The political myth of a single, united Arab people, combined with a shrewd exploitation of their actual suffering and discontent, have resulted in a broad recognition of the Iraqi dictator as a 'great hero' of our time.

## Kuwait

So, what *is* the meaning of the invasion and annexation of Kuwait by Iraq's dictator? On a profound level, this adventure signalled a new departure in the history of the region: one in which outright inter-Arab political and military confrontation replaced the traditional structure of relations based on 'Arab brotherhood' and solidarity. Among the most important characteristics of this newly emerging, conflict-ridden history is the fact that the nationalism of many Arab states is no longer anti-colonial and anti-Israel. Rather, the reality of nation-statehood in the Arab world has led each state to defend its own national interests against the ideological imperatives of pan-Arabism, an ideology intended to initiate, in the post-colonial era, a genuine history of the Arabs as a unified nation.

The Iraqi dictator's adventure in Kuwait was projected as an attempt to revive this dream. It will almost certainly turn out to have been the last such attempt. Compared with previous failed attempts, this one was conducted in the most cruel and deceitful manner. Its blatantly expansionist aim functioned as a vehicle for state capitalism tailored almost entirely to a military model. The militarism of the Iraqi state, which evolved rapidly during the 1980s, indicates a deep-rooted economic, political and moral crisis. In addition, of course, the Iran-Iraq war, the militarization of the Gulf region, the suppression of democracy and the complicity of some Western powers were all contributing factors to this tragic event.

## The Iraqi state

It is widely believed that the Iraqi state provides a modern alternative to the Gulf oil states. My own view is that, on the contrary, in its basic structure and rationale the difference is not as great as people think. The leader's charisma; the concentration of state power in the hands of one family; coercive interaction between the various spheres of life (e.g. between traditional morals and politics, between the economy and the state); disregard of aspirations for democracy – these are the main characteristics of the Iraqi state. Despite its 'modern' façade, the Iraqi state under Saddam Husain has never made and cannot be expected ever to make any contribution to the development of democracy, Arab unity or national liberation. Instead of establishing a civilized way of life, Iraq under Ba'thist rule has gone through an absurd and bloody ritual of installing a 'hero', although history does not welcome such figures at present. Nobody should imagine that appropriate solutions lie hidden behind the horrifying chaos created by such heroic saviours.

Indeed, it seems difficult to find objective reasons for this sort of voluntarist politics. What do the voluntarism of the Iraqi dictator and the anger of the 'wretched of the earth' have in common? The dictator's extremism has nothing in common with the romantic extremism of revolutionaries striving honourably for the impossible (a final end to the suffering of humanity). Long before the voluntarism of the dictator was taken up approvingly by propagandists of 'anti-imperialism', it had manifested itself in abnormal violence against the self (the Iraqi people). It is a great pity that the internal violence practised by the dictator's apparatus has not, so far, been studied in sufficient detail. Is it the product of a nihilistic individual, or of the whole structure of society? Is it the outcome of the construction of an ideological state, or the by-product of a political history that includes many conflicting ideologies? Is it related to an extraordinary conjuncture, or to stereotyped cultural attitudes? Does it help or hinder the upward course of history, seen from a Marxist perspective? Instead of trying to answer these questions individually I suggest the following general approach.

## Political violence

It has to be admitted, at the start, that political violence cannot be understood exclusively in terms of its objective causes. This is because the violence itself often produces results which are more damaging than the alleged justifications for resorting to it. For this reason, perhaps, great historic crimes (like those of the Nazis, or Hiroshima, or Halabja) are best attributed to some super-political phenomenon, a temporary decline of humanity into self-destructiveness or something of the sort. I believe that this interpretation may help to clarify the apparent discrepancy between cause and effect in such matters. To understand this unequal relationship between cause and effect, one needs to follow an indirect, even tortuous, line of reasoning.

Confronted with phenomena as repugnant to the human conscience as, for example, the systematic mass murder of unarmed civilians, one seems to teeter on the brink of a bottomless abyss into which normal human relations have been thrown by voluntarism and irrationality. The quest for radical answers should be tempered by recognition that the decline of a given society into the mire of barbarism is just as possible as some positive form of progress. Paradoxically enough, the subjective nihilism that provides the ground for this sort of decline is always present in politics. Once it is allowed to become dominant, however, the awesomeness of this nihilistic power makes it possible for those who exercise it to avoid discussion of universal values and make no honest distinction between motives 'beyond good and evil', so to speak.

## The nihilistic tendency

Despite the amount of time and energy it devotes to obscuring reality, the nihilistic tendency in politics does sometimes come up with an appropriate solution to a particular problem. In the masses, it elicits equal measures of enthusiasm and guilt. But why has this tendency become dominant in Iraq, especially since the late 1970s? From the outset, there is a striking resemblance between the anti-imperialist ideology of the Ba'th Party and the single-party politics of the former East European regimes. The idea of the hegemony of the people was made use of in the same way as the idea of the hegemony of the working class. In both examples the form of the political game is considered secondary to its economic and social content. The rejection of colonialism and economic exploitation has led to an unjustified rejection of one of the basic principles of modernity: democracy in its broad sense including, for example, the rule of law.

The illegitimate way in which the Iraqi Ba'th Party attained power has convinced it that any subsequent political regime will also be illegitimate. The simple logic behind this is that non-legitimacy breeds non-legitimacy, in theory and practice. It is in looking at the illegitimacy of Ba'th rule that we perceive most clearly the voluntarism alluded to earlier. With breathtaking effrontery, the voluntarist regime bestows legitimacy on its own rule, as if it were an unquestionable right. Saturated with *inqilabi* – conspiratorial spirit – which it unleashes on all opponents regardless of their actual political attitudes, a regime of this kind paves the way for the emergence of an autocratic despot at the top of the pyramid. Indeed, it makes that eventuality inevitable. The illegitimate exchange of power opens the door for the arrival of illegitimate leaders, men willing to try absolutely anything to prove their legitimacy in the eyes of their subjects. Did not the dictator, for example, draw up a family tree tracing his ancestry back to the prophet Muhammad? Did he not try to revive the ancient, forgotten tradition of *bay'a*, the act by which a certain number of persons, acting individually or collectively, recognise the authority of another person?

## Legitimacy

Every time there has been an internal political crisis (always a legitimacy crisis) – and they have occurred frequently – the dictator has resorted to looking for a de facto source of legitimacy. He used his war with Iran to lay claim to patriotic and national legitimacy; then he used the latter to prove the illegitimacy of his opponents and to justify a bellicose stance towards other neighbouring countries. More recently he has sought to suspend the deep political crisis of his rule (demands for political reform and democracy) by trying to establish leadership over the region and threatening Israel and the West. Kuwait was the victim. The sense of danger felt by the dictator impels him to threaten others with danger. He does not regain his sense of security until the Iraqi people in turn sense the danger and seek his protection from the external response to his adventure. Thus the dictator's 'frivolous' behaviour generates real necessities. Behind these necessities is a simple fact: the flagrant will of the dictator cannot be fully expressed without an ample and transparent reality which does not differ very much from fantasy. It is a reality with no political tradition, no state, no borders between things, no rules, no principles, nothing superior to the lust for power. How can we denounce violence when we do not possess a positive counter-tradition?

At the level of the Arab masses in general, the Iraqi dictator has capitalized on their mounting resentment over their conditions of life. By resorting to a fundamentalist discourse, the dictator managed to conceal, albeit only temporarily, the core of the crisis caused by the invasion of Kuwait, and to seduce the masses into defying international law and conventions. He whipped up mass sentiments and took political cover behind them, in much the same way as he took physical cover behind the bodies of the foreign hostages.

## The man in the street

Few can rival the dictator in manipulating the sensitivities of the man in the street – a creature so marginalized by the Arab machinery of repression that he has become a passive audience for idealistic and fundamentalist political slogans. If another world is promised with enough confidence by such sorts of utopian politics (whether religious or secular), then many will be eager for the demolition of a reality which is close to intolerable. For this impatient mass of people, besieged by the misery of life and the viciousness of repression, believes that any temporary loss will be permanently restored in a future paradise. The man in the street was, apparently, ready to invest all his weakness and limitations in a despot who symbolizes, more than anything else, naked power and determination. So, while the advantages and the disadvantages of this symbol are only seen later, his presence is associated with a reckless force, acting as though it were superior virtue, which inflames the imagination of the repressed mass. The resulting political relationship in this case is one of projection, and hence of exclusion, rather than of an active interaction between autonomous agents.

The alleged 'popular' support inside Iraq for the dictator's adventurous politics can, however, bear different analysis. We may assume that there was no choice left for a people in a cul-de-sac whose end wall is fascist dictatorship. Nobody can even touch this wall, let alone scale it to see the reality beyond. This being the case, the people's level of satisfaction or dissatisfaction with the regime becomes irrelevant. Nor is it useful to assess the extent to which this regime expresses deeper motivations and universal desires. These may be absent from the consciousness of the people while being wholly clear to the regime, which then feels justified in using coercive and persuasive means to bring them to the people's attention. What is important from our point of view is to focus on the *relationship* between a regime symbolized by an omnipresent leader (at least as a very effective illusion) and a mass that is castrated and rendered passive.

The first thing that confronts us in this relationship is its reliance on all-encompassing social institutions (the party and its ideological and military apparatus). While unleashing indiscriminate violence against society, these institutions retain their immunity from justice by making a virtue of their constant and unquestioning allegiance to the person of the dictator. Their authority, however, is always limited: they are just local centres of power and subjugation. Overall power is reserved for the dictator alone.

Second, this relationship is based on a reciprocal deception in which the regime moulds the mass according to principles of reward and punishment. These principles become repressive by reducing human facts and deeds to predetermined limits. When the mass has been coerced or deceived into believing that its salvation lies in accepting and even admiring the dictator's rule, the presence of the mass is reduced to a state of perpetual pretence. The role of the mass becomes one of winning the regime's trust, joyfully parroting its strategy and merging the regime with the homeland, the dictator with the people. There is a Ba'thist song which goes '16 million people and that people's name is Saddam!'

## Ridicule

Here one must also note that alongside its seriousness, sustained by a mechanism of barbaric repression, this relationship of deception involves a great deal of reciprocal ridicule. On the one hand, the regime, fearing public opinion, deliberately burdens the mass with the responsibility of one single right: the right to silence. It is a right to shoulder impossible historic tasks and achieve rare acts of heroism. Behind the exaggerated language of glorification and praise, there lies a consistent ideological deception by a regime skilled in fabricating lies and ridiculing its subjects. On the other hand, the people's inability to question the claims of the regime, leads them to exhibit absolute readiness to accept the regime's claims. The mass of fascism is that mass which adopts, in rotation, two roles only: the role of the fighter and the role of the clown. When a unilateral relationship is established between the regime and its mass, it is possible to describe the result – an example would be Iraqi society under the Ba'th – as a post-politics society. In such a society politics coincides with its objectives and hence with its end. A society like this is not a happy utopian one but on the contrary an anti-utopian or tragic society, one in which spontaneity and tension have been abolished from the mainstream of social life.

## National identity

Can we claim that in an oppressed society (like Iraq's over the last decade or so) it is possible for there to emerge, for the first time, a politically unified national identity? There are two ways of achieving national unity and consensus. The first achieves unity through a totalitarian or semi-totalitarian state whose main role is to suppress political difference and to subordinate every sphere of life to its control. The second does not impose unity from above, but lets it emerge in the process of reconciling various conflicting social interests. Unity in this sense becomes equivalent to consensus, and hence to a stable body politic in which formal principles and practical mechanisms are combined. Therefore, one could say, if the second type of state is the fruit of the general will, the first embodies the negation of the general will. But, although the second type of state has proved in practice to be more solid and adequate to human needs, none of these context-dependent types can be entirely immune to the possibility of regression or dismemberment into more primitive (and regional) entities. Before this real possibility, the dominant political discourse tends to impose, with force if necessary, the primacy of the idea of unity.

To return to our previous question concerning the national unity of Iraq under Ba'th rule: the unity achieved is less durable than people seem to have expected. Iraq's military defeat in the Gulf War has shown how fragile and contingent this form of unity was. The strong Iraqi state was not itself able to prevent the country from disintegrating along regional and ethnic lines. What finally prevented this terrifying possibility from becoming a reality was the Arab and the international interest in maintaining Iraq's territorial integrity. Partition and civil war are clear indicators of the rapidity with which a centralized totalitarian state can disintegrate into tribal, ethnic or religious forms of allegiance.

## Ideological crisis

The danger of disintegration of the national state in Iraq inaugurates the second phase of its historical failure. The first phase of this failure is exemplified by popular disenchantment with the time-honoured utopia of a unified Arab nation. This uncompromising project has proved to be illusory and impracticable but also very useful for the consolidation of the individual Arab nation-states (leading in turn to deepening divisions between these states). The second phase refers to the current situation of the nation-state which is suffering from a deep ideological crisis. It is a crisis of representation and legitimation caused by the state's outdated form and rationale in comparison to the sophisticated tasks of modernization. The failure of the pan-Arab idea, as both utopian ideal and ideology, could be translated as the failure of the political effort to establish politics in a framework of generally accepted institutions and rules. More clearly than ever before, the reality of the Arab world shows us that the Arabs were originally united under generally negative economic and political conditions but are moving relentlessly towards division. This divergence between our history and our politics poses a serious obstacle to the project of modernity in the Arab world. The negative conditions of misery and deprivation, dictatorship and repression, have so far failed to produce their proper negation. Ideas like unity, democracy, social justice and tolerance will remain in a state of suspension so long as the collective self is misrepresented. The 'heroic' adventures of Iraq's dictator will serve for a long time to come as a reminder of the dead-end possibilities of this misrepresentation.

## Notes

1. An earlier version of this chapter was first published in Arabic as 'Philosophical reflections on a frivolous adventure: the meaning of Saddam Husein's invasion of Kuwait' in *Al-Thaqafa al-Jadida* no. 228 (1990).

2. Karl Marx, *A Contribution to the Critique of Political Economy*, Collected Works, vol. 29, p. 263.

CHAPTER FIVE

# Women: Honour, Shame and Dictatorship

*Suha Omar*

In Iraq, women played an important role against imperialism and the reactionary intrigues of the Royal Family. Iraqi women now enjoy equal political rights with men and an Iraqi woman is always included as a Minister in the different cabinets. Nawal al-Saadawi, *The Hidden Face of Eve*, 1980

Rarely do women in the Arab world enjoy as much power and support as they do in Iraq. Women in Iraq are granted the full rights of citizenship, and are also expected to fulfill their role in building the country... Women occupy high political positions, including 27 out of 250 seats in the National Assembly. They pursue professional careers in labor and social services. They are organized by a strong network of the General Federation of Iraqi Women that covers almost all of the country. The 1970 Constitution affirmed the equality of all citizens before the law, and guaranteed equal opportunities without discrimination by sex. According to labor law number 71 enacted in 1987, men and women must receive equal pay for equal work. Women working in the government sector are entitled to a one year maternity leave, receiving their full salary for the first six months, and half salary for the next six months. A wife's income is recognized as independent from her husband's. Women have the right to acquire and dispose of agricultural land. In 1980, women were granted the right to vote and hold office. In 1974, education was made free at all levels, and in 1979/80 it was made compulsory for girls and boys through the age of twelve. These legal bases provide a solid framework for the promotion of women and the enhancement of their role in society. They have had a direct bearing on women's education, health, labor and social welfare. UNICEF-Iraq, *Children and Women in Iraq* 1993

There is some truth in these statements, but they give a false impression since they fail to mention that Iraqi women live under one of the most repressive regimes in the world. A 71-page Amnesty International report published in 1989, for example, dealt exclusively with children who were victims of political repression in Iraq.[1] Women's equal political rights with men are exemplified by the women's political wings of prisons such as Abu Graib and al-Rashid. Here a woman can be imprisoned for twenty-five years for making a joke in private about Saddam Husain, if she escapes being executed for that capital offence. All members of the National

Assembly, be they male or female, are appointed by the regime. Legislation takes the form of decrees issued by Saddam Husain or the Revolutionary Command Council (RCC) and there is no legal protection for victims of the regime's terrorization of the population. Women appointed to high political positions are tools of the Ba'th Party regime and adopt male ways of thinking. The General Federation of Iraqi Women (GFIW) is effectively part of the state security system, which is headed by Saddam Husain and his male relatives. In these conditions, women's equality before the law and their right to vote and hold office are sources of pain and oppression rather than pleasure and liberation.

The submissiveness which the dictatorship requires from all its citizens in the public sphere is analogous to the submissiveness which Iraqi men require from Iraqi women in the home, and both are symptomatic of fear. The oppression of Iraqi women will not, however, end with the demise of the dictatorship. A free and fully democratic Iraq will only come into being when Iraqi men and women are able to relate to each other on a basis of full equality and mutual respect within the home and outside it.

An analysis of the specific effects of the Ba'th regime upon women must begin with an understanding of the ideology of honour and shame in Iraqi society. The honour of any kinship group resides in the sexual conduct of its womenfolk. If a woman behaves immodestly or her modesty is violated she brings shame to all her kin. This applies to women – with varying degrees of severity – be they Arab, Kurd, Assyrian, Turcoman, Sunni Muslim, Shi'i Muslim, Christian, Yazidi, rural, urban, peasant, professional, Islamicist, Communist, nationalist or democrat.

Dishonouring women is therefore a powerful means of attacking social cohesion in order to secure political control. It has been a distinctive feature of the process whereby Saddam Husain and his family have come to govern Iraq, implementing their own tribal values behind the façade of and with the resources of an oil-rich nation-state. The effects of that process on the economic, social, political and cultural life of Iraq are examined elsewhere. This chapter looks at it from the point of view of Iraqi women and concludes by suggesting how their needs could be addressed in an Iraq freed from dictatorship.

## Women's rights strengthen the state

The ideal of a modern, free woman which was adopted in Iraq, above all among the urban middle classes, was influenced by the country's links with the German Democratic Republic (East Germany) and the Soviet Union. It was an integral part of Iraq's profile as a modernizing member of the international community. In the 1970s, between the Ba'thist take-over of 1968 and the outbreak of war with Iran in 1980, women benefited from increased educational and employment opportunities and legislation in their favour. According to official statistics, female students at secondary school rose from 20 per cent of the total in 1971 to 31 per cent in 1982. Women (excluding farm-workers) were only 4 per cent of the working population in 1957, but 12.5 per cent by 1975 and 17.6 per cent by 1977. By 1982, women constituted 26.9 per cent of doctors, 51.2 per cent of dentists and 65 per cent of pharmacists.[2] In 1971 pension and social security legislation gave women the right to paid maternity leave, secured free medical care for women and children and established a female retirement age of 55. Under the labour laws of 1970, and subsequent amendments, women's working hours were reduced, the right to feed babies in working hours was guaranteed and encouragement was given to the setting up of workplace nurseries. In 1975 women acquired entitlement to be taxed sepately from their husbands.

However, studies of Ba'thist social programmes carried out by Amal Rassam and Jacqueline Ismael in 1980 drew attention to the fact that changes in family law stopped short of abolishing polygamy or giving women equal rights to initiate divorce.[3] They observed that the undermining of clan control of women and the encouragement of nuclear families primarily served industrial development and the strengthening of state power. This was also the view of Suad Joseph, who argued that extension of women's rights was a key survival strategy for a regime which needed to eliminate political opposition and expand the economy to consolidate its power. 'Individualism, autonomy and independence are fostered more to undermine kin and religious-ethnic allegiance than to encourage economic or political democracy.'[4] Or, as Samir al-Khalil put it in *Republic of Fear,* 'It rankles to have fathers, brothers, uncles and cousins all lined up to exert varying degrees of real power and control over half the Iraqi population. Thus, if a new loyalty to the Leader, the party and the state is to form, women must be "freed" from the loyalties that traditionally bound them to their husbands and male kin. This was the essential purpose of the 1978 legislation on Personal Status, which diminished the power of the patriarchal family.'[5]

## Nuclear families

It is questionable both how far this purpose was thought out and deliberately adopted by the regime and how far it was achieved. Saddam Husain's legislation on women's rights was part of the international image of Iraq as a modernizing nation. Encouragement of nuclear families was seen as a significant element of modernization, regardless of the effects on women.

A study by Sana al-Khayyat conducted in the early 1980s[6] concluded that the trend towards the nuclear family weakened the position of women both at home and at work. Women interviewees across a wide social spectrum indicated that they had grown up thinking of themselves as working women. They found, however, that they retained all domestic and childcare responsibilities, without changes in cooking methods and without the material and emotional support of their extended families. Living in nuclear families they were isolated from female relatives and deprived of their help. This isolation -- recognized by researchers as a problem for women in Western societies -- could not be alleviated as in the West by involvement in sporting activities, or social clubs, or women's associations. As Beck and Keddie observed, 'female association, powerful in cultures where social institutions and values inhibit most efforts by women to establish solidarity with one another, can challenge male domination.'[7] In the transition to the nuclear family Iraqi women lost their traditional forms of female association without gaining Western ones. This allowed greater male domination of individual women.

## Pressure at work

Women were deeply affected by the *al-tasattur*, the regulation which placed citizens under an obligation to inform the authorities of any subversive or potentially subversive behavior. This included such innocuous acts as turning down the volume when Saddam Husain appeared on television. Women primary- and secondary-school teachers were particularly intimidated and were caused great distress by being required to report on the parents of children in their charge. In December 1979, for example, a letter was sent from the Ministry of Education to head-teachers of schools in Karbala', telling them that all female teachers were to be dismissed who had visited one of their colleagues to pay their respects after her two sons had been executed.[8] Pressure to inform and to join the Ba'th Party forced many women to leave good jobs for the relative safety of life at home.

## Decrees against women[9]

Since Saddam Husain became president in July 1979, many orders and decrees have been issued to control women's lives and reinforce the dictatorship. In April 1981 men married to Iraqi women 'of Iranian origin' were made eligible for government grants if they divorced their wives or if the wives were deported. The grant for civilians was 2,500 dinars and for soldiers 4,000 dinars, then the equivalent of £2000 or three times a teacher's annual salary. In October 1982 the Ministry of Defence ordered the arrest and detention of wives and children of deserters. In December 1982 the RCC decreed that Iraqi women were not allowed to marry non-Iraqis. An Iraqi woman already married to a non-Iraqi was prohibited from transferring money or property to him, he could not inherit from her and if they divorced he could not have any financial settlement or custody of the children.

In February 1990 the tribal practice of killing women for 'honour crimes' – i.e. illicit sexual relations – was reinforced and legitimized by the Iraqi regime, which was still being backed by the West as 'modern'. Decision 1110 of the RCC, signed by Saddam Husain, exempted from punishment or legal questioning men who murdered their mothers, daughters, sisters, paternal aunts, brothers' daughters or father's brothers' daughters, if they were deemed guilty of an 'honour crime'. In accordance with Bedouin tradition it was a woman's male blood relatives who acquired this legal right, not her husband.

In November 1993 the official newspaper *Babil* announced an RCC decision which used marital relations as a weapon against political opponents. A woman could now divorce her husband if he 'switched to serve the enemy'. She kept her rights as a wife and the divorce could be annulled if the husband returned to her and 'to the patriotic line' within the period of '*idda*, i.e. within three months of the divorce.

## Increasing the birth-rate

During the Iran-Iraq war women also had to face the regime's attempts to raise the birth-rate by putting a price on them so as to encourage men to take second wives, and by drastic measures to increase their fertility. The war created many widows and initially they were paid compensation. But then grants were introduced which were payable to men as financial incentives to marry war widows. This was supposedly to protect the honour of martyrs' wives who might otherwise be forced into prostitution, and to provide fathers for war orphans. Women without men clearly could not be trusted and there was a need to increase the population.

These grants gave a boost to polygamy which, although permitted in Islam, had become rare, particularly in the cities and among the middle classes. They appealed primarily to avarice. For marrying a woman with a middle-school certificate a man received a grant of 200 dinars, for a high-school graduate 300 dinars and for a university graduate 500 dinars. The effect was to further reduce the marriage market value of non-virgin women, to the advantage of men. In one case, for example, a 47-year-old married man with seven children, a bus-conductor from a working-class background, proposed to marry a secondary-school-educated, childless war widow aged 22 from a much higher social background. The matter was not discussed with the young woman and the man's wife was herself reluctant to raise objections, for fear of divorce.[10]

In the drive to increase fertility, great consternation was caused by a programme of compulsory injections given to female students and staff in secondary schools and universities. These were widely believed to be fertility drugs, although it was officially denied. As the young women involved were unmarried, it was assumed that the drugs had a long-term effect. Compulsory fertility drugs were given to women in hospital immediately after the birth of their babies, which resulted in many choosing to be delivered at home.

Contraception, which had previously been freely available, was made illegal, as was abortion, forcing women to resort to illegal abortions which risked their lives. These measures – comparable to those introduced in Nazi Germany – were promoted under the slogan 'we promise you a cradle in every home'. Every family should have five children, the president announced. Four children or less would be considered a threat to national security. Women in their forties and even fifties were pressurized into giving birth, despite the danger to their health. 'We hope,' Saddam Husain told leaders of the General Federation of Iraqi Women (GFIW), 'that a woman's inclination to go out to work will not take her away from her family or from giving birth along the lines set by our slogan.'[11]

## The General Federation of Iraqi Women (GFIW)

The General Federation of Iraqi Women (GFIW) is a government-sponsored organization with offices in towns and villages throughout Iraq (apart from those Kurdish areas which ceased to be under Baghdad's control in 1991). It is defined in one of its own publications as 'a progressive social institution representing all women of Iraq without any discrimination in connection with ethnic origin, language, social status or religion.'[12] Founded in 1968, when the Ba'thists came to power, it played an important role in projecting the international image of Iraq as modern and secular throughout the 1970s and 1980s.

During those years, however, membership of any other women's organization was a political crime subject to a fifteen-year prison sentence. This led to the 'disappearance' of, among others, A'ida Yasin, a leading figure in the Iraqi Women's League (IWL) – which had been founded in the 1950s with the backing of the Iraqi Communist Party (ICP) and whose president, Dr Naziha al-Dulaimi, became, in 1959, the first woman cabinet minister in the Arab world. Amina al-Sadr ('Bint al-Huda'), a writer and leading female figure in the Shi'i community, was executed in 1980.

In reality GFIW's role in Saddam's Iraq is to police Iraqi women. It pays lip-service to the idea of formal equality but has never developed a critique of the sexist and patriarchal attitudes to women common among Iraqi men. On the contrary, the attitude of its members to the all-male RCC, which lays down much of its policy, is unfailingly deferential. As Saddam Husain said in his speech to GFIW's seventh congress: 'There is a question which might cross the mind of each of the sisters, which is how the Revolution managed to end all the foreign petrol controls and end feudalism, but did not manage to resolve the legal rights of women... if we are to deal with women's legal rights, the Revolution as a whole will lose the support of half the population.'[13]

GFIW has long been believed to be responsible for procuring women for Ba'thist officials. This is confirmed by a confidential letter signed by Fito al-Tikriti, vice-president of the Iraqi Hunt Club in Baghdad and addressed to the General Secretary of GFIW, a copy of which was sent to GFIW's office in Najaf. Dated 4th June 1982, it requests the participation of GFIW members 'to entertain our senior officers' at a late-night party to celebrate the anniversary of the 'July 1968 Revolution...We request they do not bring any of their relatives...and we will offer a very good grant to the ladies.'[14]

## Official rape

Documents, or photocopies of documents, seized during the *intifada*, together with testimonies and the discovery by international journalists of rape rooms attached to police stations, confirm that the regime has long operated a policy of official rape. For example, an index card for a man who had a secret contract with the general security organization, file number 43,304, identified his activity as 'violation of women's honour'.[15] Rape has been used to crush the spirit of political prisoners, to recruit women into the internal spy network, and to 'break the eyes' of families and communities. To 'break someone's eyes' is a Bedouin notion which applied to the way Tikriti men in the Ottoman era notoriously destroyed the authority of any non-Tikriti official by ambushing his family and gang-raping his wife in front of him. Similarly, in the 1970s, young women from leading Baghdad families, Sunni and Shi'i, were kidnapped and held captive for several weeks.[16]

## Women in Iraqi Kurdistan

Since the 'safe haven' was established in some of the Kurdish areas of northern Iraq in 1991 it has been possible for journalists and researchers to visit and establish contact with the women's organizations and women MPs. In Iraqi Kurdistan the 'widows' towns' of Gushtapa demonstrate, sadly and dramatically, the outcome of Saddam Husain's policy of tearing apart the social fabric of those he sought to control. The Gushtapa settlements are examples of the breeze-block 'model villages' into which Kurdish villagers, in this case members of the Barzani tribe, were forcibly resettled in the 1970s – far from their fertile apple orchards, cereal fields and dairy farms. In 1983 Iraqi soldiers came to Gushtapa and took away every man and boy over the age of ten. In all, some 8,000 Barzanis disappeared.

Stripped of the male protection which assured their livelihood and respectability, the women and children of Gushtapa were exposed and vulnerable. Girls lost any hope of a decent marriage, and wives were left in a limbo as their husbands had 'disappeared' but were not definitely dead. Unused to contact with people outside their tribe, young and old alike had to earn money to live. Coralled into the settlements by Iraqi soldiers, they became labourers for local landowners or escaped to survive in the city of Arbil as street traders or factory workers, thereby dishonouring the Barzani name. Some younger women formed relationships with non-Barzani men, but in so doing they ran the risk of being killed by older women who believed that was the only way to purge 'unclean hearts'.[17]

While traumatized women in Gushtapa suffocated their pregnant daughters as they slept, in the hope of regaining the honour taken from them by the Ba'thist regime, Kurdish women MPs and others worked on a women's agenda for the fragile parliamentary system established by the elections of May 1992. In the weeks before the elections, women from the women's committees of the Patriotic Union of Kurdistan (PUK), the Kurdish Democratic Party (KDP), the Communist Party and a new party formed from the amalgamation of the Socialist Party of Kurdistan, the Democratic Independent Party of Kurdistan, and the People's Party of Kurdistan came together in a women-only committee to draft proposals for reform of family law. The proposals were taken to schools and hospitals throughout Iraqi Kurdistan with a petition for women to sign in support.

By August 1992, when the proposals were informally presented to the new parliament, 3,372 women had signed the petition; a year later there were approximately 30,000 signatures. For a law reform proposal to be formally presented to parliament a minimum of ten MPs must have signed it. By September 1993, 35 PUK MPs had signed; but the KDP, being the more conservative of the two main parties, opposed the proposals, and none of its MPs signed. The next step was for the proposals to go before senior parliamentarians who would decide if it was 'the right time' to put them to parliament. The women's committee was pessimistic about the likely decision but determined to try again in future if necessary.

The family law at present in force is that of the Iraqi state, as developed by the Ba'thist regime from Islamic law. The proposed reforms are in three main areas: marriage, divorce and inheritance. The proposed marriage law reform would reduce the number of wives a man may have from four to two. He would still have to establish before a judge that he could financially support more than one wife, but would also have to establish that the first wife was sterile or suffering from an incurable psychiatric disease. The proposed divorce law reform would abolition the *talaq* method, by which a man can divorce his wife simply by saying three times 'I divorce you'. The proposed inheritance law reform would abolish the rule whereby male relatives of someone who dies intestate receive twice as much as female relatives. This last proposal was so controversial that the women's committee felt it was bound to be defeated and so decided not to try to put it before parliament until a later date. Other proposals under consideration but still to be worked out in detail include the outlawing of forced prostitution and domestic violence, and new provisions in criminal law which would mean that the adulterous husband would face the same penalties currently faced by the adulterous wife.[18]

## After the Gulf War

Since the Gulf War most Iraqi women have been primarily occupied with trying to feed their families and preserve some form of home life. The catastrophic impact upon them of war and sanctions was made alarmingly clear in a grassroots study conducted by independent observers which was published in September 1991.[19] As Victoria Brittain of the *Guardian* commented: 'Over and over again leaders of the allied forces and their officials in the United Nations said that there was "no quarrel with the people of Iraq". But the testimonies from within these homes show, as nothing has before, just how devastating has been the price of Allied policies for the Iraqi people.'[20] The study revealed a fourfold increase in child mortality and a high incidence of health problems among women, including psychosomatic conditions such as sleeplessness and mental disorder.

Immediately after the war there was a general increase in lawlessness. Gangs of demobilized men roamed the streets and many women were raped. War-traumatized conscripts returned home to take out their aggression, frustration, distress and anger on wives, daughters, mothers and sisters. In a popular love-song a male singer supposedly expressed female sentiment with the lyrics: 'oh wreck! break! smash up! dispose of! destroy! play with my nerves!' Women had to pick up the pieces when men were physically and psychologically damaged by war. Not only was there no clinical support for them in shouldering this burden, but they also faced a drastically worsened economic situation as victims of the pauperization of Iraqi society.

Women left with no male relative or income had to assume the role of head of household and become breadwinners. For many this meant standing outside their homes to sell the gold and jewellery they had received in their *mahar*, or marriage contract, which is intended as security for their old age. Socialized to be submissive, women have had to take new initiatives and develop great resourcefulness in obtaining food, firewood and water for their families. Reports indicate that most are increasingly pessimistic; the worst affected are the young, who see no future for themselves.

## Conclusions

For most Iraqi men the Saddam Husain Ba'thist dictatorship has meant violent exclusion from political power, conscription into two disastrous wars, and economic decline, in which the career and financial prospects that were so promising in the 1970s have been lost forever. Iraqi women, however, have arguably been at the centre of the process of social traumatization which has taken place. 'The revolutionary, radical Ba'th...have torn to shreds the inherited traditional social fabric, giving rise to a twisted new kind of Iraqi modernity that is neither traditional nor modern...Iraq has been left with the worst of everything: its society is suspended in a void, no longer having any real traditions (Islamic or otherwise) from which it can at least draw temporary comfort. This conclusion has enormous political implications for the shape of things to come in the post-Saddam era.'[21]

Throughout the 1950s, 1960s and 1970s, more and more women entered the public sphere doing office and professional jobs. The Iran-Iraq war reversed this trend. Due to labour shortages women began to do 'men's work' such as driving lorries, attending petrol pumps and directing traffic, but the over-riding pressure was to return to the home to have large families. Whereas paid work was once seen as essential for educated women, by the outbreak of the Gulf War many female graduates were opting for full-time motherhood supported by their husbands. The years of war have left women having to cope with damaged husbands, sons and fathers, or surviving without male relatives. Their situation is exacerbated by international sanctions.

Probably the most distressing effect of the dictatorship for most women has been the damage to family life resulting from repression, forced deportation, war and economic impoverishment. Family life is very important to women in the Middle East, as is recognized by feminist writers among them, but conditions within the family have further deteriorated since the Gulf War. There have been many reports of increased domestic violence and an intensification of patriarchal attitudes and practices. Even men who are politically opposed to the terror and repression of the regime rarely listen to women. They show little or no understanding of how women feel themselves to be oppressed in their personal relationships, or of how men's attitudes to women might need to change.

If the Iraqi oppposition wishes to win the hearts and minds of the Ba'thized population within Iraq, it must address the issue of women, which it has conspicuously failed to do. When the Iraqi National Congress (INC) was launched in Vienna in June 1992, five women were elected to its general assembly, but there was no mention in its documents of social policies that would affect women. Women's support requires a women's agenda.

Common ground needs to be found through dialogue between religious and secular women. Regardless of their political affiliation, women opposed to dictatorship share an interest in healthcare, education, training, employment and business opportunities for women, and the right to privacy and safety, particularly in their own homes. They share an abhorrence of brainwashing and spying in schools, and a revulsion against the obsessive lying and secretiveness, as well as the violence of government officials.

A women's agenda cannot conflict head-on with Islam but has to look for ideas within Islam, which allows for interpretation (*ijtihad*) according to the needs of society at a particular time. There are many statements in the Qur'an and the Hadith which order men to be lawful and kind to women and which can clearly be interpreted as supporting women's interests. It is the distortion of Islam which has oppressed women, as has the distortion of modernization imposed by the Ba'thist regime.

The essence of a democratic Iraq will be new choices and freedoms on offer to women. A programme of positive action – for example training widows for paid employment – will provide alternatives to polygamy, which is not a satisfactory solution, from women's point of view, for the demographic imbalance resulting from war. In a democratic Iraq women will wear various modes of dress in the street, from *hijab* to modern fashions. The *hijab* will remain an option, but it will be worn by choice, not only out of obedience to male religious leaders or because women feel that wearing modern dress makes them vulnerable to sexual harassment or damages their chances of marriage.

It is essential that women play the rightful part in public life which they have been denied. It is also important for them to feel able to express their needs within the household, where there is now very little democracy. The transition from a society where people live in fear to one where women enjoy social equality and respect in the home, and are fully involved in the processes of government, will require enormous changes and take many years to achieve. But it is a transition which all who wish to see a future democratic Iraq can but hope for and work towards.

## Notes

1. Amnesty International, *Iraq – Children: Innocent Victims of Political Repression*, 1980 (AI Index MDE 14/04/89).

2. GFIW, *Conference on Women's Role in Development*, 1982.

3. Cited in Suad Joseph, 'The Mobilization of Iraqi Women into the Wage Labour Force', *Studies in Third World Societies* no. 16 (1982), p. 84.

4. Ibid. pp. 69-90, p. 82.

5. Samir al-Khalil, *Republic of Fear: The Politics of Modern Iraq* (London 1989), p. 92.

6. Sana al-Khayyat, *Honour and Shame: Women in Modern Iraq* (London 1990).

7. Lois Beck and Nikki Keddie (eds), *Women in the Muslim World* (Harvard University Press, 1980)

8. A photocopy of this letter was supplied by Ghanim Jawad of the opposition Iraqi Broadcasting Corporation.

9. Photocopies of these decrees and orders were supplied by Ghanim Jawad.

10. Sana al-Khayyat, *Honor and Shame* pp. 171-172.

11. Published speech of Saddam Husain to the executive committee of GFIW, May 1986.

12. GFIW, *The Iraqi Woman* (Baghdad 1975) p. 36.

13. Hala al-Badri, *Iraqi Women* 1980 (in Arabic).

14. A photocopy of this letter was supplied by Ghanim Jawad.

15. Kanan Makiya, *Cruelty and Silence* (London 1993) p. 287.

16. Ibid. pp. 289-90.

17. Based on a report by Clare Pointon, *The Times* magazine 13 March 1993

18. Based on research by Teresa Thornhill in Iraqi Kurdistan in August-September 1993.

19. Bela Bhatia, Mary Kawar and Mariam Shahin, 'Unheard Voices: Iraqi Women on War and Sanctions', *Harvard Study Team Report* September 1991.

20. Ibid., quoted in frontispiece.

21. Kanan Makiya, *Cruelty and Silence* pp. 293-294.

CHAPTER SIX

# Economic Devastation, Underdevelopment and Outlook

*Abbas Alnasrawi*

No sooner had Iraq invaded Kuwait in August 1990 than the US-led industrialized countries succeeded in having the United Nations Security Council impose a total embargo on all trade with Iraq. The blanket exclusion of Iraq from the world economy was followed on 16 January 1991 by a concentrated bombing campaign which virtually destroyed Iraq's infrastructure and disorganized its economy. And when the bombing stopped, at the end of February, a country-wide spontaneous *intifada* broke out against the Ba'th Party regime. The harsh and indiscriminate manner in which the armed forces crushed the *intifada* aggravated the problems of the shattered economy.

It is important to note also that these war-related problems were superimposed on an economy that was still in the midst of the unprecedented crisis in which Iraq found itself as a result of the 1980-88 Iran-Iraq war. An appreciation of Iraq's current economic crisis, as well as the prospects for recovery, must, therefore, start with an examination of some of the economic consequences of that war.

## Impact of the Iran-Iraq war on the Iraqi economy

The years 1972-74 constitute an important turning point for the Iraqi economy and the role of the state in it. The 1972 nationalization of the foreign-owned Iraq Petroleum Company (IPC) together with the OPEC-led oil price revolution of 1973 had the effect of raising Iraq's oil revenue by more than eightfold—from US$1 billion in 1972 to $8.2 billion in 1975. This sharp increase in revenue solidified the centrality of the role of the state in the economy by making it the primary link between the oil sector and the rest of the economy. This change gave the state an unprecedented power to allocate economic resources among various sectors of the economy and among different social classes and groups. It also empowered the state to channel resources to, or withhold them from, this or that geographical area. While governments in non-oil-producing countries had to rely on taxation to finance their programmes, governments in oil-producing countries were freed from the constraints and burdens of having to face the consequences of their taxation policies. In short, the Iraqi government, that is to say the Ba'th Party, became the primary determinant of employment, income distribution, and sectoral and regional development. Moreover, the sharp increase in oil revenue provided the government with the opportunity to expand and modernize the military and internal security forces while implementing its development and social programmes.

The outbreak of the war with Iran in September 1980 did not slow down the pace of spending. This was because of the availability of foreign reserves and the fiscal assistance which Sa'udi Arabia and Kuwait extended to Iraq to help it in its war against Iran. This availability of funds explains Iraq's ability to increase its military and non-military imports between 1978 and 1981 from $4.2 billion to $20.5 billion. No less dramatic was the value of contracts with foreign enterprises for non-military projects, which rose from $14.8 billion in 1980 to $24.3 billion in 1981.[1]

Such high levels of spending could not be sustained, however, due to the destruction of Iraq's major oil-exporting facilities and the sharp fall in the price of oil. The combined effect of these changes led to a drastic decline in Iraq's oil revenue from a peak of $26.3 billion in 1980 to $7.8 billion in 1983, which caused Iraq's balance of trade to swing from a surplus of $12.4 billion in 1980 to a combined deficit of $34.7 billion in the period 1981-83, thus wiping out Iraq's foreign reserves which had stood at $32-35 billion on the eve of the war.[2]

The emergent economic crisis and the rising demand of an enlarged military forced the government to resort to policies of economic retrenchment and austerity which took the form of drastic cuts in non-defence spending, reduction of imports, a freeze on new infrastructural projects, and cutbacks in investment in the industrial and agricultural sectors. Iraq's economic plight had the additional effect of weakening its position as a major force in the Arab region, especially among other Arab oil-producing countries. This change was reflected in the marked decline in its development spending, as measured by the value of projects contracted. Thus while Iraq's share of such contracts had peaked at 31 per cent of all contracts by Arab oil-producing countries, it dropped sharply to only 2 per cent by 1983.[3] As the war lasted much longer than Iraq had envisaged, and as oil revenue continued to decline, Iraq found its international status transformed from a creditor country to a debtor country. In addition to having to borrow on the international capital market, loans were extended to it from Kuwait and Sa'udi Arabia, on average $1 billion per month for the first two years of the war.[4]

Iraq's economic losses attributable to the Iran-Iraq war were estimated by Kamran Mofid at $452.6 billion, broken down as follows: damage to infrastructure and commodity-producing sectors $67 billion; GNP losses $222.1 billion (including $198 billion in lost oil revenue); the loss of Iraq's accumulated $35 billion foreign exchange reserves at the start of the war plus lost earnings on the original $35 billion; $80 billion in war-related military expenditures above and beyond defence spending under non-war conditions; and $4.7 billion for the cost of re-routing imports.[5] The magnitude of the war losses and their implications for the future of the economy and the people of Iraq can be appreciated if we realize that Iraq's war losses amounted to 435 per cent of its oil revenue during the war years, or the equivalent of 112 per cent of its GNP every year for the eight-year period of the war, 1980-88.[6]

## Economic crisis and the failure of privatization policies

In 1982, as the war front moved to Iraqi soil, Syria closed Iraq's oil pipelines across its territory, and the government was forced to shelve its high spending policy. One of the more significant policy reorientations of the ruling Ba'th Party in response to the 1982 debacle was over the issue of the role of the private sector in a state-run economy. At its July 1982 conference the Ba'th Party adopted a political decision to promote the private sector.

This decision was endorsed publicly by Saddam Husain in 1984 and then again in 1986, when he declared: 'All activities of the private sector form part of the national wealth, and are as important as the activities of the socialist sector.'[7] He reiterated this in even stronger terms the following year when he asserted: 'Our brand of socialism cannot live without the private sector whether now, or after the war.'[8] The policy of promoting the private sector was further enforced with the introduction in February 1987 of an ambitious economic liberalization and privatization pro- gramme.

While certain industries such as oil, defence, steel, petrochemicals, banking and insurance, railways, and public utilities were retained by the state, others were to be sold to the private sector. The new measures were characterized by the *Middle East Economic Digest* as representing a turnaround of the official ideology propounded since the Ba'th came to power in 1968. The main features of the new measures included selling state land, farms and factories to the private sector; encouraging private enterprise; and deregulation of the labour market by abolishing labour law.[9] Other measures to benefit private enterprise included the reorgani- zation of state enterprises and restructuring of ministries and commissions, creation of companies to run state enterprises, enactment of laws to induce the flow of Arab capital, introduction of limited competition in banking, freedom to use foreign-held balances to finance imports, and the encour- agement of private initiative in agriculture.[10] Iraq's rising food dependency under the Ba'th, together with the failure of import substitution industrialization, the impact of the war, the close relationship with the United States, and Saddam's need to consolidate and broaden his power base beyond the Ba'th were among the factors that contributed to the new policies of privatization.[11]

However, these new measures seem largely to have exacerbated Iraq's economic problems. In the agricultural sector output failed to increase. Foreign trade failed to respond to the liberalization measures, as holders of foreign balances opted not to repatriate their foreign-held assets. Instead they engaged in trade schemes which entailed large-scale export of the Iraqi dinar to neighbouring countries in order to buy consumer goods to resell in Iraq at inflated prices. This practice encouraged other firms to charge higher prices thus setting the stage for ever higher inflation rates.[12] And in attempting to reduce claims on its declining oil income, the state contributed to the inflationary spiral by relaxing its policies of providing subsidies to state enterprises as well as the policies that had sought to set price ceilings on a large number of goods.

In its haste to join the fashionable parade of privatization and turn over state enterprises to the private sector, the Iraqi government did not take the time to create and develop the necessary legal, economic, and financial frameworks for the new private sector era. Indeed, the expediency of the entire policy is attested by the fact that the government sold its enterprises to the private sector at prices that were below their book value or replacement value. 'In most cases, the prices paid barely covered the market cost of the land the factories were built on. The government required only a down payment of 40 per cent, to be transferred in increments.'[13]

The transfer of state enterprises to the private sector, the removal of subsidies, the discontinuation of the practice of setting price ceilings, the failure of government policies to control inflation, and the inability of the weakened economy to provide employment, were among the forces that aggravated the economic crisis. The consequent erosion in purchasing power meant that the new policies lowered the living standards of the majority of the Iraqi people.

In the face of these failures the government was forced to retreat from its declared policy when it decided in 1989 to increase the salaries of civil servants, lower certain commodity prices, freeze prices of all consumer goods and services produced by the public sector, lower profit margins of state-owned and mixed-sector enterprises, and increase the subsidies paid to producers of agricultural products.[14]

Such reactive expedient policies could not, however, address the deeply embedded economic crisis. This remained focused on low oil revenue, a heavy foreign debt burden, the failure of the economy to increase its agricultural and industrial output, high rates of inflation and unemployment, the concentration of wealth in relatively few hands, the failure of privatization, and the general worsening stagnation of the economy. The failure of the 1989 measures to solve the deepening economic crisis seems to have persuaded the government to look southward for a solution – to Kuwait.

## Oil, Iraq's economic crisis and the invasion of Kuwait

In theory Iraq's oil prices and exports are set by the decisions taken by OPEC. But in order for such decisions to be effective they need to be implemented by all member countries, as non-compliance otherwise affects other countries' exports and income. Following the 1986 collapse of the oil price, OPEC decided to re-establish the system of output quotas and set a reference price of $18 per barrel. The actual price, however, averaged $16.92 per barrel in 1987, $13.22 in 1988, and $15.69 in 1989, as a number of countries produced more than their assigned shares. Since Iraq, like Algeria, Nigeria, Iran, Libya, and Venezuela, was not in a position to expand output, it found it necessary to focus its policy on prices as the only means to increase or at least stabilize oil revenue. While these countries focused on price maximization, other countries such as Kuwait, Sa'udi Arabia and the United Arab Emirates (UAE) tended to focus on production. The large size of their oil reserves combined with a relatively small population placed them in a position where they could pay less attention to the oil price. In addition to its oil reserves Kuwait had other advantages which distinguished it from other OPEC countries, such as a sizeable foreign investment portfolio which yielded considerable annual income. Kuwait also owned oil refining and marketing outlets abroad, which meant that it made little financial sense for it not to supply these outlets with low-cost oil extracted from its own oil fields.[15] But to produce this oil, Kuwait would have to encroach upon the market shares of other member countries.

The inherent conflict between the interests of price maximizers such as Iraq and output maximizers such as Kuwait was brought into sharp relief by the way each reacted to the oil price changes in 1989 and the first half of 1990. OPEC's goal of establishing a reference price of $18 per barrel remained elusive for the years 1987-89, as indicated earlier. It was not until December 1989 that that goal was reached, with a market price of $18.84 per barrel, 84 cents above the OPEC reference price. This upward price movement continued into January 1990, when the price peaked at $19.98 per barrel, after which it dropped by 30 per cent by June, to $13.67 per barrel, causing a major decline in the oil income of Iraq and other oil producers. And since Iraq was exporting close to 2.8 million barrels per day (MBD) its losses were estimated to be over $7 billion per year – a loss that had the disastrous effect of worsening the deep crisis of the economy.

The desperate state of the Iraqi economy was revealed by Saddam Husain when he said: 'a few billion dollars could solve much that has been at a standstill or postponed in the life of Iraqis.'[16] The seriousness with which the Iraqi government viewed the price decline attributed to Kuwait's policy of overproduction was expressed by the Iraqi president at the Arab Emergency Summit Conference in Baghdad in May 1990, when he said that he considered the damage it had caused to the Iraqi economy to be nothing other than an economic war of aggression. He went on to say that this type of economic warfare against Iraq could not be tolerated, and that Iraq had reached a state of affairs where it could take the pressure no longer.[17]

In addition to the oil issues, Iraq demanded that the loans which Kuwait had extended to Iraq in the course of the Iran-Iraq war be written off since the war had been waged to defend not only the territorial integrity of Iraq but that of Kuwait and the other Gulf states as well. Iraq's failure to receive the relief it sought on these issues prompted its government to use its military power. Thus on 27 July, with the shadow of Iraqi troops along the Iraq-Kuwait border looming large, OPEC decided to raise the reference price of oil from $18 to $21 per barrel and voted to adopt new quotas, with the injunction that no member country was allowed to exceed its allocated share for any reason whatsoever.[18] A few days after the adoption of the new agreement Iraq invaded Kuwait.

## Economic consequences of the invasion

There is clearly no single explanation for the Iraqi invasion of Kuwait. An attempt to deal with all the factors which led to the invasion are beyond the scope of this chapter. Yet there can be little doubt that Iraq's multiple economic crises played a decisive, if not *the* decisive, role in the decision to invade Kuwait. The endemic nature of the crisis may be appreciated by reviewing some of the following economic indicators.

In the first place the destruction of a significant portion of Iraq's oil-exporting capacity, and changing oil market conditions, led to a drastic decline in Iraq's oil revenue. On a per capita basis Iraq's oil revenue declined from $2,000 per capita in 1980, when total revenue amounted $26.3 billion, to $792 per capita in 1989, when total revenue declined to $14.5 billion. These figures understate the loss since they do not take into consideration the decline in purchasing power due to inflation and currency depreciation.

Gross Domestic Product (GDP) per capita, which may be used as a measure of living standards, is another indicator. In 1977, the last normal year prior to the Iranian revolution, per capita GDP in Iraq was $1,600. By 1989 it had increased to $2,818: an increase of 76 per cent. But such an increase becomes meaningless when we consider that the 1980s were a time of rampant inflation, with annual rates of up to 40 per cent.[19]

GDP per capita in real terms becomes, therefore, a more useful measure of what happened to the standard of living of the people. According to United Nations data, real GDP per capita stood at $1,674 in 1980 and averaged $1,145 for the six-year period 1983-88, reflecting a decline in purchasing power of 32 per cent. No less disturbing was the fact that GDP per capita was lower in 1988 than in 1975 – a strong testimony to the vast economic losses which the people had had to endure.[20] Indeed the picture is much bleaker, since a major portion of the country's income was absorbed by military expenditure, which increased from 30 per cent of GDP per capita in the period 1975-79 to 60 per cent in 1980-86. Another indicator of growing economic hardship may be found in the relationship between rates of population growth and agricultural output. Thus between 1980 and 1989, while the Iraqi population increased by 38 per cent, the agricultural production index increased by only 34 per cent. The picture becomes worse when it is realized that the index of cereal production in 1989 actually declined to 72 per cent of its 1980 level. On a per capita basis the cereal production index in 1989 was only 52 per cent of its 1980 level.[21]

It can be seen from these indicators that by 1990 the Iraqi economy had reached a dead end, with no prospect for recovery. And it was in this context that Kuwait's economic resources looked like an expedient solution to the Iraqi economy's endemic crisis. Indeed, Kuwait's economic importance for Iraq was underscored by Iraq's deputy prime minister soon after the invasion, when he said that Iraq would now be able to repay its debt in less than five years; that its oil reserves had doubled; that the 'new Iraq' would have an oil production quota of 4.6 MBD instead of 3.1 MBD; that its oil income would reach $38 billion per year, rising to $60 billion in the near future; that there would be considerable expansion in the private sector once the two economies were integrated; and that Iraq would be able vastly to increase its spending on development projects and imports.[22]

But instead of providing economic relief the invasion deepened Iraq's economic crisis, as the freezing of assets and the United Nations tight system of embargo on its exports and imports cut off the economy from the rest of the world. A measure of the effectiveness of the embargo is shown by the 86 per cent fall in Iraq's oil output, from 3.3 MBD before the invasion to less than 0.5 MBD in subsequent months – only enough to meet the needs of local consumption.

Over the years, but especially during the period of the oil boom and the war with Iran, the Iraqi economy has become highly dependent on imports of agricultural products and other food items and other consumer goods. It has also become dependent on imports of inputs and capital goods for its industrial and other sectors of the economy. It was natural, therefore, that the effects of the embargo were felt throughout the economy soon after the invasion. In a 5 December 1990 testimony before the US Senate Foreign Relations Committee it was reported that the embargo has effectively shut off 90 per cent of Iraq's imports and 97 per cent of its exports, resulting in serious disruptions to the economy and hardship for the people.[23] The damage which the embargo inflicted upon the economy in the six-month period prior to the January 1991 bombing was estimated by the Iraqi government at $10-17 billion in lost oil exports; $5.1 billion in production cuts; $1 billion in increased production costs; $.7 billion in losses resulting from delays in development projects; and $1.3 billion for other losses.[24] A different source, however, estimated that between 1989 and 1990 Iraq's GDP declined by $31 billion – from $66 billion to $35 billion.[25] But such economic disruptions and hardships were, in retrospect, minor relative to the destruction imposed upon Iraq by the 1991 Gulf War.

The bombing was targeted not only at military installations but also at such assets as civilian infrastructure, transport and telecommunications networks, fertilizer plants, power stations, oil facilities, iron and steel plants, bridges, hospitals, storage facilities, industrial plants, and civilian buildings. And the assets that were not bombed were made dysfunctional by the destruction of power-generating facilities. The intensity and scale of the bombing moved a special United Nations mission to Iraq to make the following assessment:

> It should, however, be said at once that nothing that we had seen or read had quite prepared us for the particular form of devastation which has now befallen the country. The recent conflict had wrought near-apocalyptic results upon what had been, until January 1991, a rather highly urbanized and mechanized society. Now, most means of modern life support have been destroyed or rendered tenuous. Iraq has, for some time to come, been relegated to a pre-industrial age, but with all the disabilities of post-industrial dependency on an intensive use of energy and technology.[26]

## Estimated human and economic destruction

Neither the US or Iraqi governments nor the United Nations has seen fit to release data on the extent of the human and material losses caused by the war. Any estimate of the extent of the destruction will have to be considered at best provisional. Human losses caused by the war fall into three categories: military and civilian losses during the war itself; civilian and military human losses during the *intifada*; and civilian losses that can be attributed to the effects of the destruction of infrastructure and the continued embargo.

Estimates of military losses indicate that anywhere between 50,000 and

120,000 Iraqi soldiers were killed in the 43-day Gulf War.[27] Iraqi civilian losses were estimated to range between 5,000 and 15,000. But in the month-long *intifada* against the government which followed the war, it is estimated that between 20,000 and 100,000 civilians lost their lives. In addition it is estimated that 15,000 to 30,000 Kurds and other displaced people died in refugee camps and on the road and that another 4,000 to 16,000 Iraqis died of starvation and disease.[28] These figures show that in total between 94,000 and 281,000 Iraqis lost their lives during the war and the *intifada* which followed it.

In addition to the loss of human lives, the war and its aftermath inflicted on the civilian population other forms of human misery which are difficult to quantify. No data for instance have been released regarding the number of injured, maimed and traumatized, or the extent of their plight. Similarly it is difficult to estimate the losses endured by the large numbers of refugees and persons displaced by the government's crushing of the March 1991 *intifada*. Suffice it to say that in late March 1991 more than two million people 'got up and left their homes in less than six days', fleeing to Iran and Turkey or to seek refuge in the marshes near the Iraq-Iran border.[29] Another group of affected persons are those civilians who were drafted into the war only to be demobilized and return to a devastated and inflation-ravaged economy capable of offering only starvation and unemployment.[30]

The breakdown in healthcare delivery systems, the lack of food, medicine and purified water, and the destruction of power generating plants contributed to further deaths among Iraqi civilians, especially children. This phenomenon was stressed in the May 1991 Harvard Study Team Report which projected that some 170,000 under the age of five would die over the next year from the effects of the war, a doubling of pre-war figures.[31] Moreover, the Gulf War will undoubtedly have an impact on life expectancy similar to the Iran-Iraq war, which lowered life expectancy for Iraqi males by a full ten years.[32] In short, a loss of well over 100,000 active persons, in addition to the much higher losses sustained in the Iran-Iraq war and the large numbers of injured, will affect the size and skill structure of the labour-force, and consequently the future growth and size of the Iraqi economy.

As to the extent of economic losses, it will be recalled that when the Iraqi government decided to invade Kuwait the economy was in the midst of a crisis which was a direct result of the bankrupting effects of the Iran-Iraq war. The economic damage caused by the Gulf War was superimposed on an economy that was suffering from the consequences of the earlier war. Such economic damage took several forms.

In the first place there was the destruction of military and non-military assets. The massive damage to the infrastructure as assessed by the United Nations was referred to earlier: the severity of the destruction was a consequence of the constant escalation of the bombing by the USA and its allies. Thus when Iraq invaded Kuwait, US military planners had designated 57 sites in Iraq as strategic targets. But in the course of the war the list was expanded to include 700 targets, so as to amplify the economic and psychological impact of the UN sanctions.[33] Indeed, some targets were deliberately destroyed in order to increase Iraq's dependency on the West after the war:

> Some targets, especially late in the war, were bombed primarily to create postwar leverage over Iraq, not to influence the course of the conflict itself. Planners now say their intent was to destroy or damage valuable facilities that Baghdad could not repair without foreign assistance.[34]

The kind of bombing that was certain to increase Iraqi dependency in the postwar period was the obliteration of Iraq's electrical system, which could not be repaired or replaced without imported equipment.[35] A United Nations report estimated that the complete replacement of Iraq's power generating system would cost $20 billion.[36] Another study estimated the replacement cost of assets destroyed during the war at $200 billion.[37]

## Impact on personal income and cost of living

The combined impact of bombing, sanctions, *intifada*, inflation, unemployment, and general economic stagnation and social disorganization led to an economic collapse and forced the overwhelming majority of the people to contend with even more severe conditions of poverty and deprivation. The depth and breadth of the deterioration in living conditions are reflected in the findings of the International Study Team.[38] Having analysed the behaviour of prices, incomes and patterns of employment for the year ending August 1991, the study noted that:

> While there has been a shift in the distribution of employment from the formal to the informal sectors of the economy monthly earnings remained stagnant.
> Consumer prices during the same period increased considerably especially the food price index which increased by 1,500 to 2,000 per cent in that year.

Based on these and other findings the study concluded that:

> Real monthly earnings or the food purchasing power of private income has declined by a factor of 15 or 20, or to 5-7 per cent of its August 1990 level.
> These monthly earnings are lower than the benchmark used by the Iraqi

government before 1990 to identify 'destitute households' eligible for
government support.

These earnings are lower than the monthly earnings of unskilled agricultural workers in India – one of the poorest countries in the world.

In addition to the losses mentioned above one must take into account the
loss in national output which can be attributed to the crisis which erupted
in August 1990. The embargo and the war resulted in lost output, the most
obvious and most readily measurable being that of lost oil revenue. The
fall in the output of goods and services can be related to a variety of factors,
including the destruction of infrastructure, depreciation of the Iraqi dinar,
lack of inputs, general deterioration of health, and higher rates of unemployment and inflation.

Such problems tend to be magnified due to the influence of the
multiplier effect on the economy. Taking all these factors into consideration, a provisional estimate shows that Iraq's real GDP declined from
nearly $20 billion in 1989, to $14.5 billion in 1990, and to $8.4 billion in
1991. On a per capita basis the respective decline was from $1,088 to $780
and to $438.[39] These figures indicate that the Iraqi people's living stand-
ards were thrown back to the levels they were at when the Ba'th regime
came to power in 1968.

## Iraq's economic prospects

The previous analysis gives a picture of the current state of the Iraqi
economy. The picture to be sure is not precise, but is at least indicative of
the magnitude of the destruction and the Herculean effort that will be
required to return the economy to some resemblance of normality. Iraq's
problems, it should be stressed, are compounded by the losses and the
destruction which its economy had to endure during the eight-year Iran-
Iraq war.

Any attempt to speculate about Iraq's prospects for economic reconstruction, recovery, and growth must recognize that such prospects are
externally determined and beyond the grasp of the Saddam Husain regime.
This is so because Iraq's prospects for economic recovery will be shaped
by three factors. These are: (a) oil revenue, (b) foreign debt and (c) the
duration of the UN-imposed economic sanctions.

### Oil revenue

Iraq, like all other OPEC member-countries, has to sell its oil in order
survive. The war with Iran and the invasion of Kuwait have shown how
vulnerable the country is to any interruption of the flow of its oil. As was

noted earlier, it was the decline in oil revenue in the aftermath of the war with Iran that ultimately pushed Iraq to invade Kuwait.

Leaving aside for the moment the impact of sanctions, it can be said that Iraq's oil revenue will be determined in the final analysis by how much it will be able to sell and at what price, which in turn will be determined by the world demand for OPEC oil and by Iraq's share of OPEC's total output, i.e. Iraq's quota as determined by OPEC. But given the pattern of OPEC member countries' market shares as it has evolved since the outbreak of the crisis in 1990, and given the predominant share of Sa'udi Arabia, with nearly one-third of all OPEC output, it can be safely said that Iraq will find it extremely difficult if not impossible to export as much as it did prior to August 1990. The other variable which will determine Iraq's oil revenue will be the price of oil. Although OPEC decided in mid-1990 to set the price at $21 per barrel, the price, aside from the early months of the crisis, has actually been below that level. The primary explanation for this is the unwillingness of OPEC, under the leadership of Sa'udi Arabia, to regulate output to the point where the price of $21 per barrel is reached. Indeed, as of July 1993 the price of OPEC oil was only $15.96 per barrel.[40]

But if for the sake of argument we say that Iraq will be granted by OPEC its prewar quota, that it will be able to produce at prewar capacity, and that the price will be $21 per barrel, then Iraq should be able to generate $21.5 billion per year or $107.5 billion for the five-year period 1993-97. But this is only one half of the $214.4 billion which the Iraqi government estimated its foreign exchange requirements to be to cover the following expenditures: $75.1 billion for the payment of foreign debt; $48.5 billion for imports; $55.4 billion for development plan projects; $20.6 billion for the repair of war-damaged infrastructure; $12.6 billion for services; and $2.4 billion for reconstitution of stocks.[41] It is worth noting that the Iraqi government projected an annual rate of economic growth of 3.4 per cent. But with a population growth rate of 2.8 per cent per year this means that during this five-year period per capita income is projected to rise only by 0.6 per cent per year.[42] Yet even the 3.4 per cent growth may prove to be unattainable, given the inevitable resource gap between Iraq's foreign exchange requirements and its projected foreign exchange receipts. It is obvious that it will take Iraq decades to recover its past higher rates of economic growth.

## Foreign debt

Iraq has been a foreign debt free country since the early 1950s. But in the early phases of the Iran-Iraq war it exhausted its accumulated foreign reserves of $35 billion and also incurred heavy foreign debts. Although there are no precise figures on Iraq's foreign debt obligations, or even an agreement on precisely what constitutes debt, there are reliable estimates of magnitudes. Iraq's foreign debt to Western governments and banks was estimated to have reached $35-36 billion by the end of 1990; $11 billion to the former Soviet Union and Eastern Europe; and $40 billion to other Arab countries.[43]

The Iraqi government has adopted the position that the funds it received from the Gulf states during the war with Iran were a grant. Iraq made this clear to the United Nations when it stated: 'Iraq's total external debt and obligations as of 13 December 1990 amounted to 13.1 billion Iraqi dinars or the equivalent of $42.1 billion excluding interest.'[44] Even if we accept the lower figure as Iraq's actual debt obligation this will still mean that if Iraq were to repay its debt within five years it would have to pay a total of $75.1 billion, an annual average of $15 billion or 71 per cent of its potential oil earnings.

How Iraq's creditors will deal with Iraq's obligations – rescheduling, write-off, exchange of debt for equity – will influence the amount of foreign exchange that Iraq will have at its disposal and therefore its prospects for recovery. As was indicated earlier, debt payments are like oil revenue in that their levels are externally determined. The third external force that will shape Iraq's economic future will be the duration and status of the UN-imposed sanctions.

## United Nations sanctions

Since the invasion of Kuwait the economy of Iraq has been virtually cut off from the world economy. UN Security Council sanctions and embargo measures were imposed in order to force Iraq's withdrawal from Kuwait. And although Iraq withdrew from Kuwait, sanctions are still in effect. Following the ceasefire, the UN Security Council adopted a series of resolutions intended to regulate the level and composition of trade that Iraq may engage in.

One of the most important features of the UN sanctions regime was that which requires Iraq to apply to the UN Security Council for permission to engage in trade – how much oil it could sell, which exporting terminals such oil may go through, how much and what to import, etc. Furthermore, the ceasefire resolution (Security Council Resolution 687, April 1991) stipulated that a special UN-administered Compensation Fund (the Fund) be created to which 30 per cent of Iraq's oil revenue is to be diverted to pay compensation for claims against Iraq for any direct loss or damage, including environmental damage and depletion of natural resources, injury to foreign governments, nationals and corporations, as a result of the invasion of Kuwait. By accepting the resolution, Iraq in effect agreed to mortgage its oil revenues for the indefinite future.

In a July 1991 mission report to the UN Secretary General it was estimated that Iraq would need $6.85 billion for the following twelve months to cover essential imports. These imports were deemed necessary in order to provide two-fifths of the prewar per capita levels of clean drinking water and to put a corresponding proportion of the damaged sewage treatment capacity back in operation, to fund enough imports to restore health services to prewar levels, to import enough food to sustain a disaster-stricken population, to provide supplementary feeding programmes to meet the nutritional needs of malnourished children and pregnant and lactating mothers, to restore power generation to one half of prewar level, and to repair refineries and oil facilities in northern Iraq. The mission went on to say that a four-month programme would call for the spending of $2.65 billion.[45]

Instead of approving the annual allocation of $6.85 billion or the four-month allocation of $2.65 as recommended by the mission, the UN Security Council decided to allow Iraq to sell $1.6 billion of oil. The extent of the control that the UN Security Council intends to exert over Iraq's economic future was reflected in the restrictions which the 15 August 1991 Security Council Resolution imposed on Iraq. Under the terms of the resolution Iraq was allowed a limited one-time sale of $1.6 billion worth of oil over a six-month period to fund the purchase of humanitarian items needed for the Iraqi people and to repair war damages. Although Iraq was to select the buyers, the UN Sanctions Committee was to approve each contract.

The UN resolutions stipulated other restrictions. These include the deposit by the oil purchaser of the full amount of each purchase into an escrow account set up and administered by the United Nations, and that oil be exported via the pipeline which runs through Turkey with UN monitors posted along the pipeline and the loading terminal to ensure compliance with the resolution. Moreover, Iraq was not to have access to the full revenue from the sale since the resolution stipulated that 30 per cent of the proceeds, $480 million, be placed in the Compensation Fund and another $186 million set aside to cover the cost of the activities of various UN agencies in Iraq.[46] The remaining $934 million would be used by Iraq, but with approval of the UN Sanctions Committee, to buy food, medicinal supplies and other essential civilian needs for distribution in Iraq, with payments for such purchases to be approved by the Secretary General from the escrow account mentioned earlier. In other words, none of the oil money would go through the hands of the Iraqi government. With such restrictions on its freedom of action it was not inaccurate on the part of the Iraqi ambassador to the United Nations to say that the plan would make 'a trusteeship of Iraq'.[47]

## Conclusion

It can be seen from the previous analysis that regardless of whether Iraq is free or not to sell its oil, its prospects for economic recovery are poor. This is so because of the huge resource-gap between its earnings and its foreign exchange requirements. Iraq's oil revenue is not expected to reach prewar levels for a long time to come; its new status as a major debtor country will severely narrow its options; and the war claims it will have to pay will overburden the economy in the future. In short, Iraq will labour under a vicious cycle of debt and underdevelopment. This is so because for the Iraqi economy to grow it must save in order to invest in its goods-producing sectors. But to generate savings Iraq must be able to have a level of income that would exceed total private and public consumption. Under present conditions the prospects for doing that are simply nonexistent.[48]

Regardless of how the Iraqi government attempts to conduct its economic policy in the coming years, its real options are few and narrow. It took Iraq four to five decades, with vast amounts of oil revenue and considerable foreign expertise, to build its national assets. Furthermore, when it turned to oil to finance its development projects in the early 1950s it had a population of 5 million. Before the end of the 1990s its population will reach 26 million. Its national assets, however, were virtually destroyed in the Gulf War bombing campaign of 1991. The combined effects of this war and the Iran-Iraq war resulted not only in the destruction of economic assets but also in the fiscal bankruptcy of the country, impoverishment of the people, underdevelopment of the economy, and deepening dependency on the West. A bleak outlook indeed for a country that in the early 1980s stood on the brink of joining the major advanced industrial nations.

## Tables

Table 1
### Iraq's population, labour-force and Gross Domestic Product, 1970-91

| Year | Population (millions) | Labour-Force (millions) | GDP Market Prices ($ billion) |
|------|------------|-------------|--------------|
| 1970 | 9.4 | 2.4 | 3.6 |
| 1975 | 11.1 | 2.8 | 13.2 |
| 1976 | 11.5 | 2.9 | 16.4 |
| 1977 | 12.0 | 3.0 | 19.2 |
| 1978 | 12.4 | 3.1 | 23.1 |
| 1979 | 12.8 | 3.2 | 38.2 |
| 1980 | 13.2 | 3.2 | 51.0 |
| 1981 | 13.6 | 3.3 | 35.0 |
| 1982 | 14.1 | 3.8 | 40.6 |
| 1983 | 14.8 | 4.0 | 42.5 |
| 1984 | 15.4 | 4.1 | 47.6 |
| 1985 | 15.9 | 4.2 | 49.5 |
| 1986 | 16.5 | 4.4 | 47.9 |
| 1987 | 17.0 | 4.5 | 57.6 |
| 1988 | 17.6 | 4.7 | 55.9 |
| 1989 | 18.1 | 4.9 | 64.5 |
| 1990 | 18.6 | 5.0 | 47.5 |
| 1991 | 19.2 | 5.1 | 27.5 |

*Notes:* (1) 1989 was assumed to have grown by 15.3 per cent, see *Country Reports-Iraq*, no. 1, 1991, p. 3. (2) The GDP in 1990 was arrived at by subtracting from the 1989 GDP the $17 billion or 26.4 per cent losses in output which the Iraqi government attributed to the embargo and the sanctions. (3) The 1991 was estimated by deducting from the 1990 GDP only the loss in oil revenue estimated at $20 billion or 42.1 per cent of GDP in 1990. Actual decline in GDP must have been steeper, of course, since the value of lost non-oil GDP is not taken into consideration as the data were not available at the time of writing.

*Sources*: World Bank, *World Tables* (3rd ed) (Baltimore: The Johns Hopkins University Press, 1983); League of Arab States et al., *Joint Arab Economic Report* (Annual); and United Nations, *Monthly Bulletin of Statistics*.

## Table 2
### GDP in current prices and in constant 1975 prices, 1970-91

| | GDP | | GDP per capita | |
| | Current prices | 1975 prices | Current prices | 1975 prices |
| Year | ($ billion) | ($ billion) | ($) | ($) |
|---|---|---|---|---|
| 1970 | 3.6 | 8.5 | 383 | 904 |
| 1975 | 13.6 | 12.8 | 1,225 | 1,153 |
| 1980 | 51.0 | 22.1 | 3,864 | 1,674 |
| 1983 | 42.5 | 16.9 | 2,872 | 1,142 |
| 1984 | 47.6 | 17.1 | 3,091 | 1,110 |
| 1985 | 49.5 | 17.1 | 3,113 | 1,075 |
| 1986 | 47.9 | 18.4 | 2,903 | 1,081 |
| 1987 | 57.6 | 22.3 | 3,388 | 1,311 |
| 1988 | 55.9 | 20.2 | 3,176 | 1,148 |
| 1989 | 64.5 | 19.7 | 3,564 | 1,088 |
| 1990 | 47.5 | 14.5 | 2,554 | 780 |
| 1991 | 27.5 | 8.4 | 1,432 | 438 |

*Note*: The 1990 and 1991 rates of declines in real GDP were assumed to be the same as the rates of decline in current GDP. See notes 2 and 3, Table 1.
*Sources*: See Table 1.

## Table 3
### Exports, imports, and arms imports, 1970-90 ($billion)

| Year | Total exports | Total imports | Arms imports | Ratio of arms to total imports (%) |
|---|---|---|---|---|
| 1970 | 0.8 | 0.5 | 0.1 | 20.0 |
| 1975 | 7.4 | 4.2 | 0 5 | 11.9 |
| 1980 | 26.3 | 13.8 | 2.4 | 17.4 |
| 1981 | 10.6 | 20.5 | 4.2 | 20.5 |
| 1982 | 10.3 | 21.5 | 7.1 | 33.0 |
| 1983 | 9.4 | 10.3 | 7.0 | 68.0 |
| 1984 | 9.4 | 9.9 | 9.2 | 93.0 |
| 1985 | 10.7 | 10.5 | 4.7 | 44.8 |
| 1986 | 7.6 | 8.7 | 5.7 | 65.5 |
| 1987 | 11.4 | 7.4 | 5.5 | 74.3 |
| 1988 | 11.0 | 10.6 | 4.6 | 45.0 |
| 1989 | 14.5 | 13.8 | 2.7 | 19.6 |
| 1990 | 9.5 | 7.5 | N/A | N/A |

*Sources*: International Monetary Fund, *Direction of Trade Statistics* (Annual); US Arms Control and Disarmament Agency, *World Military Expenditures and Arms Transfers* (Annual).

### Table 4
**Relative importance of military expenditures and
the armed forces, 1970-88**

| Year | Armed forces (thousands) | Ratio of armed force to labour force (%) | Military expenditure ($ billion) | Ratio of military expenditure to GDP (%) |
|------|------|------|------|------|
| 1970 | 62 | 2.9 | 0.7 | 19.4 |
| 1975 | 82 | 2.9 | 3.1 | 23.5 |
| 1980 | 430 | 13.4 | 19.8 | 38.8 |
| 1981 | 392 | 11.9 | 24.6 | 70.1 |
| 1982 | 404 | 10.6 | 25.1 | 61.8 |
| 1983 | 434 | 10.9 | 25.3 | 59.5 |
| 1984 | 788 | 19.2 | 25.9 | 54.4 |
| 1985 | 788 | 18.8 | 19.0 | 38.4 |
| 1986 | 800 | 18.2 | N/A | N/A |
| 1987 | 900 | 20.0 | N/A | N/A |
| 1988 | 1,000 | 21.3 | N/A | N/A |

*Sources*: Derived from Tables 1 and 3.

### Table 5
**Relationship between oil revenues and military expenditure, 1975-90**

| Year | Oil revenue $ billion | Oil revenue per capita $ | Ratio of military expenditure to oil revenue (%) | Military expenditure per capita $ |
|------|------|------|------|------|
| 1970 | 0.8 | 85 | 88 | 74 |
| 1975 | 8.2 | 738 | 38 | 279 |
| 1980 | 26.4 | 2,000 | 75 | 1,500 |
| 1981 | 10.4 | 764 | 237 | 1,809 |
| 1982 | 10.1 | 716 | 249 | 1,780 |
| 1983 | 7.8 | 527 | 325 | 1,709 |
| 1984 | 9.4 | 610 | 276 | 1,682 |
| 1985 | 10.7 | 673 | 178 | 1,195 |
| 1986 | 6.9 | 418 | N/A | N/A |
| 1987 | 11.4 | 670 | N/A | N/A |
| 1988 | 11.0 | 625 | N/A | N/A |
| 1989 | 14.5 | 801 | N/A | N/A |
| 1990 | 11.5 | 612 | N/A | N/A |

*Sources*: Derived from Tables 1 and 4.

*Iraq since the Gulf War*

## Table 6
### Food price increases in Iraq since sanctions began

| Food Item | Price per unit[a] (ID) | | Percentage increase over 1 year |
|---|---|---|---|
| | Aug 90 | Aug 91 | |
| Wheat-flour | 0.05 | 2.42 | 4,531 |
| Milk (powdered) | 0.75 | 27.33 | 3,661 |
| Bread (per piece) | 0.01 | 0.33 | 2,857 |
| Baby milk (450g tin) | 0.45 | 10.00 | 2,222 |
| Sugar | 0.20 | 4.42 | 2,208 |
| Cooking oil | 0.48 | 10.33 | 2,138 |
| Rice | 0.23 | 4.08 | 1,801 |
| Tea | 1.70 | 23.67 | 1,392 |
| Tomato | 0.27 | 1.25 | 469 |
| Chickpeas | 0.65 | 2.92 | 449 |
| Potatos | 0.45 | 1.92 | 426 |
| Eggs (carton of 30) | 3.83 | 12.50 | 350 |
| Onions | 0.37 | 1.25 | 341 |
| Dates | 0.52 | 1.75 | 339 |
| Meat (lamb) | 7.00 | 16.33 | 233 |
| Meat (beef) | 6.83 | 16.90 | 247 |
| All items[50] (high case) | | | 2,004 |
| All items[2] (low case) | | | 1,546 |
| Cost (at current prices)* | 66.00 | 6,010.00 | 1,546 |

* average 1990 food basket for a family of six ('low case' assumptions)

*Notes*: (a) The commodity unit is 1 kg unless stated otherwise. For each commodity, the stated price is an unweighted average of the prices reported in Mosul (northern Iraq), Baghdad (central Iraq) and Basra (southern Iraq); (b) Food price indices are weighted averages of individual commodity prices; the weights are the corresponding shares of total food expenditure in 1990. Incomplete information on 1990 expenditure patterns was supplemented with more detailed information for 1971. The 'high case' and 'low case' correspond to different assumptions about the evolution of expenditure patterns between these two dates.

*Source: Jean Dreze and Haris Gazar, 'Income and Economic Survey', in International Study Team, Health and Welfare in Iraq After the Gulf Crisis: An In-Depth Assessment, October 1991.*

### Table 7
#### Composition, cost and implicit value of food rations, August 1991

| Commodity | Quantity supplied[a] (kg) | Ration price (ID) | Market price (ID) | Implicit value (ID) |
|---|---|---|---|---|
| Wheat-flour | 8.00 | 0.115 | 2.417 | 18.416 |
| Rice | 1.50 | 0.325 | 4.083 | 5.637 |
| Sugar | 1.50 | 0.225 | 4.417 | 6.288 |
| Cooking oil | 0.25 | 0.410 | 10.333 | 2.481 |
| Tea | 0.05 | 2.000 | 23.667 | 1.083 |
| Baby milk | 1.80 | 0.750 | 22.222 | 38.650 |
| Full ration* | | 11.088 | 219.263 | 208.175 |

* basket for a family of six (one child under one year).

*Note*: (a) Per person per month.
*Source*: Jean Dreze and Haris Gazar, 'Income and Economic Survey', in International Study Team, *Health and Welfare in Iraq After the Gulf Crisis: An In-Depth Assessment*, October 1991.

### Table 8
#### Estimated monthly wages by occupation, August 1991

| Occupation | Monthly wages (ID) | Index[a] |
|---|---|---|
| Conscript, starting | 85 | 65 |
| Clerk, government | 120 | 92 |
| Casual street vending[b] | 120 | 92 |
| Unskilled worker, public sector | 130 | 100 |
| Medical assistant | 130 | 100 |
| Conscript, experienced | 165 | 127 |
| Unskilled worker, private sector | 175 | 135 |
| Postman | 180 | 138 |
| Daily-wage labour (unskilled)[b] | 180 | 138 |
| Primary teacher, public sector | 180 | 138 |
| Civil service official (mid) | 200 | 154 |
| Professional soldier | 220 | 169 |
| Electrician, public sector | 225 | 173 |
| Semi-skilled worker, private | 225 | 173 |
| Skilled technician, private | 600 | 462 |
| Blacksmith[b] | 625 | 481 |
| Bus driver, self-employed | 1,000 | 769 |
| Taxi driver, self-employed[b] | 1,375 | 1,058 |
| Engineer, private sector | 2,000 | 1,538 |

*Notes*: (a) Unskilled worker int he public sector = 100; (b) Monthly wage figure
　　obtained by combining information on daily wages with estimates of the
　　number of days of employment per month.
*Source: Jean Dreze and Haris Gazar, 'Income and Economic Survey', in Interna-
　　tional Study Team,* Health and Welfare in Iraq After the Gulf Crisis: An
　　In-Depth Assessment, *October 1991.*

### Table 9
**Nominal and 'effective' earnings by occupation, August 1991**
**(Monthly earnings (ID) for 6-member households with 2 earning adults)**

| Occupation | Nominal earnings | 'Effective' earnings[a] |
|---|---|---|
| Conscript, starting | 170 | 378 |
| Clerk, government | 240 | 448 |
| Casual street vending | 240 | 448 |
| Unskilled worker, public sector | 260 | 468 |
| Medical assistant | 260 | 468 |
| Conscript, experienced | 330 | 538 |
| Unskilled worker, private sector | 350 | 558 |
| Postman | 360 | 568 |
| Daily-wage labour (unskilled) | 360 | 568 |
| Primary teacher, public sector | 360 | 568 |
| Civil service official (middle ranking) | 400 | 608 |
| Professional soldier | 440 | 648 |
| Electrician, public sector | 550 | 658 |
| Semi-skilled worker, private sector | 1,200 | 1,408 |
| Blacksmith | 1,200 | 1,458 |
| Bus driver, self-employed | 2,000 | 2,208 |
| Taxi driver, self-employed | 2,750 | 2,958 |
| Engineer, private sector | 4,000 | 4,208 |

*Note*: (a) Effective earnings are obtained by adding the implicit value of food
　　rations (see Table 6) to normal earnings.
*Source: Jean Dreze and Haris Gazar, 'Income and Economic Survey', in Interna-
　　tional Study Team,* Health and Welfare in Iraq After the Gulf Crisis: An
　　In-Depth Assessment, *October 1991.*

**Table 10**

**Estimates of labour earnings in Iraq (August 1991), compared with various benchmarks**

| Description of the estimated variable | Estimate[a] (ID/month) | Index |
|---|---|---|
| Nominal monthly earnings, unskilled labour (public sector) | 260 | 100 |
| 'Effective' monthly earnings, unskilled labour (public sector) | 468 | 180 |
| Monthly earnings of unskilled labour in India (incalorie-purchasing-power equivalent) | 482 | 185 |
| Value of the Indian poverty line in terms of 'calorie-purchasing-power equivalence' | 667 | 257 |
| Value of the 'destitution line' which the government of Iraq used before August 1990 to identify households eligible for social security payments[b] | 835 | 321 |
| Value of the average 1990 food basket | 1,010 | 388 |
| Value of *pre-crisis* real earnings of unskilled labour (public sector)[b] | 4,022 | 1,547 |

*Notes:* (a) All figures are in monthly terms, for a household of size 6 with 2 earning adults; (b) The lower estimate of the food price index has been used as deflator.
*Source: Jean Dreze and Haris Gazar, 'Income and Economic Survey', in International Study Team,* Health and Welfare in Iraq After the Gulf Crisis: An In-Depth Assessment, *October 1991.*

# Notes

1. For a detailed analysis of these issues see Abbas Alnasrawi, 'Economic Consequences of the Iraq-Iran War', *Third World Quarterly*, vol. 8, no. 3 (July 1986), pp. 869-95.
2. See *Middle East Economic Digest* (MEED), various issues.
3. See OPEC, *Secretary General's Annual Report*, Kuwait.
4. See The Economist Intelligence Unit, *Quarterly Economic Review of Iraq*, no. 2, 1983, p. 7; *Middle East Economic Survey* (MEES), March 14, April 4, May 23, and July 11, 1983; Kamran Mofid, *The Economic Consequences of the Gulf War*, (London: Routledge, 1990), p. 41.
5. See Mofid, *The Economic Consequences*, pp. 127-35.
6. It should be noted that the $452.6 billion was only the quantifiable monetary loss. Other economic losses include inflation cost, loss of services and earnings of those who were killed or disabled by the war, loss of potential earnings due to the postponement of development projects, cost of delayed education,training and employment, and the social and economic burden of those who were disabled. See Ibid.

7. *MEED*, 15 February 1986, p. 17.

8. Ibid., 28 March 1987, p. 18.

9. Ibid., 15 August 1987, pp. 6-7.

10. It should be noted that the privatization decisions of the 1980s were a logical next step to the Ba'th Party's earlier decisions to privatize the agricultural sector, which were taken in 1979 when it realized that the goal of food self-sufficiency proclaimed under the 1976-80 five year plan will not be achieved. See Robert Springborg, 'Iraqi Infitah: Agrarian Transformation and Growth of the Private Sector', *The Middle East Journal*, vol. 40, no. 1 (Winter 1986), pp. 33-52.

11. Springborg, Ibid. An important indicator of the new policy and the government's need for investment funds was its decision to entice foreign oil companies to re-enter Iraq's oil industry to develop new oil fields using their own capital. See *MEES*, 12 February 1990, p. A10.

12. Estimates of inflation rates vary. According to data cited by al-Khafaji the consumer price index (CPI) increased between 17 per cent and 45 per cent in the period 1980-86. The Economist Intelligence Unit places the CPI increase at between 25 per cent and 45 per cent for the period 1985-89, while the Iraqi government uses an average annual increase CPI of 17.7 per cent for the period 1985-89. See al-Khafaji', The War and the Iraqi Economy', p. 6; Economist Intelligence Unit, *Country Report: Iraq*, no. 4 (1990), p. 3; and 'Economic Prospects', p. D8.

13. See Kirn Aziz Chaudhry, 'On the Way to Market: Economic Liberalization and Iraq's Invasion of Kuwait', *Middle East Report* (May-June 1991), p.18. See also Economist Intelligence Unit, *Country Report: Iraq*, no.1 (1990), pp. 10-11.

14. See *MEES*, 23 January 1989 pp. B3-4; and *MEES*, 18 September 1989, pp. B1-2.

15. See *MEES*, 15 January 1991, pp. B2-3.

16. See 'Documentation on Iraq-Kuwait Crisis' *MEES*, 22 July 1991, pp. D1-9.

17. Ibid.

18. See *OPEC Bulletin* September 1990 p. 7.

19. The lower inflation rate was reported by the government while the higher rate was estimated by outside agencies. For inflation rates for the period 1980-83 estimated by the government to have increased by 77 per cent, see Ministry of Planning, *Annual Abstract of Statistics 1983*, p. 143. For the period 1985-90 the government reported a rise in the consumer price index of 126 per cent. See 'Economic Prospects', p. D8. The much higher inflation rates may be found in Economist Intelligence Unit, *Country Report: Iraq*, various issues.

20. For GDP data see United Nations, *Monthly Bulletin of Statistics*, July 1991, p. 278.

21. See Food and Agriculture Organization, *FAO Yearbook: Production, 1989*, pp. 85-102.

22. See 'Iraq: Dreams and Figures', *Tareeq al Shaab*, October 1990 p. 5.

23. See *New York Times*, 6 December 1990, p. A16.

24. See *MEED*, 30 August 1991, p. 22.

25. *Country Report Iraq*, no. 1, 1990, p. 3.

26. See *Report to the Secretary-General on humanitarian needs in Kuwait and Iraq in the immediate post-crisis environment by a mission to the area led by Mr.*

*Matti Ahtisaari, Under Secretary-General for Administration and Management,* dated 20 March 1991, p. 5

27. An explanation for this wide range in the military losses may be attributed to the overestimate by the US of the size of Iraq's army in Kuwait on the eve of the ground war. For such estimates see US House Armed Services Committee, *A Defense for A New Era: Lessons of the Persian Gulf War* (Washington: 1992), pp. 29-33.

28. See Caryle Murphy, 'Iraqi Death Toll Remains Clouded', *The Washington Post,* 23 June 1991 and Ruth Sinai, 'Greenpeace Says 200,000 Die in War', *The Burlington Free Press,* 30 May 1990. A source in the US Census Bureau calculated that, as of the end of 1991, 86,194 men, 39,612 women and 32,195 children had died at the hands of the American-led coalition forces, during the domestic rebellions that followed, and from postwar deprivation. See *Inquiry,* March/April 1992, p. 15.

29. Judith Miller, 'Displaced in the Gulf War: 5 Million Refugees', *New York Times,* 16 June 1991.

30. For a brief review of some of the problems experienced by families and children of soldiers who lost their lives in the conflict see Kathleen Evans, 'Years of War Wrack Iraqi Families', *The Christian Science Monitor,* 6 June 1991.

31. Harvard Study Team Report, *Public Health in Iraq After the Gulf War,* May 1991, p. 1.

32. Carl Haub, 'A Demographic Disaster', *Guardian Weekly,* 10 March 1991.

33. Barton Gellman, 'Allied Air War Struck Broadly in Iraq: Officials Acknowledge Strategy Went Beyond Purely Military Targets', *The Washington Post,* 23 June 1991.

34. Ibid.

35. See Harvard Study Team Report, Table 6.

36. *MEES,* 29 July 1991, p. D6.

37. See Amy Kasslow, 'Shifting Fortunes in the Arab World', *The Christian Science Monitor,* 26 June 1991, p. 7.

38. See Jean Dreze and Haris Gazdar, 'Income and Economic Survey', in International Study Team, *Health and Welfare in Iraq After the Gulf Crisis: An In-Depth Assessment,* October 1991, pp. 10-32.

39. See Table 2 for the data. It is worth noting that the dollar value of the destruction of civilian and military facilities, infrastructure, power stations, and oilfields has been estimated to be more than $450 billion. See *Joint Arab Economic Report, 1991* (Abu Dhabi: Arab Monetary Fund, 1992) p. 133.

40. For this and other monthly price quotations see OPEC, *OPEC Bulletin,* (monthly).

41. The government's projected foreign exchange requirements were for the period 1991-95. See 'Iraq Outlines Dire Economic Prospects In Plea To The UN For Five-Year Moratorium on War Reparations', *MEES,* 13 May 1991, pp. D6-9.

42. Ibid., p. D7 for economic and population growth rates.

43. See Keith Bradsher, War Damages and Old Debts Could Exhaust Iraq's Assets', *New York Times,* 1 March 1991.

44. *MEES,* 13 May 1991, p. D6.

45. See United Nations; *Report to the Secretary-General on humanitarian*

*needs in Iraq by a mission led by Sadruddin Aga Khan, Executive Delegate of the Secretary-General, dated 15 July 1991*, p. 8.

46. For the text of the resolution see *US Department of State Dispatch*, 23 September 1991, pp. 696-97.

47. See Jerry Gray, 'U.N. Decides to Permit Iraq Oil Sale of $1.6 Billion', *The New York Times*, 16 August 1991, p. A8; and Marian Houk, 'Plan To Allow Iraqi Oil Sale Puts UN Chief in Charge, And Iraqi Officials Bristle', *The Christian Science Monitor*, 19 August 1991, p. 6.

48. For an analysis of the prospects of various economic growth under different assumptions see Sinan Al-Shabibi, 'Iraq's Financial Obligations Could Cripple Economic Prospects', *MEES*, November 4, 1991, pp. B1-2.

# CHAPTER SEVEN

# Why the *Intifada* Failed[1]

### *Faleh 'Abd al-Jabbar*

In March 1991, following Iraq's defeat in the Gulf War, the Kurds of northern Iraq and Arabs of the south rose up against the Ba'th regime. For two brief weeks, the uprisings were phenomenally successful. Government administration in the towns was overthrown and local army garrisons were left in disarray. Yet by the end of the month the rebellions had been crushed and the rebels scattered, fleeing across the nearest borders into Turkey or into Iraq's southern marshes. Many of those who could not flee were killed in summary mass executions.

Despite the calls made during the Gulf War by Western leaders for Iraqis to rise up and dispose of Saddam Husain, these dramatic and ultimately tragic events were the last thing any outside powers anticipated. Did the *intifada* also take the Iraqi people by surprise? There is good cause to think so. Iraqi opposition leaders had long been calling for a 'popular uprising' which would end the war with Iran and the deprivation and tyranny foisted upon them by Saddam's regime. Yet when the moment did arrive, the opposition was totally unprepared. The conditions for success quite simply did not exist.

The Gulf crisis of 1990-91 was paradoxically a favourable period for the regime. However, the roots of the failure of the March *intifada* are to be found in the period of the war between Iran and Iraq, when the opposition developed a belief that war and revolution were indivisibly linked. But if war is to lead to revolution, the internal social struggle must take precedence over the external, national struggle. This, generally speaking, is the European model from the early part of the century – the two Russian revolutions, the 1918 revolt in Germany, the first Hungarian rebellion in 1919, and the Italian workers' revolt in the 1920s. In each case, the nationalism of the ruling classes was seen to have failed, and people placed their loyalty elsewhere.

The Iraqi opposition, fervently hoping that the course of the Iran-Iraq war would bring such a breakdown, deeply underestimated the extent to which Saddam Husain had succeeded in forging a new Iraqi patriotism of national self-defence. Even many Kurds and Shi'i had seen the war as their own: some 250,000 Kurds joined the Salah al-Din Forces, a militia which helped the army to keep the Iranians out of Iraqi Kurdistan; battalions with a majority of Shi'i soldiers mounted a similar defence in the south-east.

Chastened by its disappointment, the opposition learned the wrong lessons. Some factions turned to conciliations with the Ba'th in 1988 and 1989, after the stalemate and ceasefire, precisely when the regime was at its weakest and most vulnerable. Then, during the Gulf crisis and Gulf War, it overcompensated for its previous misjudgment by overestimating the strength of Saddam's appeal to Iraqi patriotism. The opposition was therefore completely unprepared for the spontaneous and truly 'popular' uprisings of March 1991. In that lack of preparation lay the seeds of the failure of the *intifada*.

## The Iran-Iraq war and the opposition

One of the startling features of the Iran-Iraq war was Saddam Husain's ability to refashion his regime's ideology to incorporate widely varied appeals to the many different forces who might support him. The Ba'th's pan-Arab ideology naturally helped bolster his posture as the defender of the Arab nation against the Persian threat, which was important in securing backing from other Arab countries. For the powers beyond the Gulf, all of whom supported Iraq in one way or another, Ba'thism's secular, modernizing aspects made it an attractive potential neutralizer of Khumaini's radical Islamism.

Yet simultaneously, Saddam was able to enlist the loyalty of large numbers of Iraqi Arabs who were Shi'i, and of the non-Arab Kurdish population. During the war, Ba'th ideology became a new synthesis of Arabism, Islamism and, above all, Iraqi patriotism. This patriotism, a new invention, reached deep into the past for heroes like Nebuchadnezzar, who had invaded ancient Palestine, and Salah al-Din al-Ayubi, the Kurd who had challenged the Crusaders in Jerusalem. It developed particularly after 1983, when the war changed from an offensive to a defensive effort. In character with the history of Ba'thist rule, it was wedded to a ruthless internal campaign against dissenters, including the expulsion of up to 250,000 Shi'i from the south.[2]

Among the organized opposition, three positions crystallized in response to the new war-dominated society: pro-Iranian (some Kurds and Shi'i groups); pro-Iraqi (chiefly the pro-Syrian Ba'th splinter party and a faction within the Iraqi Communist Party); and against both Iran and Iraq (the main body of the ICP). Only the Ba'th splinter party decisively supported the Iraqi army and regime, but did not seek an alliance with Saddam Husain. Their hearts were set on a coup d'état which would install in power the 'true' Ba'th, which they claimed to represent.

The Islamist Shi'i parties had traditionally prioritized religious identity, or an ideal projection of it, over national identity. They were waiting for the 'zero hour' of the 'Islamic upheaval' – their version of the popular uprising. The Supreme Council of the Islamic Revolution in Iraq (SCIRI), led by Muhammad Baqir al-Hakim, an umbrella group founded in 1982 and incorporating the Islamic Action Organization (IAO) and the Islamic Masses Movement (IMM), had little political experience to rely on.[3] Another SCIRI component, al-Da'wa al-Islamiyya (Islamic Call), was an exception: it led anti-regime mass demonstrations in 1977 and took to the streets again in 1979.

All the Islamists took a pro-Iran position during the 1980–88 war, mistakenly assuming that they possessed a religious legitimacy in the eyes of the majority of Shi'i which would justify such an alliance. Nationalism was missing as a factor in their calculations. They failed to assess the extent to which the Islamic revolution in Iran arose from a sense of national indignity and bitterness at the Shah's fealty to Washington, and forgot that Ayatullah Khumaini began his own political career as an advocate of Iranian nationalism. They also suffered disastrously from the Iraqi version of pan-Arab nationalism, which saw Iraqi Shi'ism as an extension of Iranian influence.[4] Yet for those people of southern Iraq whose sympathies had not been enlisted by radical Islam, Saddam was still able to extend an appeal based on his new-found Iraqi nationalism and its defence of national borders.

Some Kurdish parties also supported Iran, but from a different historical background. As a large but marginalized national group within Iraq, their political calculations were always influenced by the need for external support in their battles for autonomy against Baghdad. In the early 1970s, they accepted the Shah's money and arms to fight a proxy war which troubled the Ba'th regime deeply in its early, unconsolidated years. In 1975, however, Iran dropped them at a stroke, leaving Baghdad free to wage a bloody campaign of suppression. By once again tying themselves to Iran after 1980, these Kurds were forgetting how their earlier costly experience had isolated them from the Iraqi democratic movement, such as it was. As with the Shi'i parties, this tie to a foreign nationalism brought further repression while detaching them from many of their own people who supported national self-defence.

The Communists, once the most influential of the opposition parties, opposed both Iraq and Iran while planning for a popular uprising (which in 1985 they recognized that the war had 'delayed'[5]). The strain of this position showed itself in the emergence, within the ICP and in leftist circles in exile, of a minor wing which saw that it would be meaningless to call on the people to turn their guns on the regime which was leading the 'defence of the homeland'.[6]

Thus none of the organized parties with the potential to threaten the regime and to form a democratic movement was able to formulate a position which synthesized both the urgent need for democracy, to throw off the yoke of tyranny and war, and the powerful appeal to nationalism which the regime had usurped on the basis of the necessity of defending Iraq.

## Seeds of the Gulf War

Saddam's patriotic posture had thrown the opposition into disarray. During the war years of 1980-88, the opposition was cut off from the major urban centres – Baghdad, Basra and Mosul – which contain almost half of the Iraqi population. Their organizational structures in the cities were largely destroyed, and in some cases wiped out completely. The Kurds and the Communists retained bases in the northern mountains, with some ties to small towns and to the Kurdish cities of Sulaimaniyya and Arbil. The Islamists' only organized bases were in Iran.

Before the Iran-Iraq war, many parties did exist in the cities, especially in Baghdad, but political and social discontent was then at a minimum. With the war over and internal discontent intensifying, the opposition parties quite simply had no reliable organizational structures. The regime was in crisis, but so was the opposition. During the worst period for the Ba'th regime since it came to power, most parties opted for a policy of conciliation.[7]

The Islamists who had put their faith in Iranian tanks, or had even gone so far as to join the Iranian Basij units, were dismayed. Their activities were subject to restriction by Tehran. Their followers in other Arab countries, such as Syria, who used to pack their bags to return to Iraq at each new Iranian offensive, now packed for asylum in Sweden or other European countries. The Kurdish parties opted for conciliation in the hope of conserving whatever they could. The ICP, for its part, attempted to set conditions: any dialogue with the government should be collective and public, and a goodwill gesture should precede it, such as the release of political prisoners.[8] Up until just a few days before the invasion of Kuwait, most Iraqi opposition leaders were busy considering the best way to strike a face-saving bargain with the regime.[9]

## The exhaustion of Iraqi patriotism

During the Iran-Iraq war, a naive and obvious patriotism was the overwhelming mood: defending one's country against invasion. But after the ceasefire, when social and economic problems multiplied, and then after the invasion of Kuwait, when Saddam Husain again gave up the Shatt al-'Arab waterway as an objective in order to neutralize Iran, a second form of patriotism arose; one that joined national defence with opposition to the ruling regime and its foolish, dangerous policies.

To put it more accurately, there are two kinds of nationalism: state nationalism and popular nationalism. These two forms may run together or go different ways, and ultimately turn against each other. During the Iran-Iraq war the two forms coincided to a great extent, particularly during the defensive phase of the war. In the Gulf War, however, this coincidence was over. State nationalism retained its outward orientation. Popular nationalism turned inward, against the ruling elite.

The opposition looked at the invasion of Kuwait and shuddered at the prospect of renewed Iraqi patriotism, not realizing that this time it would be inward-oriented. People did not want this new war. When it did break out, they accepted it submissively but hoped that the destruction would carry one compensation: the fall of Saddam Husain.[10]

It was clear from the way Saddam conducted his ideological campaign during this period that he had an inkling of this mood. He tried desperately to renew his ideological appeal with a new but well-contrived Islamic vocabulary. He had 'defeated' Khumaini, and attributed his victory to his being the 'Deputy of God'. The Iraqi people were in no mood to swallow this act, but the opposition was ill-placed to measure the extent to which mass discontent had grown. The means to measure the popular mood were lacking. There was no significant economic or social research on the country. Only fragments of political news leaked out now and then, which opposition figures scrutinized in vain. Some got into the habit of judging popular feeling by their own personal reaction to events, like the gassing of Halabja. Yet three years later it became clear that most Kurds had first heard of it only after the *intifada*, when rebels publicly showed videos of the gassing. There were scenes then of disbelief and mass weeping whenever it was shown.

The real discontent was fuelled by the crisis in the economy. A quarter of Iraq's 4 million labour-force were under arms; the vast majority ordinary conscripts who were growing restive. During the war against Iran, Iraq's hard currency reserve had fallen from $37 billion to less than $2 billion. Yet the import bill remained at $11 billion per year, much of it stemming from the need to import 80 per cent of the country's food requirements. For the first time under Saddam's rule, feeding the people became a serious problem. The price of basics soared, lowering living standards not just for the poorer strata but also for the middle classes.

Sa'dun Hammadi, then finance minister, appeared on state television after the invasion of Kuwait to tell hungry Iraqis that the occupation of Kuwait would enable them to repay their colossal foreign debts in a mere two to four years. A range of official media took up this theme, yet the public discounted almost entirely any such idea. Above all, they did not want another war, and freely gave that opinion to Western reporters on the streets of Baghdad. Other reports reaching the Iraqi opposition abroad began to speak of social unrest – in Basra, Mosul and the al-Thawra district of Baghdad. Mosul had had the highest casualty rate among young officers in the war with Iran, and Basra had suffered the greatest number of civilian casualties and the worst physical damage. Al-Thawra contained many students who had led attempts to resist conscription. Now students in elementary, secondary and intermediate schools in Baghdad distributed handwritten leaflets against the coming war. In November 1990, a massive student demonstration against the government took place in Baghdad.[11] Samir al-Shaikhli, then interior minister, devised a simple solution: evacuate two million of the capital's inhabitants. (He succeeded in evacuating fewer than 1 million.)

## Exhaustion of the Army

Discontent had begun to grow in the army, which since 1977 had grown from 140,000 to around 1 million. A further 700,000 civilians were recruited into the temporary forces of the so-called Popular Army. The swollen armed forces now included substantial anti-government elements. Kurdish tribesmen formed the Salah al-Din Forces of the Popular Army, mobilized by their chieftains in return for a payment per head. Arabs in the Popular Army were no longer only Ba'th Party members, though Ba'th cadres controlled them. As for the regular army, Shi'i Arabs accounted for 85 per cent of the fighting ranks, but only 20 per cent of its officers.[12]

From 1973 to 1980, as Saddam's personal power grew, key army posts had been filled with clan relatives from his home province. During the Iran-Iraq war, though, the Tikritis found it imperative to enlarge the officer class in order to utilize all available military expertise, including bringing people out of retirement. This meant diluting Tikriti power and influence.

For these reasons the army, or large sections of it, was the greatest problem for the regime in the brief interlude between the wars. It had acquired a truly popular base, but at great cost economically and politically for the regime. One symptom of the malaise in the army was the removal, in November 1990, of Nizar al-Khazraji as chief of staff, followed by Defence Minister Jabbar Shanshal in December. Shanshal's offence was telling the president that his senior military commanders feared the Iraqi army was no match for the allied forces.[13]

A strong anti-Saddam bloc emerged in the higher levels of the military, though it advanced its criticisms in the most cautious and coded terms. Some supported the invasion of Kuwait but not the timing: Iraq had given the West time to group its forces through the winter and launch an offensive before the heat returned, whereas a March invasion would have delayed an allied counter-offensive until the next winter. Others opposed the invasion of Kuwait as precluding any attack on Israel. They anticipated that other states would exploit the battle to their own ends – a Turkish bid for the Kirkuk oil fields, an Israeli jump into Jordan, or perhaps Iran grabbing Mandali or Basra. Only a small minority foresaw success, counting on Arab enthusiasm for Iraq to overthrow the regimes of Syria and Egypt and detach Europe from the USA.[14] Initially Saddam encouraged discussion at the meetings of the senior military commanders, as a way of checking for himself the accuracy of sycophantic reports that the majority backed their leader. But executions soon followed: approximately six hundred officers were killed in November 1990, according to contemporary Kurdish reports.

At lower levels, men who had in some cases been fighting for the best part of a decade were simply exhausted. The case of Ahmad, a corporal, was typical.

I forged an ID with a new profession – peasant – to evade being recruited again. I was relieved, along with tens of thousands of others who turned out overnight as false peasants to plant and cultivate the crops needed to foil the sanctions. But after two months the order to exempt peasants from military service was rescinded. I tried hard, using my mother's gold ornaments, even her wedding ring, to buy a vacation, but in vain: it was too costly. The officers got rich. Lucky soldiers could buy transfer orders, getting assignments far from the Kuwaiti theatre. We were trapped. But hope came when a conscript from the Albu Hijam tribe which lives in the Hur al-Hammar marsh whispered that he was going to desert and seek shelter in the marsh, as he had done before. He invited me to go with him on the condition that I tell no one. I did.

In a letter to relatives abroad, a deserter named M. Ali wrote: 'The smugglers who did trade in tea, sheep and cigarettes were idle before the invasion of Kuwait; now their area, the Iraqi-Turkish border, became prosperous. Not only were food items in demand but a new commodity was on the market: deserters. You had to pay 500 Iraqi dinars if you were a soldier, 1,000 if you were an officer. Around one hundred were smuggled into Turkey, including two officers.'[15]

Hoshiar Zibari, a leading member of the KDP, quoted Kurdish officers and conscript deserters as saying that their units on the Kuwait-Sa'udi border were hemmed in by mines planted by another regiment who were then moved to another position. The mines were not there for protection, but to 'prevent soldiers from defecting to the other side of the front line'.

Kurdish opposition parties in Iraq estimated that the number of deserters even before the war ran into thousands. The Revolutionary Command Council (RCC), Iraq's ruling body, issued Decree no. 11078 on deserters ordering that defectors' wives, children and other relatives be detained. Confidential memorandums from the general staff ordered continued surveillance of suspect elements in the army and their removal from any sensitive command headquarters. They warned unit commanders against 'soldiers showing negative attitudes, namely complaining to Kuwaiti civilians about the food shortages, or even exchanging weapons and ammunition for food.'

## Regime fantasies, opposition blindnesss

On these unpromising foundations Saddam set about mobilizing his reluctant people. Redeploying Iraqi patriotism, he enriched it with a strong dose of Islamic fervour. In this he was helped by the Arab world's Islamist movements, including the Islamic Salvation Front in Algeria, Hasan al-Turabi's National Islamic Front in Sudan, Rashid Ghannushi's al-Nahda in Tunisia, Jordan's Muslim Brotherhood and the Palestinian Hammas. He sought to inflame Arab enthusism by advertising himself as the only leader strong and determined enough to threaten Israel.[16] Saddam also had to convince Iraqis that the West would suffer. The president was ready to pay a heavy price – he even predicted casualty rates of up to 50 per cent – in the hope of inflicting 30-40,000 casualties among the Allies.

Saddam's state of mind during the countdown to war, and the outlines of his strategic thinking, have been the subject of intense speculation. It appears he was truly convinced that he had scored a great victory over Khumaini during his previous adventure. A transcript of a secret meeting of senior officers inside Kuwait in October 1990 reveals that many of them were surprised to find the president there – a clear indication of Saddam's lack of trust in his generals. In the course of the meeting, Saddam claimed he was given orders from heaven to invade Kuwait: 'May God be my witness, that it is the Lord who wanted what happened to happen,' Saddam declared. 'This decision we received almost ready-made from God. ... Our role in the decision was almost zero.'

Predicting that the war would start with allied air raids, Saddam counselled his commanders to 'stay motionless under the ground just a little time. If you do this, their shooting will be in vain. ... On the ground the battle will be another story. On the ground the Americans will not be able to muster forces as strong as you are.' In the final analysis, he said, the power of oil would prevail: 'We have 20 per cent of world reserves. Sanctions will be lifted not for the sake of our eyes, but for the sake of our oil.'[17]

If the generals could not do other than murmur their assent, the opposition was also finding it difficult to articulate its dissent. Still licking their wounds from their failure to gauge the strength of patriotic feeling in the Iran-Iraq war, too isolated now to know how far the pendulum had swung the other way, they did not want to make the same mistake again. All of them had denounced the invasion and annexation of Kuwait, and demanded Iraqi withdrawal. None had lost their hope that Saddam might be displaced. But most feared they would lose their moral right to oppose the regime if they did not side with 'Iraq' against the West.

In a communiqué from Beirut dated 19 January 1991, two days after the air war began, Muhammad Baqir al-Hakim ordered his followers in

SCIRI to join the 'Recruitment Forces', the military wing of his organization, and instructed those based near Iran's border with Iraq to stand firm
against 'United States aggression'. The ICP also denounced US aggression. Mas'ud Barzani, leader of the KDP, opposed both the war option and
the western military build-up; and the Iraqi Kurdistan Front (IKF), a
coalition of Kurdish parties and the Kurdish section of the ICP, halted all
military actions against the Iraqi army in Kurdistan so as not to 'stab the
army in the back'. As the situation ripened towards a mass uprising, the
opposition parties had ceased to expect any such thing.

## The people rise up

Assuming Saddam's true 'strategy' was the one he outlined at the meeting
in Kuwait – there is no evidence of any other – it was a colossal blunder.
The air campaign, which he thought would last two or three days, lasted
more than a month. The Israelis did not react. The Europeans stood fast
alongside the Bush administration. No oil famine occurred. The ground
battle Saddam so confidently awaited never materialized. Instead there
was a rout. The Iraqi army was unlikely to have fought even if the order
had been given. The devastation wreaked upon the country surpassed
imagination.

From the ruins Baghdad radio spoke of the war as 'a great achievement', and called the withdrawal 'heroic'. Baghdad's official version of
events reminded Iraqis of the story of an Italian general defeated at
el-Alamain by Field-Marshal Montgomery. When reproached for having
allowed whole sections of his forces to flee the battle, he solemnly
remarked: 'Yes, we ran away – but like lions.' To the peasant conscripts
who made up the vast bulk of the Iraqi armed forces, no such implausible
irony was possible. For them the experience of flight ended in carnage,
such as that on the 'highway of death' at al-Mutla.[18]

Amidst this chaos the Iraqi people rose up to defy the dictator. In the
throes of a devastating battlefield defeat they reached out for victory inside
their own wrecked and wretched nation. It was the 'popular uprising' for
which every opposition leader, from modern leftist to traditional cleric,
had been calling throughout the Iran-Iraq war. Yet most had given up hope
of it and none were remotely prepared for putting it into practice.

The most common opposition scenarios involved a running series of
political demonstrations at a time of crisis, when the ruling party and the
security services were politically isolated and structurally ruptured. These
mass protests would unify the people, further isolate the regime, and win
over the army rank and file. Only then would the stage of armed revolt
occur, culminating in a battle for the capital. Such a strategy would require
a field leadership with extensive networks of cadres and supporters to
gather intelligence, react swiftly to developments, carefully assess the

mood of the civilians and the military, and plan the positioning and actions of various units. It would need a sober and highly disciplined leadership to overcome the ethnic, religious and communal fragmentation of the Iraqi nation. The crisis did not arrive as expected. The army, which had lost a third of its troops, disintegrated. More importantly, so did the security services, which had suddenly lost all control of the situation. The popular explosion, building since 1988, was detonated by the retreating soldiers and officers who had survived the horrors of al-Mutla.

The first sparks of the rebellion were in the Sunni towns of Abu'l-Khasib and Zubair, about 60-70 kilometres south of Basra. It was the last day of February 1991, three days before the formal Iraqi surrender to General Schwarzkopf at Safwan. The revolt gained momentum immediately, and other cities followed suit: Basra, March 1; Suq al-Shuyukh, March 2; Nasiriyya, Najaf and Kufa, March 4; Karbala', March 7; and then 'Amara, Hilla, Kut, and on throughout the south. In the north the sequence was: Raniyya and Chawar Qurna, March 5; Koi Sanjaq, March 6; Sulaimaniyya, March 7 and 8; Halabja and Arabat, March 9; Arbil, March 11; Dohuk, Zakho and other small townships, March 10 and 13; and finally Kirkuk, March 20.

A detailed account of what happened in each city and township is impossible, but reports in various outlawed Iraqi publications speak of a series of events that were remarkably similar to one another. Masses would gather in the streets to denounce Saddam Husain and Ba'thist rule, then march to seize the mayor's office, the Ba'th Party headquarters, the secret police (*mukhabarat*) building, the prison and the city's garrison (if there was one). As they marched, people would shoot at posters or wall reliefs of the dictator. As the cities came under rebel control, the insurgents 'cleaned out' Ba'thists and *mukhabarat*. This is the general picture, but details, where known, often differed. Poor lines of communication and limited transportation meant that not only nearby towns but frequently adjacent neighbourhoods within the same town (Basra, for example) did not know what was going on in each other's quarter.

Even with hindsight, any assessment of the *intifada* must be cautious. Many of the dramatis personae were killed or are now in hiding in Sa'udi Arabia or Iraq, fearful that their families will be brutalized if they do not remain anonymous. Those who carried the burden of the *intifada*, especially in the first days, were ordinary people whose accounts were often neglected by the opposition press. The situation is further complicated by the fact that the opposition parties often claimed credit for this or that mutiny during the early days, but when failure set in they distanced themselves, saying it had been the spontaneous work of the masses.[19]

## An approximate record

Despite these problems, we have enough evidence to set down an approximate record of the *intifada*, dividing Iraq into three zones: the predominantly Shi'i south; the north, comprising the Kurdish sector; and the middle swathe made up of Baghdad and its environs, together with the towns of the so-called 'Sunni triangle' running from Baghdad north along the Tigris River to Mosul and west to the Syrian border. Each zone is distinguished not only by its own ethnic, religious and communal identity, but also by the degree of political awareness, the quantity of free-flowing information, the extent of organizational capacity, and the balance of the military forces.

In the south, the hypothetical scenario of the *intifada* which the opposition parties had once sketched out was stood on its head. Armed mutiny was the first, not the last, link in the chain. Following the revolt in Zubair and Abu'l-Khasib, Basra too took up arms, led by angry retreating soldiers and followed by a mass of equally angry civilians.

'The Iraqi army cannot bear the responsibility of the defeat because it did not fight. Saddam is responsible', charged Khalil Juwaibar, an armoured vehicle driver who was among the soldiers who left Zubair for Basra to stoke the fires of revolt. An officer described the mood in Zubair and Abu'l-Khasib:

> We were anxious to withdraw, to end the mad adventure, when Saddam announced withdrawal within 24 hours – though without any formal agreement with the allies to ensure the safety of the retreating forces. We understood that he wanted the allies to wipe us out: he had already withdrawn the Republican Guard to safety. We had to desert our tanks and vehicles to avoid aerial attacks. We walked 100 kilometres towards the Iraqi territories; hungry, thirsty and exhausted. In Zubair we decided to put an end to Saddam and his regime. We shot at his posters. Hundreds of retreating soldiers came to the city and joined the revolt: by the afternoon, there were thousands of us. Civilians supported us and demonstrations started. We attacked the party building and the security services headquarters. Within a few hours, the uprising spread to Basra, at exactly three o'clock on the morning of the first of March.

The Basra revolt was led at first by Muhammad Ibrahim Wali, an Iraqi officer who gathered a force of tanks, armoured vehicles and trucks to attack the mayor's office, Ba'th Party offices and security headquarters. The vast majority of the Basra population backed the revolt. Most of the active participants in the clashes were between 14 and 35 years old. Almost all the soldiers took part, including Mechanized Regiment no. 24 stationed near Tannuma. Below the BATA shoe company premises, opposite the mayor's office, they found a secret prison. Hundreds of prisoners were released, some shouting 'Down with al-Bakr', referring to Ahmad Hasan al-Bakr, who had resigned as president of Iraq in 1979.

This spontaneous rebellion in Basra did not have a well forged leadership, an integrated organization, or a political or military programme. Many brave soldiers lamented the fact that cannons, tanks and other weapons were scattered here and there; and that there was no plan to move to Baghdad and no contact with officers and soldiers in other units, who as yet had no idea what had happened in Kuwait apart from the cease-fire. Indeed, when the first officer sent to crush the *intifada* hoisted a white flag and entered the city to join its ranks, he was humiliated and expelled.

The Basra rebellion detonated the Iraqi uprising in general. The people of Suq al-Shuyukh were the next to rise. Three groups of armed men attacked the city, backed by the marsh tribes of Hur al-Hammar and led by the chieftains of Albu Hisham and Albu Ghassid. Virtually all citizens took to the streets and joined the battle for the centres of power. 'Abd al-Shabacha, a member of the National Assembly and an ex-Ba'thist, led the movement in its first days.

## Disastrous slogans

As the revolt spread, it became clear that the south was up against some critical disadvantages. First, it was close to the front lines where some Republican Guard units were still stationed. Second, while the conscripted military was ripe for rebellion, it was politically immature. And thirdly, the Islamists, in the euphoria of early apparent success, joined in and raised a disastrous slogan: Ja'fari (Shi'i) rule.

The rebellion had been taking place under the watchful eyes of Iraqi Shi'i dissidents living in Iran. At SCIRI headquarters in a school in Khorramshahr, where his followers hoisted aloft both his photo and that of the late Ayatullah Khumaini, Muhammad Baqir al-Hakim told Western reporters that he looked forward to a general election in which the Iraqi people would choose their own government, adding that he had no intention of imposing Islamic rule. Inside Iraq, events told another story. 'In Suq al-Shuykh Islamic slogans and posters ... had been erected where giant portraits of Saddam Husain once stood.'[20] With Basra and 'Amara open cities after the rebellion, it was easy for Iraqi dissidents in exile to cross the borders and return home, and many did arrive in Nasiriyya, 'Amara, Najaf and Karbala' to see their families again. Many were bent on revenge, and as a result many unnecessary killings took place in the south.

Although the SCIRI veterans were only one element of the forces who seized the cities in the south, they spoke and acted as if they were the decision-makers. Al-Hakim's military command issued directions stating that 'all Iraqi armed forces should submit to and obey [SCIRI] orders ... No action outside this context is allowed; all parties working from the Iranian territories should also obey al-Hakim's orders; no party is allowed to recruit volunteers; no ideas except the rightful Islamic ones should be disseminated.'[21]

According to Dr Muwaffaq al-Ruba'i, a Da'wa Party leader based in London, those who returned to the south bearing posters of al-Hakim and Khumaini contributed to the failure of the *intifada*. They concentrated their efforts in the holy cities of Najaf and Karbala', 'but by this they gave the uprising a very narrow character, as if were a family affair.' The successful rebels, al-Ruba'i admitted, were a disparate crew, including elements of the Sunni military, Ba'thists, leftists and people from all walks of life.

Al-Hakim should have known that Islamic rule is a nightmare scenario for all their allies in the Iraqi opposition (whether Kurds, Communists or Arab nationalists), not to mention Sa'udi Arabia, Egypt and the USA. In addition, the notion of Islamic rule in Iraq carries connotations of communal strife. Thus it provided an opportunity for Saddam to garner domestic support and regain some implicit if undeclared international sympathy.

## A different landscape

In the north the political landscape was different. Sulaimaniyya was more than 1,000 kilometres from the front line, but its links with the nationalist and leftist parties made it better placed than most northern cities to know what had occurred on the battlefield. The Kurds en masse quickly grasped the meaning of the army's defeat, the subsequent disintegration of the *mukhabarat*, and the rapidly spreading rebellion. This was the moment of reckoning. The battle for Sulaimaniyya erupted within a few days of the Basra insurrection. Negative international and regional responses – US fears of Iranian intervention, the alarm signals sent out by Ankara – were still tentative. The Kurds opened a second front and did so with greater boldness, cunning and discipline than the rebels in the south.

Tension had been growing for some days. Security agents were hunting down deserters in Raniyya, a township near Sulaimaniyya, and provoking armed clashes. Demonstrations followed, police and security units opened fire and civilians defended themselves. Armed masses took control of Raniyya within an hour, but the intelligence service held out for another eight hours before collapsing, losing 34 men in the process. Crucially, Kurdish 'light regiments', the Salah al-Din Forces (the Kurds called them *jash*, meaning 'donkey', playing on *jaysh*, the word for 'army'), went over to the side of the people. Division no. 24, stationed at Chawar Qurna, did not fire a single bullet at the rebels and surrendered peacefully. The *peshmerga* (guerrillas) helped the rebels by occupying the hills overlooking the town.

The news spread to Koi Sanjaq, where a fierce battle was fought against the special commando units backed by Qassim Agha, chief of the *jash*. It took two days until the town was captured on March 6. Bazian and Basloja followed suit. By now, Sulaimaniyya itself was on the verge of an explosion. Thousands of young deserters were discussing the situation, publicly criticizing Saddam Husain, and vandalizing his posters. On March 6 the authorities announced a curfew; security and army units patrolled the town, backed by light armoured vehicles. But on March 7 the city was filled with demonstrators, with women and children in the forefront. One by one the official centres of power surrendered. The battle for the headquarters of the Ba'th and the Popular Army in the Bakhtiari neighbourhood lasted from 3.00 to 7.30 in the evening, when the building was razed to the ground. Fighting then shifted to the Aqari neighbourhood, site of the new security service directorate. More than nine hundred *mukhabarat* were killed, including their director, Colonel Khalaf al-Hadithi, along with some hundred and fifty rebels.

Arbil, the capital of Kurdistan, was simultaneously preparing for rebellion. This time the demonstrations were timed in co-ordination with the *peshmerga* of the Patriotic Union of Kurdistan and the Communists. On March 11, armed crowds swarmed the streets and controlled the town within three hours. A chain reaction followed in Koi, Chamchamal, Kifri, 'Aqra, Tuz Khurmatli, Dohuk and the other towns of the north.

Unlike the situation in the south, these armed takeovers were preceded by public demonstrations lasting sometimes for several days, and bearing clear political slogans: democracy for Iraq and autonomy for Kurdistan. The Kurds were in a position to forge a wider unity: Mas'ud Barzani, leader of the Kurdish Democratic Party, approached the Salah al-Din Forces and tens of thousands thronged to the rebels' side. Barzani also forged cordial personal relations with many high-ranking commanders from the six regular army divisions deployed in Kurdistan.

The *peshmerga* played a more tactical role than the retreating remnants of the conscript army had been able to play in the south. Having helped to seize control of a town, the *peshmerga* would withdraw, leaving it under the control of a locally selected administration. Such a gesture delivered three messages: first, that the cities were liberated not from the outside but from within; second, that the military's pride should not be wounded; and, third, that the Turkish government should not fear Kurdish secession. These tactics paid off as the rebellion snowballed and reached the oil city of Kirkuk, just three hours' drive from Baghdad.

More than fifty thousand soldiers left their units without fighting back, and were soon seen in the streets of the Kurdish cities, welcomed, fed and sheltered by Kurdish families. The rebels' own armed actions were carefully limited to punishing security servicemen and leading Ba'th cadres. Revenge attacks could not always be prevented as the long-awaited moment for the people to vent their anger materialized, but the scale of retaliation was much smaller than in the south.

## The uprising that wasn't

What became of the middle sector of the country? It was essential for any lasting success that the masses in Baghdad bridge the wide gulf separating the north and south, between which there was clearly no adequate political, military or organizational co-ordination. But the rebels were to be disappointed. Baghdad remained idle and quiet.

One key factor was the flow of information, or rather the lack of it. Witnesses testify that it was extremely difficult to travel even across the capital, never mind through the countryside. News was slow to arrive. The real situation at the front was not known in Baghdad, as it was in Basra and even in Sulaimaniyya. It took five days, according to one leftist, before they were sure that Basra was in rebellion.

Even then the *intifada* created only a peculiar sort of passivity: Baghdadis were waiting for it to come to them. This false hope was encouraged by some opposition leaders, notably Jalal Talabani, who proposed an attack on Mosul and then on Baghdad. Al-Hakim also broadcast that the revolt was on its way. From interviews with at least a dozen Baghdadis who later left Iraq, it seems that the news spread either by the opposition leaders through Tehran radio or on the BBC and other channels was exaggerated and sometimes even unfounded. One dissident made tremendous efforts to move around Baghdad to check out news about mass arrests in, for example, the Kadhimiyya or al-Thawra districts (poor neighbourhoods of mainly Shi'i residents): 'Each time I got to the place indicated only to find nothing there', he complained.

The main cause of the passivity, however, goes back to the lack of organizational structures inside the capital. It was easy to penetrate 'Amara, Basra and Nasiriyya across the permeable borders with Iran; the Kurds could, even when times were hardest, manage to move in and out of their cities. Baghdad was a critical exception. Only three parties could, in theory, have filled the gap: the Communists, the Da'wa, or the pro-Syrian Ba'th splinter party. But the Communists had locked themselves in the mountains of Kurdistan and identified themselves closely with the Kurdish cause. From 1980 to 1989, they confined themselves to one form of armed struggle, the least effective in Iraqi conditions: Guevara-style country-to-city elite warfare. Any idea of forming armed units in the cities was dismissed as heretical or anti-revolutionary. No real attempt was made to build up cells in Baghdad. When guerrilla bases were destroyed in 1988, bringing the struggle in the countryside to an end, critics jumped to the conclusion that any form of armed struggle was irrelevant and the best way forward was to strike a deal with the regime. The Da'wa had enough strength and expertise to build underground networks, but had been intoxicated with the reverent Islamic belief that trust in God also meant trust in the Iranian tanks, and failed to make significant preparations of their own. The pro-Syrian Ba'thists held similar hope that the tanks of Damascus would one day carry them on to Baghdad. As a result, there was not a single leader ready to give the signal to Baghdad's four million people.

Additionally, the slogans of radical Islam emanating from the south caused much concern. One Shi'i dissident told how his Sunni relatives took shelter at his house as a precaution against the indiscriminate retaliations they feared would follow in the wake of the revolt. Such fears were not rare and must have helped Saddam to enhance his position, especially in the more backward areas of the 'Sunni triangle'.

This may well explain, in part, the situation in Baghdad. Two other factors help explain why any uprising had little chance of success. First, the regime had concentrated its security efforts in the capital. And second, nearly one million Baghdadis had been evacuated before the outbreak of the war.

## All silenced

Deprived of the capital's support, and lacking organizational, tactical and political coordination, the rebellious towns fell one by one. True, some cities in the south changed hands several times, but in the end all were silenced.

The relative ease with which the remnants of the Iraqi army saved the regime shocked opposition leaders. It also awakened them to the fact that the US was interested in reducing the Iraqi military threat in the region only, not internally. That was understood to be the reason for bombing the retreating units which were to play a vital role in the uprising. These were the very units suspected by Saddam Husain of potential trouble. Half of the Iraqi units were stationed in and around the Kuwaiti theatre. The other, loyal, half was divided into four groups: one in Kurdistan (which surrendered without putting up much of a fight); another in Mosul (six divisions); another in Tikrit, with the task of foiling any attempt in Baghdad; and the last in Baghdad itself to thwart any attempt from the south.

In the 1930s, King Faisal had said that the Iraqi army should be strong enough to quell two mutinies at the same time. By 1991, Saddam Husain arranged his forces to face a three-edged threat – from the north, from the south and from inside the capital – presuming that at least one area would rise in military insurrection. In *From the House of War*, BBC correspondent John Simpson describes the astonishing appearance of Tikrit on the eve of the war. It was a fortress in the strict sense of the word, although it was more than 1,000 kilometres from the front lines. In short, Iraq's pre-war security arrangements were chiefly concerned with countering internal elements.

The approach pursued by the USA tended to help rather than weaken the regime's arrangements. Although the Iraqi military defeat helped detonate the popular revolt, the manner in which the defeat was inflicted undermined it. The rout relieved Saddam of the most troublesome part of his army and preserved the most loyal divisions.

To add to the problems, the Shi'i character given to the rebellion by Western and Arab media from the beginning was confirmed by unwise overstatements made by some Shi'i leaders. Furthermore, mass revenge killings of Ba'thists – to some extent in the north and to a greater extent in the south – rallied the majority of party cadres behind Saddam Husain. These killings were a clear message to Ba'thists that they were wanted dead, not alive, and they predictably resisted to the end.

The task of the rebels was to divide not only the Ba'thists but the Tikritis as well. The Tikriti clan provides state, party and security-service leaders and key cadres; but it is also the main source of high- and medium-ranking army officers – an estimated 2,000 or so. In an army reduced to one-third of its former size, this Tikriti elite is a decisive core. In addition to political and ideological ties, and economic interests, kinship lends this group an almost monolithic character. Yet political differences had caused some cracks, as in 1979 when President Ahmad Hasan al-Bakr was unseated by Saddam Husain, or in 1989 when Saddam Husain's brother-in-law, Defence Minister Adnan Khairullah Tulfa, was assassinated. To widen such divisions and invest them with an active political significance remains one of the most vital tasks confronting the opposition as a whole.

For Iraq's regional neighbours (apart from Iran) and the USA, it seemed as though the situation had returned to its starting point in 1980, when Iran was bent on exporting its revolution. A war had been fought for eight years to reduce that threat. A second war, to remove the resulting malgrowth and new disequilibrium, had just been waged. The Islamic nightmare changed regional and international attitudes. Perhaps this is why the rebels were, according to Colonel Qattan, denied access to Iraqi weaponry and ammunition dumps under US control across the river in Nasiriyya. It should be added that, in the eyes of most ruling elites in the Middle East, the word 'democracy' is more dangerous than Saddam's tanks. The Iraqi *intifada* was the first popular upheaval unwelcome to Arab opposition and Arab rulers alike. The rulers feared a spread of so-called revolutionary arson. The opposition feared divergence from their own outward-oriented, anti-Western, nationalist sentiments.

The *intifada* was drowned in blood. The scenes of mass executions showed the world an Iraq that is still a wonderland of terror. Yet Arab leftists and philanthropic liberals turned a blind eye and a deaf ear to the cries of a nation victimized. Their anti-imperialist rhetoric was loudest precisely when it was necessary to listen not to oneself but to those who were asked to line up behind the patriarch, even if he was in his 'autumn'. The fatal error in the arguments of the Arab and, by extension the international, Left was to neglect the longing of the Iraqi people for democracy. This left the cause of peace and democracy to the manipulation of the USA and other Western powers. The rightful condemnation of US schemes and hidden agendas should have been complemented by a defence of the Iraqi people's legitimate right to democratic freedoms and their right to decide matters of peace and war.

## Changes and prospects

War, sanctions, uprisings and reprisals generated dramatic changes. The nation that entered the Gulf War barely resembles the nation that came out of it. The state has been deprived of the vast oil revenues it earlier enjoyed and was able to use for war preparation, social bribery and building up the security apparatus. It has only a quarter of its previous armed forces, and a security apparatus weaker in terms of manpower, equipment and infrastructure. The credibility and legitimacy of the ruling elite have suffered greatly. The ruling Ba'th Party – which has since the Gulf War hastily convened its 10th Congress – lost almost 40 per cent of its cadres and membership (originally 1.1 million). The result is a feebler control system.

Control systems are the product of a host of integrative material, economic, political, social and cultural factors. When all these factors sustain damage, the whole system ceases to work properly or collapses. In the case of Iraq the control system – much to the misfortune of those who oppose it – combines two elements: the single party and the single family. This dual monopoly gives it an extra potency.

The weaker the state, the stronger the tendency to rely on Saddam's inner family. The Iraqi state now looks more like a family enterprise than ever before. Watban, Saddam's half-brother, is minister of the interior. Sab'aui, also his half-brother, is director-general of the security directorate. 'Uday, his elder son, is in charge of information, culture and youth. Qusayy, his younger son, is director-general of the special security agency. 'Ali Hasan al-Majid, his paternal cousin, is minister of defence. Husain Kamil, his son-in-law, is minister of military industries. Saddam, the latter's brother and President Saddam Husain's son-in-law, is director-general of the presidential security agency (*jihaz al-himaya*). There is also a strong Tikriti presence in the general staff of the army and air force.

The more the state is a family-run project, the stronger the cohesion of the ruling elite. But the more the ruling elite's cohesion is on family lines, the greater is its alienation from the people. State culture is essentially universal. As an agency monopolizing legitimate means of violence, the state protects universal rights such as property, life, order, and law-enforcement. Family culture is by definition particular. The clash between the two cultures means that the family cohesion of the ruling elite is a temporary strength but a chronic weakness.

Confronting the reality of its own crisis, the ruling family initiated an organized retreat on almost all fronts except the ideological – that is, adherence to worn-out state nationalism. The decision to withdraw the armed forces and central administration from Iraqi Kurdistan was part of this tactical retreat. Among the new tendencies is a rapprochment with the old tribal shaikhs and landlords, to whom Saddam has apologized for the agrarian reforms of the 1958 revolution. The telegrams of support sent to the president on Army Day and National Day are no longer from trade unions, students organizations, professional societies, political parties or other modern social groups. Nowadays they are signed by tribal shaikhs whose tribes are named and even the number of their tribe members is given. The revival of old social classes seems clearly intended to forge new social alliances, particularly in the south.

Iraqi society has undergone severe fragmentation. In its present condition of hyper-fragmentation it is increasingly resorting to old forms of solidarity and traditional networks: tribal, communal, familial.This is because the state is omnipresent, and civil society so extremely marginalized. The state monopolizes vast areas of economic, social and cultural production and activity; civil society is thus almost totally deprived of the modern means of self-expression and therefore relapses into any available 'free zones'.

The weaker the control system becomes, the more the relation between civil society and the state changes. This leads, in the long run, to the demise of the old power forms and structures. Iraq is at present undergoing this process. In other words, the emergence of direct family rule resulted from the partial collapse of the pre-Gulf War state structure, particularly the control system. However, it will itself cause deeper change in the state structure. The current strengthening of family rule is but a transitory moment in this change. A new relation between state and society is in the making. Whether or not the new relation will be democratic remains to be seen.

## Notes

1. This chapter is an updated version of an article first published in *MERIP*, May-June 1992.

2. Only two parties have exact figures: the Iraqi security services which deported the Shi'i, and the Iranian agencies which received them (minus those who died *en route*.) This figure is an average based on ever-increasing numbers coming out of Iran. Iraqi opposition groups give even higher figures. An investigation I carried out in Iran in the spring of 1982 leads me to believe this is a conservative

figure. Some 40,000 of those originally deported to Iran have since resettled in Syria.

3. From interviews with Mudarrisi, Muhammad Baqir al-Hakim and others in Tehran in the spring of 1982. See my *Materialism and Modern Islamic Thought* (in Arabic), 2nd edition (Beirut, 1985).

4. Contemporary Iraqi writers, among them Hasan 'Alawi, Wamidh Omar Nadhmi and Karim al-Izri, indicate that pan-Arab thought had much in common with Ottoman anti-Iranian and, by extension, anti-Shi'i positions. If Shi'ism was seen by the Ottomans as an extension of the Safavid and Qajar dynasties; it is viewed now as an extension of the contemporary Iranian state.

5. See the speech of ICP general secretary Aziz Muhamad in *Documents of the 4th Party Congress* (n.d.), p. 93.

6. Among the prominent figures of this trend is the Communist veteran Zaki Khairi, author of *Problems of Revolution and Defence of the Nation* (Damascus, n.d.).Khairi remained within the party, but others left and published the monthly *Communist Tribune*. Later the group almost disintegrated and some of its key figures returned to Baghdad. On the whole they took the same stand in the Gulf War.

7. For more details, see my essay in Victoria Brittain (ed.), *The Gulf Between Us: The Gulf War and Beyond* (London: Virago Press, 1991).

8. ICP Annual Meeting Report, March 1989, pp. 27-32.

9. Zaki Khairi and his wife, Suad Khairi, campaigned for a return to Baghdad on the model of the Turkish Communist Party, whose leaders returned to Ankara accompanied by a host of MPs and reporters. Channels of dialogue were initiated by Mukarram Talabani, former minister of irrigation and former member of the ICP's Central Committee, who has been living under undeclared house arrest in Baghdad since the collapse of the Ba'thist-Communist alliance in early 1979. The Kurds favored conciliation; the Communists were more cautious: there was no unanimity. There was also an anti-regime dialogue among the opposition forces. The Islamist movements delayed the process, rejecting on ideological grounds terms like democracy, nationalism, secularism and even patriotism. At that time Saddam Husain offered but did not deliver a reform package: economic liberalism and a multi-party system. Instead he had himself elected president-for-life. For more details about the state of mind of the opposition in this period see Rahim Ajina and Fakhri Karim in *Al-Thakafa al-Jadida* (1991).

10. Among the ironies is that while the leadership of the ICP was criticized by sections of their membership abroad for having no firm stand against the US invasion, it was more severely criticized by its membership inside the country (either in the mountains or in underground networks) for opposing the allies and forgetting the urgent need to topple the regime: the divergence is typical. It was asserted in interviews with two ICP leaders whom I cannot name without their permission. Other letters and interviews with Iraqis fleeing the country since the ceasefire support this view.

11. This information is contained in a leter from Muhammad Baqir al-Hakim to London-based Arab dailies and also in an ICP press release. The Iraqi Ministry of the Interior corroborated the information in a backhanded way when it broadcast on Baghdad TV interviews with a dozen or so teenage students from a so-called

'Black Hand Gang' who confessed to writing leaflets and threatening other students.

12. Colonel Ahmad Zubaidi, 'The Structure of the Iraqi Armed Forces' cited in *al-Thakafa al-Jadida* no. 237 (September 1991).

13. On the eve of war, President Saddam Husain established a bipolar equilibrium in the armed forces. The ministry of defence and the Republican Guard command were entrusted to non-Tikritis, Marshal Sa'di Tu'ma Abbas al-Jaburi and General Mukhlif al-Rawi; while the positions of chief of staff, airforce commander and minister of military industries remained in the hands of Tikritis, generals Husain al-Rashid, Mezahim Sa'ib and Husain Kamil. Military and political intelligence and security services are controlled by Saddam's own half brothers, Sab'aui, Watban and Barzan. This division of power makes any attempt to seize power dependent on cooperation between the two poles or the unlikely neutralization of one. After the defeat, reliance on the inner family circle was the choice.

14. This is primarily based on reports by the late Salim al-Fakhri, a prominent ex-military expatriate living in London who passed away shortly before the air campaign began.

15. Risking the death penalty, countless numbers of Iraqi soldiers and junior officers sent letters to opposition forces, relatives and friends in exile to seek a way out. The stream of stories is colossal indeed and merits a separate study.

16. For more about the role of political Islam in the conflict, see my essay, 'The Gulf War and Ideology: The Double-Edged Sword of Islam' in H. Bresheeth and N.Y. Davis (eds.), *The Gulf War and the New World Order* (London: Zed Press, 1991).

17. I published an almost complete version of the text in the London-based Arab daily *al-Hayat* (9 June 1991) and a briefer version in *The Guardian* (10 June 1991).

18. See the account in Victoria Brittain's introduction to *The Gulf Between Us*, p. x.

19. That, for example, was what ICP politburo member Fakhri Karim asserted in a lecture in London shortly after the end of the uprisings saying, contrary to earlier claims, that they were spontaneous and their failure was of their own making.

20. *Newsweek*, 1 April 1991.

21. A copy of the directive was furnished by the Information Bulletin of the ICP, no. 175 (13 May 1991). The weekly *al-Badil al-Islami* (Islamic Alternative) printed the full text on 9 May 1991.

# CHAPTER EIGHT

# The Kurdish Parliament

## Falaq al-Din Kakai MP

In this chapter the establishment and survival of a parliamentary system in Iraqi Kurdistan since the Gulf War is described by someone who was personally involved in that historical experience. It begins with the Act for Electing the Parliament in Iraqi Kurdistan, passed on 8 April 1992, and goes on to provide a statistical analysis of the parliament which was elected in May 1992. A description of the coalition formula devised by the two main parties is followed by a summary of the programme of work which the prime minister presented to parliament in July 1992. The issue of electing the head of the national liberation movement is examined, and the chapter concludes with the parliament's declaration of federal union with Iraq, made on 4 October 1992.

## Free and fair elections

The Act for Electing the Parliament in Iraqi Kurdistan contained Rule 1 of the Iraqi Kurdistan Front (IKF). It was signed by the first secretaries of each of the eight political parties that made up the IKF. These were the Kurdish Democratic Party (KDP), the Patriotic Union of Kurdistan (PUK), the Socialist Party of Kurdistan (PASOK), the Socialist Party of Iraqi Kurdish (SPIK), the Iraqi Communist Party (ICP), the Kurdistan Popular Democratic Party (KPDP), the Kurdish Toilers Party (KTP) and the Assyrian Democratic Movement (ADM).[1]

In addition to its contemporary political significance the act has great historical and cultural meaning for the Kurdish people. It is the first law in the history of modern Iraq to be enacted by a de facto Kurdish authority exercising power and assuming decision-making rights within the Kurdish region of Iraq, irrespective of the central government in Baghdad. The resolution to hold a general election in Iraqi Kurdistan in May 1992 was a crucial element in this assertion of authority.

Elections were held, parliament then assembled and began to debate, a council of ministers took office, ministries and other state organs were reorganized. The political bodies which resulted from the election insist that the Kurdish region remains part of the state of Iraq. Yet they themselves are not part of the Iraqi political system. They are democratic legislative, executive and judicial institutions which are alien, because of their representative nature, to the official regime in Iraq.

A dual political system has thus emerged in Iraq. There is the central government which claims the absolute right to represent Iraq internationally and in fact still has diplomatic legitimacy, and there is the administration in the Kurdish region which does not claim to represent all Iraq but is striving to function as a federal authority within the Iraqi state.

The central government is based on a long-established single-party system. It has been denounced again and again for violation of human rights, civil liberties, Kurdish national rights and the rights of ethnic and religious minorities. The government in Iraqi Kurdistan is based on pluralism, respect for civil liberties and human rights, and consolidation of the democratic experience.

Pursuing different ends by different means, the two regimes contradict each other in terms of conception, thought, values and practice. But they are symbiotic within a single state whose unity the world community vows to protect. Such coexistence cannot last forever. One of the two regimes has to outlive the other. Which it will be depends upon domestic, regional and, most decisively, international factors.

According to logic and natural justice, democracy should triumph. If this happens an oppressed people, the Kurds, will have played an extraordinary historical role in toppling a dictatorship that overpowered them in every way. They will be able to extend their democratic experience beyond the geographical, demographic and historical boundaries of the signatories of the Elections Act. Although such far-reaching effects were hardly imaginable by those signatories at the start, the outcome may well provide a democratic model for the rest of Iraq. This, at least, is what is hoped for by those seeking a better and more decent life for the Iraqi people.

The majority of the non-Kurdish Iraqi opposition parties (mainly in exile) were sceptical, hesitant or simply against the IKF's takeover of political administration from April 1991 (that is, long before the May 1992 elections). Even after the elections this attitude persisted. But when the IKF showed that it had a strong commitment to change and that the Kurdish people were firmly behind it, many non-Kurdish Iraqi opposition parties changed their attitude and began supporting the parliamentary system in Iraqi Kurdistan.

The elections were based on proportional representation and one of the results was that most of the signatories to the Elections Act did not gain the 7 per cent quota of votes needed to be represented in parliament. All parties were identified by colours, and the election turned out to be a competition between the yellow of the KDP and the green of the PUK, with other colours fading away. The sole exception was the purple of the Assyrians, and the Christians in general, who voted separately for five allocated seats.

The parties which failed to win seats underwent severe internal crises after the election. This led to a new polarization and realignment within the Kurdish political arena. Some of the losers merged to form a bigger party. Segments of other parties joined the winners. The process was still in full swing a year later (May 1993), with each group trying to expand its popular base within a peaceful and democratic atmosphere.

The Elections Act which initiated this process was itself part of a dramatic sequence of events. The Gulf War had ended with the Iraqi popular uprising of March 1991 (the *intifada*). The Iraqi government's violent counter-attack against the *intifada* led to the mass exodus of Iraqi Kurds into Iran and Turkey. Despite the agonies of the mass exodus, the *intifada* in Iraqi Kurdistan was not a failure.

There were two factors that primarily contributed to its positive outcome. One was international support on the basis of UN Security Council Resolution 688. The other was the active manoeuvring of the Kurdish leadership, who were well organized and well-equipped to deal with the twists and turns of political events. During the *intifada*, the exodus, the negotiations, the imposition of the no-fly zone and the creation of safe havens, the IKF became, unintentionally, the de facto ruling power. This was recognized in the following text from the Elections Act.

The Iraqi government has recently carried out an unprecedented measure, namely the withdrawal of its administrative units and personnel from Kurdistan,[2] thereby creating a unique administrative and legislative vacuum. The IKF, which was conducting negotiations with the central government, has thus been thrown into a very complicated and challenging situation.

It is a norm that any community of human beings has to organize itself to secure the rule of law so as to protect the lives, property, liberty, rights and dignity of citizens. There must be a system of justice. Food and medical care must be provided. These goals cannot be achieved by individuals acting alone, which would lead to antagonisms and chaos. Collective work is needed to organize social affairs, for the rule of law and justice to be established by elected representatives of society.

Humanity has for centuries recognized democracy as a way of expressing the hopes and aspirations of society and of electing deputies to administer power. The democratic principle has been shown to have universal validity. No other principle has survived to become the distinctive method and style of modern times. When the historical page of dictatorial regimes has been turned over a new world order can be built on the twin pillars of democracy and respect for human rights.

The IKF, as a de facto ruling power, is determined to take up this challenge.[3] It has resolved to draw inspiration from the spirit of our age and translate it into a living reality in Iraqi Kurdistan. It is taking the first step to catch the train of the civilized world. It intends to reconstruct Kurdish society on the basis of democracy and respect for human rights in accordance with international norms and agreements. It will demonstrate to the world that the people of Iraqi Kurdistan are capable of such self-government.

The IKF decided as early as 1988[4] to establish a Kurdish parliament that would exercise power and express the views of Kurds. But circumstances in the years up to the *intifada* of March 1991 and in the year after it did not allow this decision to be implemented. Events moved fast, from the *intifada* to the mass exodus to the negotiations.[5]

The negotiations achieved none of the IKF's demands because the Iraqi government kept up its tactics of buying time and going back on its promises made in Baghdad at the beginning of the negotiations. There were also various military, economic, financial, psychological and other pressures in violation of any human norm in our civilized world.[6]

Since democracy means the rule of people by their elected representatives who create specialized state organs on the basis of separate legislative, executive and judicial power in order to fill the legal vacuum, build the administration in Kurdistan and define relations with the central authorities, and since these aims cannot be achieved without free and fair elections, this Act has been laid down.

The Elections Act shows clearly that the Kurdish people are capable of self-government in accordance with universally recognized norms. But it might appear to be a leap into the unknown, a political adventure. A parliamentary system requires specialized cadres and a mature population with a wide stratum of literate and educated individuals. What do Iraqi Kurds have?

Despite wars, ordeals and long deprivation, significant professionalism and expertise have accumulated in Iraqi Kurdistan. Among a population of 3-4 million there are approximately 35,000 teachers, 400,000-500,000 pupils, 15,000 university students, 450-500 lawyers, 2,000 jurists, 3,000-3,500 engineers, 400-500 artists, 350-400 writers, 500 geologists, 70-80 translators and 2,000 Islamic scholars. Most of the last are members of the Kurdish Muslim Ulama Union, an organization which supports the Kurdish regional government and its programme; some are deputies in the parliament.

Furthermore, Iraqi Kurds have developed 40 specialist popular organizations such as the students' union and the writers' society. In Iraqi Kurdistan two daily newspapers and five regular weeklies and monthlies are published. There are 15 radio and television networks including some which broadcast throughout the region. Kurdish society, in short, does not lack the skills required for self-government. If international protection is provided to prevent encroachment by the central regime, Iraqi Kurds can succeed.

## The parliament

The administration established after the May 1992 elections reflects the high level of competence in Kurdish society as a whole. The level of competence was high even though key leaders of the KDP and PUK did not participate in the parliament and council of ministers but left those responsibilities to second line party cadres and independent figures. This can be demonstrated by a statistical analysis of the parliament.[7]

The parliament is composed of 105 deputies, of whom 99 are men and 6 are women. The women make up 5.7 per cent of the total. One is from Arbil, two are from Kirkuk and three are from Sulaimaniyya. Men make up 94.3 per cent of the total. 30 are from Arbil, 15 are from Kirkuk, 34 are from Sulaimaniyya and 20 are from Dohuk. The percentages of all deputies according to province are as follows: 30.3 per cent from Arbil, 15.2 per cent from Kirkuk, 34.3 per cent from Sulaimaniyya and 20.2 per cent from Dohuk. The Dohuk figures include those born in Mosul and the Kirkuk figures include those born in Khanaqin and Kifri because the Dohuk and Kirkuk provinces cover four electoral regions. The highest percentage of KDP deputies is from Dohuk. The percentage from Arbil is lower, the percentage from Sulaimaniyya is lower still and the lowest percentage is from Kirkuk. The difference between the highest and lowest percentage is seven seats. The highest percentage of PUK deputies is from Sulaimaniyya. The percentage from Arbil is lower, the percentage from Kirkuk is lower still and the lowest percentage is from Dohuk. The difference between the highest and lowest percentage is 24 seats.

All the deputies belong to one of the party lists. These are the lists of the KDP, the PUK and the Christians/Assyrians. Each list, however, contains both party and non-party deputies (i.e. the independents). The latter form 68 per cent of KDP deputies, 53 per cent of PUK deputies and 40 per cent of Christian/Assyrian deputies. The Kurdish Toilers Party is an example of a small party included in the list of a big party, the PUK.

The average age of deputies when the parliament first asssembled was 46.4 years. Hasan Kanibi from Sulaimaniyya was the oldest at 68. The three youngest, all aged 30, were 'Ayad Hajji Namiq Majid from Arbil, Sarkis Aghajan Mamand from Arbil, and Hasan Husain Bafri from Kirkuk. Seventy-seven per cent of the deputies were aged between 35 and 54. The average age of KDP deputies was 47.2, of PUK deputies 46.2 and of Christian/Assyrian deputies 38.

Half the deputies have BA degrees. Many have MA or PhD degrees. Many are high-school graduates. Only 3.8 per cent have no more than elementary school education. Of the KDP deputies 54 per cent have a BA, 14 per cent have an MA or a PhD and 16 per cent are high-school graduates. Of the PUK deputies 44 per cent have a BA, 16 per cent have an MA or PhD and 16 per cent are high-school graduates. The academic specialities include jurisprudence, literature, engineering and administrative sciences such as economics and planning.

By occupation, many of the deputies are schoolteachers, lecturers, university professors and lawyers. A high proportion are party workers, professional politicians, military commanders and former *peshmergas* (guerrillas). This is hardly surprising, given that the parliament grew from a national liberation movement engaged in armed struggle for decades.

## Coalition

The parliamentary election of May 1992 effectively resulted in a draw between the KDP and the PUK. They agreed to divide the 100 seats between them (the five additional seats were allocated to the Christians/Assyrians) and adopted a coalition formula to make up the government. The head of parliament is a member of the KDP. The head of council of ministers (the prime minister) is a member of PUK. Each has a deputy from the other party. The ministries were formed in a similar way: as a general rule, a minister from one party has a deputy from the other. There are also ministers from the Assyrian Democratic Movement and the Iraqi Communist Party. The minister of justice is an independent appointed by full mutual agreement between the KDP and PUK. There is a commitment to try to involve other parties in the government, such as representatives of the Turcomans. The original composition of the Council of Ministers was as follows.

| *Name* | *Ministry* | *Party* |
| --- | --- | --- |
| 1. Dr Fu'ad Ma'sum | Prime Minister | PUK |
| Dr Rosch Shawais | Deputy Prime Minister | KDP |
| 2. Mr Amin Mawlud | Industry & Electricity | PUK |
| Ameen Abdulrahman | Deputy | KDP |
| 3. Mr Sherko Bekass | Culture and Information | PUK |
| Mr Ahmad Salar | Deputy | KDP |
| 4. Dr Muhammad Tawfiq | Humanitarian Aid | PUK |
| Dr Kamal Kirkuki | Deputy | KDP |
| 5. Dr Idris Hadi | Communication and Transport | KDP |
| Dr Faridun Rafiq | Deputy | PUK |
| 6. Mr Yonadam Yusif | Housing and Public Works | ADM |
| Mr Tayyib Jabir Amin | Deputy | PUK |
| 7. Dr Nasih Ghafur | Education | KDP |

| Name | Ministry | Party |
|------|----------|-------|
| Mr 'Uthman Hasan | Deputy | PUK |
| 8. Mr Qadir 'Aziz | Agriculture | KTP/PUK |
| Mr Akram 'Izzat | Deputy | KDP |
| 9. Mr Kamal Mufti | Peshmerga Affairs | PUK |
| Mr Azad Fattah | Deputy | KDP |
| 10. Mr Ma'ruf Ra'uf | Justice | Independent |
| 11. Dr Salah al-Din Hafidh | Finance and Economy | PUK |
| Mr Salah Dalu | Deputy | KDP |
| 12. Mrs Kafia Sulaiman | Municipalities and Tourism | PUK |
| Mr Salih Ahmad | Deputy | KDP |
| 13. Dr Kamal Shakir | Health | ICP |
| Dr 'Abd al-Ahad Afram | Deputy | KDP |
| 14. Mr Muhammad Mulla Qadir | Endowment (Religious Affairs) | KDP |
| Mr Muhammad Salih | Deputy | PUK |
| 15. Mr Ma'mun Brifcany | Reconstruction and Development | KDP |
| Mr Husain Taha Sinjari | Deputy | PUK |
| 16. Mr Yu'nis Rushbayani | Interior | KDP |
| Mr Ahmad Sharif | Deputy | PUK |

The coalition formula adopted by the KDP and PUK ensures a joint approach to government, with continual dual meetings to address problems and make decisions. A disadvantage of the coalition formula is the possibility that sharing responsibility will slow down the development and implementation of policy. Also, a change in the even balance of power in parliament after a future election would necessitate structural changes in the ministries. On the whole, however, the coalition formula strengthens national unity, facilitates the overcoming of sensitivities left from past clashes and encourages an atmosphere of tolerance and working together to achieve a common purpose.

## Council of Ministers' programme

The prime minister and his deputy were named by the parliament after it was formed on 4 June 1992 and the composition of the first Council of Ministers of the Iraqi Kurdistan Region was announced on 22 July. The next day the programme of the Council of Ministers was presented to parliament by the prime minister, Dr Fuad Ma'soum, with the following introduction.

> Respected Sir, Head of the Kurdistan Parliament, respected Members of Parliament ... In any people's history there are turning points and events which cannot be forgotten. And naturally in the chronicles of the Kurdish people there are happenings and tragedies which leave their mark. Some cause us joy and pride, either when they occur or when they are settled in history. One such event is the election of the parliament and creation of the council of ministers of the Kurdistan Region. You have given us our historic task and so we present our programme to you ...
>
> The Iraqi regime has used different policies against the Kurdish people to annihilate them and eliminate all traces of their nationality, language, culture and way of life. But the Kurdish people confronted these policies and were able to keep their national character and increase their love for their homeland, day after day, insisting on its development and progress.
>
> The election of the Kurdistan parliament was a great victory for our people. Our enemies anticipated that we would drown in a sea of blood. The Iraqi regime hoped that the people would side with it so that Saddam Husain could claim a victory to cover his defeat. But, as we expected, the people stayed true to their traditions and the national liberation movement rose to the occasion.
>
> The election succeeded. Thousands stood in long queues from early morning to vote. Because of the success of the election you decided to form the Council of Ministers, albeit under very difficult conditions. The infrastructure has collapsed and Kurdistan has been transformed into a wasteland, particularly since the Iraqi regime stopped negotiating with the IKF, withdrew its administration and imposed an economic blockade. The people who fought for many years for freedom and democracy now want bread. They want daily life to be organized. They need security and laws. This can only be achieved with continual hard work.

The wide range of political, economic and social problems addressed in the programme begins with the relationships of Iraqi Kurdistan with the central government of Iraq, with neighbouring states and with the international community. The first is to be organized on the basis of voluntary union within a democratic Iraq that recognizes the rights of the people of Iraqi Kurdistan. Good relations are sought with Iran, Syria and Turkey, with whom there are historical and cultural bonds, based on non-interference and serving the interests of all Iraqi people. Through the United Nations and its organizations efforts are to be made to achieve four aims: lifting Iraq's embargo on Kurdistan; exempting Kurdistan from the international embargo on Iraq; allocating some of Iraq's assets frozen abroad for economic relief in Kurdistan; extending the no-fly zone beyond the 36th parallel so that it includes more of the area under Kurdish control.

Freedom, democracy and human rights are high on the political agenda.

All laws, decisions, regulations and special directives issued by the central government that strengthen dictatorship and destroy the spirit of freedom in Kurdistan are frozen. The rule of law is to be imposed with an independent judiciary and interference in the course of the law prevented. Human rights are to be protected in accordance with international declarations. These include freedom of thought and the right to express and act upon, within legal limits, political, religious, national, journalistic and trade-union views. The cultural rights of minorities in Kurdistan – Arabs, Assyrians and Turcomans – are guaranteed.

In the interests of internal security, gun control is to be introduced. Many civilians have complained about the unauthorized carrying of weapons and it has caused many problems, particularly in the cities. The police force is to be recreated and enlarged, to protect lives and property. This will provide a career option for suitably qualified *peshmerga*.

Special attention is to be given to the *peshmerga*, who have made huge sacrifices for Kurdistan and are now its defenders. Because each party has armed forces under its command it is difficult to establish centralized control of the region. The *peshmerga* have to be brought together under one leadership and be given special camps and sites close to the armed forces' headquarters and the cities. The number of *peshmerga* necessary for Kurdistan has to be specified. To guarantee their livelihood they have to be trained and transformed into a regular force, taking into account their years of service in regard to appointments, promotion, allowances and pensions. For this there needs to be a ministry for *peshmerga* affairs, and the cooperation of the political parties. Special care has to be taken of disabled *peshmerga* and the families of those who sacrificed their lives.

On the economic front, humanitarian and development aid is sought from foreign governments and agencies as well as from Kurds living abroad, with attempts made to coordinate reconstruction projects and follow up their achievements. For agriculture to revive there needs to be a plan to encourage farmers to return to their villages. The land problem must be tackled in a way that achieves justice between them and the landowners.

In order to develop, the free market economy needs supportive government initiatives. These include establishing a banking system; assisting the revival of productive enterprises, whether state-owned or privately owned; conducting a census and study of economic needs; organizing taxation (including customs) and state expenditure; encouraging joint foreign-Kurdish ventures by renting government-owned premises and obtaining payment for water, electricity and telephones; seeking foreign credit and investment; and developing international trade, particularly with neighbouring states. There needs to be a functioning postal service internally and with the outside world. The telephone, telegram, telex and fax systems need to be greatly improved. Transportation needs to be reorganized.

Education policy objectives include expanding the number of teachers, developing Salah al-Din University, and working towards opening institutes in Arbil and Sulaimaniyya so as to have adequate places for high-school graduates. On the general cultural level there is to be freedom within the law to publish newspapers, magazines and books; and to organize radio and TV networks. There is a commitment to support Kurdish studies and humanitarian creative work; to protect archaeological sites; to encourage sport; to take care of minority cultures; and to establish a printing and publishing house.

On health there is a commitment to protect public health, to make medicines and medical instruments available, and to establish a Kurdish Red Crescent. On social affairs, the objectives are to identify social problems and find solutions for them; to take care of women's issues and protect their rights; and to support disabled and homeless people, particularly refugees and the survivors of massacres and the Anfal campaign. On religious affairs, care is to be taken of mosques and religious schools. There is a commitment to work towards establishing a college for Islamic studies. A special council is to be set up for Christians and Yazidis, to supervise their temples, property, religious schools and affairs in general, according to law. 'We do not want to give a picture of life as a fresh spring,' the prime minister concluded, 'but the horizon is not dark and not all doors are closed to us.'[8]

The presentation of the Council of Ministers' programme was a historic landmark in the implementation of the IKF's Rule 1, which decreed the election of parliament. Rule 2, which decreed the election of the head of the national liberation movement, proved more contentious. It states that 'the people of Iraqi Kurdistan through direct, secret, universal suffrage elect the head of the national liberation movement to represent them and speak on their behalf on internal and external matters.'

## Head of the national liberation movement

There were four candidates in the election for the head of the national liberation movement, which took place in May 1992 at the same time as the parliamentary election: Mas'ud Barzani, Jalal Talabani, Dr Mahmood Othman and Shaikh Othman Abdul-Aziz. Mas'ud Barzani secured the highest number of votes but not the absolute majority required to win the election. The IKF, which was still the de facto legislative authority, took an immediate decision that there should be a second election between Barzani and Talabani. The election, however, did not take place. At the end of October (by which time both parliament and Council of Ministers were functioning) the IKF took its last legislative decision. This was to further postpone the election to an unspecified date.

The head of the national liberation movement has many consitutional responsibilities in relation to the legislative and executive bodies. They include (under Rule 10): convening parliament; ratifying agreements approved by parliament; issuing laws and regulations agreed by parliament; issuing decisions that have the strength of law during the parliamentary recess or in emergency situations, on condition that they be presented to parliament when it next meets for ratification; presenting draft laws; inviting the electorate to elect parliament fifteen days from the end of the parliamentary term or when parliament dissolves itself. Under Rule 11 the head of the national liberation movement also has to: issue an order to those whom parliament has named to form the council of ministers; issue orders appointing or discharging senior officials and accept their resignations.

These are important responsibilities. In the absence of an elected head of the national liberation movement how are they being carried out? How is the legal gap being filled? According to Article 14 of Rule 2: 'If the head of the national liberation movement post is vacant, for whatever reason, the head of parliament exercises the powers of that post until a new head of the national liberation movement is elected within a month of the post becoming vacant.'

The present parliament has considered the non-election of the head of the national liberation movement to constitute the post being vacant. The IKF has exercised its authority to postpone the election beyond the agreed time and the head of parliament is now discharging the responsibilities of the head of the national liberation movement. For example, laws and regulations are being issued in the name of the head of parliament.

Nevertheless, while the post of head of the national liberation movement – which is intended for a top-rank political leader – remains vacant, a vacuum exists which is not filled by either the legislative or the executive authority. Iraqi Kurdistan needs a spokesperson on 'internal and external issues'. This is particularly so because of the unresolved constitutional relationship between the central government of Iraq and the regional authority in Iraqi Kurdistan. There were legal and political difficulties with the election of the head of the national liberation movement from the outset. The KDP and some members of the IKF defended the need for Rule 2 and its implementation; while the PUK and other members of the IKF demanded its cancellation or modification. They wanted, for example, the title to be changed to regional governor so as to indicate the executive nature of the post.

A year's experience of the parliamentary system and the coalition formula functioning in practice resulted in an implicit agreement not to raise the issue, for the sake of unity. The practical need for the post and a postholder remains, however, and increases as the parliamentary system becomes more firmly established and its regional and international relations develop.

The post is also of internal importance because it creates a balance in the field of executive power. The Kurdish parliament has the right to nominate one of its members to form the council of ministers, from which it can give or withdraw confidence. The head of the national liberation movement has the reciprocal right to issue laws in certain conditions and the general commander of the Kurdistan armed forces has the right to appoint senior officials and accept their resignations.

This is similar to many other democratic systems, as explained by Jawher Namiq, head of the parliament, in the *Khabat* newspaper in September 1992. 'The duality of executive authority is considered as a safety valve preventing parliament from marginalising the role and status of the council of ministers or dominating it.'

The Kurdish peculiarity is only the title – head of the national liberation movement – which is appropriate in the current situation for two reasons. First, the Kurdish political forces are on the threshold of achieving their national and patriotic goals but have not done so. Second, the legal formula for the relationship between Iraqi Kurdistan and the government of Iraq has yet to be worked out.[9]

## Federation

'The most suitable formula in our situation,' wrote Jawhar Namiq, 'given our political system and the huge sacrifices our people have made, is federation, within the framework of Iraq. The federal formula is in tune with both Kurdish aspirations and the local, regional and international situations. It emphasizes the unity of the Iraqi people and their territory and avoids misinterpretation of our goals. The issue must be left to the Kurdish parliament, which alone has the right to make a decision on it.'

On 4 October 1992, parliament issued the following communiqué declaring the federal union of Iraqi Kurdistan with the rest of Iraq.

With the end of the First World War, the Kurdish nation, like all those colonized under Ottoman rule, looked forward to establishing its own self-governing entity. But the various interests of the victorious forces, who held the levers of power and authority, decided to deprive this ancient nation of its legitimate right to independence. Furthermore, they divided the nation between five neighbouring entities. This was done regardlesss of Kurdish protests and uprisings, and despite Articles 62 and 64 of the fourth part of the Treaty of Sèvres, signed on 10 August 1920.

The Treaty of Sèvres recognized the Kurdish right to nationhood and said that right should be transformed, in the course of a year, into complete independence for a Kurdish nation-state, consisting of all parts of Kurdistan.

This included south Kurdistan, which later became Iraqi Kurdistan, whose people could chose to join the independent Kurdish state.

These hopes were dashed by the Lausanne Treaty, concluded on 24 June 1923, by which the Mosul *wilayat* was added to the newly formed state of Iraq on 16 December 1925. This was done even though the relevant League of Nations committee reported that the demographic reality supported recognition of an independent Kurdish state 'since the Kurds represent five-eighths of the population'. The League of Nations settled for Kurdish rights to self-government in administration, justice and language.

Thus south Kurdistan became part of Iraq despite the opposition movement led by Shaikh Mahmud and his recognition by the British as Hukumdar[10] in 1919 and 1922. The state of Iraq was under the British Mandate and a joint statement was issued by the British and Iraqi governments recognizing the rights of Kurds living within Iraqi borders to establish a Kurdish government within those borders. They said they hoped the different Kurdish elements would agree about the shape of the intended government and its borders and would send envoys to Baghdad authorized to discuss political and economic relations with them.

These remained commitments on paper only. On 3 October 1932 Iraq was admitted as an independent member of the League of Nations, but only on condition that it signed guarantees to respect the administrative, cultural and human rights of the Kurds and minorities living in the provinces of Mosul, Arbil, Kirkuk and Sulaimaniyya. Article 16 of the League's last decision, made on 18 April 1946, reaffirmed those guarantees upon which Iraq's independence and territorial integrity depended. Iraq's obligations to the League of Nations transferred to the United Nations, but successive Iraqi governments failed to abide by them. The United Nations reaffirmed the obligations on 5 April 1991 with Security Council Resolution 688, with the decision of the Social and Economic Council made at Session 48 and with various decisions taken on 5 March 1992.

Kurdish history is full of uprisings and revolutions. On 11 September 1961 the Kurdish people rose up under the leadership of the legendary Mustafa Barzani. This was in response to the failure of the 'Abd al-Karim Qasim government to abide by Article 3 of the temporary constitution issued after the Iraqi revolution of 14 July 1958, according to which Arabs and Kurds are partners within Iraq. The 1961 revolt was a Kurdish national movement for popular demands and legitimate aspirations. It led to the historic agreement of 11 March 1970, which reaffirmed the temporary constitution and recognized the Kurdish right to autonomy. The Iraqi government did not, however, respect the agreement. In 1975, after secret international negotiations, Saddam Husain, in the Algiers Agreement, made territorial concessions to Iran in order to suppress the Kurdish national movement. The Kurds continued their struggle to prove to the world that they are a proud people who cannot be suppressed.

The United Nations Charter forbids the denial of basic human rights and upholds the dignity and status of individual men and women be they rich or poor. The introduction to the Charter affirms, in the third paragraph of Chapter 1, the necessity of establishing relationships between nations based on the principle of equality of rights between peoples. The right of peoples to decide their own destiny is affirmed in the first paragraph of the first article of the two international commitments concerning social, economic and cultural rights. It was reaffirmed in the statement on political and civil rights issued by the General Assembly in 1966, to which Iraq subscribed on 25 January 1971.

The second article of the United Nations Charter specifies the principles according to which the organization works to achieve its goals. Member nations enjoy rights and privileges, including respect for sovereignty and territorial integrity, and accept the obligations laid down in the Charter.

However, since the establishment of the state of Iraq, in 1921, successive Iraqi governments have denied the most basic economic, social, cultural and human rights. The right to life itself has been denied, let alone political rights. The oppression has intensively and regularly destroyed agriculture, animal life and the natural environment as well as people. The long record of criminal acts has been crowned by one of the worst campaigns of annihilation in human history.

Three hundred thousand Fa'ili Kurds have been deported and the fate of 7,500 of their young people who have been arrested is still unknown. More than 5,000 innocent women, children and old people were killed by the chemical weapons bombardment of Halabja in March 1988. Chemical weapons were also used to kill civilians in Balisan, Bahdinan, Kramyan and other parts of Kurdistan. In the 1987-88 Anfal campaign of starvation, rape, torture and mass burials of people still alive, more than 180,000 perished. More than 4,500 villages throughout 90 per cent of the Kurdish countryside have been systematically and thoroughly destroyed. Ethnic minorities such as Assyrians and Turcomans have suffered alongside Kurds. These are crimes against humanity under international law.

A long period of silence and inaction by governments worldwide ended when international sympathy for the Kurds was aroused by TV pictures of the mass exodus which took place after the crushing of the *intifada* in spring 1991. For the first time since the Treaty of Sèvres the international community acted in support of the Kurds, when the Security Council passed Resolution 688. The suppression of the Kurds was condemned and a safe haven was established in part of Iraqi Kurdistan to protect them from aggression by the Iraqi regime.

Despite the pain, the tragedies and the campaigns of annihilation, our people have always accepted in good faith any initiative for a peaceful solution to their problems. They negotiated in 1963, 1966 and 1984, but good faith was met with deceit, treachery and disavowal of agreements signed by different Iraqi regimes. The latest example of this was in 1991, when the Iraqi regime disavowed promises made at the start of the negotiations, then withdrew its administration and imposed an economic blockade on Kurdistan.

In response we Kurds held free elections, as decided by the IKF as the de facto authority, with the people voting on 19 May 1992 for their representatives to form the parliament. On 5 July 1992 the first government of the Kurdistan region was formed and received the confidence of parliament to fill the administrative vacuum. Rule 1 of April 1992 – the law for electing the parliament of Iraqi Kurdistan – stated, in paragraph 2 of Article 56, the duties of parliament. These include deciding the crucial issues facing the people of Iraqi Kurdistan; specifying the legal relationship with the central government; protecting and strengthening the national unity of Iraq; and maintaining the historical brotherly relationship between the Kurdish and Arab peoples.

Parliament's fulfilment of its duties is compatible with the decisions of the Iraqi opposition agreed in Vienna [June 1992] and in Iraqi Kurdistan [September 1992]. These emphasized the legal principle of recognizing the right of the Kurdish people to decide their own destiny and its mutual benefit to the Kurdish and Arab peoples. It also recognized the national, cultural, administrative and constitutional rights of the Turcomans and Assyrians.

Thus the parliament, in exercising its duties and its right to decide the destiny of Iraqi Kurdistan in accordance with international commitments and conventions, has agreed unanimously to specify the legal relationship with the central government of Iraq as one of federal union within a parliamentary, democratic Iraq based on a multi-party system and respect for human rights.

## Notes

1. The parties are listed in the same order as in the *Perleman* newspaper, September 1992. *Perleman* is the official publication of the Kurdish parliament and local government. Its first issue appeared under the name *Anjuman*, meaning 'Assembly'. From the second issue it was entitled *Perleman*, meaning 'Parliament'.

2. The process of withdrawal began in autumn 1991, and ended with the imposition of a complete economic embargo against Iraqi Kurdistan by the Baghdad government.

3. After the embargo was imposed the IKF said it intended to hold elections, i.e. in January 1992.

4. The IKF was formed in November-December 1987. Its formation was announced in May 1988. Its basic rules and programme were approved a month later.

5. The negotiations between the IKF and the central government began in April 1991. There were sporadic and irregular KDP contacts into early 1992. These stopped after the Kurdish elections of 19 May 1992.

6. The IKF had proposed a draft autonomy programme. The central government rejected it and presented a counter programme. This aborted the whole process. The negotiations finally broke down after the central government imposed the economic embargo on Kurdistan.

7. This analysis was prepared by a university professor who published it under the pseudonym Abu Salar in the *Khabat* (The Struggle) newspaper, no. 635, September 1992. *Khabat* was then a monthly publication.

8. Following discussions in the PUK leadership, Fu'ad Ma'sum resigned as prime minister on 17 March 1993 and was replaced by Abdullah Rasul ('Kosrat'). In the reshuffle there were four other important ministerial changes. The new

ministers appointed were: Finance Minister Daru Shaikh Nuri; Justice Minister Qadir Jabari; Agriculture Minister Sa'di Pira; Minister for Peshmerga Affairs Jabar Farman. [Editor's note, September 1993.]

9. In December 1993 the parliament agreed to form a council of eight members to fulfil the role of head of the national liberation movement until a new election can be held for the post. The council consists of Jalal Talabani, Mas'ud Barzani, the speaker of the parliament; the prime minister and two members from each of the politburos of the two main parties, the PUK and the KDP. [Editor's note, January 1994.]

10. The Hukumdar Shaikh Mahmud Barzinji was the governor of Sulaimaniyya and surrounding areas.

CHAPTER NINE

# Suppression and Survival of Iraqi Shi'is

*Hussein al-Shahristani*

Survival in southern Iraq since the Gulf War has become progressively more arduous. This account is based on regular contacts with hundreds of refugees who have recently fled Iraq, on work with families of the 'disappeared', on interviews with victims of Ba'thist atrocities, and on reports by relief workers who take aid inside Iraq. The people of southern Iraq are overwhelmingly Shi'i Muslims and include, as well as the Marsh Arabs, the townsfolk of Diyala, Kut, Hilla, Diwaniya, Samawa, Nasiriyya, 'Amara, the port of Basra and the holy cities of Najaf and Karbala'. Two-thirds of all Iraqis are Shi'is and in Baghdad alone there are three million, living in suburbs such as Kadhimiyya, al-Thawra, al-Sha'la and al-Hurriya.

Although Iraq is a mosaic of ethnic, religious and cultural groups, most have historically been excluded from power, which was concentrated in the hands of a minority Sunni Arab elite. This political discrimination against the Shi'i Arab majority, the Kurds and minorities such as Turcomans and Christians, became systematic repression after the Ba'th regime came to power in July 1968, and worsened dramatically after Saddam Husain took the presidency in July 1979. Tens of thousands of Iraqi citizens were executed or disappeared, many of them the professionals and graduates who were the hope of the nation. Documented, undeniable genocide took place with the Anfal campaign of 1988, in which up to 200,000 Kurdish villagers were exterminated; and during the suppression of the March 1991 *intifada*, when, it was claimed by one government official, 300,000 Shi'is were slaughtered in a month.

## Najaf and Karbala'

The carnage following the *intifada* was the culmination of a twenty-year Ba'thist campaign against the Shi'i community, its religious and political leaders, and its spiritual centres, Najaf and Karbala'. These two holy cities are as meaningful to Shi'i Muslims as Rome is to Catholics. They were, into modern times, places of pilgrimage for Shi'is from as far as India, Afghanistan and Turkey. They have a tradition of independence from Baghdad and of promoting the tolerant values of Islam which have stirred the wrath of Saddam. For example, *fatwas* (binding religious decrees) were issued by leading Shi'i scholars forbidding the killing of Kurds and denouncing aggression against Kuwait.

By 1991 the clergy of Najaf had been reduced through executions, imprisonment and exile from ten thousand to a few hundred. After the *intifada* the shrine of Imam 'Ali was attacked, its sacred precinct was occupied by army tanks, and its treasures and libraries were looted. The great cemetery outside Najaf was deliberately desecrated and partially concreted over. Karbala' suffered even worse physical damage. The old souk between the shrines of 'Abbas and Imam Husain, and all the homes around it, were levelled. The famous palm groves were destroyed. Over seventy mosques, religious schools, libraries and prayer halls were demolished.

The devastating assault on Iraqi Shi'ism in the interests of Saddam Husain's political control is of world historical significance. Iraqi Shi'is are heir to the many rich cultures which have thrived in Iraq before and since the coming of Islam. In philosophy, metaphysics, art, poetry and social customs Najaf and Karbala' represent a living continuity with ancient times. More significant than the cultural achievements of Shi'is, however, is the fact that modern 'civilized' nations can stand by from only a few miles away and passively watch the butchery of hundreds of thousands of people.

## Marsh Arabs

The ruthlessness of Saddam Husain's Ba'thist regime against Shi'i Arabs is vividly illustrated by the coodinated operations against the Marsh Arabs and their marsh homeland. The water-based rural economy and culture pursued by the Marsh Arabs – which dates back at least five thousand years – has been savaged and faces extinction. In 1988, at the end of the Iran-Iraq war, there were about half a million Marsh Arabs. By early 1994 almost all had been forced from their homes as Saddam Husain asserts his control of the area with massive drainage programmes and relentless military attacks.

The marsh waters have been poisoned; mines have been planted in reed beds and in villages; artillery bombardments and army advances are the norm. The Marsh Arabs have become nomads in search of water. Some seek anonymity in the towns, although this is extremely dangerous given the detailed documentation required of all Iraqi citizens. Many have been forcibly resettled on artificial waterways or on the dykes built to separate one marsh region from another. Here their movements are closely supervised by the Iraqi army – just as Kurds in the north were controlled in 'model villages' constructed close to main roads.

Productive farmlands to the east of the Tigris (south-east of the 'Amara) have been flooded by 3 metres of water diverted from the marshlands, leaving thousands of families stranded on elevated roads surrounded by fast-flowing water. Some parts of the roads and the reed homes built on them have been carried away by the floods. Each family, including children and livestock, has an area of only about 4 metres by 10 metres in which to live. Some are from the flooded farmlands. Others have escaped from the dried-out marshes.

It will never be known how many people have died from malnutrition or disease resulting from destruction of their homeland. Or how many have been executed after arbitrary arrest or killed in military operations.

Since June 1993 well over ten thousand Marsh Arabs have succeeded in fleeing to the Iranian side of the Howeiza Marsh to live as refugees in a desolate roadside settlement at Himmet. They describe how Allied planes imposing the no-fly zone merely observe – many use the term 'supervise' – blatant genocidal attacks on people and their homes, rather than enforcing the withdrawal of Saddam's army and destruction of the dams which have gradually dried the marshes out. Their only hope is that these dams will be destroyed – if not by outside military intervention then by Marsh Arabs themselves, whenever the army and security forces are withdrawn. Past experience indicates that if the water is allowed to flow again the natural habitat can regenerate itself.

Now, in March 1994, a new influx of refugees is expected in Iran from the regions that border the marshlands, particularly from Msharra, Kahla and villages nearby. These are farming communities which have been destroyed by flood waters. Recent video films show that only a few centimetres remain between the flood waters and the surfaces of roads being used as refuges by displaced farmers. Very soon these people will have to flee for their lives.

## Surviving in the cities

One effect of the regime's repression is that many people have little reliable knowledge except about their own experiences. Nevertheless, it is possible to piece together a clear picture of the suppression and survival of Iraqi Shi'is in the cities since the latest war. People from the southernmost towns of 'Amara, Basra and Nasiriyya, and the surrounding areas, have escaped through the marshlands. Those from towns such as Hilla, Diwaniya, Kut and Baghdad do not have access to these routes and far fewer of them have been able to escape to freedom. Despite the limited contact all these people have had with each other, their accounts are remarkably consistent.

The towns and cities of southern Iraq (i.e., of Shi'i Arabs) were largely neglected in the oil boom of the 1970s. They were left without many basic services such as regular garbage collection and essential infrastructural developments, while costly projects were implemented in Baghdad and favoured regions to the north. Huge sums were spent on strengthening the military might that was used as much against the citizenry as in naked aggression against Iraq's neighbours. Much of the damage inflicted by the allies during the Gulf War and by the Iraqi army during the suppression of the *intifada* has not been adequately repaired. Imposition of a 'no-fly zone' exacerbated the situation because the regime's forces rapidly asset-stripped equipment and supplies from factories, farms and hospitals, and removed them to Baghdad and Tikrit.

Despite United Nations regulations that allow the importation of food and medicine, Saddam Husain continues to starve the Iraqi people and deprive them of essential medical services. Monthly food rations bought from government officials last at most two-and-a-half weeks. They must be supplemented by food bought on the open market at exorbitant prices, far beyond the means of most people. A typical family of six with a monthly income of 400 dinars (a civil servant's salary) will pay about 120 dinars for their rations and then must pay 5 dinars for one egg, 25 dinars for a kilogram of rice, 30 dinars for a kilogram of tomatoes (once plentiful in southern Iraq), 180 dinars for a kilogram of meat, and 12 dinars for a kilogram of 'black' flour. This flour is 'filled out' with sawdust, ground date pips and powdered corn cobs, making it difficult for adults to digest, let alone children. Ba'thist officials offer 'white United Nations flour' in return for cooperation with the regime.

As well as hindering the importation of food by refusing to comply with UN resolutions, Saddam Husain is destroying vital Iraqi farmlands. These include areas to the west of the Tigris – such as al-Majar, al-Salaam, al-'Adl and al-Maimoona – which have been rendered useless by the marshes drainage project, and areas to the east of the Tigris – such as Msharra, Shatt al-Amma, al-'Atwaniya, and al-A'aiwaj – which have been deliberately flooded with fast-flowing water. Water, such a precious resource in the Middle East, is being used as a double-edged weapon against the population, to decrease agricultural output either by draining or by flooding, and then being sent away down the Shatt al-'Arab.

Shortages of medicines and severely limited medical care have led to a drastic rise in child mortality and in deaths from treatable heart, diabetic and blood-pressure conditions. It is an open secret that warehouses are filled with medicines and medical equipment but government policy forbids the issuing of these. Hefty bribes, however, to the appropriate persons, provide any medicines requested. The rising incidence of viral liver infections disturbs doctors because the regime refuses to make available appropriate medication. Only the most urgent surgery is performed, due to lack of anaesthetics. A Baghdad paediatrician reports giving sick children only one spoonful of their required medicine and then sending them home. Although Iraq had several factories producing excellent syringes until the Gulf War, now veterinary syringes are being used in some hospitals. The government could, if it wished, make food and medicines readily available. Instead, with cruel irony, it uses the suffering of Iraqi citizens as a propaganda weapon.

Education has also deteriorated. Standards began a steady decline in the 1970s which continued throughout the Iran-Iraq war. Now hunger, poor clothing, lack of books and stationery make both teaching and learning difficult. Girls and boys are forced to leave school early. Young women at institutes of higher learning are pressurized by the regime's students' union or Ba'thist agents to renounce the traditional conservative values of the society. Immorality, and the resulting family breakdown, is made to seem 'modern'.

Transportation costs are soaring. Rent for the simplest accommodation in Baghdad is at least 1000 dinars monthly. Clothing is of extremely poor quality and sold at exorbitant prices. Iraqis used to be noted for personal integrity and honesty in business dealings, but now illegal practices, as well as bribes, 'commissions', etc., are the norm. Increasing numbers of women sell their 'personal services'. Parents offer a child for sale, in order to buy enough food to keep the other children alive.

Travel is restricted and dangerous. Between the northern city of Mosul and the capital Baghdad there are four checkpoints manned by combined units of military police, military intelligence and the security forces. The treatment motorists receive at these checkpoints changes on the approach to Baghdad and is worse still south of Baghdad, travelling for example to Hilla or Karbala'. Further south, in the no-fly zone, they are liable to be detained and abused until their families pay a bribe to secure their release.

## Security forces

Extensive networks of internal spies are deeply entrenched in Iraqi society. Most agents become involved as a result of coercion or blackmail. Their activities range from writing reports on neighbours and colleagues, to signing detention orders, to actually participating in interrogations. More 'committed' agents receive frequent gifts and quota payments for the number of persons detained and who sign 'confessions'. So many individual citizens have been wronged, tortured, disappeared or killed that no security agent feels safe. Assassination of agents and security officials is not very common, but such people usually let their wives or children open the front door, have strong lighting outside their homes and are provided with bodyguards.

It is common knowledge that the security forces are deeply involved in theft and burglary. In a country with so much hunger, theft is on the increase and petty thieves are liable to execution. However, most burglaries (an informed estimate is 80 per cent) are committed by gangs composed of or led by security officials in order to support their lavish lifestyles. Typically five or six men arrive at a house wearing the dark green uniform of the security police and announce they are there to 'search the premises'. No warrant is shown. While the residents are held at gunpoint, the 'search' continues until no valuables, appliances, etc., are left in the house. Witnesses to such burglaries note that gang members refer tol their leader as *sayyidi*, a term of deference used to acknowledge rank among senior Ba'thists and when addressing officers of the security forces. While some such burglaries do not seem to be organized by the regime, they are certainly not discouraged.

In every town and city there are official and unofficial detention centres, often ordinary-looking houses. Torture is routine. People are taken from the streets, even if their papers are in order. After interrogation they may be released, still bearing the signs of torture, or they may be detained for years. Either way, the effect is to terrorize the population. An inordinate number of young women are arrested. By the end of 1993 there were reports of tens of thousands of arrests in Baghdad and the southern cities.

It is impossible to estimate accurately how many persons die under torture or are executed. In most cases bodies are never returned, nor death certificates issued. But mass executions may be publicized, as when forty-three merchants were executed in July 1993. Sometimes the sheer numbers shake the entire population, as in August 1993 when at least six hundred bodies were returned, all to Shi'i families, identifiable only by the name-tags on their wrists.

Victims of terror and repression have no legal protection. Former inmates of the Rudhwaniya concentration camp have independently reported that victims who begged for mercy were told by their torturers that their innocence was not in doubt but they had to be made examples to others. A magistrate who was brought to the camp to review the cases and refused to forward any of them, on the grounds that there was no evidence to support the forced confessions, was taken away to an unknown fate, and a different magistrate was brought in who continued, personally, the torture of those who had 'confessed'.

Despite the ubiquitous repression and terrorization, the regime clearly fears another *intifada*. Workers made redundant from military-industrial establishments have been re-employed. Ministries have been instructed to disperse files previously kept in central locations, to stockpile petrol and heating fuel, to upgrade the security of government buildings and to train staff in civil defence procedures. Ba'th Party members are being trained in street fighting.

## Democracy in post-Saddam Iraq

The Shi'i tradition itself has a powerful reciprocal relationship between the general population and religious leaders. A *mujtahid* (interpreter of religious law) rises in competence and gains a reputation among his peers, but ultimately his influence depends on the number of people who follow his interpretation and support him. As more people recognize his competence so his reputation grows. The religious laws do not allow people to follow the decrees of a dead scholar, and the succession to a scholar's role is not assignable but is based on popular recognition and acknowledgement. Therefore religious leadership is an ongoing, fluid process always related to current popular endorsement. An important result of the continuing interaction between religious leaders and the Shi'i masses who affirm or refute their competence is an inherent affinity for popular rule.

While educated Iraqis discuss democracy among themselves, the great majority of southern Iraqis use the term *hurriyya*, or freedom. For them the word *dimokritiyya* is associated with the Western powers which have cruelly mocked and oppressed the Iraqi people by supporting and strengthening the Ba'thist regime. 'They want democracy for themselves,' is a commonly stated view, 'but we don't count as human beings to them. They don't want democracy for others. They just want our oil. Our blood, our suffering mean nothing to them. Just oil.'

If these people, many of them newly escaped from Iraq or living in camps, are asked what they want, they will immediately reply 'freedom'. They have sacrificed families, jobs, homes and all possessions, and now survive as refugees awaiting the next distribution of food and clothing. But if challenged that they were fools to leave behind so much for so little, their response is consistently the same. 'I want my home, I want my family, I want my country. I want to go back to Iraq, but not while Saddam is there, not with the Ba'thists. Here I don't have much, but I'm not afraid. I can say what I want. I can sleep at night. There is freedom.'

What is acceptable to the majority of Iraqis may be disputed by different political groupings because currently there is no democratically elected representation. However, the slogans raised by the Shi'i masses who rebelled in March 1991 – in a spontaneous, unsynchronized movement that freed twelve of Iraq's 18 povinces – clearly indicate that they wanted freedom from totalitarianism and a government that would establish the Islamic ideals of justice, equality and fraternity.

Any government in Iraq that does not properly represent proportionally the Shi'i Muslims and Kurds cannot claim to be democratic or legitimate. It would lack the acceptance and support of the majority of the Iraqi people. To remain in power it would have to force the majority to submit to it, thereby becoming another repressive dictatorship

Countless Iraqi men and women have sacrificed their lives in the struggle against tyranny. These sacrifices must be honoured. It is a grave injustice to deny the Iraqi people the freedom for which so many have fought and died, and the right to self-determination.

# CHAPTER TEN

# Destruction of the Southern Marshes

## *Hamid al-Bayati*

The Mesopotamian marshes are the site of a human and ecological war of horrific proportions. To get rid of the Marsh Arabs who have lived in the area for over five thousand years, along with the refugees and freedom fighters, Saddam Husain is destroying their homeland by draining and poisoning the water and bombing the area.

The draining of the marshes of southern Iraq, now being carried out by the Iraqi regime, is not a new plan. These works owe their origin to plans made by British engineers after the Second World War, when the civil service was run largely by the British. Parts of the 'Third River' canal, which runs from south of Baghdad to Basra were begun under British supervision in 1953. More was completed in the 1970s under the supervision of the British consultancy Mott MacDonald , who constructed about twenty kilometres of the canal at Dalmaj. 'At the time the purpose of the Third River', stressed Bill Pemberton, of Mott MacDonald, 'was to drain saline waters from the waterlogged farmland north and west of the marshes – not to drain the marshes themselves.'

The strategic thinking, however, behind the draining of the marshes goes back to 1951 and the publication of the Haigh Report, written by a senior engineer formerly with the British Indian administration, Frank Haigh. Haigh, like most of the engineers at the time, argued that water allowed to dissipate in the marshes was wasted. He wanted to capture the marshlands water for irrigation, and proposed concentrating the flow of the Tigris into a few embanked channels that would not overflow into the marshes. He proposed one large canal through the main 'Amara marsh.

The strategy of Saddam Husain has a striking resemblance to this plan. However, instead of being implemented to reclaim land for much needed food production and to increase the volume of water available for irrigation, the massive engineering schemes, which affect an area roughly the size of Wales, are viewed by many observers as a way of draining large areas of the southern marshes to deprive opponents of the Iraqi regime of cover and bring the populace to heel.

## The Marsh Arabs

The marshes – home to an estimated half-million people – occupy an extensive area around the confluence of the Tigris and Euphrates rivers, broadly delineated by a triangle with its points at the towns of 'Amara in the north, Nasiriyya in the south-west and Basra in the south, with an eastern edge that coincides roughly with the Iran-Iraq border. The marshlands of Iraq are among the largest in the world, described by the World Conservation Monitoring Centre as a site of primary ecological interest. It is a most important area for threatened birds, including pygmy cormorants, marbled teal, imperial eagles and grey hypocolius. It also includes an abundance of freshwater fish, wild boar, otters and terrapins. The Hawr al-Hammar Lake, the Nasiriyya marshes and the Shatra marshes have all been internationally recommended for special protection as sites of particular importance for bird life and vegetation.

The overwhelming majority of the population of southern Iraq are Shi'i Arabs, including the Marsh Arabs. The number of Iraqi Shi'i is estimated at approximately 10.5 million. They are found mostly in the south of the country, but there is also a large Shi'i community in Baghdad. Although the Shi'i comprise 55-65 per cent of the total population, they have been systematically discriminated against by the Sunni-dominated government of the country and are continuing to experience many of the problems commonly encountered by minorities.

When the Iran-Iraq war started in 1980, the support of the Marsh Arabs was important to the Iraqi government, as much of the fighting took place in and around the marshes. With their knowledge of the waterways, the Marsh Arabs could easily have acted as spies and fifth columnists for the Shi'i Iranians. Saddam Husain cleverly emphasized the bond of shared nationhood and played down sectarian differences. At this time, people thought of themselves first and foremost as Iraqis, and no longer considered their religious identities to be of primary importance. But official attitudes began to change after the suppression of the popular uprising in March 1991 in the wake of the Gulf War.

## The *intifada*

During the Gulf War, US planes showered leaflets over Iraq urging the population to topple the Iraqi dictator with slogans such as 'Act Against Saddam Now'. The Americans also broadcast radio messages to civilians in southern Iraq urging them to overthrow the tyrant. But, when the uprising started, the Allies' response was incomprehensible. They watched from secure positions on the edge of important towns in southern Iraq while Saddam's forces brutally crushed the *intifada*. Iraqi opposition groups documented many reliable eyewitness accounts of how the Allies helped Saddam's forces to crush the uprising, for instance by allowing the heavily armed Republican Guards to pass through their checkpoints, or failing to prevent Saddam's helicopter gunships from massacring Iraqi civilians who were taking part in the uprising.

After the revolt had been crushed, groups of popular forces and large numbers of civilians took refuge in the marshes. Saddam ordered an assault on the area and Iraqi military units effectively encircled it, enforcing a total economic blockade and cutting off escape routes to Iran. An official Iraqi government document which was in the possession of an engineer captured by resistance forces provided extensive details of the siege. It contained instructions to 'withdraw all foodstuffs, ban the sale of fish and prohibit transport to and from the areas'. Mass arrests, assassinations, poisoning the water and burning villages were also ordered by the Iraqi regime.

## Canal-building: drainage projects

The devastation of the area was also carried out through the prompt revival of the 'Third River' project. Saddam and his engineers modified Haigh's plans to suit their own political purposes. After languishing half-finished for many years, the canal was completed in the record time of one year. Five hundred and fifty kilometres long and ninety miles wide at its seaward end, it joins the Shatt al-Basra Canal, and eventually flows into the Persian Gulf.

The 'Fourth River', another major component of the drainage project was also completed at the same time. This river drastically reduces the water flowing into al-Hammar Marsh. It takes water from the Euphrates upstream of al-Nasiriyya, reducing pressure on the new dam and then empties into the Khawr al-Zubair. Drawings captured from a government water engineer in October 1992 show that since the Gulf crisis a new canal has been built running east-southeast from a point near al Salam to meet the water entering the marshes from the north and draining into the Euphrates.

The Islamic resistance group SCIRI, active in southern Iraq, reported that forty streams, which previously flowed into al-'Amara marshes, had been diverted. Independent observers confirmed that this diversion of the waters from the marshes to the al-'Amara canal had helped speed up the drainage process. Analyses of satellite images confirm SCIRI's reports. The pictures, taken at night when water is warmer than land, strongly suggest that the area is drying out.

In an interview with *Geographical*, Shaikh Human Hammudi, political consultant to the head of SCIRI, Ayatullah Sayyid Muhammad Baqir al-Hakim, alleges that two-thirds of the marshlands area is now dry. He also said that large swathes of formerly viable farmland in southern Iraq have been rendered useless because government construction engineers have used the topsoil for building dykes.

Baghdad has denied that anything untoward is happening in the marshes, but visitors to the region, including the United Nations special reporter on human rights, Max van der Stoel, claimed that in 1993 the regime's engineering works prevented water reaching up to two-thirds of the marshes. SCIRI's claims have also been substantiated by Middle East Watch, the human rights monitoring group based in Washington DC, which predicted that by the summer of 1993 the damage was likely to be irreversible, with disastrous ecological, social and human consequences for the region.

For Baghdad the drainage schemes are a top priority but progress has been severely slowed by several factors: sabotage by resistance fighters who succeeded in damaging the earthworks; unusually heavy rains in the winter of 1992-93; and Kurdish resistance in northern Iraq, which successfully released large amounts of water from behind the Dukhan dam on the Tigris to slow down Saddam's destruction of the marshlands.

## Human rights abuses

International organizations such as Amnesty International and Middle East Watch have drawn attention to widespread human rights abuses in southern Iraq. They have documented the placing of a tight army cordon around the marshes, the control of main access roads, and the imposition of a tight economic blockade. Food and medicines are not allowed into the area, and the inhabitants are not allowed to collect the basic food rations to which all Iraqis have been entitled since the imposition of sanctions in August 1990.

Amnesty International confirms that rat poison has been used by the Iraqi army to pollute the water in the marshlands. Napalm has been dropped on civilian homes, and human rights workers from international organizations report that while air attacks have ceased, ground assaults on the marshes have escalated dramatically since the imposition of the no-fly zone which forbids the Iraqi government from flying fixed-wing aircraft and helicopters south of the 32nd parallel. The ground attacks have been accompanied by widespread arbitrary arrests and the torture or execution of detainees. Amnesty International received details of repeated artillery and mortar attacks on scores of villages and towns in the vicinity of 'Amara, al-Nasiriyya and Basra which started the day after the implementation of the no-fly zone.

During the following two months several thousand Shi'is were arrested. Whole families were transferred to unknown destinations and it is believed that many detainees were executed extrajudicially while in custody. Others may have died under torture. The attacks continued unabated throughout the winter of 1992-93, when people began to flee with their few worldly goods towards the Iran-Iraq border. As many as 100,000 may still be trapped in the marshes. Those unable to flee often hide deep in the marshes and are surviving in primitive rush shelters. They have been forced to eat grass to stay alive. Many women and children whose menfolk were killed travelled through the night covering themselves with mud and hiding in fetid pools during the day. Several different routes took them to Hemmet, a raised section of dried land in the Huwaiza Marsh on the Iranian border. By August 1993, the number of refugees had reached 55,000.

## Refugees

I visited the refugee camp at Hemmet in August 1993 accompanied by Emma Nicholson MP, BBC reporter George Alagiah and *Times* reporter Tom Rhodes. Rhodes wrote a detailed article about 5,000 refugees from the marshlands living on the asphalt road which runs from the marshes to the border. He described their wretched existence in shanties made from reeds which provide little or no protection from extreme temperatures of up to 55 degrees centigrade.

For its part, the Iranian government provides food and fresh water and has set up an emergency clinic. Many of the refugees are suffering from bloody diarrhoea or amoebic dysentry and cholera. Emergency medical supplies are also being provided by the AMAR appeal chaired by Emma Nicholson, who launched the AMAR appeal in the aftermath of the Gulf War to provide relief for Iraqi refugees in south-west Iran. The Iranian government may demand that the international community takes action against the Iraqi regime if refugee numbers continue to swell, as the burden of taking care of these wretched human beings is borne almost entirely by Tehran.

In their discussions with reporters the refugees said they fled from their homes in the marshlands as the area had been dried out and they could not survive without food and fresh water and under continuous heavy mortar and artillery bombardment. After their villages had been razed to the ground many refugees had to swim for part of their escape journey. There are no accurate estimates of the numbers who perished along the way, succumbing to their injuries or to hunger and thirst in temperatures averaging 45 degrees centigrade.

Constant campaigning by the head of SCIRI has prompted the UN Secretary General to announce that he will send an envoy to the southern marshlands to monitor the situation. The UN may in fact be able to enforce human rights monitoring in southern Iraq in accordance with Security Council Resolution 688. This resolution calls on the Iraqi government to provide free access to United Nations and non-governmental humanitarian agencies to all parts of the marshes so that essential humanitarian assistance can be provided.

## Oil

Oil reserves in and around the marshes in areas such as Majnun, Nahr al-'Umar and Halfaya are also affecting the Iraqi government's policies. It is estimated that the level of oil production could be raised from 3.2 million to 5.6 million barrels a day, if these resources were fully exploited. This could also account for the regime's desire to drain the marshes. Despite the economic embargo two French oil companies, Elf Aquitane and Total, are close to concluding an agreement with the Iraqi government to begin exploitation of the resources as soon as the sanctions are lifted. For them it is business as usual. Iraqi opposition groups see the regime's efforts to lure the oil companies as an attempt to prompt France to put pressure on the UN to lift the sanctions.

## Conclusion

As the Minority Rights Group concludes, the Marsh Arabs are among Iraq's most vulnerable citizens, deprived of control over their future and living in a society which is exhausted by war and divided against itself by an oppressive regime. Immediate action is needed to ensure that their unique way of life is protected from continuous, gross human rights violations. A comprehensive, independent assessment of the effects of Saddam's drainage schemes needs to be made before the Marsh Arabs are annihilated and a unique way of life, which has survived since Babylonian times, is eradicated forever by the insane acts of an evil dictator.

## References

*Geographical*, July 1993.

Minority Rights Group, *The Marsh Arabs*, February 1993.

Amnesty International, *Iraq – Summary of Concerns*, September 1992.

Amnesty International, *Iraq – Written Statement to the 49th Session of the United Nations Commission on Human Rights*.

Middle East Watch, *Current Human Rights Conditions Among the Iraqi Shi'i – Summary of Findings of a Middle East Watch Commission, 28 January-14 February 1993*.

Barbara Stapleton, *The Shi'is of Iraq – An historical perspective of the present human rights situation*, Interparliamentary Human Rights Group, March 1993.

Statement of Max van der Stoel to the UN Human Rights Commission, 22 March 1993.

Shyam Bhatia, 'Murder in the Marshes', *The Observer*, 28 February 1993.

Oliver Tickell, 'Genocide by Ecocide', *BBC Wildlife*, May 1993.

Tom Rhodes, 'Saddam Hounds Shi'is to Deadly Refuge', *The Times*, 2 August 1993.

# CHAPTER ELEVEN

# Human Rights, Sanctions and Sovereignty

*Laith Kubba*

When Iraq invaded Kuwait on 2 August 1990 the United Nations responded to this attack on one of its members by adopting a series of Security Council Resolutions (SCRs) against the aggressor nation. SCR 661 imposed a total trade embargo on Iraq. Food and medicine were then excluded by SCR 666. SCR 706 allowed Iraq to sell limited amounts of oil to pay for food and medicine under strict UN guidelines laid down in SCR 712. SCR 715 stipulated inspection procedures for Iraq's military programme.

SCR 688, adopted on 6 April 1991, called on the government of Iraq to desist from committing human rights violations against Iraqi citizens. It made a significant distinction between the government and the civilian population but it is not mandatory. Neither were human rights an item in the lengthy and at times very tense UN-Iraq negotiations that have taken place since the Gulf War.

In November 1993 Iraq finally agreed to comply with SCR 715 on military inspection procedures, thereby fulfilling an important condition for the lifting of sanctions. But Saddam Husain – Iraq's sole decision-maker on matters of national interest – has categorically refused to comply with SRCs 706 and 712. These resolutions, he argues, by restricting the sale of Iraqi oil and putting the revenue under UN supervision, violate his country's sovereignty.

His concern, however, is not with the principle of sovereignty but with keeping his power over the Iraqi people. He has already traded much of Iraq's sovereignty for the survival of his regime. He gave away sovereignty over the Shatt al-'Arab waterway to Iran. He agreed to Turkish military operations on Iraqi territory. He accepted the safe haven in the north and the no-fly zone in the south. Where he stands firm is against the raising of reveue through oil sales in order that food, medicine and other non-military necessities be bought for the long-suffering people of Iraq. It remains to be seen whether the UN will resist his power to threaten the Iraqi people with starvation, a power given to him by its imposition of sanctions.

The technical and legal jargon of the UN is open to interpretation by the permanent members of the Security Council and others in the political and moral debate on sanctions, sovereignty and human rights. The result is controversy and inconsistensy within the UN both in defence of sovereignty and in the application of resolutions. The inviolability of national sovereignty is used to justify international indifference towards the suffering of Iraqis at the hands of the Saddam Husain regime. But at the same time that regime uses the principle of sovereignty to justify its rejection of SCRs 688 and 712 (human rights and UN supervision of oil revenue) – the two resolutions directly relevent to the well-being of the Iraqi population.

The Western allies have expressed their commitment to Iraq's sovereignty and territorial integrity but their policy of maintaining sanctions whilst ignoring the regime's gross abuse of human rights is having the opposite effect. Iraq as a nation is withering away, crushed by the combined burden of Saddam Husain's dictatorship and UN sanctions. Saddam Husain, by rejecting UN supervision of the revenue, is able to deny Iraqis access to their oil at the moment at which they desperately need it. In a cynical ploy, he then uses their economic plight to appeal to the world's conscience for the lifting of sanctions.

The international policy-makers who imposed the sanctions should not underestimate the devastating effects upon millions of Iraqis caught in the crossfire between the UN and Saddam Husain. Their victimization has been of little concern to member states of the Security Council and the UN as a whole, and matters even less to the Iraqi regime. The Iraqi dinar is now (March 1994) worth one-eightieth of its pre-Gulf War value, and continues to devalue. Most Iraqis can barely afford to buy food on the open market and have become dependent on the rations sold by the regime at subsidized prices. Thousands of babies, children and vulnerable adults die every month due to shortages of basic medicines. Crime, corruption, prostitution and other social ills are increasing at an alarming rate.

Ironically, both the Iraqi regime and the US administration use this suffering in their rhetoric to justify policies which serve their own ends but do not seriously address the needs of the Iraqi people. Iraq, in the name of national sovereignty and the suffering of innocents, calls for the lifting of sanctions and condemns the UN as a pawn in the hands of the US. For its part, the US has, belatedly, made human rights improvements in Iraq a condition for the lifting of sanctions. The politics of sanctions, however, have little to do with suffering and human rights and much to do with power. Saddam Husain needs the sanctions to be lifted so that he can again use Iraq's oil wealth to finance the police state that protects his personal dictatorship. The US and its allies need the sanctions to remain as a restraint on a ruthless aggressor with territorial ambitions which threaten their own oil supplies.

It was not the intention of the UN in August 1990 to impose indefinite and unconditional sanctions on Iraq which might cause it to collapse into chaos, becoming another Afghanistan, Somalia or Bosnia. But if the current economic and social disintegration continues, internal forces will be unleashed in bloody conflicts and a total breakdown of law and order which no internal or external force will be able to control. Such a scenario is highly undesirable both for neighbouring countries and for the West, which needs stability at the heart of the Middle East and north of the Gulf oil fields. If this scenario is allowed to develop, historians and analysts will be left to apportion responsibility for the outcome well into the future.

It is clear to all concerned about the future of Iraq that the suffering of a the Iraqi people, the political implications of the current economic deterioration and Saddam Husain's partial but incomplete compliance with SCRs are all reasons why the sanctions policy needs to be reviewed and its objectives questioned. It has to be asked whether or not the sanctions are working; whether or not they should be lifted or modified and, if so, under what conditions. So far, the views of dissident Iraqis on these matters have been effectively excluded from the technical, political and moral debate.

Turkey, France and Russia strongly favour the lifting of sanctions, driven by their trade interests. The US and the UK strongly oppose the lifting of sanctions while Saddam Husain remains in power, and they can be expected to deploy delaying tactics at the UN Security Council. China and India are for political reasons resisting US and UK attempts to delay the lifting of sanctions. For Kuwait and Sa'udi Arabia the lifting of sanctions is a nightmare prospect because it would revive Saddam Husain as a regional power, despite UN monitoring of his military programme.

Many Iraqi groups which staunchly oppose Saddam Husain are now questioning the validity of sanctions. An assessment of the costs and benefits of the options available provides no simple answer. Maintaining sanctions is a desirable option for regional and Western governments, which see them as a cost-effective measure to keep Saddam Husain in check. The costs of that option, however, are Iraq's future as a country and the ongoing suffering of its population: these make it unacceptable to many Iraqis. Lifting sanctions, on the other hand, will strengthen Saddam Husain's power and lead to further regional instability.

Iraqis know that the sanctions regime was not intended to overthrow Saddam Husain or protect human rights in Iraq. For more than three years the UN made the disposal of Iraq's arsenal the main condition for lifting sanctions, while human rights abuses were ignored. The US bombed Baghdad, killing innocent civilians, so as to cut Saddam Husain down to size militarily. More than 60 UN weapons inspection teams were sent to Iraq to secure compliance with SCR 715. But neither the UN nor the US showed similar resolve or even concern over the human rights and humanitarian needs of the Iraqi people. Hence the last-minute pitch by the Security Council to maintain sanctions because of Iraq's defiance of SCR 688 (on human rights) adds insult to injury for millions of innocent Iraqis.

Maintaining sanctions on Iraq as a whole without devising measures to bring down the Saddam Husain regime does not make sense politically to the people of Iraq and their relatives and friends abroad. They view the use of the regime's human rights record to justify maintaining sanctions – with all their inhumane consequences – as hypocritical. The continuous talk about SCR 688 with no accompanying action to curtail Saddam Husain's abuses is, to their mind, of no benefit.

Iraqis, Iraq's neighbouring countries and Western governments all agree that Saddam Husain is the main threat to stability in the region and must not be given the chance to regain his dominance. They disagree, however, as to the means and costs of containing him. The current situation in which a weak Saddam Husain remains in power while the Iraqi people bear the brunt of sanctions may be acceptable to some countries but it is unacceptable to the majority of Iraqis.

Iraqis have long called for the immediate removal of Saddam Husain as the first and most important step for rebuilding Iraq and ensuring stability in the region. But many Western governments fear an Iraq without a strong central government. That was why the March 1991 *intifada* and many attempted coups were not given critical support by the Allies and failed accordingly.

However, the successful state of affairs in northern Iraq – where three provinces are administered by Iraqi Kurds in a free zone – provides a glimmer of hope for a country in deep despair. It is an idicator of the potential future development of Iraq. The three provinces (Dohuk, Arbil and Sulaimaniyya) suffer from double sanctions – i.e. those imposed by the UN on Iraq and an internal blockade imposed by Saddam Husain. Nevertheless economic conditions there are far better than in the rest of Iraq. In March 1994 the Iraqi dinar was trading against other currencies at four times its value in Baghdad. The local free market has ensured the availability of food at affordable prices. The Kurdish administration has managed to provide basic medical services and calls for the lifting of UN sanctions over its region so that development programmes can be implemented.

The Iraqi people have endured war, UN sanctions, violations of their national sovereignty and the bloody aftermath of a crushed revolt against Saddam Husain, always with the hope that these traumatic events would lead to his downfall. Unlike the situation in other war-torn zones, the conditions in Iraq are largely the consequence of a UN-backed war and UN-imposed sanctions. The US and its allies cannot escape the disastrous moral and legal effects of their inconsistent policy of supporting Saddam Husain in the 1980s and then leaving him to rule the land they ruined in the 1990s. Their anti-Saddam rhetoric is not taken seriously by Iraqis, who see Iraq breaking up under continued dictatorship and international sanctions. The credibility of the Iraqi opposition, such as the Iraqi National Congress (INC), is undermined by close affiliation with current Western policies on Iraq.

Protection of human rights in Iraq is very low on the agenda of international policy-makers. In the 1980s the regime's appalling human rights record had a negligible influence on Iraq-West relations. Similarly the current suffering of Iraqis cannot be expected to detract from the merits of maintaining sanctions as an effective instrument for restraining Saddam Husain from further regional misadventures. However, such unrelieved suffering in Iraq can be expected to bring serious instability to the region in the long term.

Even though the UN Security Council does not consider the views and interests of the Iraqi people as distinct from those presented by the regime, it is important that Iraqis publicize their attitudes to sanctions. Members of the Iraqi opposition may shy away from criticizing sanctions because they rely heavily on Western support, or because they do not wish to see Saddam Husain benefit from the stands they take. However, Iraqis should not be intimidated into remaining silent or endorsing policies which do not serve their country.

Iraqis must promote a policy of isolating Saddam Husain, holding him accountable for his crimes and accelerating his downfall. Lifting sanctions will not accelerate his downfall, but neither will passively maintaining sanctions, which are doing Iraq more harm than good. Sanctions may be tolerated as a temporary measure for ridding Iraq of Saddam Husain if they are linked to other measures with the same aim, such as

- imposing UN human rights monitors throughout Iraq;
- exempting the liberated zone in the north and the no-fly zone in the south from UN sanctions;
- indicting Saddam Husain for war crimes and crimes against humanity; and
- providing support to Iraqis in their attempt to overthrow the dictatorship.

Iraqis have little to gain from an unconditional lifting of sanctions, which would leave Saddam Husain in total control of the oil revenue and distribution of food. His rehabilitation is very bad news for them, and would be strongly resisted. However, lifting sanctions would improve the Iraqi economy, and the dinar would cease to be devalued. The people would benefit from better economic conditions even though they would continue to suffer under the dictatorship.

Iraqis should not call for the lifting of sanctions as their first option but should strongly condemn the current policy of maintaining sanctions. They should call for modification of the sanctions regime as their first preference. But if the UN fails to implement the necessary modifying measures then Iraqis should accept the lifting of sanctions as the lesser of two evils, and condemn the policy which does more harm to Iraq and its people than to Saddam Husain and his regime.

# CHAPTER TWELVE

# The Opposition[1]

*Rend Rahim Francke*

The clandestine Iraqi political opposition, severely repressed and restricted before Saddam Husain's invasion of Kuwait in August 1990,
transformed very rapidly thereafter into a crowded public forum in which
many new factions emerged and individual dissenting voices were raised
for the first time. By late 1991 the clamour of activity had produced at least
seventy different Iraqi opposition groups in exile.

There are an estimated 2 million Iraqis living outside Iraq today,
roughly 11 per cent of a population of 18 million. The exodus of hundreds
of thousands during the 1970s and 1980s – to settle in the Gulf, Europe
and America – was not driven by economic forces. Indeed many made
material sacrifices to leave. Whether it was explicitly acknowledged or
not, they almost all left for political reasons: actual or threatened persecution, gratuitous harassment, intensifying discrimination, fear in the climate
of Ba'thist repression and desire for a modicum of freedom completely
absent in Iraq.

Successive military coups d'état, seizure of power by small groups
often unknown but well organized, and control of the country by un-
accountable cabals have marginalized individual citizens, alienating them
from the process of government and from political activity. Among the
mass of Iraqis, at home and abroad, fear was so firmly part of their lives
that political discontent could not be openly expressed. After 1968 assassinations became routine and political involvement was justifiably seen as
extremely dangerous even by those outside the country. Given the widespread support the Iraqi regime received within the region and from the
West, particularly during the Iran-Iraq war (1980-88), any opposition
seemed futile to most Iraqis, at the very time when persecution was
reaching a very high level.

Political activity was, however, carried out in these years by Kurds,
Islamists and communists. The last two groups had been severely attacked
and many of their members forced into exile by the early 1980s, but they
continued to function in both rural and urban areas. The Kurds, too, were
fiercely attacked but retained their territorial strongholds in the mountains
of northern Iraq. The main havens for opposition Iraqis were Iran, Syria
and the Kurdish areas. Kurds and Communists found refuge in Kurdistan;
Islamist groups in Iran and Arab nationalists and communists in Syria. But
international and Arab support for the Iraqi government during the Iran-

Iraq war made the position of exiles in Iran and Syria increasingly difficult. Of the thousands of Iraqis who had moved to Europe since 1958 many were settled in England, and on the eve of the Gulf War London emerged as a centre of opposition activity.

The end of the Iran-Iraq war saw a resurgence of popular disaffection in Iraq which coincided with rising Arab and international mistrust of the Ba'th regime. For Iraqis, the only tangible results of the war were half a million casualties and a devastated economy with an international debt of one hundred billion dollars. There were no discernible benefits or even a credible military victory. A new restlessness affected hitherto unpoliticized Iraqis and invigorated existing dissenting groups. However, although the ground was being prepared in 1988-89, there was as yet no concerted political activity against the regime and no coalescence of opposition forces. Regional and Western support for the regime was still in effect, even if less enthusiastic. It was sufficient for reports of chemical gas attacks on Kurdish villages to be stifled or ignored. Iraqis critical of the regime still could not obtain a hearing in the Arab world, Europe or the United States.

A dramatic reversal occurred on 2 August 1990. The invasion of Kuwait and the ensuing Gulf War totally transformed the political environment for the frustrated Iraqi opposition in two crucial ways. First, the Gulf War was waged against Iraq by the very countries that had long been its staunchest supporters and largest creditors. The network of international relationships that had supported Saddam Husain for two decades unravelled with breathtaking speed. Iraqi opposition forces ceased to be outcasts going against the grain and became part of mainstream opinion condemning their long-time enemy. Second, there was the upheaval that the Gulf War caused within Iraqi society both inside and outside the country. It was a cataclysmic event for Iraqis, producing in their collective psyche a watershed between 'before' and 'after'. Saddam Husain was seen as having wilfully brought about the ultimate destruction of the country, its army, its people, its economy, and its international standing. Coming on the heels of a dirty eight-year war with Iran from which the nation had hardly begun to recover, the Gulf War's wantonness was incomprehensible and intolerable to ordinary citizens. They condemned the ferocity of Allied bombing attacks on Iraq's troops and infrastructure, but some suspected collusion between Saddam Husain, the West and Israel to destroy the country's military and economic capabilities. There was at any rate a universal conviction that it was Saddam Husain's megalomania that had precipitated this unbearable national debasement.

Iraq's defeat and the international humiliation of the regime resulted in unprecedented breaking of political taboos. Saddam Husain lost his aura of invincibility, fear diminished and popular anger was expressed violently and uncontrollably during the *intifada* of March 1991. Condemnation of the regime became commonplace and a new critical attitude emerged even among its traditional allies within Iraqi society. The process of reevaluation did not stop at the Gulf War, but delved back into the futility and losses of the Iran-Iraq war and the previous twenty-five years of repression and persecution. Public opinion, hitherto unheard of in Iraq, examined corruption and nepotism in government, the disenfranchisement of all but a select few, and the extreme poverty of large sectors of the population in contrast to the vast wealth amassed by Saddam Husain's family and favourites.

Thus the transformation of international opinion from hostility to sympathy, and of Iraqi popular sentiment from fear and apathy to active condemnation, combined to strengthen the Iraqi opposition in exile. New groupings formed and new figures emerged. The proliferation expanded debate and brought forward new, frequently disparate, analyses, ideas and approaches along with new alignments and disagreements.

The popular uprising which raged for two weeks and engulfed three-quarters of Iraq's territory (the insurgents at one point controlling as many as 12 of the 18 Iraqi governorates) was crushed by Republican Guards and helicopter gunships, which had not been prohibited in the Gulf War ceasefire agreement, despite initial encouragement of the insurgents by Washington. Inside Iraq resistance has continued since March 1991, albeit on a limited scale, particularly in the southern marshes. While disaffection with the regime continues, its expression has been cut back by the return of customary state violence and a renewed climate of fear which is heaviest in Baghdad and other cities.

Only Iraqi Kurdistan, thanks to Western allied protection enforced after April 1991, has evaded the control of the central government and maintains a measure of political and administrative autonomy, which culminated in the election of a regional parliament in May 1992. Despite the precariousness of its security arrangements, Iraqi Kurdistan is now an important centre for a number of Iraqi opposition groups. Among those are the various Assyrian and Turcoman parties, which generally have amicable and co-operative relations with the Kurdish administration and other Iraqi parties.

## Survey of the opposition

The Iraqi opposition consists of five broad currents: Islamist, Arab nationalist, Kurdish, Communist and democratic. To these can be added the political parties formed by minorities such as Assyrians and Turcomen. Of the five, the first four are traditional in that they are organized around parties which played a part in shaping the politics of modern Iraq, particuarly after 1958. The democratic current, whose intellectual roots predate the 1958 revolution, failed to develop an effective party structure and was submerged in the mid-1960s. Each of the five currents includes various parties, groups and individuals, and has its own internal dynamics of alliances and differences. At the same time, there are areas of overlap where the lines between currents are blurred, and many individuals provide links between one group and another.

Despite their differences, all five currents publicly agree on four main points:

1. They regard the overthrow of Saddam Husain and the group surrounding him as a precondition for change;
2. They endorse the territorial integrity of Iraq;
3. They accept the principle of democratic elections and constitutional government;
4. They accept the need for a special status for the Kurds based on a degree of self-government.

However, these five major currents diverge and offer different alternatives to the Iraqi nation in their conceptions of the mechanism of change, their projections for Iraq's future and their definitions of Iraq's identity.

## Islamists

The Islamist movement in Iraq is predominantly Shi'i, although Sunni Islamist groups also have a decades-long history. The predominance of Shi'ism among the Islamist groups is in part due to the fact that the Shi'i are the overall majority of the population, with particularly heavy concentration in the southern and the south-central areas around the holy cities of Najaf and Karbala'. Despite their numerical majority, the Shi'i have historically been offered few opportunities in Iraqi political life, which has tended to be dominated by Sunni career politicians or the Sunni army officer corps.

After the First World War the British adopted a policy of dependence on a small circle of Sunni ex-officers of the Ottoman army to provide a governing elite; a policy which continued as a tradition throughout the period of the monarchy (1920-58). The army officer corps, during and after the monarchy, remained almost exclusively Sunni. As a consequence, the successive military coups d'état carried out by army officers from 1958 onwards perpetuated the Sunni control of government. Even the brief tenure of power in 1963 by the Ba'th Party – which had a civilian leadership and many Shi'i members – relied heavily on Sunni army officers and therefore did not significantly change the established pattern. Following the second Ba'thist takeover, in July 1968, access to power continued to shrink, as ever larger sections of the population were excluded. Participation in government – increasingly conditional upon obedience and personal loyalty – became restricted to a small circle drawn from Sunni clans close to that of Ahmad Hasan al-Bakr, the president, and Saddam Husain, then vice-president.

The historical exclusion of Shi'is from the political process bred a crisis of allegiance and identity. Two alternatives were available around which their grievances could crystallize and to which their allegiance could be given. The first was Communist ideology, which took root in Iraq with the establishment of the Iraqi Communist Party (ICP) in 1934. Communism appealed to secular Shi'is because it was confessionally indiscriminate and intellectually satisfying. It was opposed to Western imperialism, seen by many as the ally of the Sunni elite, and spoke a language of social equality which appealed to those whose political dispossession was accompanied by economic deprivation. Consequently, southern Iraq became a hotbed of Communist organization and activism.

The second alternative, Islam, was traditional and indigenous. The Shi'i *'ulama'* in Iraq, often Sayyids (descendants of the Prophet Muhammad), exercised a strong spiritual and emotional pull on the Shi'i population. This was not always out of strict piety but from reverence and respect for their learning and lineage. The Shi'i doctrine prevalent in Iraq, that of the Twelvers, believes in an awaited hidden Imam (a messiah). It admits the representation of the hidden Imam by a hierarchy of religious scholars (*'ulama'*) who, by virtue of their proxy status, have authority to interpret the Qur'an and the *shari'a* (religious laws). Thus the *'ulama'* are often consulted on secular matters as well as on religious observance, and are integrated into the community through their involvement in its daily life. During the British mandate in Iraq, and particularly in the 1920s, Shi'i *'ulama'* played a major role in expressing popular aspirations for national independence and participation in the political process, although such leadership did not evolve into an organized movement.

Pressure for a Shi'i political identity increased with the successful appeal of Communism and Ba'thism to Shi'i youth, particularly after the mid-1950s. Enthusiastic committment to these secularist ideologies eroded conservative values, undercut the spiritual and social ties that had held the community together for centuries, and threatened the status of the *'ulama'*. After 1968 the Ba'th regime adopted a policy of anti-clericalism and ruthlessly sought to bring what had previously been the traditionally independent Shi'i religious institutions under its control.

The 1960s upsurge of Arab nationalism in Iraq and throughout the Middle East arguably also threatened conservative sectors of the Shi'i community with a further undermining of its interests by Sunni Arab hegemony. But the defeat of Arab armies in the 1967 Arab-Israeli war and the loss of Jerusalem was an emotional shock to devout Muslims, causing them to question the integrity, commitment and competence of their governments, and to seek an alternative to corrupt regimes and imported ideologies. The presence in Iraq's holy cities of Najaf and Karbala' of universally acknowledged and revered clerics such as Sayyid Muhsin al-Hakim and Sayyid Muhammad Baqir al-Sadr enhanced the attraction of political Islam as an activist ideology rooted in a cultural tradition, responsive to political and social needs, and promising to raise Muslims above failure.

## Da'wa Party

One of the earliest and most visible manifestations of Islamic political organization was the Da'wa Party, officially founded in 1968 under the guidance of Sayyid Muhammad Baqir al-Sadr. Its origins date back to 1957, when Sayyid Muhammad Baqir al-Sadr began to formulate a social and political philosophy out of Islamic doctrine and the *shari'a*. The Da'wa Party was a clandestine movement organized, like the Communist Party, around tightly-knit secret cells and a strict hierarchy. The number of its adherents at any given time cannot be reliably verified, but it is known that the three sons of Sayyid Muhsin al-Hakim – an important Shi'i *marji'* (authority) – were principal figures of the Da'wa Party, lending it considerable weight.

In the late 1970s and early 1980s, the Da'wa Party openly confronted the Ba'th regime. In 1979 it organized demonstrations in several southern cities. It carried out attacks on government centres and installations, and in 1980 made an attempt on the life of Tariq 'Aziz, then deputy premier. It succeeded in establishing cells in other Arab countries such as Kuwait and Bahrain, but the political leadership and spiritual guidance remained firmly Iraqi.

The regime's policy of harassment and persecution which had been launched in the early 1970s developed after the 1979 demonstrations into a vigorous campaign of extermination. The Da'wa Party was banned and allegiance to it became a capital offence. Many suspected members or sympathizers, including women and prominent *'ulama'*, were hunted down, jailed, tortured and killed. The regime conducted a purge against the family of Sayyid Muhsin al-Hakim and in April 1980 Sayyid Muhammad Baqir al-Sadr (who had assumed a more spiritual than political role) and his sister, Bint al-Huda, were seized and executed.

Not content with pursuing Da'wa Party members, the Iraqi government began to target non-political Shi'i families. A campaign of wholesale deportations to Iran begun in the 1970s continued into the early 1980s. Victims were accused of *taba'iya*, or being of Iranian descent. Over 300,000 people were deported, their property confiscated and their sons detained by the Iraqi authorities, later to disappear without trace.

The campaign of persecution and the death of Sayyid Muhammad Baqir al-Sadr left the Da'wa Party weakened and in disarray, but did not eradicate it. Members of the party, including Sayyid Muhammad Baqir al-Hakim (son of Sayyid Muhsin al-Hakim), fled to Iran or elsewhere, and attempted to regroup. In 1981 a crisis developed within the party over two issues. The first was the question of whether it should retain its Iraqi identity and leadership, or whether, as an Islamist party, it should identify more closely with the Islamic Republic of Iran as a forerunner of a greater Islamic nation. The second issue was the selection of the leadership. The party proposed holding elections for a leadership council, but a splinter group rejected the principle of elections as being contrary to *shari'a* law. The elections went ahead with the support of over 70 per cent of the membership, and the splinter group formed a new party, the Islamic Da'wa.

In spite of the early establishment of cells outside Iraq, the Da'wa Party has always retained a firm nationalist identity. Since the execution in 1980 of its mentor, Sayyid Muhammad Baqir al-Sadr, no single individual has wielded full spiritual and temporal power over it, although Shaikh Muhammad Mahdi al-Asifi is acknowledged as its most senior cleric. This is partly because the spiritual momentum for Shi'ism moved from Iraq to Iran in 1979-80, following the Iranian revolution that brought the Ayatullah Khumaini to power, and partly because of the expulsion and execution of Iraqi clerics by the Ba'thist regime. In order to seek the type of guidance provided by Sayyid Muhammad Baqir al-Sadr, the Da'wa Party would have had to look to Iran, causing a shift in orientation that would contradict its nationalist nature.

The Da'wa Party is distinguished from other Islamist groups in having had, since its inception, a defined political programme. This is based on an Islamic interpretation of Iraq's history and social structure, and calls for a government that derives its constitution and laws from the *shari'a* and will implement an Islamic economic and social programme. However, unlike Islamic political philosophy in Iran, the Da'wa Party' s programme does not accept the principle of *wilayat al-faqih*, i.e. guardianship of the jurisconsult, a concept somewhat akin to papal rule in Catholicism.

After the losses and dispersal of the 1980s, the regrouped Da'wa Party concentrated on internal organization and recruitment. At the same time it had to adjust to new political factors, such as its international and regional image, its problematic relationship with Iran, and, more recently, Kurdish demands for federation. Like almost all opposition groups, it has adopted a relatively pragmatic stand and has accepted the need for a democratic form of government in Iraq, allowing for free elections. At present, members of the Da'wa Party maintain that Islamic rule should not be imposed from the top down and implemented by coercion, but should emanate from popular conviction and the will of the majority expressed through national elections. In response to Kurdish demands for federation, the Da'wa Party has made a counter-proposal suggesting a decentralized system of government deriving from the ancient *wilayat* system in operation during the Islamic period and under Ottoman rule. The decentralization they propose would be based on geographic regions rather than ethnic or sectarian distribution. The Da'wa Party claims to have large numbers of adherents and supporters inside Iraq, particularly in the southern governorates, who concentrate on intelligence-gathering and organization-building, and publish a clandestine periodical, *al-Jihad*.

## Supreme Council for the Islamic Revolution in Iraq

Following the persecution of suspected Da'wa Party members and sympathizers in the late 1970s and early 1980s, and the expulsion of hundreds of thousands of Shi'i lay families to Iran, a sizeable body of Iraqi Shi'i *'ulama'* took refuge with the newly established Islamic government of Ayatullah Khumaini. With its support, a coalition of Iraqi Islamic movements was created in 1982, headed by Sayyid Muhammad Baqir al-Hakim and known as the Supreme Council (or Assembly) of the Islamic Revolution in Iraq (SCIRI). SCIRI was to be a representative coalition, and included the followers of Sayyid Muhammad Baqir al-Hakim, the Da'wa Party, the Islamic Action Organization and other smaller groups. SCIRI derives its weight from the stature of its leader, who commands the respect of many Iraqis both in his own right and from veneration for his late father, Sayyid Muhsin al-Hakim.

As an umbrella group, SCIRI has a seventeen-member *shura* (advisory) council, including unaffiliated Iraqi clerics and members of Iraqi Islamist groups based in Iran. However, it is a loose structure and does not have an articulated political programme. After the end of the Iran-Iraq war, a rift developed between the Da'wa Party and SCIRI over the issue of Iran's role in supporting the Iraqi Islamic movement. The Da'wa Party has effectively frozen its participation in SCIRI. As a result of the rift, SCIRI now in effect represents the followers of Sayyid Muhammad Baqir al-Hakim, and its relationship with other Islamist groups appears to have become largely formal.

Like other Islamicist movements around the Arab world, SCIRI's followers work at the grassroots level, particularly with Iraqi refugees in Iran and in southern rural areas. Because of its generally good relations with Iran, it has access to the Iraqi marshes. This enables it to maintain contact with the marsh inhabitants, offer rudimentary assistance and gather intelligence through its supporters. It has thus served, in the past two years, as a conduit of information on the resistance activity that persists in southern Iraq. It has also developed a number of administrative offices, including an information centre and a document-gathering centre, and has representatives in Syria, Iraqi Kurdistan and several European countries. It also publishes papers and periodicals in Arabic and English.

SCIRI representatives claim to have strong political support in southern

Iraq, and the organization is certainly well placed for access into Iraq from Iran. As in the case of the Da'wa Party's claims, it is impossible to confirm the level of its political support in Iraq. Although Sayyid Muhammad Baqir al-Hakim enjoys respect among many Iraqi Shi'i, it is difficult to gauge how far he is regarded as a political leader or spiritual guide. Significantly, he holds himself up not as not only a Shi'i leader, but as a leader for all Iraqis, regardless of religion or ethnicity – a claim that is disputed by others, including other Islamists. SCIRI cooperates with non-Islamist Iraqi opposition forces and has adopted a platform calling for elections and constitutional government in Iraq. However, like other Islamist groups, it regards the Western-inspired democratic system as outside the Islamic tradition. While conceding areas of compatibility between Islam and democracy, Islamists wish to see Islamic doctrine used as the framework within which some democratic practices, such as representation and decentralization, can be implemented.

## Other Islamist Groups

The Islamist current of the Iraqi opposition encompasses other, smaller groups based in Iran or Syria, most notably the Islamic Action Organization. There are also prominent Islamist individuals who accept democratic practices beyond elections and constitutionalism, and are receptive to the principles of political tolerance and pluralism.

## Arab Nationalists

The term Arab nationalist (or pan-Arab nationalist) applies to many individuals, groups and parties now within the opposition but previously part of mainstream Iraqi politics following the 1958 revolution. It covers Ba'thists and all who see Iraq's regional and international relations as rooted in the Arab context. For Arab nationalists, Arabism is not only a cultural concept but a political imperative in Iraqi affairs.

Arab nationalism as an ideology has in one form or another dominated Arab political discourse and rhetoric – though not perhaps Arab political action – since the emergence of Arab statehood in the 1920s. It holds that the Arab states are based on an artificial division of what is in reality a single nation. These states are but staging posts towards the ultimate union of the Arab world into one great nation-state, a goal which it is the duty of every Arab politician to pursue vigorously.

In the 1940s and 1950s this ideology was boosted with the spread of Ba'thist and Nasserite ideas built around belief in a single Arab state. But the shared aspirations of Arab nationalists did not prevent them from breaking up into rival or even hostile groups. The Nasserites, who counted among their ranks many army officers, were a fluid and loose conglomeration of several fractured groups. Relations between them and the Ba'thists in Iraq and Syria were in the 1960s and 1970s confontational, in spite of temporary and tactical alliances formed primarily to stage coups d'état. More dramatically, the Ba'th Party itself split in 1966 into a Syrian camp and an Iraqi camp. The principal founder and ideologue of Ba'thism, Michel 'Aflaq, moved to Iraq from his native Syria and transferred his support to the Iraqi Ba'th Party which came to power in 1968 under Ahmad Hasan al-Bakr and Saddam Husain.

The Iraqi Ba'thists' antagonism with the Syrian Ba'thists had affected their unity and caused defections, friction and purges. After 1968 widespread periodic executions and purges of both military and civilian Ba'thists were carried out to ensure allegiance and conformity. Many left Iraq fearing for their lives, and took up residence in Syria or Europe. Saddam Husain's increasing control over the Ba'th Party culminated in his rise to the presidency in 1979. The diminishing role of party members thereafter further aggravated rifts within party ranks. Meanwhile, the Nasserites, who had enjoyed a brief ascendancy under the two 'Arif governments (1963-68), were also silenced and left Iraq. Lacking a party organization, they eventually lost their impetus as a group, but remain active in the opposition as individuals within the broad Arab nationalist framework.

The invasion of Kuwait triggered renewed political activism among dissenting Ba'thists, and a reassessment of Ba'thist doctrines and practices. Since the Gulf War two distinct factions have emerged. A 'revisionist' group still adheres to a basic Ba'thist platform, but recognizes errors of outlook and strategy committed in the past and calls for reform and ideological flexibility. This group forms the majority of the Arab nationalists who have gravitated towards Syria. The second group comprises ex-Ba'thists who regard Ba'thism as a failed experiment and condemn its rigid ideological doctrines. They retain a belief, however, in the Arab identity of Iraq and the need to work politically within an Arab context.

Both Ba'thist revisionists and ex-Ba'thists claim to have discarded the concept of the 'leading party', a cornerstone of Ba'thist ideology used to justify Ba'thist domination of society and the suppression of other political views. They also agree that after Saddam Husain became president in 1979 the Ba'th Party was excluded from power, and its decision-making capability transferred to the presidency or, to a lesser extent, to the Revolutionary Command Council (RCC). Without necessarily exonerating the party, few in either group would blame it for the events of the past fifteen years.

The two groups differ over three main issues. First, there is the question of whether Ba'thist ideology – with its stress on Arabism and socialism – imposed an unrealistic formula on Iraq by ignoring its distinctive social and economic features. On this the ex-Ba'thists tend to be more pragmatic and flexible than the Ba'thist revisionsists in arguing in favour of recognizing Iraq's diversity. Second, the ex-Ba'thists also consider that the organizational policies of the party – such as its secrecy, hierarchy and rigid orthodoxy – by their nature made it prone to authoritarianism and permitted the rise of dictatorship. Third, there is the issue of Iraq's relations with the West. Ba'thist revisionists and other traditional Arab nationalists regard the West with a suspicion that lingers from the days of anti-imperialist fervour. They see the interests of the West in the Arab world as self-serving and therefore likely to conflict with the interests of Arab countries, including Iraq. Ex-Ba'thists, on the other hand, are more willing to deal with the West and tend to see a coincidence of interests, at least in the foreseeable future.

In general, Arab nationalist groups tend to be formed around personal connections and shared histories rather than party agendas. With a few exceptions their political programmes are nebulous and no political philosophy has been developed to replace the old Arab nationalist socialist doctrine of the early Ba'thists and the Nasserites, although there are the beginnings of party formation in some quarters which could do so. Groups composed of ex-Ba'thists (in contrast to other Arab nationalists) usually benefit from a tradition of organizational capability. In part because of their small size they have abandoned the strict hierarchial order characteristic of the Ba'th Party, whilst retaining its elitism and cabalistic operating style.

The Arab nationalist groups within the Iraqi opposition have toned down the emotive language long common to Arab nationalism in favour of a more realistic approach, acknowledging that the rhetoric has been used to cover up real problems in Iraq and elsewhere in the Arab world. Like other Iraqi opposition groups, the Arab nationalists – including the Ba'thists – increasingly use a democratic vocabulary and advocate democratic practices. This gives rise to a certain degree of scepticism among other Iraqis because the early Ba'th Party, like the Iraqi Communist Party, always expressed its political opposition to contemporary regimes as a call for democracy and freedom. Despite the new pragmatism, there is controversy within the Arab nationalist camp over Iraq's relations with the West; the degree of conformity to mainstream Arab politics; the status of the Kurds within Iraq; questions of decentralization or federation versus a strong central government; and the role of the army.

Arab nationalist groups believe that any change in Iraq must inevitably be carried out by disaffected elements within the existing power structure – the army, the security apparatus and the Ba'th party – rather than by a popular uprising or foreign intervention. Moreover, they regard the involvement of such elements as desirable and necessary to preserve Iraq's unity, maintain order and avoid bloodshed in the aftermath of change.

Whereas other opposition groups consider the Ba'th Party to have so discredited itself in Iraq that there is little likelihood of its participation in shaping the country's future, Arab nationalists believe there is room for a reformed Ba'th Party in a democratic Iraq and argue that the party was corrupted and subverted by Saddam Husain's regime. They expect to play a significant role in the process of change because of their continuing ties to factions in the army and to the administration. They believe that, despite the need to adopt a more Iraqi particularist orientation, they still represent the strong current of nationalist sentiment and interest that is dominant in Iraqi society and is a continuous thread in Iraq's modern history. They present their platform as indigenous, arising from Iraq's cultural, regional and historical identity, and capable of unifying Iraqi society above its sectarian divisions.

## Kurds

The Kurds in Iraq have a long history of opposition to the central government in Baghdad. Apart from brief interludes of negotiation and appeasement, opposition by at least some sections of the Kurdish movement has been the norm, particularly since 1960. From time to time it has broken out into open warfare, particularly between 1961 and 1975, exhausting both the Kurdish population and the central government. Until 1975 Kurdish political and military force was mobilized by the Kurdistan Democratic Party (KDP). The struggle for leadership of the Iraqi KDP shifted back and forth between a tribal and an urban base. On the whole, however, the party was dominated by Mulla Mustafa Barzani – a traditional leader who was highly regarded among the tribes and commanded essential fighting troops – and eventually it became identified with him.

The Kurdish opposition movement in Iraq has been influenced by two main factors: its ties to Iran (Iraq's historical rival in the region) and factionalism. Ties to Iran subjected the Kurds to the vicissitudes of Iranian-Iraqi relations, rendering them vulnerable whenever there was a rapprochement between the rival states, however temporary. Thus in March 1975, following the Algiers accord between Iran and Iraq, Kurdish fighters found themselves suddenly deprived of the Iranian support on which they had depended. Additionally, during the Iran-Iraq war the Kurds were perceived by the Iraqi government as supporting Iraq's enemy, a charge that incurred brutal reprisals by the army and security forces. These included the razing of thousands of frontier villages and the internal deportation and disappearance of tens of thousands of Kurdish men, women and children in the now notorious Anfal campaigns of 1987 and 1988.

Factionalism persisted for decades among the Kurdish tribes as well as between the traditional tribal leaders like Mustafa Barzani and the more left-leaning intelligentsia led by Ibrahim Ahmad and Jalal Talabani. It contributed to the fragmentation of the Kurdish movement and weakened its ability to pursue a coordinated strategy. From 1960 to 1975 the Iraqi government exploited the factionalism by periodically engaging in negotiation and rapprochement with one faction at the expense of others. Furthermore, until the Gulf War of 1991 the government successfully recruited a 'fifth column' among Kurds to subvert their resistance movement.

The signing of the 1975 Algiers Accord by the Shah of Iran and Saddam Husain led to the withdrawal of Iranian (and US) support for the Kurds and a new political party, the Patriotic Union of Kurdistan (PUK), split off from the KDP under the leadership of Jalal Talabani. The split formalized disagreements within the old KDP on issues such as support base, operations and tactics. The PUK appealed to the urban population, particularly in Sulaimaniyya, and incorporated a socialist component in its political philosophy.

In 1979 Mulla Mustafa Barzani died, and leadership of the KDP was assumed by his son, Mas'ud. During the 1980s Kurdistan provided a refuge for Iraqi Communists and armed resistance continued sporadically against the central government. The operations of the Iraqi army and security forces against the Kurds during the Iran-Iraq war culminated in the bombardment of villages with chemical weapons which began in spring 1987 and became widely known internationally after the gassing of Halabja in March 1988. The use of chemical weapons, destruction of thousands of villages and the widespread, systematic killing of civilians in the Anfal campaigns further radicalized Kurdish dissent and drew the fractious Kurdish groups together. In May 1988 the Kurdish groups formed the Iraqi Kurdistan Front (IKF), an umbrella organization comprising five groups in addition to the KDP and the PUK.

The IKF faced its strongest challenge in March 1991. The Gulf War, devastating as it was, had failed to topple Saddam Husain's regime; the uprisings in the south and the north had collapsed; and hundreds of thousands of Kurds were fleeing over snow-bound mountains into Turkey and Iran in appalling conditions. The allied forces had not offered the Kurds any guarantee of safety, and the Iraqi regime, weakened but still in power, was urging negotiations upon the Kurdish leadership. In a move widely criticized by the rest of the Iraqi opposition, leaders of the IKF, including Mas'ud Barzani and Jalal Talabani, travelled to Baghdad in April for talks with Saddam Husain and the Iraqi government. The talks quickly reached an impasse over three main issues: namely, the inclusion of the oil-producing Kirkuk province in a Kurdish autonomous region; the limits of authority for an autonomous Kurdish administration; and Kurdish demands for democratic government in Iraq as a whole. Given the centrality of these issues, the negotiations inevitably broke down. Since then no formal talks have taken place between Baghdad and the Kurdish leadership. There have, however, been several overtures from Baghdad, and the possibility of such talks is raised periodically in the face of the precarious political situation and economic hardship in Kurdistan.

While the IKF leadership went to Baghdad for talks in April 1991, the United Nations Security Council, in response to the merciless retaliation of the regime against the *intifada* and the pitiful condition of fleeing Kurds, adopted Resolution 688, which demanded that the Iraqi government cease its repression of the Iraqi people. The United States, Britain and France used the spirit of this resolution to declare the skies above the 36th parallel closed to Iraqi aircraft and establish a 'safe haven' zone in a swathe of Kurdistan across the north and north-east of Iraq, to be guarded by the Allies from bases in south-east Turkey. This limited zone was extended de facto to most of Iraqi Kurdistan soon after, when the Iraqi army withdrew from Kurdish cities and countryside. In October 1991, the Iraqi government also withdrew its civilian administration from the zone evacuated by the army, and declared an economic embargo on the area. This security arrangement for the Kurds, albeit temporary, has remained in force since April 1991, and has provided them with a high degree of safety and freedom, despite occasional Iraqi army incursions and acts of sabotage.

The IKF used this unprecedented freedom to declare its intention to hold elections for a Kurdish regional parliament which would represent the three million inhabitants of the region. The elections would create a political framework for resolving differences among the Kurdish parties and establish a Kurdish administrative structure to replace the one removed by the Iraqi government. The elections were delayed a number of times, and there was fear of factional conflict. However, they took place in May 1992, monitored by dozens of international observers. They were reported free and fair by these observers, although dissatisfaction was expressed by some of the participating parties, such as the Communists, the socialists and the Islamicists. Some 900,000 voters cast their ballots, and the results were predictably and broadly, if not totally, satisfactory to the Kurdish parties. The KDP and the PUK won an almost equal number of votes and shared the seats in parliament, since none of the smaller parties in the IKF obtained the minimum 7 per cent required for a seat under the proportional representation system adopted. A few seats were allocated to Assyrians and other non-Kurdish groups. As a result of their defeat in the elections, the smaller Kurdish parties have consolidated and remain part of the IKF.

Within a few months of the elections the new parliament voted in favour of seeking a federated status within Iraq. This was a departure from the autonomous status that had hitherto been the focus of Kurdish demands and discussions with the Iraqi government. The Kurdish parliament and leadership have stressed that federation would be implemented within a unified Iraq, and the Kurdish parties remain committed to their partnership in the Iraqi opposition movement. However, despite repeated Kurdish assurances, the announcement of federal status has caused misgivings in Turkey, Iran and Syria, as well as among segments of the Iraqi opposition, including some of the nationalist and Islamic groups. They see the proposal for federation as a first step towards Kurdish secession from Iraq and the creation of an independent Kurdistan. Neighbouring countries with Kurdish minorities fear that an Iraqi Kurdish state would form the nucleus for, or set an example to, other Kurdish separatist drives.

The Kurdish parliament has also successfully created a unified corps out of the two parties' *peshmerga*, or irregular fighting force, numbering about thirty-five thousand. The extreme, even revolutionary, nature of the Kurdish experience in the three years after the Gulf War seemed to produce a greater level of cooperation and concerted action between the KDP and the PUK and their respective leaders, Mas'ud Barzani and Jalal Talabani. Despite setbacks and limited resources, the new parliament and administration have managed to return a degree of normality to life in Kurdistan and begin small-scale reconstruction efforts and repatriation of refugees. A number of Kurdish non-governmental organizations have been set up to supplement the work of the administration and international agencies in repairing the physical and human damage caused by several years of war.

The Kurdish parties have several unique advantages over the other Iraqi opposition groups. Thanks to the 1992 elections, the parties and their leaders are able to substantiate their claim to represent a sector of the people of Iraq, whereas the claims of other opposition currents remain a matter of conjecture and debate. Moreover, the Kurdish current is the only one operating on its own territory inside Iraq, with few constraints although with an uncertain future. Because of these advantages, the Kurdish parties form an indispensable political and strategic element of the Iraqi opposition. The Kurdish administration has welcomed the presence of other Iraqi opposition forces in its area, and encouraged the improvement of working relations with them.

## Communists

The Iraqi Communist Party (ICP), formed in 1934, is the oldest party on the Iraqi political stage. Its history is one of harassment and outright persecution by most of the governments that have ruled Iraq, including those under the monarchy prior to 1958, the first Ba'thist regime of 1963, the two 'Arif regimes from 1963 to 1968, and the second Ba'th regime, particularly after Saddam Husain became president in 1979. Under the 'Abd al-Karim Qasim presidency the ICP enjoyed a short-lived period of political ascendancy curtailed by its own excesses and Qasim's vacillating favour.

From the start, the ICP attracted the young in the Shi'i community and much of its recruitment and activity took place in Iraq's southern cities. It appealed to the educated but politically and economically disadvantaged members of the community, who welcomed its universalist message and call for political and social equality. During the 1960s it gained considerable support among middle-class professionals, and harnessed the discontent of the rural poor. It was never able to gain significant power in government but occasionally tried to increase its leverage by alliance with other groups (usually those in opposition), such as the National Democratic Party (NDP) or, later, the Ba'thists. In 1973, during the second Ba'th regime, the ICP and the Ba'th Party formed the National Front, but when this collapsed in 1978 the ICP was again suppressed and its members severely persecuted. In 1979 it took up armed struggle against the regime.

The ICP had established a presence in Kurdistan, and close relations with the KDP and later the PUK. It survived repeated attempts to suppress and liquidate it partly because its leadership and cadres were able to take refuge in the Kurdish mountains beyond the reach of the Iraqi government. The alliance with the Kurds resulted in many non-Kurdish Iraqi Communists fighting alongside the *peshmerga* against government forces. Following the 1987-88 government campaigns against the Kurds, the Communists were forced to move again, this time to Syria. The ICP's relationship with the Kurds remains good, particularly since it is a vocal advocate of Kurdish rights and, according to party members, was the first opposition group to suggest the idea of Kurdish federalism. It participated in the Kurdish elections of May 1992 within a Democratic Front alliance, but failed to obtain the minimum 7 per cent of votes required for a parliamentary seat.

The ICP's fourth congress, held in Iraqi Kurdistan in 1985, engaged in a critique of its strategies and tactics, and evaluated proposals for internal party democracy. These proposals were rejected as inappropriate to the conditions of armed struggle which it faced. After 1989, it embarked on an intellectual and organizational reform which questioned the Marxist-Leninist ideology at the very heart of Communist thinking. In 1990, the party leadership put forward for discussion issues directly affecting the political philosophy of the party, its methods of operation and internal organization, and its relations to other opposition groups. The views expressed in discussion ranged from steadfast Marxist commitment to a desire for a complete overhaul of the intellectual and operational foundations of the party, including changing its name. The prevailing opinion appeared to favour preserving the party while revising its ideological platform away from class struggle, centralization and other aspects of classical Marxism, towards leftist socialism. This shift was accompanied by a greater tolerance for the concepts of political pluralism and liberal democracy.

At the ICP's fifth congress, held in Iraqi Kurdistan in October 1993, the focus was 'democracy and renewal' but a name-change proposal was overwhelmingly defeated. The role of private enterprise in post-Saddam reconstruction was recognized, and there was a 50 per cent change in membership of the central committee. The congress adopted a policy of working for the lifting of international sanctions coupled with increasing isolation of the Iraqi regime through implementation of UN Security Council Resolution 688. In common with other parties and groups in the Iraqi opposition the ICP stresses the need for communicating with and mobilizing the Iraqi people, especially those in Baghdad, with its population of around 5 million. It accepts that it is no longer the dominant opposition force and, although active inside the country, is not in a position to determine events. It is unlikely to pursue its past policies of autocratic control of its members and hegemony over civil institutions such as trade unions, but will probably seek instead to create a broad front with other socialist and democratic forces.

## Democrats

Singling out certain groups within the Iraqi opposition as democrats is somewhat misleading because all currents of the opposition advocate the adoption of at least some democratic procedures, such as free elections and constitutional government. At the same time, several opposition parties use the word 'democratic' as part of their name to give greater definition to their underlying nationalist or socialist orinentation. In this survey, groups and individuals are identified as democrats on the grounds of the priority they give to the principles of liberal democracy over other considerations, such as nationalism or ethnicity or religion. It might therefore be more accurate to refer to this current as the liberal democrats, but in Western terminology liberalism has acquired political and social implications which may not apply to the outlook of these groups.

A democratic movement existed in Iraq prior to 1958 among young upper-middle-class professionals. It first found expression not as a political party but as a group of intellectuals connected to a paper called *al-Ahali*, which began publication in the 1930s and articulated liberal, secularist, socialist and democratic views. In the mid-1940s, some members of the *al-Ahali* group, notably Kamil Chadirchi and Muhammad Hadid among others, formed the National Democratic Party (NDP), which was to survive, albeit in opposition, into the mid-1960s through the vicissitudes of Iraqi politics. Members of the NDP took an active part in Iraqi politics during this period, and occupied ministerial posts in their individual capacity in the governments formed under 'Abd al-Karim Qasim's presidency (1958-63). The NDP did not represent a mass movement, as did the Communists or the Nasserites, and their base of support was limited to educated professionals. The only way that the NDP could gain leverage was through alliances, which it frequently formed with other opposition groups, including the Communists and the early Ba'thists. The NDP also served a useful role as mediator among the opposition groups, or occasionally between opposition groups and the government, and as a barometer for measuring deviation from democratic standards by the Iraqi government.

Ideologically, the NDP and other unaffiliated liberal democrats were out of the mainstream of Iraqi and Arab politics of the period, particularly after 1950. The Iraqi political scene was dominated by the emotionally charged appeals of Arab nationalism on the one hand, and Communism on the other, both of which played to the tunes of the Cold War, the Arab-Israeli conflict, feudal exploitation, anti-imperialism, and other politically sensitive issues of the period. Meanwhile, the growing Islamist movement taking shape in the 1960s provided its own emotive appeal as an alternative to other ideologies. Thus, by the end of the 1960s, the Iraqi political scene was dominated by competing radical ideologies, and the moderating democratic voice had become increasingly weak. Little remained of the NDP by 1968, when the Ba'thists took over.

The upsurge in support for democratic ideas which occurred around the world in the late 1980s and early 1990s, even in a few Arab countries, has revitalized the Iraqi democrats and increased their numbers. Disenchantment with the political parties, rigid ideologies and authoritarian systems that have held sway over Iraq in the past thirty years has prompted a search for fresh ideas and new models, from which the democratic current has gnerally benefited. The collapse of the Soviet Union and world Communism provoked a reevaluation of their positions by some erstwhile Communists and socialists. Similarly, many previous members of the Ba'th Party have rejected its philosophy as incapable of providing answers to Iraq's many social and political problems. Deserters from these two camps have tended to join the ranks of the liberal democrats rather than parties or groups that have only modified their previous positions. Individuals from the left of the political spectrum form the bulk of the converts, giving the democratic current mildly socialist leanings.

Organized democratic parties have been lacking in the Iraqi opposition spectrum, although an Iraqi Democratic Party was formed in late 1993, and many groups are active in Europe and the Arab world which could eventually coalesce to form a powerful liberal bloc. The many Shi'is in the liberal democratic current provide a counterweight to the Shi'i component of the Islamist current, challenging their claim to represent the entire Iraqi Shi'i community. Liberal democrats, as secularists and particularists (i.e. with a specifically Iraqi orientation), are distinct from even the most democratic Islamists and Arab nationalists, who have broader and more global allegiances. They present themselves as the only unifying Iraqi voice, not bound by the religious, ethnic or supra-national identities which, they charge, have undermined Iraqi society. Other groups, they argue, superimpose on the Iraqi situation homogenizing programmes which have proved in practice divisive rather than unifying. Their attitudes to Iraqi Kurdistan are sympathetic to Kurdish demands and advances towards democracy, creating a natural alliance between democrats and the Kurdish opposition.

Despite their present lack of party organization, the democrats have succeeded in defining the frame of reference for political discussion among the Iraqi opposition. They have raised the issues of political pluralism, individual freedoms, civil liberties and government account-ability – principles which have at best been given only lip-service in Iraq's political past. The other currents in the Iraqi opposition continue to be challenged for responses to these principles. However, in addition to the absence of formal organization, the democrats suffer from a lack of recent government experience, and therefore cannot be expected to have lines of communication with individuals in the present regime, unlike some ex-Ba'thist groups. In appealing to the Iraqi people, the democrats have to assume that the bitter experiences of three-and-a-half decades of dictator-ship and failed ideologies have alienated them from the traditional parties and predisposed them towards democracy. On the basis of this assumption, the democrats claim to represent the 'silent majority' of Iraqis, a claim no more verifiable in the existing circumstances than that of any other group.

## Efforts at unification

The first public and comprehensive conference of the opposition took place in Beirut at the end of the Gulf War in March 1991, attended by more than three hundred Iraqis, from across the political spectrum, including Arab nationalists, Kurds, Islamists, Communists and democrats, as well as independents with no defined affiliation. The conference was organized by the Joint Action Committee (JAC), a Damascus-based coalition of opposition groups and dissidents formed in December 1990 under the protective canopy of Syria. It was inconclusive and contentious, but the final declaration expressed a shared commitment to the overthrow of Saddam Husain's regime, to democratic freedoms and political pluralism, and to the preservation of Iraq's unity and sovereignty.

After Beirut the JAC tried to organize a second conference but encoun-tered difficulties. Some stemmed from the antagonsims and rivalries exposed at the Beirut meeting. Others arose because Iraqi exiles in coun-tries as diverse as Syria, Iran, Sa'udi Arabia, Britain and the USA were inevitably influenced by the political outlooks and regional agendas of their hosts, who did not have a shared approach to Iraq's future. In addition, the philosophical disparity between, for example, Arab nationalism and Kurdish rights, or democratic secularism and Islamic doctrines, was exacerbated by the fact that groups had not had sufficient dialogue over the years to develop compromises and still claimed the rights of exclusive leadership. Moreover, the failure of the March uprising in Iraq led to mutual recriminations which deepened mistrust.

As JAC members shuttled between Damascus and other Arab and European cities, it became increasingly difficult to pull together all the strands, draw up an acceptable agenda or even decide on a venue. It had been agreed within JAC that political currents should be represented in proportion to the allegiance they were deemed to command within Iraq, but claims and demands by each group were hotly contested by other groups and conference preparations became bogged down in arguments over quotas. The choice of venue was also a sensitive matter, since many feared that host countries might influence the direction and decisions of the conference. The JAC went through months of postponements and debate, trying to draw everyone into the fold.

Following the Kurdish elections in May 1992, a group of JAC members, along with the Kurdish parties, resolved to hold a conference in Vienna, regardless of comprehensive participation. The decison was criticized by some Arab nationalist groups, including the Ba'thists in Syria, and by SCIRI and the Da'wa Party, all of whom refused to participate. They were dissatisfied with the quotas assigned to them and to others, and objected to the conference agenda, which included the rights of the Kurds to self-determination. Furthermore, the Vienna conference participants were accused of yielding to American and British influence after failing to gain regional endorsement.

The Vienna conference, which took place from 16 to 20 June 1992, founded the Iraqi National Congress (INC). It was attended by nearly two hundred delegates divided according to a pre-agreed quota formula. Although it was boycotted by SCIRI, the Da'wa Party, the Communists and the Syrian-based Arab nationalists, it did include smaller Islamic groups and independent Islamists, other Arab nationalists, the PUK and the KDP, democrats and unaffiliated individuals. Its tone was moderate and non-doctrinal, but the procedures it followed sacrificed democracy for expediency and consensus. In addition to a general assembly, it elected an executive committee of twenty-five charged with carrying out its recommendations. Groups and individuals normally mutually suspicious or antagonistic were able to work out compromises and agree on common ground. The closing statement established some basic principles: that constitutional government, parliamentary representation and the rule of law should guide Iraq's political future; that Iraq's territorial integrity should be preserved; and that the Iraqi Kurds should have the right of self-determination within a unified Iraqi state. The INC embarked on a public relations campaign in the Middle East and the West, and intensified its efforts to draw in those Iraqis who had boycotted the Vienna conference.

In September 1992 a committee including INC and non-INC members met in Iraqi Kurdistan at the invitation of Mas'ud Barzani to prepare for a second, broader-based INC conference. Following intense bargaining and some compromises, the second conference was held in Salah al-Din in Iraqi Kurdistan on 27-31 October 1992. This larger conference, also based on a quota formula, included representatives from SCIRI, the Da'wa Party and smaller Islamist groups, as well as Communists and an increased Arab nationalist participation. The general assembly of the INC was considerably enlarged and a new 26-member executive committee was elected (both according to the agreed system). A three-man leadership council was also elected, composed of a Shi'i cleric, a Sunni army general and the leader of the KDP. Tensions arose over two main issues: the Kurdish demand for federation within Iraq (announced by the Kurdish parliament weeks before the conference); and the composition of the INC leadership council. These and other, less contentious issues, were eventually resolved, but not necessarily to unanimous satisfaction. The literature emanating from the conference did not deviate in its essential principles from those established in Vienna. It condemned the regime in Iraq; stressed the need for democratic reform, constitutional government, free elections and pluralism in Iraq; and reaffirmed the unity of Iraq while declaring federalism to be a possible formula for a future administrative system.

After the second conference, the expanded INC established offices in Salah al-Din to bolster its presence on Iraqi territory and created an organizational apparatus with an information network, a broadcasting station and other operations. Tensions persisted within the INC and the Da'wa Party withdrew from the coalition in September 1993. However, despite the tensions and defections the resilient INC has in general been able to resolve differences and arrive at decisions in a collegial manner. It remains the only body of Iraqi opposition that has succeeded in creating a unified structure and developing a political platform that deals with specific issues. Next to the Kurdish parties, it is also the largest opposition grouping with an active presence on Iraqi territory. In the summer of 1993, the INC scored diplomatic gains when it was officially received at high levels in the United States, Britain, Sa'udi Arabia and Kuwait, and sent delegations to a number of regional, non-aligned and European countries. The process of negotiation, compromise and mutual accommodation through which the INC evolved offers a potentially successful means of resolving differences within the Iraqi opposition, and in a post-Saddam Iraq.

Since September 1993 the INC coalition has been expanding its presence in Iraqi Kurdistan and concentrating its efforts on organization within

Iraq. The most visible achievement of the INC is in the field of propaganda. Its weekly newspaper is distributed in government controlled areas and the radio broadcasts of its affiliate – the Iraqi Broadcasting Corporation – can now be heard throughout the country. Less visible is the considerable intelligence work that the INC carries out, gathering information on the Iraqi regime's activities and institutions. While such penetration indicates an ability to win over and mobilize people, defections, especially from the military, do not appear to have occurred in any significant numbers. The coalition may be required to prove its credentials with more substantial work sustained over a longer period of time before it can become a powerful magnet for Iraqis seeking a political alternative.

Those outside the INC (other than the withdrawn Da'wa Party) are Ba'thists and Arab nationalists, and some Communists, largely in Syria and Europe. They have misgivings over the INC's political platform, its imputed allegiances and its procedures for representation. In their view, the INC has conceded too much to Kurdish demands, in accepting the principle of federation adopted by the Kurdish parliament. Furthermore, it has also placed too much emphasis on Shi'i Islamist representation and too little on the nationalist representation which they regard as politically and strategically indispensible. The method of proportional representation used by the INC in selecting its governing bodies is criticized for ignoring Iraqi political differentiation and consecrating the ethnic and sectarian divisions in Iraqi society. Perhaps the most serious charge concerns the perception that the INC is too dependent on western support (which, in the view of these groups, has proven unreliable), whilst it underestimates the importance of neighbouring countries. Essentially, the same criticisms levelled at the INC at the time of the Vienna conference persist in relation to the expanded INC.

Several attempts have been made by the dissenting nationalist groups to form rival alliances, including the establishment in Damascus in 1992 of a Committee for National Coordination, and in 1993 of a nationalist democratic front. These alliances have held several meetings in Syria, but have so far not established a comprehensive national front that could absorb or dissolve the INC or provide a material counterbalance to it. Alongside these rival attempts, groups within and outside the INC have, since the Salah al-Din conference of October 1992, maintained good bilateral relations and continued dialogue aimed at finding common ground for an all-encompassing coalition of opposition forces.

It is also worth noting that 1993 saw the emergence of a royalist front, advocating the restoration of constitutional monarchy in Iraq under a Hashemite candidate, Sharif 'Ali ibn al-Husain, a second cousin of King Faisal II who was assassinated during the 1958 revolution. The royalists argue that after thirty-five years of turbulent politics and divisive government policies, which have fragmented the Iraqi nation, a constitutional monarchy would signal a return to legitimacy in government and represent a stability and continuity that could repair the social fissures and provide a symbol of unity for all Iraqis. Politically, the royalist platform is general, moderate and democratic, but lacks a clearly conceived strategy for change. At present there does not appear to be any friction between the INC and the royalist front, which includes some INC members.

## Facing the future

The Iraqi opposition, including the INC, faces some stern tests of its credibility. The first is the level of acceptance it receives from Iraqis. Despite the claims by many groups that they have support inside Iraq, such support cannot be measured or verified, except in the case of the Kurdish parties. Translating the INC's international diplomatic success of 1992 and 1993 into success in gaining the confidence of the Iraqi people is a major challenge. Groups outside the INC will not have an easier time, since on the whole they represent only sections of the Iraqi population and lack the diversity required for a wider appeal. The necessary credibility is more likely to be achieved if the coalition represented by the INC can expand to include all the opposition groups and present a unified, comprehensive national front. In any event, tightening and orchestrating the relationships between the émigré and exile opposition, on the one hand, and the opposition (actual or potential) inside Iraq, on the other, is a formidable and risky task.

A second challenge lies in achieving a change of regime in a manner consistent with the opposition's declared commitment to democracy and the rule of law. Quite apart from the logistical difficulties entailed, the opposition groups are not united on what constitute possible or desirable methods for achieving change. Some groups, particularly those which have old connections to the Ba'th, favour the military or palace coup scenario, seeing in it a solution that will maintain order, prevent bloodshed and preserve the country's unity. Others, such as the Islamists, put their faith in guerrilla tactics and a popular uprising which they hope will have greater discipline and be better organized than that of March 1991. The Kurds and democrats are more inclined to believe that change has to be a collaborative effort between the people and the military. None of these groups has publicly declared a programme of action designed to bring about change.

On the political level, the opposition has to resolve problems ingrained in Iraq since 1958, if not since the country's creation in the 1920s. Successive Iraqi governments have managed to ignore these problems by diverting attention to the external threats, whether real or imaginary, from colonialism, imperialism, Israel, Iran and – most recently – alleged plots to partition Iraq. Most opposition groups acknowledge that there are chronic flaws in the state system, such as the status of Iraqi Kurdistan, the politicization of Iraq's military, the entrenchment of the state security apparatus, and the relative exclusion of the Shi'i from power. However, attention to these problems is still in a diagnostic stage, with only a few suggested remedies being currently debated. One of these is the proposal for a federated state. The Kurds have called for an Arab-Kurdish federation regardless of what other system is used in the rest of Iraq. Some Islamists oppose the word 'federation' and propose a decentralized system based on five or more *wilayat*, which would be drawn on geographic rather than ethnic lines. The Arab nationalists agree to a limited degree of local government throughout Iraq, but wish to defer the Kurdish issue for a future decision. The INC's statements in favour of federation make a declaration of principle but do not expand on the details, and in any case have drawn criticism from the nationalists.

Beyond these difficulties lies the problem of political identity which has long plagued Iraq. The parties and currents found within the Iraqi opposition movement are implicitly parties of exclusion: the Kurdish parties are not designed to include Arabs; the Arab nationalist groups are unlikely to win Kurdish, Assyrian or Turcoman membership; the Shi'i Islamist groups are by definition closed to people of other religions as well as to Sunni Muslims. Only the Communists and the democrats offer platforms that are non-ethnic and non-sectarian, and cut across these many lines of differentiation. Therefore, one of the more intractable tasks facing the Iraqi opposition is the forging of a national programme, or alternative national programmes, to which all Iraqis can subscribe regardless of race or ethnicity. The INC has come closest to presenting a unified Iraqi agenda, but it remains to be seen whether the endorsement of the agenda by the groups within the INC is wholehearted or only tactical. Whatever the national agenda, it must deal with the lingering Kurdish and minorities problem. The Arab nationalist groups especially will have to define their understanding of the relationship between Arabs and Kurds in Iraq not only to their satisfaction but to the satisfaction of their partners, the Kurds, and indeed to the satisfaction of minorities in Iraq such as Assyrians and Turcomans.

Underlying these problems are the basic questions of what kind of Iraq the opposition groups wish to see, and whether the Iraqi state is regarded as an end in itself or as a stepping-stone towards wider ethnic or religious allegiance. The answers to these questions will largely determine the success or failure of the Iraqi opposition, both in achieving the kind of democratic change it proposes for Iraq and securing peaceful and stable conditions after any such change occurs.

## Notes

1. This chapter is based on interviews with individual Iraqi opposition figures, news reports and statements made by Iraqi opposition groups. I am particularly indebted to Gareth Smyth for assistance with the interviews. I am grateful to the following for interviews granted to me or to Gareth Smyth: Muhammad 'Abd al-Jubbur, 29 April 1993; Salem 'Ali, 4 June 1993; 'Ayad 'Allawi, 4 June 1993; Muhsin al-Athari, 3 July 1993; Hamid al-Bayati, 11 January 1993; Ahmad Chalabi, 26 January 1993; Hani al-Fikaiki, 8 and 11 January, 23 March 1993; 'Aziz 'Ulayan, 29 April 1993; Latif Rashid, 6 January 1993; Muwuffuq al-Ruba'i, 4 January, 5 and 6 June 1993; Salah 'Umar al-'Ali, 19 January 1993; Hoshiar Zibari, 15 January 1993. A number of bibliographical sources were also used in the writing of the chapter.

## References

Hanna Batatu, *The Old Social Classes and the Revolutionary Movements of Iraq* (Princeton, 1978).

Majid Khadduri, *Republican Iraq* (Oxford, 1969).

Cardri (ed.), *Saddam's Iraq* (London 1989).

Efrain Karsh and Inari Routsi, *Saddam Hussein – A Political Biography* (New York, 1991).

Edith and E.F. Penrose, *Iraq: International Relations and National Development* (London 1978).

# CHAPTER THIRTEEN

# Attitudes to the West, Arabs and Fellow Iraqis

### *Ayad Rahim*

This survey of attitudes provides a glimpse into the global Iraqi village of exiles, refugees, visitors and political activists. As a US citizen of Iraqi origin I was exposed to various conflicting pressures after 2 August 1990. My political roots are in the progressive, anti-imperialist left and at the time of the invasion of Kuwait I was living in Jerusalem, where I worked for a year and a half as a journalist on behalf of the Palestinian cause. I point out these personal and seemingly tangential facts because I believe my individual journey illustrates the complexity of sentiments, views, attitudes and debates swirling among Iraqis since the Gulf War, and helps put them in context.

## Iraqi Attitudes to the United States and the West

In Jerusalem during the occupation of Kuwait I was not so much moved by the plight of Kuwaitis as caught up with the implications of the Gulf crisis for Palestinians and the possibility that they might gain from a peaceful solution to it. Surrounded by the nationalist, anti-imperialist rhetoric that is the common currency of the Arab world, I always registered my opposition to Saddam Husain. Many Palestinians welcomed his take-over of Kuwait, but I tried to impress upon people the brutality of the man and his regime. I resolved, however, that if it did come to war between Iraq and the US, which I was sure it would not,[1] I would stand with the people of Iraq, but not the Iraqi regime, against the US, and I would want a great number of American soldiers to be killed. This came from a self-proclaimed pacifist.

During the allied bombing of Iraq,[2] the Iraqis I was in contact with (who were living abroad, mostly in the UK and US) watched their television screens ceaselessly and with horror as the raids persisted, day after day, with seemingly no end in sight. We all wondered what was left to be bombed. One friend had written to me beforehand that what had taken thousands of years to build could be destroyed in a few seconds. During the bombing my brother remarked sarcastically that the US would not stop until there was a MacDonalds in Baghdad. It turns out, though, that most Iraqis inside the country viewed things differently.

Many of the refugees I met at the Iraq-Turkey border in May 1991[3] said that when Saddam invaded Kuwait they saw it as an adventure too far and thought that maybe now he would get his come-uppance. These two dozen Kurds and Assyrians all said they had wanted international action against the regime which would include its overthrow. They saw international action as a salvation for their plight, albeit at a very high cost. To this day the US army would almost certainly be welcomed by the overwhelming majority of people in Baghdad and the rest of Iraq, I believe. Iraqis are waiting for a saviour, any saviour to defeat Saddam, no matter the source or the motive. In the Iran-Iraq war, for example, many privately cheered Iraqi defeats in battle. Most living inside the country equate patriotism and the Iraqi state with Saddam and war, and view the defeat of Saddam as an end to war.

Among the first things I am asked by Iraqis, especially those out of Iraq for brief respites abroad,[4] are: 'What are they [the US] going to do?' and 'Are they going to keep him?' meaning: Will the US allow Saddam Husain to stay in power? The belief that the US (and, for many, the CIA in particular) controls everything in the world is still deeply held by many Iraqis. Most who hold this world view see the US as the source of all evil. They feel, for example, that the US-led operation in Somalia was in fact an effort to colonize that country. With the converse view of the US as the omnipotent arbiter of all affairs it is asked, 'Why did America save the Kuwaitis but not us?' Sometimes, after the customary exchange of old and new horror stories from Iraq, it is said, 'Isn't that human rights? Why doesn't America do something about that?' Such idealism, though, is rare among Iraqis. The past twenty years, and especially the eight-year war with Iran, have shattered most ideals with a sobering and brutal reality. Overall, the most common Iraqi response to US involvement in Iraq is: 'Why didn't America complete it?'. That is, continue to prosecute the war to Baghdad and finish off Saddam. The answer most often supplied to that question is a conspiratorial one.

Conspiracy theories and stories abound among Iraqis. The allied bombing campaign and economic sanctions are a deliberate policy by the West to destroy Iraq and its people (particularly the younger generation), including its resources, potential and spirit. Depending on one's religious or political faith this policy is seen as targeted at Islam and Muslims or at the Arab nation. The US came to Saddam's aid during the *intifada* by flying its planes above Iraqi planes to form a protective shield, and by allowing Republican Guards through allied lines to counter-attack against the rebels. Some Iraqis claim that allied troops reached Baghdad at the end of the war and formed a defensive circle around the presidential palace to protect Saddam. The US, and even the rest of the world, want Saddam in place because he serves their interests, such as retention of military bases in the Gulf. Iraq and the US may have been in cahoots from the start. A common refrain heard covertly inside Iraq is: 'Saddam is an American', meaning he is a US agent, doing its bidding in the region. The West is afraid of Shi'is and Islam. Here again, some see Saddam as serving US/Western interests by being not only a countweight to Iran and the Islam it represents, but a future offensive weapon against that state and Islam. By accepting thousands of Iraqi refugees after the war, the US is draining Iraqi brain-power as another piece in its grand plot to destroy Iraq, the Arab nation or Islam. Some go further with regards to US intentions vis-a-vis the refugees. They have been dispersed across the cities of the US to weaken their bonds of solidarity and patriotic and revolutionary spirit. They will be trained by the US government for future use as agents inside Iraq.

What is mainly behind this conspiratorial way of thinking is a cynicism that governs most Iraqis' outlook on the world and drives them to be mistrustful of others' actions. Iraqis are, however, far less conspiratorial in their thinking than they used to be, say ten or fifteen years ago, while the conspiratorial proclivities of other Arabs are becoming more pronounced. The conspiracies outlined above are heard much more often from Arabs of other nationalities than from Iraqis.

This knee-jerk anti-Americanism (the 'Great Satan' view of the West) was evident in Iraqi responses to the August 1991 coup against the Soviet president Mikhail Gorbachev. Many still viewed the ex-Soviet Union as a positive counterweight to US hegemony in the Middle East and its bias on the Palestinian issue. Such people were overjoyed by the coup. They were mainly adherents of the traditional anti-Western (in particular anti-American) Stalinist-type parties and ideological currents that dominated Iraqi politics from the 1940s. That is to say, Communists, Arab nationalists and Islamists. By contrast, others watching the announcement of the 'emergency council' coup against Gorbachev were reminded of the day Saddam Husain was pronouced on Iraqi television as the successor to Ahmad Hasan al-Bakr.[5] In that broadcast in July 1979 the icy long faces of the members of the Revolutionary Command Council (RCC) revealed their knowledge of the horrors taking place, their foreboding of horrors soon to take place away from public view, and their complicity in those horrors. As a result of that memory, some Iraqis (many of them Communists) were moved to tears by the coup against Gorbachev. They were terrified by the prospect of a cycle of terror and violence taking place in the Soviet Union similar to that in Iraq.

Saddam's regime is so discredited inside the country that people tend to disbelieve anything it says and believe the opposite to be true. For example, support for the no-fly zone over the south declared by the Western allies in August 1992 is widespread, despite government proclamations to the contrary. Most Iraqis think the no-fly zone does not go far enough in protecting the residents of the south and weakening Saddam's grip on power. Many were dismayed that the UN and the West compromised in the confrontation over inspection of the Ministry of Agriculture building in July 1992. 'They should not be dealing with him!' one Baghdadi said in Jordan a month later.

On the other hand, most Iraqis wonder what the UN has done for them. Some even wonder what the UN weapons inspectors have achieved. The extreme view is that not a single weapon has been destroyed in the UN-supervised campaign.[6] Those still living under Saddam Husain's rule have not witnessed much in the way of positive change in their lives as a result of UN activities. They continue to be brutally repressed and people are still being butchered. In addition, the previously high standard of living has deteriorated dramatically.

Iraqis are nonetheless friendly to Americans and Westerners in general. An American film-maker who went to Iraq in autumn 1992, and who was often mistakenly thought by Iraqis to be with the UN, noted that when people asked him about his work, they did not express hostility or bitterness towards the UN. 'They were more intereted in talking,' he said, 'and just thirsting for information. They were gracious to us. I didn't fear telling those we meet in the street that I was an American. There was a genuine desire to make contact. They'd bring up politics because I wouldn't.' Things were quite different before the Kuwait crisis. One diplomatic wife observed that throughout her two years in Baghdad, much of which were spent pushing baby-buggies, not a single Iraqi stopped in the street to smile at her babies or utter so much as a 'koochie-koochie-koo'. This was in stark contrast to the friendliness found in other Middle Eastern countries, especially towards children. She concluded: 'They were scared even to be seen talking to babies.'[7]

Another aspect of Iraqi attitudes to the West is the fact that many – especially professionals, educated people, the young, Christians and other minorities – badly want to emigrate to the West. Younger Iraqis in particular are frustrated by life in Iraq and see no hope there for the future, much of which will have to be devoted to reconstruction, not only of the economy and its infrastructure, but also of society and its values, and of individuals.[8]

I believe it is somewhat self-indulgent for Americans, Britons or other Westerners to focus on how they are perceived by Iraqis and then make those perceptions the basis for their behaviour toward Iraq.[9] Whatever the effect of the Gulf War on Iraqi-Western relations, it had a more dramatic and profound effect on relations between Iraqi and non-Iraqi Arabs, and – as I discovered on a trip to Kurdistan in October 1992 – between Iraqi and non-Iraqi Kurds.[10]

## Unfriendly neighbours

I first heard news of the invasion of Kuwait from a Palestinian actor friend who years earlier had been horrifically tortured in a Baghdad prison. I was stupified by the news but did not immediately absorb its significance, and most certainly did not empathize with the Kuwaitis. For several months before the invasion I had been hailed as a hero wherever I went in the West Bank and Gaza Strip. Once strangers learned I was an Iraqi they would call out to me 'Saddam Husain! Saddam Husain!'.[11] After the invasion I was faced daily with Palestinians singing Saddam Husain's praises and extolling his latest deed. The most frequently played song in the outdoor markets of the old city of Jerusalem, through which I walked to work, was 'Oh Saddam, the Hero, the Arabs' Confronter!'. Confronter, or collider, is the literal meaning of the word 'saddam'. On the day of the invasion, it was reported, a flight from London to Amman was 'crowded with Palestinian businessmen drunkenly toasting Saddam Husain'.[12] At the newspaper where I worked a gentle and sensitive middle-aged colleague – whose poetry had been widely published and whom I admired – deeply disappointed me by remarking after one of Saddam's 'linkage' overtures: 'A thousand George Bushes wouldn't be worth a pair of Saddam's shoes.' This same man had responded to my account of conditions in Iraq after a visit in January 1990 by wondering whether Palestinians living under Israeli rule were not better off than Iraqis. Now, in the Gaza Strip, peddlers hawked long loaves of bread as 'Saddam's rockets'. Palestinian friends and acquaintances stopped me in the street – as they had done even before the invasion – to ask when Saddam would use his chemical weapons against Israel. I was infuriated by all of this and replied that I had nothing to do with Saddam; that he was a butcher and a criminal. Even so, I did not take in the enormity of what was happening to Kuwait and its people, something for which I now feel ashamed.[13]

I am not alone among Iraqis in my feelings of alienation towards Palestinians. Most Iraqis have been deeply enraged and disappointed by Palestinian sympathies for Saddam Husain, often expressed enthusiastically, unreservedly and directly to them. I had, since childhood, devoted most of my work, studies, social activities, emotion, energy and hope to the Palestinian cause. Such devotion is not unusual for an Arab. Arabs have been weaned for generations on anti-Zionism and the Palestinian cause. Iraqis in particular have felt deeply committed, possibly because in the past couple of decades they have had to reroute their political energies away from Iraq. My feelings of anger, betrayal and bitterness towards Palestinians were echoed by Iraqi soldiers interviewed by a journalist friend in Amman.

Palestinian friends have made many offensive remarks about Iraq since the invasion of Kuwait. One pointed out that 'Shi'i rebels killed a hundred

Ba'thists in one day, something Saddam Husain didn't do throughout his rule' and that the country would have been far worse off if the rebels had succeeded. Another friend remarked, during the mass exodus of terror-filled Kurds following the failed *intifada*, that he could not believe the Iraqi state would harm its people, as was being alleged. On another occasion, when a special UN report on human rights violations in the south was being highlighted in the news, he wondered why so much attention was being paid to Iraq when massacres were going on in Bosnia. On yet other occasion, he said he could not believe that an operation such as the Anfal campaign could have been carried out.[14] What has pervaded the attitudes of these friends and other Arabs is an assumption of superior knowledge about Iraq and an eagerness to enlighten me on Iraqi affairs.

One possible explanation for such reactions is that the Palestinian cause has been the focus of Arab attention and passion for the past forty years and the Kuwait crisis caused attention to be directed elsewhere. Most Palestinians and their sympathizers did not take kindly to this. But Palestinians are not alone in demanding that attention and sympathy be focused on their plight. Self-pity on the part of Palestinians, Shi'is or Arabs generally is standard fare in the Middle East. Much of it comes from an inability or unwillingness to do something to change one's state of affairs. It is extremely difficult for a person who has a sense of being under attack or victimized to sympathize with another person and their pain. Palestinians cheered when they saw Iraqi bombs flying overhead. Now Israelis would have to run from war and find a safe place to sleep as Palestinians had often had to in the past.

Other Arabs and Muslims (to say nothing of Western leftists) have likewise exhibited what Iraqis perceive as antagonism towards and ignorance of their plight and recent history. For example, one Sudanese man with a doctorate in public health, who had gone to Iraq from the US with the Gulf Peace Team following the war, tried to rationalize to several expatriates the execution of forty-two merchants in Baghdad in July 1992. He also stated that Saddam would have improved, liberalized and democratized the country were it not for the war with Iran.

As a result of the near-monolithic views of Arabs about Iraq, I for one have come to the conclusion that non-Iraqi Arabs just will not understand what Iraqis – Arabs, Kurds and others – have been through, or what it is like to live in Iraq. They simply refuse to believe the facts and the stories. By way of a personal illustration, an Iraqi Kurdish woman living in the US whose husband died in a car accident in autumn 1922 was persistently urged by her Arab friends to take her young children and go to live with her family in Iraq, without her opinion on the matter ever being sought.

On the other hand, while most Arabs and Muslims (and others from the Third World) have become extremely alienated in the West since the Kuwait crisis, most Iraqis have not. One 10-year-old girl in the US, for instance, was able to say in school for the first time, during the Gulf War, that she was part Iraqi, and she spoke about her background and her feelings without any fear of retribution or alienation from her fellow students.

## Kuwait

Kuwait is an issue where differences among Iraqis are well pronounced. Many, including prominent opposition figures, hold firm to the view that Kuwait is historically part of Iraq and that there was just cause for Saddam's invasion. UN Security Council Resolution 773 redraws the Iraq/Kuwait border. Tariq 'Aziz, representing Iraq, told members of the Security Council in November 1992 that Iraq accepted the border but members of the opposition and the Iraqi public at large are divided on the issue. Many refuse to surrender an inch of territory, even if accepting the new border would give outside support for the Iraqi National Congress (INC) in its bid to replace the Saddam regime.[14] In spite of that, the feelings of patriotism and nationalism which lie behind such positions are weak and most people quickly affirm the priority of ousting the regime. Those Iraqis who do have a strong sense of national pride often refuse to believe that Iraqi soldiers – and many Iraqi civilians – systematically looted, vandalized and brutalized Kuwaitis and their country in the way they did. Finally, I have heard only one Iraqi wonder what would have happened – to Kuwait, to Iraq and to the Middle East – if Saddam Husain had succeeded in keeping Kuwait.

## Iraqis Inside

The emotional disposition of Iraqis inside the country can be summed up in two words: desparate and cynical. They are desparate because their conditions are extremely grave. In addition to the accumulated pressure of living under a totalitarian tyranny for more than twenty years, they have suffered economically in the past few years, deprived of the bounty which previously eased the denial of basic human rights. The economic situation is growing worse daily, with the poor scraping along by whatever means are at their disposal and the large middle class falling into relative poverty. Iraqis are cynical because they have been lied to and 'sloganeered to death' by their rulers. Their cynicism is exacerbated by the perception that nobody in the world – not the US, not the West, not the UN and certainly not Arabs – has come to their aid. Above all, they feel, nobody is helping them address the immediate need for improving the situation in Iraq, namely a change in the ruling regime.

Although Iraqis are traditionally a highly politicized and culturally active people, the prison-like existence of life in Iraq has meant that broad swathes of political, social, intellectual and artistic forms of thought and expression have been denied them. It is staggering to contemplate the distance they now have to travel to catch up with some of the most basic social and political developments around the world in such fields as ecology, decentralization and feminism, not to mention the countless theoretical and technical advances in the sciences and arts.

Iraqis have nevertheless chanelled their energies in other directions – mainly career and professional – and developed personal strengths and traits previously untapped in the culture, such as forthrightness, assertiveness and individuality. Meeting the younger generation of Iraqis (recently out of Iraq or in free Iraqi Kurdistan) has been very uplifting for me. They are, on the whole, bright, self-reliant, independent-thinking and extremely resourceful. For example, a refugee who was a Master's student in media studies purchased a computer, as did many others, while in one of the two camps for Iraqis in Sa'udi Arabia. With his computer he carried out research into refugees' religious attitudes and Iraqi opposition radio broadcasts. Previously, while a student at Baghdad University, he had produced his own magazine by taking apart an existing magazine then rearranging the letters and gluing them together as articles, all of which he wrote himself. Private ownership of typewriters and photocopiers is strictly prohibited in Saddam's Iraq. The refugees who began arriving in the US in autumn 1992 have shown themselves to be hard-working, committed and driven individuals. It is possible that through the increased personal strength, individuality and independence resulting from the experience of the Ba'thist years, Iraqis have come to learn that no one can have your interests more at heart than yourself and that you must depend on yourself to achieve what you want. This is an approach to life diametrically opposed to the traditional tribal-based norms that have governed Iraqi society. It has no room for the supremacist notion that Arabs – a once glorious people eternally destined for greatness – are owed much. The Saddam generation have suffered tremendously and experienced tremendous bitterness during this learning process.

Most Iraqis have responded to Saddam Husain's totalitarianism by rejecting, silently, almost every aspect of it. So, for instance, they had no freedom of expression and now they demand total freedom of expression. They had no freedom to travel and now they demand unlimited freedom. Whatever the Ba'th did, people now demand the opposite. The danger here, though, is that this reflexive, uncritical contrariness toward the Saddam Husain and the Ba'th – which is part and parcel of treating them as an evil force alien to the society and imposed from without – does not take a nuanced view of what they have done. The Ba'th aimed to modernize Iraq by creating 'a new man' in 'a new society'. Among positive consequences of their modernization programme have been the improved position of women in terms of access to education and work, higher literacy rates, free and higher standards of education and healthcare, and a general modernization of the economic infrastructure. However, there is no clear view among most Iraqis of the transformations that have taken place in Iraqi society over the past quarter-century. The critical and responsible examination by Iraqis of their society and history, in order to find the roots and causes of the rise to power of a totalitarian Ba'thist regime, is a process that has barely begun.

During the conferences of the Iraqi oppostion abroad, and in discussions among Iraqis the world over, much debate has revolved around the issue of the future leadership of Iraq, and in particular the ethnic identity of that leadership. So, for instance, the most extensive debate at the October 1992 conference of the Iraqi National Congress (INC) in Salah al-Din, in northern Iraq, centred on the number and make-up of something called 'the leadership committee'. The members of this committee would act as representatives of the INC around the world, and as a possible leadership in the transitional period. Much time was spent by delegates at the conference debating the number of members of the committee should have. The initial proposed number was three. It was understood that this meant one Kurd, one Shi'i and one Sunni, although the ethnic and religious identity of the members was not explicitly stated. Secularists called for a single leader. Shi'i Islamists called for a larger committee – demands ranged from four to twelve – in which the proportion of Shi'is would reflect that in the population.[16]

Most Iraqis inside the country, however, do not care who replaces Saddam or what their religious and ethnic identity is. It was reported that one graffito found in Baghdad in 1992 proclaimed: 'No to Saddam. Yes to Shamir.' The prevailing anti-Zionist propaganda was similarly disposed of by a nurse in Karbala' who was filmed shouting in horror at the death and devastation all around her during the massive government bombardment to crush the *intifada* in the south. 'America didn't do it like this,' she cried out, referring to the allied bombing of Iraq. 'America is more honourable. The Jews [meaning Israel] are more honourable.'

Genuine feelings of nationalism and patriotism are rare among Iraqis who have lived inside the country for much of the past twenty years. Many soldiers are ashamed of being Iraqi, perhaps more so than civilians. Quite a few who participated in the failed *intifada* in the south, and then fled to Sa'udi Arabia, have related that they claimed another nationality when asked by people in the streets there. This comes as a great shock to Iraqis outside, who traditionally harbour strong feelings of national pride. Much of this feeling of shame is the standard reaction of a humiliated soldiery. But Iraqi soldiers – many of whose lives have been devastated by upwards of ten years of fighting – have little love for the army. One would be hard pressed to find anybody who wants to fight another war, for any cause.

This contempt for the army was reflected in an initial battle cry of the soldier-sparked intifada in Basra, the day after the Gulf War cease-fire: 'Saddam is finished, all the army is dead.'

## Iraqis Outside

Even the nigh-on two million Iraqis living abroad have been cowed into silence by the Ba'thist regime. Only since the March 1991 *intifada* have they begun to find their voice and strength. Residual effects of state terror and repression remain in almost all of them. Many, especially those with immediate family in the Saddam-ruled part of Iraq, refuse to speak out publicly or have their names associated with anything which could be construed as political, or critical of the regime.

Nevertheless, there has been a tremendous explosion of activity by Iraqis all over the world since the *intifada*. They meet and talk to each other (something they were previously afraid to do). Groups have formed, dozens of newspapers have been founded, conferences have been held. Petitions, manifestos, a bill of rights and a charter have been written, debated and circulated for signatures. Maybe the most significant change sparked in Iraqis by the *intifada* has been that they no longer fear each other.

The fear that previously dominated Iraqis abroad can be illustrated in many ways. Soon after the Gulf War, a conference about the Middle East was held in London by the National Peace Council (NPC), an anti-war coalition. At one women's discussion group half a dozen or so of the participants were Iraqi, all long out of Iraq and settled in the UK. They did not know each other before the discussion began and avoided each other assiduously. They each went to the English woman who had invited them to enquire about the others. At the start of the discussion they were silent but, roused by comments sypathetic to the regime from another participant, they opened up and remarkably similar individual stories of disappearances and torture poured out. After the discussion they began talking to each other enthusiastically. On a personal note, when I was growing up in the US, my siblings and I were under strict instructions from our parents completely to avoid any Iraqis on the college campuses we attended. A relative who migrated to the US in the late 1970s was afraid to talk politics – any politics – for several years after he arrived, even if those present were friends of the family.

Now Iraqis abroad bear the responsibility of speaking on behalf of those inside the country, who cannot speak freely. In March 1991, those inside did speak out, loudly proclaiming their rage and rejection of tyranny. They were quickly stilled. Unfortunately, those outside have been out of touch with the lives and conditions of those inside, cut off from the dramatically changed realities.

As is often the case with émigres, Iraqis abroad tend to live in mini-Iraqs around the world, socializing almost exclusively with fellow Iraqis and attempting to recreate in their daily lives and customs a version of Iraqi life. These mini-Iraqs are inevitably derived from the past. Most people imagine an idealized Iraq that never existed. They are stuck in the common émigre rut which does not allow their native country to evolve in any way that disrupts their idealized image. The fact of the matter is, however, that much has changed in Iraq, particularly in people's ways of thinking and behaving. Iraqis abroad, divorced from that changed reality, often project their romanticised views and ideologies on Iraqis inside through their pronouncements and actions concerning the country's condition and future.

On the other hand, many émigrés, especially those who have left Iraq only recently, have immersed themselves in the social and political history of modern Iraq. To some, this immersion seems an obsession, as if they are unable get out of their systems the years of Ba'thist rule through which they have lived. They want to know as much as possible about what actually happened in Iraq; devouring information and analysing past events and behavioural patterns.

## All Iraqis

For all Iraqis, the genie is out of the bottle. It seems beyond the realms of possibility that they will return to the submissiveness of the past. They are tired of war, of fighting, of confrontation, of chasing illusory dreams. They now tend to be much more honest about their world: more realistic, pragmatic and up-front, and far less absolutist and sloganeering than they were in the past. For example, a young man who arrived in Amman from Baghdad soon after the war and *intifada* was met by Jordanians and Palestinians eulogizing Saddam and Iraq. He would have none of their glorification and hyperbole and derided their notions of 'the beauty of Baghdad' and 'the greatness and glory of the Iraqi people' by decribing the facts on the ground.

One phenomenon I've observed among Iraqis is an increased polarization on a range of issues and attitudes. Chief among these are religious faith and the tribalist or particularist-versus-universalist divide. While many have 'found religion' or become more religious in the face of increased powerlessness, voicelessness and hopelessness, others have lost their faith and become religiously sceptical.[17] People who fled from Saddam's retaliation against the *intifada* by seeking refuge in the holy shrines of Karbala' and Najaf, and the Kadhimain mosque in Baghdad, did not expect to be attacked within those religious sanctuaries, which presumably would be protected by God. In fact, not only were they bombed and the shrines, cemeteries and libraries devastated, but the Islamic world and the victims' Islamic brethren did almost nothing in response to the outrage. Furthermore, almost all the predominantly Muslim states – including Indonesia, Malaysia and the north African countries – which were offered an exhibition documenting Iraq's human rights violations turned it down. The sole exceptions – and not without much prompting – were Egypt and Pakistan.[18] I was told that one Iraqi refugee who prayed seventy-two times a day when he first arrived in Sa'udi Arabia after the *intifada,* was praying no longer when he flew to the US a year and a half later.

Just as there has occurred polarization in matters of religious faith, so, too, have Iraqis been pulled to extremes of nationalist sentiment. A minority have become more patriotic and proud of being Iraqi. They seek the company and comfort of like-minded Arabs abroad to support them in the face of the great humiliation suffered by Iraq, which is seen by many as a blow to Arab dignity. As one friend put it, in response to the January 1993 bombings and to the UN weapons inspections which she perceived as invasive, 'Iraq has become like a thing to be slapped around'. Such people listen avidly to Arab music and prefer to eat Arab food. Others have reacted in the opposite direction, turning away from all things Iraqi and Arab and reaching out to other cultures and influences.

While most Arabs have continued to blame the West and Israel for their maladies, many Iraqis have been looking inward, exploring themselves and Iraqi society for clues as to how and why Iraq got into such a mess. However, most Iraqis – and I've witnessed this particularly among those living abroad – are not facing up to their historic responsibility for the country's current condition. They would rather treat the ruling regime (and thereby the catastrophe it has brought upon the country) as a foreign creation imposed from outside. They do this, of course, because it is simply much easier and more comforting to deal with an external cause for one's problems than to look within for faults and causes. Saddam Husain is seen as a monster, alien to the society and culture, inflicted upon Iraqis by non-Iraqis. Suspicions that the CIA backed the 1963 Ba'thist coup are often dredged out to support this viewpoint.

In a critique of a television programme about Joseph Stalin, the American reviewer John Leonard said, 'The monster theory is just the great-man theory turned upside down: the devil made them do it'. The view contrary to the monster theory was expressed by one Iraqi, a Kurd, who said, 'All of us are Saddam.' His wife elaborated; 'We're all dictators. We think we're right and everybody else is wrong, and when we come to power we impose our will on everybody else. We grow up with this attitude from the time we're little children. We don't have democracy in our tradition, we're not raised in democratic ways and our schools aren't democratic.'

Iraqi, and especially Baghdadi, life and society have traditionally been characterized by social inter-mixing and marriage across ethnic and confessional lines. Iraqis are rightly proud of that tradition but it has been on the decline since the early 1980s. Accompanying that decline has been a rising resentment and a vague, nebulous and growing rift between Sunni Arabs and the rest of the population. A strong underlying possibility exists of sectarian and ethnic strife in a post-Saddam Iraq. There are in Iraq not only the pent-up resentments of the historically 'out' groups – similar to those that sparked the Lebanese civil war – but also layer upon layer of brutal treatment by Ba'thists, whose leaders are mainly Sunni Arabs. The pain of that treatment has been suppressed over the years and is now bursting to be expressed. Vengeance lurks in peoples' hearts, waiting for an opportunity to explode, as it did during the March 1991 *intifada*, when Ba'th Party members, torturers, informers, interrogators and others were crucified, decapitated and dismembered, and tortured into confessing their political allegiance and identity.

Most Iraqis, particularly members of minority groups, harbour fears of that explosion taking place and agree it would be on a grand and bloody scale. However, this fear goes mostly unexpressed, for to express it would be to acknowledge the presence in each of us of a large reservoir of hatred and violence. Acknowledging that Iraqis have prejudices and sectarian sentiments shatters an illusion held by many. But in fact Iraqis can be both chauvinist and racist in their attitudes and behaviour. For example, anti-Jewish diatribes and conspiracy theories about Jews and Israel are rampant among them. I not only hear frequently the unquestioned mantras of 'Jewish control' of the Western media, 'Jewish manipulation' of the US government, and Israel 'calling the shots' around the world, but have also been told at times, 'Remember who your enemy is!'. Stereotyping of Kurds, most prevalent in the form of ubiquitous and demeaning 'Kurdish jokes', is the rule, with Kurds generally cast by Arabs as the epitome of stupidity and bumbling. Kurds have similar jokes about Arabs.

Perhaps most significantly, the pains and fears of minorities, women and other individuals – including Ba'th Party members and security personnel – go unrecognized and unacknowledged by the majority Shi'is, who will shoulder much of the responsibility of leadership in a future Iraq. In the course of a discussion with relatives about why the suffering of Shi'is has not been much represented in the West, I ventured to claim that during the first fifteen to twenty years of Ba'thist rule many Sunni Arabs were subjected to political persecution. In response it was said, 'The Shi'is have been persecuted more than the Kurds ever have' and 'For every Sunni Arab killed, one thousand Shi'is have been killed.' The need to consider the pains and fears of minorities also applies in relation to Turcomen, Assyrians, Armenians, Yazidis and others within the predominantly Kurdish northeast of the country.

Sectarianism, while not dealt with openly, nevertheless surfaces in social interaction. Shi'is, who make up the majority of Iraq's population, say things to each other, often about Sunnis, that they would not dare to say in the company of a Sunni (and vice versa, I am told). Shi'is in the Rafha refugee camp in Sa'udi Arabia purified the camp first of non-Islamic opposition elements and then of 'immoral' individuals. After this the several hundred Sunnis in the camp felt they could no longer stay and asked the Sa'udi authorities to remove them.[19]

With regard to Kurds, Iraq's largest minority, Arab Iraqis acknowledge their special suffering, but they still relate to them in an arrogant and bigoted manner. Added to that there is the resentment and jealousy they harbour – Sunnis as well as Sh'is – because of the attention, sympathy and support which Kurds have elicited worldwide. This resentment and jealousy can be found in some of the brightest and most kind-hearted of people, individuals whom I would expect to be able to see beyond their 'tribe's' affliction and take a broader view of things. Instead, some people – and this applies to Assyrians and Turcomen as well as Arabs – wince at the mention of atrocities against Kurds, such as the 1988 Anfal campaign of genocide. They tend to comdemn such reports as focusing too much attention on them.

Another point of bitterness among many Arab Iraqis is the Kurds' negotiations with the regime, symbolized by the kissing of Saddam by top Kurdish leaders at the outset of those negotiations in April 1991. It is possible that anti-Kurdish sentiments are more common abroad than inside Saddam-controlled Iraq. Only a few illustrative incidents have come to my notice, but I believe they are significant. A Kurdish woman studying at Baghdad University related when she was in Kurdistan that she had been berated by her Arab fellow students for not voting in the Kurdish elections in May 1992.[20] Some young Arab Iraqis who have only recently left Iraq greatly admire what the Kurds have achieved for themselves and express no qualms about Kurds separating and establishing their own country.

An ominous sign of how sectarianism may develop is the fact that more and more Iraqis have been retreating into particular clans or sects. This tendency was encouraged by the regime following the *intifada*, in an effort to increase fear and suspicion, and thereby gain support for its rule from frightened minorities, and on grounds of national unity. The retreat into clannishness has caused many to see a multi-ethnic and diverse society as untenable, not recognizing what the American author Dorothy Allison calls 'the energy [that] comes from contradiction.' Clannishness has been long in the making in Iraq. Tony Horwitz recorded the effect of fear and atomization on one particular Baghdadi who, like most Iraqis, had stopped seeing anyone but his family and closest friends. 'Who else can I trust?' he asked rhetorically. 'And can I even trust them?' This man had earlier told Horowitz in his office, after raising the volume on his radio: 'My phone is tapped. This office is bugged. For all I know my grandmother is wired for sound.'[21]

Iraqis probably have Saddam Husain to thank for making them more assertive, self-confident and honest individuals. Most Iraqis are better, stronger people for having survived what they have been through. They are more outgoing than they used to be, less afraid to speak out and be themselves. For although Iraqis have not been free to speak out about their reality, they have had it laid before them. Saddam Husain can rightly be regarded as the man who awoke Iraqis from their twenty-year slumber and launched them on a process of exploration and self-examination.

## Notes

1. This belief was representative of most Arabs' sense of reality at the time. A United Nations political officer in New York (who previously worked for seven years at the UN Division of Palestinian Rights) told me in August 1992 that she was astonished that all her Arab colleagues at the UN were absolutely convinced, following the invasion of Kuwait, that there would not be war over it, while all her non-Arab colleagues were certain there would be.

2. I had left Jerusalem on 10 January 1991 (seven days before the allied bombing began) to placate my parents' fears for my safety. I was still certain there would not be war and wanted to stay in Jerusalem with Palestinians, even if it came to war. As a conciliatory step, my partner and I decided to go to Egypt for a couple of weeks until the whole affair blew over and then return to our work in 'Palestine'. I finally sensed the onset of war only two days before the bombing began, from which point I longed to be with Iraqis. After Egypt I spent two weeks in the UK, the duration of the war in the US, and I have moved between the UK and the US since then, mainly spending time with Iraqis.

3. These were among the 2 million Iraqis who escaped Iraq in the terror-filled mass exodus that followed the failed *intifada* of March 1991, creating the largest refugee crisis since the Second World War.

4. Over the course of the crisis I met with Iraqis in Jordan, the UK, the US, and northern Iraq.

5. Bakr was pushed out of power in a silent coup on the pretext of poor health. The coup quickly turned into a bloody purge of hundreds of top party officials who had exhibited insufficient enthusiasm for Saddam.

6. Almost all Iraqis who have lived inside Iraq in the past twenty years welcome the destruction of the country's military capability. A small minority, however, continues to cling to the notion still dominant in the Arab world that military might is the gauge of one's strength, self-worth and value, and is especially necessary in 'the struggle against Israel'.

7. Tony Horwitz, *Baghdad Without a Map and other misadventures in Arabia*, Plume, 1992. p 108

8. For more on the alienation and depoliticization of young, educated Iraqis, see the excellent article by Andrea Lorenz, 'What Young Iraqis Don't Dare Say to Each Other: Iraq's apolitical generation', *The Washington Report on Middle East Affairs*, August/September 1991.

9. On this and on the necessity for the Left and people from the Third World to change their views of the US and transform their working relationships with it,

see Fred Halliday's seminal article, 'Yankee Doodle Dandy', *Marxism Today*, August 1991.

10. Non-Iraqi Kurds appeared to resent the worldwide attention and sypathy elicited by Iraqi Kurds, and their accomplishments. See below for a discussion of the parallel resentments and jealousies of Palestinians (and other Arabs) as a result of attention being drawn away from the Palestinian issue by the occupation of Kuwait.

11. Although I heard about another non-Jewish Iraqi living in Israel/Palestine (a woman married to a Palestinian resident of the West Bank, I was told), I did not meet any. I did meet many Jewish Iraqis, however, which was a novel and thrilling experience for me.

12. Horwitz, p267

13. I even wrote an article about human rights conditions in occupied Kuwait based on the accounts of eyewitnesses who were interviewed in Amman for Human Rights Watch by Muna Rishawi, a Palestinian lawyer. The accounts showed the behaviour of the Iraqis to be almost benign, but Ms Rishawi urged that they be put into the context of the Human Rights Warch overall report, which was based on a larger and wider pool of interviews and was much more damning of Iraqi behaviour in Kuwait.

14. 'Anfal' was the official Iraqi government code-name for a campaign that began in February 1988 with the explicit purpose of eliminating all life in the rural areas of Iraqi Kurdistan. During the eight months of the planned, systematic and well-documented campaign – which was only halted because of excessive foreign media attention – some 1,200 villages were destroyed. Almost all were Kurdish but many were Assyrian. Between 100,000 and 300,000 people disappeared. All are presumed dead, having been shot and buried in mass graves along the Iraqi/Sa'udi border.

15. The Iraqi National Congress (INC) was founded in June 1992 with a conference held in Vienna which was boycotted by Iraqis based in Iran, Syria and Sa'udi Arabia. The INC's second conference, which was not boycotted by any major party, was held in Salah al-Din, in Iraqi Kurdistan, in October 1992, the first broad public meeting of Iraqi opposition forces on Iraqi soil.

16. It is also interesting to note here the understanding of some Shi'is and other Iraqis of the meaning of democracy. One often hears among Shi'is that if democracy is allowed to function in Iraq, then a Shi'i and Shi'is will rule the country, and for that reason the West will not permit democracy in Iraq.

17. The Iraqi brand of religiousity is notoriously mild and not puritanical. Alcohol is widely and publicly sold and consumed in much of Iraq (excepting the holy cities of Najaf and Karbala'). Moreover, even among devoutly religious people, music is rarely prohibited, and religious taboos against such things as men and women shaking hands are observed more by emigres than by Iraqis who have lived inside the country over the years. In addition, it is not uncommon to find within a family communists and Islamists, secularists and believers.

18. I was told about these rejections by an former Iraqi diplomat who toured with the exhibition in 1992.

19. This sequence of events was related to me with pride by an Iraqi refugee soon after he arrived in the US from the Rafha camp.

20. Story told by Laurie Mylroie, who interviewed the woman on a trip to Kurdistan in autumn 1992.

21. Horwitz, p 11.

# CHAPTER FOURTEEN

# Intolerance and Identity[1]

## Kanan Makiya ('Samir al-Khalil')

## Intolerance

Intolerance became an issue in Western culture and political thought in the shape of religious intolerance, and in the Judaeo-Christian tradition the archetypal form of religious intolerance was anti-semitism. Today we think of intolerance as being national, ethnic, tribal, communal, ideological, political, racial, personal and sexual. It has, or rather it should have, all these different forms in the sensibilities of a modern man or woman. But the original form in which human beings appropriated the idea of intolerance and made it part of their common cultural inheritance is religious intolerance, beginning in particular with anti-semitism. During the sixteenth and seventeenth centuries religious intolerance, which had started in the history of the West with the persecution of a defenceless minority on the margins of social life in medieval Christendom, came to a head with the outbreak of religious wars all over Europe. Now intolerance was touching everyone.

In looking at intolerance in the modern Middle East, it is useful and important to remind ourselves what a wild and cruel place Europe became in the seventeenth century. Germany lost half its population. Whole tracts of land were laid waste, along with all their villages and the people in them. The impress of all of this destruction could still be felt in German culture and politics in the twentieth century. Religion was the only possible ideology. Yet the attempts to suppress religious dissent always failed in practice. In the meantime, in the name of Catholic, Protestant or Huguenot ideals, ordinary people died like flies. Everyone was threatened and it looked like no one had a future. Above all, absolutely no value was placed on human life.

However, towards the end of this most intolerant of all centuries – bar only our own twentieth century – and as a reaction to all the devastation and destruction of the previous hundred years, a wonderful new idea was born – that of toleration. This new idea came into the world suddenly, hard on the heels of all of Europe's woes. Within a very short time, it seems to have taken root. The new idea was and remains deceptive in its utter simplicity. If devotion could not be suppressed, the thought went, maybe it could be accommodated in a new kind of political structure, one which separated out the spheres of private belief and political obligation. The new idea developed by thinkers like John Locke and Voltaire was that of placing the highest possible value on forbearance or putting up with things that one does not actually like and may consider to be immoral or possibly even evil in some way. (No one tolerates what they actually enjoy or positively approve of.)

For toleration to arise, the thought went, two things needed to combine in a person's mind. First, I must believe that your soul is going to roast in hell because of the false gods that you happen to believe in. Second, I must also believe that there is a higher value in my putting up with this sorry state of affairs than there is in my attempting to shed your blood in the always noble attempt to save your soul through the application of my steel and fire.

In other words, toleration begins in modern Western thought with the impulse for survival -- survival in the face of a dramatic upward surge in the periodic tendency of our species to rush pell mell towards its own self-destruction. Voltaire put it beautifully. Toleration, he said, arises 'as a necessary consequence of our being human. We are all products of frailty; fallible and prone to error. So let us mutually pardon each other's follies. This is the first principle of all human rights.' Toleration in its deepest essence is founded on this view of human nature, a view that, in the nature of things, impresses itself most urgently upon us at the moments of our greatest destructiveness.

### The modern Middle East

How does this apply to the modern Middle East? Through the historical prism sketched above, consider the countries of the Mashreq, east of Egypt. In recent years, these have become as violent and wild a place as Europe was in the seventeenth century. Cruelty is rampant in all those countries of the Mashreq that experienced wars, civil wars, occupations, collective punishments, armed guerrilla organizations, national liberation movements, terrorist attacks, mass deportations, and expanding state bureaucracies for whom the principle of torture is always the norm.

In Hama, Syria, during one month in 1982, 20-40,000 people died. How did they die? The army had encircled the town, supposedly to crush an Islamic rebellion. The rebels and ordinary citizens flooded into the old quarter known as the Kaylania district. This was an extraordinarily beautiful part of the old city, with catacombs and twisted alleyways, a kind of casbah of the eastern Mediterranean. There the people hid. The army surrounded them and pounded the area with artillery until it all turned to rubble. A friend of mine, a Hamawi, who had fled all of this destruction in 1982 and stayed abroad for ten years, finally plucked up the courage to return to Hama in 1991. He went to Kaylania where he had been brought up as a child. He looked at what he thought was his neighbourhood from the other side of the river. At first he thought he was in the wrong place. The sight that confronted him was both familiar and terribly unfamiliar. He shut his eyes and tried to imagine the scene in his mind's eye as he knew it ought to look. Then he opened them and looked once again. Yes, no doubt about it, he was looking at the old neighbourhood of Kaylania. But instead of all the beautiful old houses with their twisted alleyways and underground pathways, there was a bald hill; a modern Syrian urban park. And rising up out of the middle of this hill, which entombed 20-40,000 dead Hamawis, many of whom he might have known in happier days, my friend saw a brand new eleven-storey Meridien hotel.

It is a fact that 3,642 car bombs exploded during the Lebanese civil war. The official casualty toll for fifteen years of civil strife is 144,240 killed, 197,506 wounded and 17,415 still missing. All this in a tiny country of three million people, one-third of whom have now emigrated to the West.

In the progressive and forward-looking country of South Yemen, on the morning of 13 January 1986, while tea was being served to the fifteen members of the ruling politburo, President 'Ali Nassir initiated a gang-land-style massacre of his rivals. One of the guards holding the leader's Samsonite attaché case whipped out his Skorpion machine pistol, and began raking the minister of defence up and down his back with bullets. Two weeks of street fighting then ensued, which left 13,000 dead, with many bloated bodies lying in the streets. The sad thing is that most Arabs have forgotten that this happened. Hardly anyone bothers to write or talk about it.

After liberation, Kuwait not only expelled its 300,000-strong Palestinian community – most of whom never knew Palestine or any country other than Kuwait – but semi-official vigilante groups hunted down hundreds if not thousands of Palestinians after liberation and arbitrarily arrested them. If they did not 'disappear' it was because they had been gunned down in public or tortured and killed. It is as though the Kuwaitis were intent on doing to the Palestinians what the Iraqis had done to them during the occupation.

Which brings me finally to the subject of Iraq. Over an eight-year period, the Iran-Iraq war cost between half a million and one million dead. These numbers are proportionally the same as the number of French dead in the First World War. A visit to those extraordinary cemeteries in France, with their rows of perfectly planned white crosses stretching out into the horizon as far as the eye can see, gives some idea of the scale of the human devastation caused by the Iran-Iraq war.

While the Iraqi and Iranian dead were accumulating, thousands of Kurdish villages were being wiped out by the Iraqi government in a zone which starts 140 kilometres from Baghdad. Between 1986 and 1988, just under 2,000 villages were destroyed. Altogether, since 1975 something like 3,500 villages have been wiped out in northern Iraq. During a period of seven months in 1988, in the course of the so-called Anfal operations, at least 150,000 non-combatant Kurds were murdered in a systematically organized government campaign which bears the hallmarks of genocide. This is the regime that so many Arab intellectuals thought was going to help them to liberate Palestine.

## Language of silence

What on earth is going on here? What is the meaning of this unprecedented high level of cruelty and intolerance reached in the modern Middle East? It was not always like this, and there are many, many factors involved. But I do want to ask one question. Have Arab intellectuals confronted this rising curve of cruelty in the Mashreq in anything like the way in which their seventeenth-century European counterparts did? Have they responded to their own drive towards self-destruction with anything like the thoughts of a Voltaire? Unfortunately the answer is that they have not, at least not yet. Instead of recognizing their own fallibility and frailty, Arabs have, on the contrary, been perfecting in the last quarter of a century a different kind of language, one that is constantly preoccupied with blaming others, in particular blaming the West and Israel for problems that are largely – although not completely – of their own making.

This language of blaming everyone other than oneself for one's tragic plight has intersected in a doubly tragic way with rising cruelty in the Middle East. As in Europe during the seventeenth century, when cruelty and fanaticism were rampant, everyone in the Middle East today feels threatened. Not only religious minorities and ethnic groups but also entire religious majorities and ethnic groups (Shi'is in Iraq; Sunnis in Syria; Kurds everywhere; Israelis; Palestinians under Israeli occupation and all over the diaspora; Maronites; Shi'is in Lebanon). When one feels threatened, regardless of whether or not the perceived threat is real, one has the choice of responding by reaching out in a spirit of reconciliation as Voltaire and others did, or turning inwards in a spirit of bitterness and recrimination. Unfortunately the Mashreq today is a world in which everybody is a victim, but more importantly most people, including in particular most intellectuals – Palestinian, Iraqi, Syrian, Israeli and Lebanese – think like victims.

I began by listing different types of intolerance: religious, racial, national, ethnic, all of which have become part of the modern vocabulary of a modern cosmopolitan intellectual regardless of his or her nationality. It is now time to add to that list a new kind of intolerance, one that arises in a particularly acute and painful way from the experience of the Middle East. I am talking about the intolerance that arises as a consequence of being a victim and thinking like a victim. Or, to put it differently, the intolerance that arises because all of us, Arabs and Israelis, constantly perceive ourselves to be victimized by others. Nothing lends itself to escalating levels of cruelty and intolerance in the Middle East as much as this.

If you attack someone for being him- or herself, the natural response for that person is to assert that he or she *is* the very thing that is being attacked. Such attacks in Europe in the interwar years against Jews heightened and politicized Jewish self-consciousness, facilitating the creation of the State of Israel in 1948. Then Palestinian nationalism was forged and hammered into the prickly and defensive thing that we see today in the crucible of its denial by Zionism. The harsher Israeli occupation policies became, the more the Palestinians grew in upon themselves and the less expansive and outward-reaching they became. These are perfectly natural, all too human responses to denial of identity through aggression. Unfortunately, however, they are also breeding grounds for nationalist, religious and ethnic fanaticism accompanied by a weakening of state ties of loyalty and allegiance. The unity of Iraq today, like that of Lebanon yesterday, is threatened by these same forces. The spiralling logic of violence in the Middle East in recent years is therefore both cause and effect of the increasing inability of individuals and political groups to establish an identity for themselves that is not exclusively reactive and hostile to others in its origins. An identity founded upon hate and the absence of empathy with the other is, to my way of seeing things, a kind of disease. In the hands of intellectuals this language of victimhood, this constant searching for someone else to blame, I call a language of silence: silence over cruelty.

What happened to my generation, the generation of Arab intellectuals brought up on the *nakdha*, the Arab defeat in the six-day war? Why didn't we rise up to the challenge of the growing cruelty of our world the way our seventeenth-century counterparts in Europe did? Why did we choose silence? Could it be that we didn't take the critique of our world far enough after 1967? Or, maybe the problem was that we went a little bit too far, breaking more taboos than society could bear – I don't really know. I have no hard and fast answers to these questions. The fact that we spoke so many different languages at the time – Marxism, Nasserism, Ba'thism, Palestinian nationalism; as well as Arabic, English and French – did not matter as things turned out. For, like intersecting circles, these ways of describing the world kept meeting on the same bit of common ground. When the boundaries of the circles began to rot and crumble away, all that remained was 'we are Arabs' or 'we are Muslims', and 'there is Israel', and 'this is the Palestinian cause' – the one and only cause of every Arab. That, if one stops to think about it, is not enough. In the end these turned out not to be different languages at all; they turned out to be a poverty of ideas, a vacuum of language. In the end Lebanon was lost; Iraq dissolved into eight years of carnage; Kuwait was invaded, sacked and annexed; and the Palestinian movement, which was the hope of so many Arabs, supported to the hilt the greatest tyrant modern Arab politics has ever known. I submit that we Arab intellectuals who generated those ideas – not that unsavoury collection of tyrannies, monarchies and autocracies that wielded the guns – we are the ones whom the next generation of young Arabs must hold principally accountable for the moral collapse of their world.

Silence of the kind I am trying to define is not born out of fear; it is born out of the poverty of thought which is itself created by an impoverishment of feeling, the all too natural consequence of so much cruelty and so much violence. Our vacuum turned out to be a spiritual vacuum, but one which could never be filled by religious belief alone. Silence is what Salman Rushdie in *Midnight's Children* called the 'hole in my heart'. And the politics of silence is that bizarre state of affairs that allows so many very fine Arab minds to meet under one umbrella in defence of 'the rights' of a tyrant not one of them would ever dream of living under. The fact that such a meeting place not only existed, but for a short while at least became so vast, holding in one terrifying embrace so many different and well-educated Arabs – this fact is the principal obstruction to the emergence of toleration as Voltaire defined it.

Arab silence is first and foremost a loss of empathy with the other, a retreat from the public realm into the comforting but suffocating embrace of smaller and smaller units of identity, like tribe, religion, sect and family allegiances. Silence is a synonym for the death of compassion in the Arab world; it is the politics of not washing your dirty laundry in public while gruesome cruelties and whole worlds of morbidity unfold all around you. Silence is choosing, ostrich-like, not to know what Arab is doing to fellow Arab, all in the name of a knee-jerk anti-Westernism which has turned into a sickness. Health 'is infinite and expansive in mode', reaching out 'to be filled with the fullness of the world', wrote Oliver Sacks. If so, then Arab silence is like a disease, 'finite and reductive in mode'. It is the language of a narcissistic inwardness, endeavouring always to reduce the world to reflections of oneself. Silence in the Arab world is intolerance; it is first and foremost silence over the cruelty that has become the norm in the Middle East.

A leader like Saddam Husain, who is in so many ways the principle of Arab cruelty incarnate, thrives on the silence of the Arab intelligentsia towards cruelty. In fact I say he is *created by that silence*. Intellectuals have a special responsibility because they created the discourse of silence. Silence is a way of talking, of writing; above all it is a way of thinking which obfuscates and covers up the cruelty that should today be a central preoccupation of those people who make talking, writing and thinking their business. Breaking with this silence is the moral obligation of every Arab, in particular the 'intellectuals' among us. Nothing else is of comparable importance – not even the 'struggle against Israel'. For all of us who love and identify with this corner of the world, it isn't easy or nice to say such things. That doesn't make them any the less true.

I do not attempt to grapple with the complicated question of how we got into such a terrible state. That kind of a project needs distance and takes years. The graves of the dead are still open in the Arab world. Maybe it isn't even possible for the proper distance to be had today. It is enough to know that things didn't have to turn out this way. And it is enough to know that we Arabs still hold in our own hands the key to reversing silence. The first step out of the morass is the ruthless and radical one of uprooting, from deep within our own sensibilities, the intellectual and moral authority that 'blaming' someone else still carries today among us. For only upon its demise can a healthy, multi-dimensional and pluralist conception of community be born. Intolerance will only go away in the Arab world when we peoples of the Middle East become incensed at the unacceptably cruel state of our world; when we become so unreasonably revolted as to lose every vestige of shame, speaking out without caring who is listening, or to what nefarious use some people will inevitably put our words.

## Identity

How does the act of speaking out or writing intersect with the most fundamental question any human being can ask of him- or herself: Who am I? I will begin by way of a personal incident. An article was published in one of the Arabic London dailies criticizing my views in the aftermath of the Gulf War. It was written by someone I do not know, who claims in the article that he used to be a great admirer of my book *Republic of Fear* – until I was exposed by my political positions. This is what he wrote:

> Were you [Samir al-Khalil] thinking of visiting your original country, Iraq, carrying your American passport after your American army had installed itself there? You have no right to speak of Iraq and of those who live in it. Iraq and its people are as innocent of you as the wolf is innocent of the blood of Yusif. You sit in the lap of luxury and in your hand is paper and pencil. This is all that you own. As for feeling and compassion [for Iraq], of that you have none. You should have denounced the attack which sent Iraq back into the twelfth century. Instead, you asked the barbarians to finish what they had started.[2]

The writer of this newspaper article has thrown down a challenge; a challenge which, it so happens, contains all the big questions raised by the issues of universalism, identity and the writer in the Arab world.

What is the connection between the passport one holds, the views one expresses, the books one writes, and one's innermost emotional and belief system which is of course what constitutes one's identity? It so happens I don't have an American passport. Nor have I ever had one. However, after years of working hard at it, I succeeded in freeing myself from the restrictions imposed by that great bane of fourteen years of my adult life, that ball and chain upon my freedom: my Iraqi passport. To be perfectly candid, the day I received the letter granting me British nationality in 1982 was one of the happiest in my life. Although I was fortunate enough to know what freedom was in many ways, on that day I tasted it. And it tasted delicious. Now I could travel without restrictions, whether those imposed by the Iraqi state or those imposed by harsh immigration policies and the occasional racist officer at Heathrow airport. Never again would I have to go to an Iraqi embassy, posting friends at the corner of the street to check up on whether or not I came out again. Many Iraqis, Syrians, and Palestinians in forced or voluntary conditions of diaspora and exile will identify with this experience.

And yet there is an unwritten rule among us Arabs that one is not supposed to speak or write about such things, as I am doing now. There is shame attached to changing one's passport; it is perceived to be an act of betrayal of some kind. That is what the author of the article meant when he wrote the words 'your American passport' and 'your American army'. The same notions of betrayal long ago found their way into the Iraqi legal system, which very explicitly associates nationality with private belief. I am a traitor, not a citizen, in the eyes of the Iraqi republic. The state will not renew my Iraqi passport and it has other laws which legitimate violence against my person because of the demonstrable fact – proven by my books – that I think non-Ba'thist thoughts.

So who am I? Am I an Arab intellectual? I write in English and that is sometimes held against me. What is an Arab or 'pro-Arab' intellectual? Why is it that we do not hear about 'pro-French' or 'pro-Latin American' intellectuals? Because they do not exist. Borges and García Márquez think of themselves as writers from Argentina and Colombia. One reads them (or not) largely because of what or how they write, not because of where they come from or the views they hold. Then there are specialists in the work of such writers who are interested in looking for connections and common preoccupations, but who would never imagine themselves as 'pro' or 'anti' Latin America. This is not the case with writers from or about the Middle East, who more often than not choose to project themselves and their work as 'Arab', 'Palestinian', or 'pro-Arab' in the politically charged connotations of those labels. As an old Palestinian friend of mine who is constantly shuttling between conferences once put it: 'I have turned into a professional Palestinian.' He was aware of the problem; most Arab and 'pro-Arab' writers are not.

The very existence of such labels is a sign of how degraded the intellectual climate on anything to do with Middle East politics has become, both in the Arab world and in the West. I think of the poisoned atmosphere inside some Middle East studies departments, especially in American universities, where the Arab-Israeli conflict often gets replayed in the pettiest of forms. Semi-professional clubs and informal networks of 'pro-Arab' and 'pro-Israel' cliques have come into being in academic life, each of which worships at a particular shrine and each of which has its childish taboos. These islands of boredom in their predictability create stereotypes far more effectively than the Western media, which at worst simply reiterate them.

Who is an Arab intellectual? This is harder to pin down than one would think, because there are no longer any coherent socio-cultural criteria which combine the quality of being an Arab with an interacting intellectual community such as one finds in a single country like Egypt. 'Arab intellectuals, or intellectuals from among the Arabs?' asks another writer in the same Arabic daily from which I quoted earlier and which supported the Iraqi regime all through the Gulf crisis. It is a good question, which the questioner succeeds in answering very poorly: 'How can a writer be an Arab intellectual, a carrier of Arabic culture as long as he footnotes his article, study or book with references that have not the remotest connection to Arabic, neither in language nor in culture nor in thought?'

Behind such a question is the bigoted assumption, widespread among us Arab intellectuals, that there is a hermetically sealed, *uniquely Arab nexus* between how one thinks and who one is, the same nexus that we encountered at the beginning: I am not *who* I think I am; I am *how* I think. Even Arabs who write in Arabic may no longer 'be' Arabs, because they read non-Arabic books and do not rely solely on Arab sources. The emphasis is not even the old classical one on language; it is on 'being' an Arab because one behaves or thinks like one, whatever these are supposed to mean. Even the Arabness of an Egyptian intellectual publishing in Arabic in Egypt can be considered suspect if he didn't take 'the right' position during the Gulf War or when Sadat visited Jerusalem. So what am I if I happen to write in English, and if I have lived largely in the West for the last quarter of a century? Who am I? And what about that burgeoning motley collection of exiles from all over the Fertile Crescent who live in Paris and London and New York, and write in Arabic for dailies, magazines and journals which are published in London and appear simultaneously in the kiosks of captial cities all over the world?

We Arabs have got ourselves tangled up in knots over these kinds of issues. Iraqis, even those who wish me well, sometimes ask: 'Who do you write for?' They want to know whether I write to please a Western audience or as an Iraqi, 'on behalf of the people of Iraq'. Others were upset when I made a film about the Kurds which revealed the scale of the Anfal operations. 'Aren't you a Shi'i?' they ask me. 'Why don't you write about us? We are suffering too.' The assumption behind the question is again that one is who one writes for, and that one writes only for who one is. All of these are polite ways of getting at the same problem as those non-Iraqi Arab-Americans or Palestinians who think of Samir al-Khalil as a 'self-hating Arab' who enjoys writing critically of the Arab world merely in order to curry favour in the West.

'I write for myself, like everyone else', is the confusing answer. By this I mean that writing has become the most important thing in the world to me. In fact you could say I am prepared to go to considerable lengths in the act of doing it. But it is not always clear to me why I write, and this I find very troubling. Always there is an uneasy tension between a clearly inner impulse which is at work in the act of writing itself, and the morality of the final outcome.

Let me try to explain myself with an example. When I interviewed the 12-year-old Kurdish boy Taimour who had survived execution in a pit by a miracle, he did not want to talk to me. He had been taught to spew out a canned speech. But I had not come three thousand miles for that. I wanted much more. And so we sat down together for two hours and I forced the boy to relive in infinitesimal detail every moment of his great six-week trauma. What right had I to do that? Is Taimour better off for it? The fact is, I may have been responsible for turning him into a prime target for assassination. Iraqi patriots and Kurds who hate Saddam Husain will approve of what I did, seeing in it the subordination of the individual good to the public good. An Arab nationalist, on the other hand, might think that my exposure of the genocidal campaign of 1988 against the Kurds will be turned by Israel or the West into an attack on all Arabs, and that is bad. My motives are therefore suspect and I should not have interviewed him. I despise both these ways of posing the moral dilemmas involved. The morality of what I did is subject to all kinds of important questions, the most interesting of which have nothing to do with who I write for, or even who I am. The real moral bind arises precisely because I write for myself and not for anyone else. Life would be simpler if I could just turn around and say 'I write on behalf of the Iraqi people', or 'in order to expose the crimes of Saddam.' The fact is, I don't. Where does this leave the 'crisis of Arab identity' which is on so many minds these days?

The ruling nationalist paradigm of the Arab intelligentsia – present in the Arabic newspaper article referred to above – cannot be understood outside the gigantic obsession over who is or is not an Arab. I was very critical of this obsession when examining the issue of intolerance.

However, criticizing someone smarting under the lash of Syrian repression or at the receiving end of constant humiliation and a brutal occupation in the West Bank, carries no force as far as I am concerned. I will never forget a scene just outside Jerusalem's Bab al-Khalil, which I witnessed during my visit there in October 1990 (a visit made possible, ironically, by the fact that I am now a British passport holder). Two Israeli policemen astride jittery horses were searching a terrified Arab boy, no more than 8 or 9 years old, by making him turn his school satchel upside down spilling all its contents onto the grass verge. In that little boy's position, scouring the dirt for for my eraser, pencil sharpener and scattered papers after the soldiers had gone, I too would look upon Saddam Husain as a saviour. Despair and disenfranchisement, when married to constant abuse and humiliation of this sort, generate illusory hopes and superstitious beliefs in any people. Nothing I have to say on the silence of the Arab intelligentsia towards the cruelty of their own world should be construed as a critique of Arabs whose dignity and very identity as human beings is daily being assaulted by Israeli policies on the West Bank.

On the other hand those cosmopolitan, Westernized Arab and 'pro'-Arab intellectuals who, more often than not, reside in the West and are in a position to write and say what they want – we are in a different category altogether. By virtue of the freedoms that we enjoy, we are in a position to do something useful for Arabs trapped inside the oppressive world of the Middle East. Yet a vast majority of us chose in 1990-91 to go along with the Iraqi dictator's political project. This was not an accidental slip, a momentary lapse in an otherwise morally smooth trajectory. It was a confirmation of the obsessive grip that the question 'Who am I?' has developed among Arabs. Something has gone horribly wrong. The problem takes the shape of a refusal to confront the Arab world as it is and face up to our own shortcomings. My purpose is not to pillory people; it is to show that a certain way of looking at the world, almost always entered into with the best of intentions, is today *morally bankrupt*. And this moral bankruptcy is the principal cause of a deep cultural malaise in the Arab world. If I write for myself as I said earlier, I also write from the standpoint of a person who wishes from the bottom of his heart to see this tragic state of affairs reversed.

## Notes

1. This chapter is based on talks given in 1992 at the Institute of Contemporary Arts (ICA) in London for two panel discussions. The first panel discussion – 'Intolerance' – was held on Wednesday 23 September and the other panellists were Aharon Applefeld, David Grossman and Emile Habiby. The second – 'Universalism, Identity and the Writer in the Arab World' – was held on Friday 25 September and the other panellists were Emile Habiby, Elias Khoury and Edward Said.

2. Usama Wathiq, 'Ba'da 'an inqaha'at al-ghumama', *al-Arab*, a London-based Arabic daily, 22 April 1991.

# CHAPTER FIFTEEN

# Charter 91

## *Arif Alwan*

Charter 91 is a statement of political principles, the focus for a signature-gathering campaign of moral persuasion, and a call for the Iraqi republic of fear to be replaced by the Iraqi republic of tolerance. It was drafted and launched by dissident Iraqi intellectuals in 1991 – a year of horror and catastrophe which no Iraqi will ever forget. If Iraqis seek salvation in new, extraordinary ideas, such as those in Charter 91, it is because their situation is too difficult to be understood by existing means. They feel compelled by a great dilemma to think, and above all to think differently, to find a mode of government to end the vicious cycle of violence.

As a writer I have long admired the ideas of tolerance, of freedom from fear, of the duties of the majority and the rights of minorities, of self-expression in a society without coercion. I am an Iraqi not ashamed to confess that my hands are too weak to hold a fellow human being by the neck, suffocate him to the last breath and force him to adore me under this threat. What is the value of love extracted from broken necks?

Some Arabs, including Iraqis, suggest that the 'current situation' in and around Iraq does not permit the emergence of a tolerant and civil society. It would be a bizarre exception. But the phrase 'current situation' is a cover-up for the impulse to control people who would free themselves from compulsory and monolithic collective consciousness. They are labelled as traitors or agents of imperialism by those who believe their own perfect ideas and objectives are polluted by the wrong ideas and objectives of others. There is no rational debate, and 'labelling' or 'smearing' your opponent is a prelude to aiming at his forehead to shoot.

There has been much political violence in Iraq's history. In ancient times Sumerians, Babylonians, Assyrians and Akkadians competed to inhabit this territory. In the middle ages the Abbassid civilization which took six centuries to develop was destroyed by Mongols in two years. Under the Ottoman Empire for five centuries the Iraqi provinces suffered chaos, confiscation of property, random executions, and so on, and Baghdad was frequently fought over by armies of the rival capitals, Istanbul and Tehran.

Foreigners have inflicted extensive injustice on Iraqis, but the injustice inflicted by Iraqis upon their own people and country has been of greater intensity. The present regime in Baghdad has taken political violence to new extremes of cruelty. If tyranny is a juggernaut wheel grinding the innocent and oiled by the blood of human victims, it must be the greatest and most savage wheel of all.

Iraqis are fed up with the bloodletting. They are overstuffed with state terror. They are punch-drunk from the dread which forces them to consider the choice between two forms of death as a gift for which hands should be kissed in gratitude. They are fearful of living in Iraq even after Saddam, when other tyrants may spring up like mushrooms. They are looking for a way out of a crisis that threatens their existence as a people and demands redefinition of their national identity.

The answer does not lie with the military. Since its establishment in 1921 the Iraqi army has been an oppressive organ used by those in power to support the police in crushing popular upheavals for freedom and bread. Since 1958 it has acted as arbiter in social and political life, with commanders running people's lives by means of tanks and military orders. The destabilization of the country through repeated coups d'état has prevented the development of civil society and a democratic political system.

If we Iraqis have any great glory we do not owe it to the army. Sheer force never creates civilization. Japan in the 1930s spent much of its national wealth and spiritual zeal in building a great army only to be defeated in the Second World War. In the decades of peaceful living since then it has thrived beyond imagination without an army.

Stability is the dream of so many Iraqis, but social systems need more than dreams and hopes. Iraqi intellectuals have a responsibility to think the unthinkable for their people so the country can rid itself of extremism and move forward to a new social era in which tolerance is a normal fact of life. The following principles outlined by Charter 91 are a step in that direction.[1]

## Charter 91 – the Text

Civil society in Iraq has been continuously violated by the state in the name of ideology. As a consequence the networks through which civility is normally produced and reproduced have been destroyed. A collapse of values in Iraq has therefore coincided with the destruction of the public realm for uncoerced human association. In these conditions, the first task of a new politics is to reject barbarism and reconstitute civility.

With this in mind, we the undersigned, a group of men and women from Iraq which comprises different nationalities, religious denominations, ideological and political convictions, hereby declare:

**1. People have rights for no other reason than that they exist as individual human beings.**

These rights can only be secured by the rule of law and due process as set out in a written constitution. Such a document comes prior to the formation of legitimate political authority. Political legitimacy must be grounded in a constitution which sets out the principles and constraints of that foundation. Any political authority arising prior to the adoption of a constitution founded on human rights is either transitory, transitional or illegitimate.

### 2. Freedom from fear is the essential prerequisite for realizing the inherent dignity of the human person.

Specifically, freedom from fear requires a new Iraqi constitution to provide that:

- The quality of being an Iraqi shall never again be held in doubt because of faith, belief or presumed loyalty.
- Citizenship becomes the irrevocable right of every individual born in Iraq, or to an Iraqi parent, or naturalized by an Iraqi state.
- No Iraqi be subjected to cruel, inhuman or degrading treatment or punishment.
- No confession of guilt, however obtained, be considered admissible in an Iraqi court of law.
- A moratorium on capital punishment be promulgated for a period of no less than ten years.
- Liability for punishment be always individual, never collective.
- Unrestricted freedom of travel within and outside the boundaries of Iraq be an absolute and inalienable right of every citizen.
- The villages, towns, cities, water sources, forests and historic and religious sites of Iraq be declared a National Trust which no political authority can capriciously destroy, disfigure or relocate.
- The Universal Declaration of Human Rights, adopted and proclaimed by the United Nations General Assembly Resolution 217A(III) of 10 December 1948, be considered binding and constitutive of the legal system of Iraq.
- Any Iraqi official found to have violated the above be dismissed and prosecuted to the fullest extent of the law.

### 3. Rebuilding civil society means elevating the principle of toleration into a new public norm soaring above all ideologies.

Toleration in matters of politics, religion, and ethnic feeling is the only true alternative to violence and the rule of fear. The full creative potential of Iraqis, in which we deeply believe, will only be realized when toleration burns as fiercely in individual hearts and minds as it does in the new constitution of Iraq.

The only acceptable constraints upon toleration are those imposed by the rule of law as secured by a constitution founded on human rights.

Toleration will not be extended to those who would abolish its rule through violence. And toleration does not mean that gross violations of human rights from the past will be forgotten.

Toleration is a solution to the fact of ethnic, religious, political and human differentiation. At bottom, it entails finding ways of accommodating or putting up with such differences. It involves putting up with things that one does not actually like, and may even consider immoral. No one 'tolerates' what they actually enjoy or positively approve of. We choose to tolerate other individuals, organizations, religions, ideas, sects or ethnic groups, because we realize that there is a much higher value in forbearance than there is in trying to eradicate difference.

Toleration is a value superior to loyalty of blood or common heritage. It is superior to ritual nationalist affirmation. Toleration celebrates the human condition because it places the highest possible premium on human life in all its forms. Toleration is the supreme civic virtue.

## 4. Representative parliamentary democracy is the rule in the republic of toleration.

Democracy requires coordinating the representation of differences among people on three levels: within civil society; between civil society and the state; and between the executive, legislative and judicial realms of government. Democracy is not only rule in the name of the people, nor is it simply majority rule. Central to democracy is the constitutionally guaranteed set of rights which protect the part from the tyranny of the whole. The fundamental idea is that the majority rules only because it is a majority, not because it has a monopoly on the truth.

In a democracy, freedom is always the right to think, work, and express oneself – as an individual or as a group – differently. It is the right to live differently, or to speak and learn in a different language. The only acceptable constraint upon freedom is that its exercise must not bring harm upon others.

The protected part may be a whole ethnic group, a minority religion or sect, or it may be a group of individuals who want to voice or organize around a particular political opinion. At the limit the part may be a single human being; and democracy consists in protecting that solitary person's right to be different from everyone else.

Democracy involves securing the freedom of everyone to participate equally in the determination of a shared political destiny. Human beings best realize themselves as individuals who propose, debate and decide. The institutionally structured activity of politics accounts for more than any final results.

**5. The notion that strength resides in large standing armies and up-to-date weapons of destruction has proved bankrupt.**

Real strength is always internal – in the creative, cultural and wealth-producing capabilities of a people. It is found in civil society, not in the army or in the state. Armies often threaten democracy; the larger they grow the more they weaken civil society. This is what happened in Iraq. Therefore, conditional upon international and regional guarantees which secure the territorial integrity of Iraq, preferably within the framework of an overall reduction in the levels of militarization of the whole Middle East, a new Iraqi constitution should:

- Abolish conscription and reorganize the army into a professional, small and purely defensive force which will never be used for internal repression.
- Set an absolute upper limit on expenditure on this new force equal to 2 per cent of Iraqi national income.
- Have as its first article the following: 'Aspiring sincerely to an international peace based on justice and order, the Iraqi people forever renounce war as a means of settling international disputes. The right of belligerency of the Iraqi state will not be recognized.'

**6. Charter 91 is a signature-gathering campaign calling for a written constitution for Iraq that arises out of a collective experience of debate and discussion.**

Charter 91 is not an organization; it has no rules or formal membership. The campaign embraces everyone who is willing to put his or her name to the words in this document.

All signatories must use their full and real names. Nothing in this Charter should be taken as binding on a future constitutional convention for Iraq. Each signatory gives permission that his or her name may be freely publicized as part of the effort to promote the Charter.

Finally, Charter 91 derives its name symbolically from a terrible year in the history of Iraq. 1991 is the year of a wantonly destructive war which laid waste the infrastructure of the country, giving rise to famine and disease unprecedented in the country's modern history. 1991 is also the year when large numbers of Iraqis rose up against the evil which had become the norm inside their country and which they held responsible for that war. And it is the year when that uprising was crushed by the brutal razing of cities and massive loss of life. No Iraqi will ever forget 1991.

Charter 91 is a different reason for remembering the year 1991. By its existence this Charter is proof that the barrier of fear has been broken. Never again will we Iraqis hang our heads in shame and let violence rule in our name.

## Notes

1. This introduction to Charter 91 is a synopsis of an article first published in *al-Hayyat* in summer 1991. The text of Charter 91 has been published in English, Arabic and Kurdish. Further information is available from:

Friends of Charter 91                    Iraq Foundation
PO Box 2724                              1919 Pennsylvania Avenue NW
London W2 4XS                           Suite 850
ENGLAND                                 Washington DC 20006, USA

CHAPTER SIXTEEN

# Federalism[1]

### *Ali Allawi*

It is becoming increasingly obvious that the crisis of the modern Iraqi state
has roots that go far beyond the horrors of the Saddam Husain era. The
structure of Ba'thist rule was not created in a political vacuum but was
based on a certain conception of what Iraq as a state was about – a
conception which was formulated in the 1920s and has continued mainly
unchallenged until the present day. In its turn, the formulation of the
identity of Iraq drew on a centuries-old pattern of rule and legitimacy
which set the framework in which the powers of the state were exercised.
Plainly put, Iraq's identity was created by a narrow, sectarian and even
non-indigenous elite without any regard to the wishes of the majority
community or the interests of the various ethnic and religious groups in
the country. At the beginning of the mandate, Iraq's character was defined
as Arab; its institutions were to be centralized so as to propagate a
self-serving notion of the Arab nature of the country; and its ruling circles
were to be drawn nearly exclusively from the Arab Sunni minority. In the
1930s a powerful army was established to defend this particular version
of the Iraqi state, its pervasive and centralizing tendency, and its supposed
role in the wider Arab world. This vision of Iraq – in whose formulation
neither the majority Shi'i community, nor the Kurdish, Turcoman or
Christian communities had participated – inexorably led to conditions
where mass murder, genocide and ethnocide could be committed and
justified in the name of protecting the integrity and identity of the Iraqi
state.

In short, the Iraqi state never sought or obtained a legitimizing consensus among its component populations. In spite of certain transparently
insincere and ineffectual attempts to 'consult' the leadership of the major
communities, the country was defined by a narrow group. The interests of
other groups were conveniently ignored and the possibility that they may
have a differing view of how and where the country was heading was never
given a second thought. By and large, this condition has persisted throughout Iraq's modern history with no effort being made – by either the ruling
circles or their opponents – to question the underlying premises of the Iraqi
state.

The end result of this hegemonic view of Iraq is a Ba'th Party run by a
tiny clique who recognize no limits to their infamous rule. They sit on an
apex of power whose base is, sadly, rooted in a sense that the historical

way of ruling Iraq is the only correct way; that there is a legitimacy to Sunni supremacy which stretches back in time to Ummayyad, Seljuk or Ottoman rule, particularly in their anti-Shi'i posturings; and the convenient disguise that Arab nationalist ideology gives to the process of dominating a multi-ethnic country where, in additon, Shi'ism is the creed of the majority.

Iraq cannot be reformed except by recasting the structure of power and the state. The overthrow of Saddam and the dismantling of the Ba'thist state cannot be successfully accomplished and replaced with a functioning and stable democracy unless and until the issue of the future of the Iraqi state is tackled head on. Paradoxically, this is better understood by Saddam than by the Iraqi oppostion. The Iraqi state is hegemonic in its institutions of rule. It will not accommodate democracy because the Arab Sunni community will equate it with a tyranny of the Shi'i, and a regime under which they will be dispossessed and stripped of their privileges. It will not accommodate Kurdish aspirations for a high degree of self-rule without raising the spectre of dismemberment. It cannot accommodate multi-culturalism without risking the dilution of the prized 'Arabness' of Iraq. This is the fate of all centralized uni-dimensional countries. In the case of Iraq this has been praised by political scientists and sociologists as the necessary condition for 'nation-building', modernization and development. The reality of Iraq exposes this for the sham that it is: a cruel and vicious system that has marginalized millions, killed hundreds of thousands, ruined countless lives, and launched two destructive wars of aggression.

The Ba'th and Saddam know that the slogans of liberal, pluralistic democracy are no match for the atavistic fears of many Arab Sunnis. It is a sad fact that the *intifada* in March 1991 in Kurdistan and southern Iraq did not spread to the Arab Sunni areas. The reason is clear: for the first time in the history of modern Iraq there was a genuine possibility that the true structure of power was about to change. Silence and non-participation does not necessarily indicate support for the existing order; they do however imply the rejection of the postulated new order. That is why it would be foolish to rely on an internal coup d'état to usher in a new world of democracy. The instruments of terror and repression are incapable of being the agents of liberalism and pluralism; neither can Sunni Arabs be expected easily to turn against a system that has, by and large, disproportionately favoured their community. On the other hand, the Kurds cannot and will not trust an Iraq that does not have built-in safeguards against a central authority gone mad. Neither will the Shi'i, only recently conscious of their powerlessness and irrelevance in the modern Iraqi state, be prepared to participate in a regime that will propagate – perhaps in a different form – yet another sectarian order.

Fear, bitterness and a sense of vengeance are deep-seated in Iraq. There is no family whose members have not suffered one way or another from the terrible consequences of the Saddam Husain years. There is a real possibility of the disintegration of the state and an attendant free-for-all whose effects can only be guessed at. The tyrant is not prepared to depart from the scene even if the country is bordering on chaos. To expect that tolerance or a common sense of an Iraqi identity will somehow prevail in the supercharged atmosphere of a post-Saddam Iraq borders on fantasy.

## The nature of Iraq

Iraq's opposition, and especially its intellectuals, must tackle the issues of Iraq directly and not through the tired clichés of party politics or through the use of coded words because of the of fear of being seen as reactionary, sectarian, or worse. I will limit myself here to considering those issues that have a fundamental bearing on the nature of Iraq.

First, it is undeniable that the ruling group in Iraq is drawn from the Arab Sunni minority. The Shi'is have always been marginalized players in Iraqi politics. A key issue that must be faced therefore is the emancipation of the Shi'is, politically and culturally. There is a growing sense among Iraq's Shi'is that they will not allow the construciton of a new order in Iraq in which they will once again be pushed to the margins. Any acceptable new state in Iraq must take into account the vital wishes and demands of the majority community. The narrow and sectarian basis of the power structure of Iraq is now accepted as one of the defining features of the country's political and social landscape; and the use of ethnicity and sectarian allegiance in the service of the Saddamist state has become explicit. Any Shi'is who might have accepted the notion of the sectarian nature of the Iraqi state are now reconciled to it as a bitter fact, particularly since the unprecedented violence and ferocity – bordering on ethnocide – that was used against the Shi'i uprising. The silence of members of the ruling community, both inside and outside Iraq, before this unequalled reign of terror against the Shi'i spoke volumes about their political priorities.

Second, the crimes committed against the Kurds are unparalleled in modern Iraqi history. The Kurds are now thoroughly alienated from the Iraqi state. One can go further and say that they have become alienated from Iraq itself. The silence of Iraqis and Arabs during Saddam's genocidal campaigns against them have convinced even the most moderate Kurds that Iraq is, in its present form, merely an entity to which they may be obliged to be attached for a short while as neighbouring countries – particularly Turkey – adjust to their semi-independence. Any future construct for Iraq must take this fact into account. The Kurds must be cajoled into a unitary state, although they will be reluctant observers initially, until such time as the balance of interest for their community propels them to accept the legitimacy of the Iraqi state.

Third, the other so-called minorities of Iraq also number in their millions. Recent estimates put the Turcoman population at two million; Iraq's various Christian communities also exceed a million. These groups have suffered seriously under Saddam, especially the Turcomans and Assyrians. A post-Ba'thist order must recognize their legitimate cultural and religious rights and constitutionally ensure their protection.

Finally, one has to contend with what is probably the biggest and most difficult issue, namely the powerful fear of the Arab Sunni community that they may lose their political, social and cultural preponderance in a new Iraq. A new order for Iraq will necessarily be obliged to dismantle the structures of the sectarian state; the Arab Sunni community will, in these terms, be seen to have 'conceded' to a new reality. There will always be a strong backlash against the dismantling of what many view as Iraq's 'mission' as the 'bastion' against non-Arab (read Persian) intrusions; as the upholder of Arab nationalist ideology; even nowadays as the defender of Islamic orthodoxy against deviationist and rejectionist tendencies (read Shi'i). No ruling group will relinquish its hold over the state voluntarily. South Africa's whites are a clear example of that. However, this is not to imply that Saddam will automatically enjoy the support of Iraq's Sunnis. He will do so in my opinion only if the alternatives being proposed are imprecise; if loose slogans empty of any meaningful content are used to placate the genuine fears of the ruling community. I do not believe that the mass of decent Arab Sunnis can possibly condone the terrible crimes of Saddam, but they may not participate as a community in his demise if their position in the framework of a new Iraqi state is not made clear beforehand.

The concept of power-sharing is quite alien to the politics of the country; but it is imperative that genuine attempts be made to articulate it and give it a leading position in the underpinning of the institutions of the reconstructed Iraqi state. The formal Iraqi opposition, groping for a formula to overthrow the Saddamist state, have been unable to recognize the critical need to rethink what Iraq should mean to its various inhabitants, and to bridge the deep fissures that exist within society.

## Kurdish view

The Kurdish parties – with their confidence greatly strengthened by their successful experiment with free elections in Iraqi Kurdistan, have probably the most developed view of the role of the Kurds within the Iraqi state. It is essentially a territorial view; one which, plainly put, envisages rights for Kurds that are constitutionally enshrined, preferably with Western guarantees, but which need not, necessarily, be applied to the rest of Iraq. The oft-heard slogan of 'Autonomy for Kurdistan; Democracy for Iraq' has had its latter part frequently truncated or ignored whenever autonomy is seen as a genuine possibility. The 'capitulations' that Iraq will afford its Kurdish citizens – in this view – do not necessarily translate into a commitment to support the struggle for rights and representation for the rest of the country. If the rest of Iraq achieves democracy and representative government, so much the better; if not, then the Kurds can live with a de-fanged and caged centralized Iraqi state.

## Islamist view

The Islamist groups envisage yet another version of the Iraqi state. In this case it is postulated that the unifying cement holding Iraq together must be its Islamic identity. Since Islam cannot and should not differentiate between believers, the nationality question is often given short shrift, and the centralizing and proselytizing features of the Islamic state are given preeminence. Kurdish and other aspirations are reduced to folkloric or cultural manifestations, and these are tolerated within the firmament of the Islamic order. Furthermore, in the context of Iraq, the Islamic parties are – and more importantly, are seen to be – essentially Shi'i parties, notwithstanding the genuine commitment to pan-Islamicism on the part of many in their leadership. Their political platform is therefore flawed when seen from an Arab Sunni perspective. It is further undermined by their (erroneous) identification in the public mind with the concept of *wilayat al-faqih* and the institutional structures of the Islamic Republic of Iran. In spite of brave attempts by some Islamic parties to give greater coherence to their notions of the Iraqi state (as in the al-Da'wa Party's manifesto 'Our Programme'), there is considerable confusion as to how the Islamists would actually deal with a multi-ethnic, multi-sectarian country. This ambiguity, coupled with the barrage of hostile and insistent campaigns against Iraq's Islamic movement in the Western and Arab media, have pushed these parties into an ideological corner that is not of their making. On the one hand, they recognize that they have evolved beyond the traditional concepts of political Islam; on the other hand, they cannot wholeheartedly embrace the language and value of liberal political democracy.

## Liberal democracy

Adherents to the principles of liberal democracy, a recent phenomenon in Iraqi politics, appear, on the surface, to hold many of the answers to the complexitites of present-day Iraq. However, the proponents of liberal democracy in Iraq are a diverse group, as are their impulses. A number of them are former Marxists and even Ba'thists. Their views range from a

mild belief in a need for representative government to extremes of thoroughgoing Westernization, pacifism and secularism. A common feature
of these new democrats – with a few notable exceptions such as the writer
and critic, Kanan Makiya and the veteran politician Sa'ad Salih Jabr – is
their recent conversion to the politics of liberal democracy. Most have had
little or no historical involvement in democratic politics prior to the Gulf
War, and their backgrounds have been frequently diametrically opposed
to the values that they now espouse. At the same time, they cannot tap into
an undercurrent of support within Iraq, and to date they have been unable,
given the conditions in Iraq, to break out of their salons and meeting halls
to create a mass following in Iraq. One cannot therefore speak of the
continuity of liberal democratic politics in Iraq. Whatever existed, effectively ended in the revolution of 1958. Iraqi liberal politics is, by and large,
a post-1988 phenomenon. A more serious criticism of the liberal opposition of Iraq is its inability to shed the politics of cabals and secret deals,
processes from which most of its members have only recently emerged.
At the Iraqi opposition conference in Vienna (June 1992) and Salah al-Din
(October 1992) – from which the expanded INC emerged – the new liberal
democratic parties and personages were well represented, but otherwise
estimable conference positions and papers were completely overshadowed
by flagrant violations of elementary rules of election and procedure. Until
this group matures further, one cannot ignore their cynical adoption of new
forms of political expression, which have arisen from the collapse of the
Soviet Empire, the bankruptcy of Ba'thist/Arab Nationalist ideology and,
unfortunately, a pandering to the perceived demands of the West.

In and of itself, the fact that members of the liberal democratic opposition are mainly latecomers to this viewpoint does not condemn the
democratic thesis on the future of Iraq. What does, however, is its inability
to deal with the concrete realities of the Iraqi political scene, and a
dogmatic, and even intolerant, interpretation of the functioning of democracy in the Iraqi context. The liberal democratic opposition is also
personalized and subject to frequent and damaging schisms.

Nevertheless, there is a widespread belief that some form of democratic
rule is necessary in the post-Saddam order, and it is this sense that society
must have its decency, tolerance and normality re-established that gives
the liberal democratic forces some continuing relevance in the Iraqi
context. However, what Iraq's erstwhile democrats have conspicuously
failed to do is to articulate their programme beyond the numbing repetition
of democratic slogans and pieties. Their fragmentation, weakness in
presentation, and schismatic tendencies have made them ineffective as the
future protectors of those who are most likely to 'lose' as a result of the
demise of the Saddamist state, namely the Arab Sunni community.

Federalism, decentralization, self-rule, automony: these are seen as
latent forces leading to disintegration and dismemberment by a not insig-

nificant segment of the Iraqi population. Spectres of Yugoslavia and the ex-Soviet Union are trotted out to warn of the imminent dangers to national unity if ethnic and other forces are given their say. The notion of the centralized, nationalist state still has many adherents. The force of inertia and the weight of historical and pan-Arab considerations continue to give this verison of the Iraqi state considerable credibility. In particular, it is still held to a large extent by the community in power, and by a segment of the exiled nationalist and Ba'thist opposition. The evils of Saddam are dismissed as an aberration and the ideological bases of nationalism and centralism are still considered valid. In this view, Iraq needs only to get rid of Saddam, his family and clan, to return to its true vocation. The institutions of the state are seen to be legitimate, although they may need a little 're-tuning'. Less violence; less terror; a smaller army perhaps; less ethnic confrontationalism; a reduction in overt sectarianism. Iraq will then be part of the 'community' of Arab nations; with a guarded indifference towards Iran; and in essence a more moderate, but essentially similar version of the historic Iraqi state.

## Visions for the future

These, in summary, are the key undercurrents in the Iraqi opposition's view of the future construct of the Iraqi state. There is one last – though still very muted and controversial – version of the future Iraqi order. This is a uncompromisingly Shi'i view, which is not rooted exclusively in the premises of political Islam. In this perspective, Iraq is seen as a reflection of the identity of the majority, where Shi'ism is changed from a simple sectarian identity to a politico-cultural platform. Iraq becomes a stage for the emancipation of the Shi'i and the state is recast in terms of the priorities of the majority population. A sense of revanchism and the need to rectify the deep historic injustices against the Shi'i of Iraq may be only part of the origin of this view. It is felt that the Shi'i of Iraq must have a state that is committed to profound affirmative action in support of the majority community. Iraq will assume the symbols and substance of Shi'ism. Its institutions – religious, cultural and political – will take on a definite Shi'i hue; in effect a substitution of the culture and symbols of the majority Arab Shi'i for those of the minority Arab Sunni.

It must have become clear by now that reconciling these profoundly conflicting views of the nature and role of the Iraqi state cannot be accomplished either justly or easily. Violence and terror have been increasingly the glue which keeps Iraq a centralized state. But the Gulf War and its aftermath have flung the windows open on the sealed interior of Iraqi political life. However, Iraqis have not been able to generate broadly acceptable political alternatives to Saddam, and the reason for this must lie partly in the mutually exclusivist visions for the future of Iraq. Liberal democracy without the underlay of tolerance will quickly lead to a tyranny of the majority (in the view of most of the Arab Sunnis). Centralism and ideological Arab nationalism are only code-words for continued Arab Sunni domination (in the view of the Shiʻi); and only a step away from genocidal impulses (from the Kurdish perspective). An Iraq dominated by essentially Shiʻi Islamic parties is unacceptable to most Arab Sunnis and the Christian community.

The condition to which Saddam's Iraq has been reduced is an unenviable one. The normal language of political dialogue has been reduced to one in which communities fear annihilation and cultures are threatened with destruciton. There is no point in denying the bestial levels to which the state has sunk. Democracy, pluralism and other concepts of governance will not take root unless we recognize the fears and aspirations of Iraq's communities and reflect them in the reconstruction of the Iraqi state. Federalism must therefore be twinned with democracy if Iraq is to avoid dismemberment or the continuation of repressive minority rule. It is in the manifest interest of all Iraq's communities to call for the dismantling of the centralized Iraqi state and to devolve power to regional units that reflect the ethnic and cultural make-up of the population. To a large extent, the excessive centralizing tendencies of the modern Iraqi state have provided the backdrop for the imposition of minority rule. All power is concentrated at the centre so that a centrally devised policy can be ruthlessly implemented without regard to regional or local sentiments. This in turn has created monstrous bureaucracies that are not responsive to local needs or to community aspirations, and are designed to implement the policies and views of those small elites who claim to define the country and its vision of itself.

## Federalism – the problems

A federal structure for Iraq would make historical and political sense. The aspirations of the Shiʻi, Kurds, and other cultural, religous, ethnic and political groups can be more easily reconciled within the framework of a decentralized state than with the centralization that has stifled all attempts to recognize the country's diversity. A regional administrative and political structure for Iraq can allow for the devolution of religious, cultural and educational policies more suited to the requirements of the population than a distorted and uni-dimensional centralism. A regional framework for conducting economic policy will also fit more easily with traditional and natural trade patterns and markets.

The exact form in which Iraq will be reconstructed as a federal entity can of course vary. There are numerous examples of successful models of highly decentralized and multi-ethnic states; as well as, to be fair, examples of how not to create federal systems. At a minimum, federalism in Iraq should meet a number of criteria, including the creation of large regional units (five perhaps: one built around Kurdistan; one including Mosul and the Jazira; one built around Karbala', Hilla and Najaf; a southern region around Basra and Nasiriyya; and a federal capital of Baghdad, which may include part of Diyala province). Federalism will imply the devolution of almost all domestic powers to the regional units, to be funded out of a percentage of oil revenues (say, up to 70 per cent) distributed directly to the regions on the basis of population; with a federal government responsible only for interregional affairs, foreign policy, defence, money and banking. The federal government will also have the constitutional responsibility for the protection of the rights of non-territorial minorities such as the Turcoman and Christian communities. Politics will be both a regional and a federal affair. Regional parliaments and executive authorities will govern the various regions; while a federal parliament and an upper house will supervise the functioning of the federal government and ensure the balance of regions at the federal level. Democracy, in the sense of universal suffrage to elect representatives to regional and federal institutions, will be the agreed mechanism for reflecting the popular will.

However, proponents of a federal or confederal solution to the identity crisis of the Iraqi state cannot rely only on the logical consistency of their positions. There are a number of undercurrents that have to be also considered if the federal solution is to gain mass support and legitimacy. The first is that the Iraqi state, despite its terribly skewed concentrations of power, has created over time a number of institutions that have effectively mixed the various communities and perhaps even diluted their sense of separateness. This has been further enforced by the fact that the state is the largest employer by far, and has not been too particular about filling local jobs with local people. The net result has been an ethnic and sectarian mixing, which when linked with the centralizing policies of the state and a limited degree of inter-ethnic and inter-sectarian marriages, has created a sense of 'Iraqiness', particularly among a segment of the middle and upper classes. As one approaches the higher reaches of power and decision-making, this 'Iraqiness' gives way to a recognition of the iniquities of the state, and a reinforcement of the always-present sectarian and ethnic identities. The vast majority of Kurds will not hesitate now in placing their ethnic loyalties way ahead of any sense of affiliation to the Iraqi state. The reaction of the Arab Shi'i, however, is far more complex. The silent majority of Shi'i probably feels a sense of regret and even bitterness that they are still victims of discrimination and harassment in a country in which they form a majority but to which they still have to demonstrate their loyalties. The Iran-Iraq war, which was supposed to have forged an Iraqi identity for the Shi'i in the 'epic' struggle between Arab and Persian, proved to be only a backdrop to the near ethnocide committed against the Shi'i of the south in March 1991. The draining of southern marshes and the campaigns against the Shi'i Marsh Arabs have further reinforced Shi'i bitterness towards the Iraqi state.

Another undercurrent with which one has to contend is the sense that federalism is only a station on the road to dismemberment, or the creation of a Lebanon-like confessional state. These are genuine concerns held not only by political centralizers but by all those who are not prepared to take a risk in uncharted waters, especially when the future of their country is at stake. While the former may have a political purpose behind their rejection of federalism, the latter are driven by real patriotic concerns. They may not want to admit that the 'experiment' of creating a non-sectarian, non-discriminatory state with genuinely open institutions, has failed. They tend to see a recognition of ethnicity and religious allegiances as somehow backward, and not worthy of being considered in the construct of modern states. The near collapse of the old order in Lebanon is to them an object-lesson in the dangerous consequences of the explicit recognition of communal aspirations and sectarianism.

## International responses

A troublesome issue, however, that faces a future federal Iraq is the attitude of its neighbours and the Western powers. Iraq is a country whose internal structure can cause profound concern and anxiety to its neighbours. The obvious matter of the potential destabilization that can affect Iran and Turkey as a result of a Kurdish/Arab federation in Iraq has been much discussed. But the drastic weakening of the Iraqi state, coupled with its potential for aggressiveness and territorial expansion (there was a land-grab aspect to both the invasion of Iran in 1980 and the invasion of Kuwait in 1990) have had a greatly disturbing impact on policymakers in neighbouring countries. They have been forced to contend with the possibility that a future Iraq may not play a role that would suit their own policy needs and ambitions. In this respect, therefore, the design of a successful federal system in Iraq must take into account – and overcome – the very serious concerns that its neighbours would have on how such a system would influence their own stability and security.

Both Kuwait and Iran have been victims of Saddam Husain's aggression and a militarily non-threatening Iraq must be among their highest national security priorities. Kuwait may be content with this, but Iran has a definite interest both in promoting the establishment of a *shari'a*-based state in Iraq and in thwarting the formation of an avowedly pro-American client state operating under the guise of liberal democracy. Sa'udi Arabia, Syria, Turkey and even Jordan each have their own – frequently conflicting – perceptions of what the Iraqi state should look like. They all reached a modus vivendi with the pre-Gulf War Iraqi state, but the situation today is vastly different. The prospect of a federal Iraq lukewarm on Arab nationalism, not overtly Sunni-dominated, without the repressive control of a military regime or police state, and in which the Kurds are truly autonomous must frighten these neighbours. Is it any wonder that their reaction to it has been uniformly hostile?

The attitude of the Western powers – especially the USA – to the future construct of the Iraqi state is also of the highest importance. The federalism being espoused by elements of the pro-American Iraqi opposition bears little resemblance to the actual policies being pursued by the USA. It would appear that American national security interests in the area – control over oil resources, maintaining the momentum towards an Israeli-dominated Levant, reversing the tide of so-called Islamic fundamentalism, preserving the centralized Turkish state – cannot accommodate a federal and democratic Iraq. I find it extremely difficult to believe that the USA, or the West in general, would abandon the tried and tested methods of control in favour of a leap into the unknown by a country as crucial to the region as Iraq. Democratic platitudes and human-rights concerns expressed by Western leaders will not be matched by affirmative policies to ensure the establishment of a federal and constitutional Iraq while doubts remain that their surrogates in Iraq can achieve and stay in power. President Bush's call to the Iraqi military to remove Saddam Husain and the apparent expenditure of millions of dollars by the CIA to engineer a coup in Baghdad contrast with the USA's ineffectual and mainly verbal backing to the liberal opposition Iraqi National Congress (INC).

## Conclusion

There is no doubt that a violent break-up of the state structure would lead to great instability and strife. However, the reform of the state should be carefully staged so that federalism is the end product of a thorough consultative process which would perhaps take the form of a constitutional conference whose recommendations would be subject to a popular vote. Restructuring the Iraqi state on the lines of equity, fairness, and long-term viability may not be an easy task, but it must be attempted in spite of the minefields through which this process must pass. In this respect, historical analogies to Yugoslavia, Lebanon and, on the opposite tack, Ethiopia, are not necessarily valid. The solution to Iraq's structure of rule must be organically and indigenously resolved, with the genuine involvement of the population.

Irrespective of the mechanism through which the principles of power devolution will be implemented, the point to be made is that decentralization, regionalism or federalism are aspects of a particular political approach to recasting the centralized Iraqi state. A prime condition for the successful devolution of power is that the balance should be tipped decisively to the regions; and that only through a new political compact between Iraq's main communities will a new Iraqi state be born. The central institutions must earn their legitimacy from the power that the main communities are prepared to give to the centre; and not the other way around. A period during which both the main disadvantaged communities – the Shi'i and the Kurds – rediscover political control over their destinies must be combined with a federalism that will safeguard the Arab Sunni community from a 'tyranny of the majority'. The new Iraqi identity will be forged over time as a result of the peaceful, mutually respectful and cooperative participation of the country's communities; and not by fear, terror and violence as has been the disastrous experience of our past.

## Notes

1. This chapter is an updated version of an article first published in *The Iraqi Review*, vol. 1, no. 3, (Winter 1991-92).

CHAPTER SEVENTEEN

# The Rule of Law[1]

## Ahmad Chalabi

This is the wounded human material out of which a new order in Iraq has
to be fashioned. The poison of Sunni-Shi'i sectarianism and of Arab-
Kurdish bitterness, either one of which is enough to kill Iraq, are today
working together to tear the country apart. The division of the country is
already being acted out in people's hearts, before it is played out on the
ground at the cost of untold numbers of Iraqi dead. No Iraqi is immune
any longer; everyone has become infected. Virulent strains of nationalism
and sectarianism are more prevalent today in Iraq than at any time in the
past. They are the driving forces for change even as the best elements in
the Iraqi opposition pretend otherwise. Where do we Iraqis go from here?[2]

Iraq is a country whose sovereignty is now compromised and whose
territory is split between two antagonistic governmental authorities, one
local and democratically elected, the other a modern dictatorship run by
gangsters. The skies of Iraq are divided by lines on the map that define
two no-fly zones – one in the north, the other in the south – enforced by
coalition air forces to protect the civilian population in those areas against
airborne attacks by their own government. The country lives under a
regime of international sanctions that restricts normal trans-border trade
to little more than food and medicine. Economic development has been
halted and even reversed. It is safe to say that the GDP of Iraq in 1994 was
less than 20 per cent of the 1989 figure. Oil production is now 15 per cent
of Iraq's quota, and only a small amount of this oil is legally exported.

Under these circumstances, it is curious that Iraqi opposition groups
are not calling for an end to international intervention. People whose
political record is replete with anti-imperialist and anti-colonialist deeds
are calling for further international involvement in Iraq, usually under the
guise of United Nations action. Iraqi patriots welcome the sight and sound
of foreign fighter aircraft flying over their country. They also welcome the
sight of UN personnel who have come to impose conditions on the Iraqi
government. Indeed, they wish there were more such international controls. Yet, these same Iraqis are bewildered by their own current attitudes
and are made uneasy by the conflicting sentiments generated by the
situation. How has this come about?

## The Iraqi regime and Iraqi society

The answer lies in the nature of the Iraqi regime. Saddam Husain has created a bloodthirsty and repressive regime, and purposefully interwoven it into the fabric of Iraqi society. The horrors of the regime were beyond the belief of the outside world prior to the invasion of Kuwait, but are now readily recognized as fact by international public opinion. The unchecked terrorism of the regime in the late 1960s developed in the 1970s into massive repression and the deportation of hundreds of thousands of Iraqi citizens. A relentless war of aggression against Iran from 1980 to 1988 was followed by attempted genocide against the Kurdish population of northern Iraq. The present decade has been marked by the invasion of Kuwait, the Gulf War, the popular uprising (*intifada*) and attempted genocide against the Shi'i population of southern Iraq, including the Marsh Arabs.

Iraqi society has been atomized by these experiences. The diverse communities of Iraq now eye each other with fear and suspicion. Civil society has long ceased to exist in the country. All forms of social organization have been usurped by the Ba'th Party. Even the nuclear family has not escaped Saddam Husain's ruthless drive towards total control. A journey through the Iraqi countryside today would be a journey of horror through a wasteland of disease, hunger, repression and war. In this rich land of oil and great agricultural potential, millions are subsisting on UN handouts. To survive winter people have sought heating and cooking fuel by cutting down the precious few trees left, depleting a scarce natural resource. Such is the present situation in Iraq.

Looking to the future, the opposition Iraqi National Congress (INC) is seeking a democratic, constitutional, parliamentary and pluralistic system, guaranteeing human rights within a federal structure as a formula for the Iraqi state. However, the disparity between the reality and the hope is vast. The task of bridging the chasm is daunting and the scepticism of learned foreign observers has taken on an inertia that is difficult to shift. How are we to get from here to there, and how can we convince the people of Iraq and the world that we are capable of doing it?

We must recall that Iraq has been brought to its present condition by Saddam Husain's systematic destruction of civil society in Iraq. From the first years of Ba'th Party rule, extraordinary measures became the normal form of government. All independent institutions, starting with private schools, were eliminated. Independent businessmen were deported. Professional organizations were either taken over or dissolved. The Kufa University Board – intellectuals attempting to create an independent educational institution – was disbanded and its money expropriated. Religious authorities, including the late Grand Ayatullah Muhsin al-

Hakim, were humiliated. Hakim's son was among those spuriously accused of spying for Israel, many of whom were executed.

## The legal system corrupted

Throughout its rule, Saddam Husain's regime has shown a complete lack of respect for legal procedure. It routinely disregarded even the Ba'th constitution, itself a terrible document outlawing all parties except the Ba'th Party and disenfranchizing millions of Iraqis. All legislative power has been vested in the Revolutionary Command Council (RCC) – a secret body appointed by another secret body, the leadership of the Ba'th Party – which lays down the law simply by issuing decrees. These decrees have included lists of people who are to be regarded as having graduated from high school and medical college with the right to practise as physicians. Another decree ruled that any Iraqi citizen whose wife was of Iranian origin (meaning that she had an Iranian ancestor up to four generation back) was entitled to financial encouragement to divorce her. Yet another decree exempted the president's wife from paying income-tax.

These laws became so embarrassing that they were published only in a secret gazette with limited distribution. The normal court system became a travesty. A lowly intelligence official could force a judge to make a judgement that suited the Ba'th Party. All important cases were arbitrarily moved to special revolutionary courts, which had exclusive jurisdiction over political offences. It was made an offence punishable by death to criticize the president, and many people were executed under this law. In the revolutionary court and the state security court decisions were mostly secret, there was no due process and no right of appeal except to Saddam Husain himself. This appalling situation was exacerbated by the Iran-Iraq war, when hundreds of thousands of Iraqi citizens, holding Iraqi passports, were deported on the grounds that their ancestors did not have Ottoman nationality when the modern state of Iraq came into being. This extra-legal deportation was one of the most disastrous developments in recent Iraqi history.

The fact that Iraq and its legal system have lost all semblance of normality indicated that the authority in power has had no internal check on its actions – there is no independent judiciary to curb violations of executive power. In Saddam's Iraq the judiciary became totally subservient. A personal experience related to me by a friend who was a judge under Saddam Husain illustrates the point. My friend the judge was instructed to appear at the security department in the middle of the night and issue some arrest warrants. He asked what the charge should be and was told, 'You make up a charge.' He asked to see the individuals to be arrested and was told, 'Hurry up and issue the warrants because they are already executed.' The judge did as he was told.

## Competing universalist ideologies

Iraq was formed as a country after the First World War from diverse ethnic and religious entities. The government of Iraq was supported by the United Kingdom and was organized as a consititutional monarchy with a modern liberal constitution. Its ethos and *raison d'être* were inspired by Arab nationalism or pan-Arabism, an ideology which threatened several population groups in Iraq, most notably the Kurds, who did not want to become an even smaller minority in an even larger Arab State. The Shi'i, although overwhelmingly Arab, were also discriminated against on the basis of their religious identity, and perceived Arab nationalism as a threat and cover for their persecution.

The situation was exacerbated when the Arab nationalists, taking their lead from the strident nationalist ideologies prevalent in Europe between the wars, adopted extreme nationalist and universalist positions. The old-style liberal Arab nationalism of King Faisal I lost the respect of the new nationalists, who were impatient for action. In response, another large group from the rising educated middle class gravitated towards Communism, as the liberal and parliamentary factions were unable to make their performance in society match their noble rhetoric. These trends were repeated in the rise of Islam as a political force, with secret societies being formed to promote exclusive Islamic ideology.

As a result of this history, the political scene in the past two decades has largely been a struggle between competing universalist ideologies, each of which claimed a monopoly on political truth and hoped to come to power by violent action. The rule of law was not part of the political programme of the parties opposed to Saddam's regime. No systematic critique of the legal system gained international attention, which was a fatal flaw in the performance of such groups and helped to limit their appeal among the people of Iraq.

Because Saddam systematically repressed all parties outside the Ba'th Party, dissenting politics were reduced to conspiracy. Political opposition tended to be limited to assassination or bombing a building, usually followed by an exaggerated claim. In this way Saddam was assured of victory. He was the best conspirator, and when he claimed to possess the whole truth he could back up his claim because he possessed all power.

## Totalitarianism and terror

Not surprisingly, people who had a sense of patriotism and decency withdrew from public life. This withdrawal was encouraged by the regime. Saddam made the penalties for political activity so severe that not only the individual and his immediate family were at risk but even their extended family could be punished. Furthermore, prospects for success were so remote as to dissuade people from getting involved in the political process. By these methods Saddam succeeded in abolishing public conscience.

A quotation from Hannah Arendt's *Origins of Totalitarianism* illustrates the position of the Iraqi people under Saddam.

> Totalitarian terror achieved its most terrible triumph when it succeeded in cutting the moral person off from the individualist escape and in making the decisions of conscience absolutely questionable and equivocal. When a man is faced with the alternative of betraying and thus murdering his friends, or of sending his wife and children, for whom he is in every sense responsible, to their death; when even suicide would mean the immediate murder of his own family – how is he to decide? The alternative is no longer between good and evil, but between murder and murder ... Through the creation of conditions under which conscience ceases to be adequate and to do good becomes utterly impossible, the consciously organized complicity of all men in the crimes of totalitarian regimes is extended to the victims and thus made really total.

This lack of any legal restraint made the perpetuation of Saddam's dictatorship easier and, at the same time, made the world even less aware of the evil inside Iraq. There was no voice from inside the country in a public position which could protest. Saddam had destroyed both the legal system and political groups. The situation became so monstrous that an arbitrary licence to kill was given to several thousand security service personnel, and their murderous actions were graced by legal sanction under the twisted laws of Saddam.

The most notorious example is that of a decree by 'Ali Hasan al-Majid, viceroy of the north, which gave licence for any person or beast to be killed by the mere fact of their presence on pre-designated territories inside Iraq. Documents now stored in the US Senate archives detail a typical example of the application of this decree. They tell the story of three shepherd boys caught in one of the forbidden zones. The first document is a record of interrogation. The boys are asked if they know that they are in a forbidden zone. They reply that they do but have no other place to graze their sheep. The next document is a death certificate attesting to the boys' death by execution. The last document is a letter to the military intelligence office reporting that these three shepherd boys were executed in accordance with the law and edict of Viceroy Majid pertaining to the forbidden zones.

## International law flouted

Iraq's adherence to international law is no better, even though Iraq is a signatory to the UN Charter, the Universal Declaration on Human Rights and the Treaty on the Prevention and Punishment of the Crime of Genocide. Iraq has repeatedly violated all those conventions of international law, as well as its bilateral treaties with other countries. Under Saddam, Iraq has committed aggression against Iran and Kuwait and continuously sponsors international terrorism against its neighbours. However, for reasons of *realpolitik*, the international community did not take Iraq to task prior to the invasion of Kuwait.

Iraq's financial regulations and obligations have also suffered under Saddam's lawlessness. The country has been looted by Saddam. To cover his tracks he ceased to publish a national budget in 1979. Even so, there is ample evidence of his theft of the Iraqi people's wealth. Under a government expenditure list item 'the transformation account', money was available from the state revenues directly to Saddam and his family. In 1978 this account contained 980 million Iraqi dinars, the equivalent of $3 billion. In another case from 1982, payment of $1.8 billion was transferred to Switzerland, ostensibly in settlement of a debt arising from a contract with Italy for naval frigates. Documents made public in the Italian parliament reveal that this money was never paid and instead was transferred to Saddam's half-brother, Barzan al-Tikriti.

Multibillion dollar contracts were awarded on the basis of influence and kick-backs, with no audit on performance or specifications. Borrowings were made illegally and without authority in a completely uncoordinated fashion. As a result, the state of Iraq could not pin down its total foreign debt. Foreign financial institutions indulged in these actions, despite their illegality, partly from a desire to win contracts and partly for fear of offending powerful regional interests.

How do we get out of this illegal morass created by Saddam Husain? We must address the root cause — his disregard for the law. Throughout his rule his government has been illegal. We must adopt the rule of law, both internally and internationally as our guide.

## United Nations

After the invasion of Kuwait, the international community moved with force to impose on Saddam a set of UN Security Council resolutions, some of them adopted under Chapter 7 authorizing the use of force. It is safe to say that Saddam has violated every one of them and continues to violate them to this day. He promises acceptance and immediately sets on a course to thwart the will of the international community. He has shown himself unwilling to obey any law or treaty that does not suit his purpose.

International action through the UN has, however, provided the necessary framework through which the opposition Iraqi National Congress (INC) can work. The institution of a safe haven and a no-fly zone in the north made possible the return of millions of Kurds to their homes, while the no-fly zone in the south provided a reduction in Saddam's ability to repress the civilian population of the area.

Resolution 688 represents a major watershed in the history of the UN Security Council international law. This resolution separates the Iraqi people from Saddam's government, recognizes that Saddam is repressing the people and demands that Iraq desist from this repression. Unfortunately, it provides no mechanism to secure the compliance of the Iraqi regime. However, Resolution 688 has worked well in the establishment of the existing safe haven and the no-fly zones. It must be enhanced and used again to justify the establishment of a safe haven in southern Iraq and to justify the deployment of human rights monitors in Iraq. The presence of UN officials all over Iraq reporting on violations will deter the regime from committing further human rights abuses.

## Iraqi National Congress (INC)

The INC believes that such action will also give heart to the Iraqi people by demonstrating that the international community is determined to impose the rule of international law on the illegal atrocities of Saddam Husain. The deployment of the monitors and their active engagement in opposing violations of human rights will severely detract from the regime's ability to oppress the people of Iraq. Such actions will help undermine the regime in a fundamental way and the people will be emboldened to denounce their oppression and engage in active opposition to the regime.

The INC also believes that the people of Iraq need food and medicine and the only effective mechanism for achieving this exists in Resolutions 706 and 712. Saddam's refusal to implement them demonstrates his priorities. He prefers to wield control over a starving and sick population rather than see a better fed and healthier population, for he knows that once the people of Iraq realise that their livelihood is independent of Saddam, then it is a short step to conclude that his removal from power is possible.

In the view of the INC, establishment of the rule of law internally in Iraq is a prerequisite for effective cooperation with international law. For if Iraq fails to make the rule of law paramount inside the county, then it will fail to negotiate the international restrictions placed upon it. At this time, Iraq economically is eating its own flesh. The country's GDP has been reduced to 20 per cent of its former level and the poor prospects of exporting oil are compounded by the state of the international oil market. The international market will not need Iraqi oil until at least 1997. In the current state of over-supply, Iraqi oil will radically depress prices. After Resolution 687 was imposed, Sa'udi Arabia took up 75 per cent of Iraqi oil exports. In effect, Sa'udi Arabia takes about two million barrels a day of the Iraqi export quota – which is equivalent to one-third of Sa'udi Arabian exports for cash. In order for Iraq to regain its quota it has to abide by all aspects of international conduct and international law. Furthermore, to accommodate itself to Resolution 687, Iraq has to negotiate within the framework of international law. These battles cannot be won unless the rule of law prevails in Iraq.

## International support

The reluctance of Western governments to break new ground in international law for Iraq is a strange phenomenon. All Western governments declare that the territorial integrity of Iraq is a principle of their policy. At the same time, in their effort to protect civilians, these same governments have created a safe haven in northern Iraq beyond Saddam's control. By this action, they have established de facto a separate entity in Iraq. Saddam Husain's reaction of imposing an internal economic blockade means that the international community's commitment to protect civilians will impel it to seek economic links with other countries for the protected area. But by the development of these links, the ties that bind the area to Iraq will become more and more tenuous. For example: international telephone links could well be developed through Turkey. It is also possible that petroleum will be refined in the protected northern area and exported without reference to Baghdad. Although Western chanceries currently resist such notions, they would be very hard put to defend their decisions in the face of concerned public opinion about Saddam Husain's victims.

The UN, under its current operating guidelines, cannot deal with the issue of the north. The problem is not a problem of relief; it is a problem of reconstruction of the infrastructure and the economic cycle. Such reconstruction and rehabilitation under current circumstances will inevitably tie the economy of the north to other countries, principally Turkey. Such a consequence cannot be good for Iraq's territorial integrity.

Therefore, to be true to their principles, the Western powers should assist the INC through action in the UN to bring about democratic political change in Iraq by the removal of Saddam Husain. The presence of Saddam Husain is the biggest threat to Iraq's territorial integrity. In the south, the no-fly zone and the continuing low level guerrilla war have signalled a weakening of Saddam Husain's control over this vast area. Army morale is low and, despite Saddam Husain's armour and artillery, his control is like that of military occupation by a foreign power. The argument that Saddam is essential for the stability of Iraq is faulty and shortsighted. Saddam's army is not getting stronger. This leaves the south prey to outside interference.

## Conclusion

In conclusion, it is difficult to see how the West can rehabilitate Saddam. The US government cannot establish any normality with a regime they have charged with war crimes against Kuwait and US citizens. As long as Saddam Husain stays in power Iraq will remain weak. Only his demise can open the door to a brighter future for Iraq and its people.

## Notes

1. This chapter is an edited version of a lecture given at the School of Oriental and African Studies, University of London, on 6 April 1993.
2. Makiya, K. *Cruelty and Silence* (London 1993).

CHAPTER EIGHTEEN

# Playing by the Rules

*Dlawer Ala'Aldeen*

The artificial boundaries of the modern state of Iraq, which were laid down by the British in the 1920s and have been protected ever since by the major powers, created a heterogeneous combination of ethnic and religious groups. The British, militarily dominant after the First World War, drew the map of Iraq by annexing the southern part of Kurdish lands – the Ottoman province of Mosul – to the Ottoman provinces of Mesopotamia inhabited mainly by Arabs, namely Baghdad and Basra. In the process, they denied the Kurdish people any right to an independent Kurdish state. The Kurds of southern Kurdistan have been through seventy years of forced co-existence with the Sunni and Shi'i Arabs under the rule of Sunni Arabs in Baghdad. The division of Kurdistan and amalgamation of these divergent groups created one of the most unstable countries in the Middle East. The plight of the Kurds (and their armed struggle for basic human rights) and the plight of the Shi'i Arabs in the south have been major contributors to instability in the entire region.

In the 1930s and 1940s, the southern Kurds somehow adapted to the new reality and started thinking in the context of modern Iraq. This was at the expense of their national identity and their human and political rights. With the overthrow of the Hashemite monarchy in 1958, Britain finally lost influence as an imperial power within Iraq and the fate of the Kurds was left entirely in the hands of a series of undemocratic Arab nationalist governments. Without exception, these regimes – all of which were supported by either, or both, Cold War superpowers – refused to recognize the Kurds' democratic rights or demand for self-determination. Since the Ba'thists came to power – first in 1963 and then in 1968 – the very existence of the Kurds has been at risk. To the superpowers, the violation of human rights and suppression of the people of Iraq were no more than 'internal affairs' so long as the regime was deemed indispensable for trade and most recently for preventing the spread of the Shi'i Islamic revolution.

The 'sacred' boundaries of Iraq and exclusively Sunni rule in Baghdad became the only recognized image of Iraq during the era of the two superpowers. All policies were worked out around those boundaries, which ensured that they remained unquestioned. However, with the emergence of the United States as the leading, or the only, master of the world, international relations have changed and old policies are no longer applicable. The clock must now turn the American way. Sadly, however, there is no evidence that the USA has developed any well thought-out policy towards Iraq. Its only obvious policy has been a reaction to events, and too little too late. Many observers have the impression that the US administration changes its policies frequently. This, and the way the USA conducted the Gulf War, demonstrates their ignorance of Iraq's social and political structure.

The USA has long valued Saddam Husain as an economic and political partner. However, following Iraq's invasion of Kuwait on 2 August 1990, it strongly indicated that he was no longer a partner and should go, hence General Schwarzkopf's desire to march all the way to Baghdad. But when, in the *intifada* of March 1991, the Iraqi people had the opportunity of removing Saddam Husain and replacing him with a Shi'i-dominated opposition, the Americans pulled away the rug and actively sought to prevent his downfall. Not having prepared a 'friendly' alternative (a military dictator with a different name), the USA accepted Saddam Husain as the 'devil they knew', preferable to the one they did not. They allowed the 'internal affairs' to carry on. The Shi'is were slaughtered in the south and the Kurds were left in the wilderness.

The British, however, are acknowledged to have a better understanding of the area, and have long conducted the policy they see as in their best interest. British policy has nevertheless time and again proved to be catastrophic for the people of Iraq and the rest of the Middle East. The British have had more knowledge, but always followed the USA, who have no thought-out policy. Fortunately for the Iraqi people, by the time of the mass exodus of refugees from Iraqi Kurdistan in April 1991, Margaret Thatcher had her own personal policy towards Saddam Husain. She had developed a deep dislike for him and, although no longer in power, was strong enough to make people listen in Britain and the USA. She initiated a sequence of events that resulted in John Major's passionate move to intervene militarily in Kurdistan (with or without the Americans). Instead of letting the British take the moral high ground, the Americans jumped in ahead and led the way into the 'quagmire' to save lives. This was a classic example of US policy. Lives were saved in Kurdistan and George Bush became Hajji Bush. But the 'safe havens' were set up only in a part of Iraqi Kurdistan, less than half the area from which the refugees had fled. As for the Shi'is in the south, their untelevized suffering remained an 'internal affair'.

## Kurdish safe haven

The Allies made a deliberate effort to limit the Kurdish safe haven to the province of Dohuk where no more than 800,000 people had been displaced. The majority of the refugees (1.2-1.5 million) were fleeing eastward towards Iran from the major cities of Kirkuk, Arbil and Sulai-maniyya. Operation 'Provide Comfort' was an attempt to appease Turkey. Great efforts were made to stop the refugees entering Turkey by providing immediate aid on the mountains. Refugees were actively encouraged to return to their homes under the impression that the Allies would stay there to protect them. Turkey closed the border from day one and succeeded in creating enough pressure to have the refugee burden shouldered interna-tionally. The Iranians, while opposed to the whole idea of the safe haven and regarding it much like a second Israel, tried to play the Turkish game and announced the closure of their border in the face of the tide of refugees. Their calls for others to shoulder the burden were largely ignored by Western governments (except for some limited aid mostly from non-gov-ernmental organizations), and fortunately they never closed the border. The Kurdish refugees along the Iranian border cried for help and for the extension of the safe haven, but they too were ignored. Masses of refugees fleeing the provinces of Kirkuk, Arbil and Sulaimaniyya remained in the open at Saddam's mercy without aid or protection. They were trapped between the Iraqi army and the border with Iran, far from the safe haven in Dohuk province to the north-west, adjoining the Turkish border. Iran did not allow international aid to cross its border. The 36th parallel, which provided air cover for less than half of Iraqi Kurdistan, was not sufficient to inhibit Iraqi army advances south of the line. Thus, Allied protection not only remained inadequate throughout the period but, more sadly, the whole of operation 'Provide Comfort' was abandoned in July 1991. The Allies left the area before their task was completed.

In October 1991, the Iraqi government suddenly withdrew from the three main Kurdish governorates of Arbil, Dohuk and Sulaimaniyya and imposed a strict embargo on the entire area, leaving the strangled Kurds as the sole authorities in charge. The purpose of the Iraqi government's gamble was not entirely obvious. It was believed to be a blackmail attempt which assumed that Iran, Turkey, Arab countries and the Allies would rush in to prevent the Kurds from running their own affairs for fear of a Kurdish independent state being established. Iran, Turkey and Syria began holding regular meetings to discuss the Kurdish situation, and publicly declared that they would not tolerate any talk of Kurdish independence or the break-up of Iraq. Nevertheless, the Kurdish parties were left alone to run a de facto state, with no income and no direct foreign support. None of the Western governments have offered direct financial support to the elected Kurdish administration which is seeking to lead, feed and police between 3.5 and 4 million people. One US government aid official attempted at a London conference in July 1993 to justify his government's lack of action, by referring to the Kurds' inability to eliminate the corruption inherited from Saddam's regime. He ignored the need for financial support to combat corruption and the fact that Western support enabled Saddam to establish such corruption in the first place.

Saddam Husain's government is able to extract, refine and sell oil. It is still able to provide people with basic services, while the Kurdish region has been deprived of the means of providing such services. No attempt has been made to relieve the sanctions on the Kurds or allow them to generate some hard-currency income. Even the small amount of money made available to the United Nations for relief in Kurdistan was wasted through Baghdad. Furthermore, non-governmental organizations (NGOs) are no longer backed to provide alternative support for the Kurds, and some have clearly been instructed not to deal directly with the legitimate, elected authorities in Kurdistan.

## Southern Iraq

The uprising in the south of Iraq had a different tragic fate. Thanks to Iranian interference with the Shi'i uprising and the Allies' lack of interference in Saddam's counter-attack, Iraqi Shi'is were badly defeated. Tens of thousands of people were massacred during and after the uprising, and the true figures of those killed may never be known. Since the *intifada*, the level of repression of the people and destruction of their historical religious institutions has intensified to such an extent that the entire Shi'i cultural legacy is in danger. The 'modernization' of mosques, construction of highways over holy cemeteries and the 'reorganization' of the structure of the Shi'i clerical school have all accelerated since 1991.

The Marsh Arabs are one of the most ancient communities in the Middle East. They are now facing total destruction of their community and way of life. Like all other Iraqi communities, they suffered a great deal from oppression and from the Iran-Iraq war. In addition, the hard-to-govern marshlands form a refuge for army deserters and opposition members. This meant they have suffered government military offensives, including air attacks, the use of chemical weapons, underwater mines, burning of reed beds and water poisoning. Having failed so far to achieve total control of the Marsh Arabs, the government's last resort has been to speed up and expand the southern desalination project (the so-called 'Third River' project). The clear purpose of this project is to drain the marshes and facilitate the government's control over the area, thereby eliminating it as a base for political opposition. However, a spin-off is the desalination of the areas between the Tigris and Euphrates and possibly the exploitation of oil-fields under the marshes. Drainage has probably reached an irreversible stage, with vast areas already drained and dried.

All this is actively taking place south of the 32nd parallel, under the nose of Allied surveillance aircraft. Protective air cover has not stopped the Iraqi regime on the ground continuing to violate both human rights and

UN Resolution 688. Saddam's bombardment of the area has, if anything, intensified since the creation of the no-fly zone. Air cover without monitoring on the ground has proved almost as inadequate as not providing any cover. A no-fly zone with no safe haven for the Shi'is in the south means continued persecution, humiliation, starvation and destruction of long-established social and religious structures.

## The opposition and the future political system

Since the creation of modern Iraq, the Sunni Arab minority has monopolized power. This was convenient for the former superpowers, but catastrophic for the Kurdish and Shi'i populations and the rest of the Middle East. With an ethnically and religiously diverse population forcibly combined within artificial boundaries, Iraqi governments failed to minimize the country's potential for disintegration by establishing a civilized constitution that would secure people's rights and strengthen the affinity between them.

For a long time, the Iraqi opposition has remained disunited. This is hardly surprising. The various groups come from different backgrounds and have distinct interests. Their diverse backers include Iran, Syria, Sa'udi Arabia, Turkey and the CIA. However, sharing a single enemy, their common sense dictates the formation of a low affinity coalition. This has never been easy.

Clearly, the sections of the Iraqi opposition that enjoy wide popular support and have a strong organizational base inside Iraq are the Kurds and the Shi'is. Alliances between Kurdish and Shi'i political organizations are therefore vital for any progress by the opposition, even though they are not monolithic groups. The rest of the opposition groups, important though they may be, are mainly loose organizations with little fame or following inside Iraq. Despite the diversity of the Iraqi opposition, there is fortunately at present a higher level of understanding among the various groups than ever before. All have accepted multi-party democracy as the only alternative to Saddam Husain, though they do not seem to have achieved unanimity on the issue of a future federal system for Iraq.

The Iraqi opposition has had to pass many tests before being able to present itself to the world as a credible alternative to Saddam Husain. It has been expected to demonstrate that it represents the views of all the people of Iraq and enjoys the moral authority to act on their behalf. But its biggest test is to demonstrate that it has understood the rules of the game and can project itself as a coalition of professional, moderate statesmen who can relate to the West. It has not passed all the tests yet. It has not been able to prove that it would contribute to peace and stability and would not disturb the balance of power in the region; that it would not pose a threat to the West's lifeline interest (the oil in the Gulf) or to Israel; that it would establish a capitalistic, pro-American free-market economy. It may even be expected to guarantee the Americans a lion's share of the future reconstruction contracts (as in Kuwait) to repair Iraq's crippled infrastructure, which is estimated at around $200 billion.

In the same way as dictatorship by the minority Sunni Arabs has proved catastrophic, the dictatorship of any other ethnic or religious groups will undoubtedly have a similar consequence. For instance, in the absence of complete democracy, a future Shi'i government based on clerical dictatorship will be suicidal. The non-Shi'i Iraqis, including Kurds, Sunni Arabs and Christians, have good reasons to fear such a dictatorship. All these groups, however, accept that a parliamentary system with a Shi'i majority is legitimate, tolerable and acceptable. Iraqi Shi'i leaders, willingly or not, seem to have accepted such a scenario, although the fundamentalists among them (and many so called 'moderate' Shi'i leaders) cannot accept Kurdish demands for limited autonomy, let alone self-determination. Many nationalist Sunni Arabs share the same feelings about the Kurds. Therefore, only a fully democratic constitution can guarantee human rights for all Iraqis and the creation of a stable country.

Since the March 1991 *intifada*, the Iraqi opposition in exile has come together and developed more mutual understanding than ever before. All parties are clearly convinced that their only chance of survival and of creating a formidable alternative to Saddam Husain's rule is to reach such consensus. This perspective is shared, albeit with varying emphasis, by all three main communities that comprise Iraqi society: Kurds, Sunni Arabs and Shi'is.

## Kurds

The Kurds have long realized the grave risk in the short term of insisting on an independent Kurdish state, and have accepted the current boundaries of Iraq. The only hope for them of securing some of their desired rights in the foreseeable future seems to lie in them committing themselves to an integral but democratic Iraq. The 'State of Kurdistan' remains the dream of every Kurd in the same way as every Palestinian dreams of the 'State of Palestine'. Nevertheless, the Kurdish political organizations are genuinely insisting on coexisting with the Arabs in Iraq. The Kurdish leaders have recently come under growing pressure from sections of the Kurdish population for greater commitment to the Kurdish right of self-determination (including independence). However, the leaders have so far skilfully and successfully managed to resist pressure, persuading people to weigh risks against interests.

Looking back at the history of Baghdad's Kurdish relations, it becomes apparent that the more aggressive the regime has been in treating the Kurds, the more demanding the Kurds have become. From the 1920s to the 1950s the Iraqi monarchy ignored the cultural and political rights of the Kurds, but treated individuals as full citizens. During those years, the Kurdish movement, for its part, restricted its political demands to little more than cultural rights. Since the 1960s, under republican rule, successive regimes have further denied Kurdish rights and stepped up their suppression. At the same time, Kurdish desire for self-rule increased and 'autonomy' became the slogan of the armed struggle.

Under Ba'thist rule and after a decade of genocidal war, coexistence with Baghdad has become increasingly difficult. The Kurds have developed a stronger desire for divorce from Baghdad. Indeed, the deteriorating relationship between Baghdad and the Kurds may soon reach a point of no return where mutual trust and coexistence become impossible. This is why only multi-party democracy with a parliamentary constitution can enhance Baghdad-Kurdish affinity, which a federal system will hopefully sustain into the foreseeable future.

### Sunni Arabs

The loose term 'Sunni Arabs' refers to a heterogeneous combination of tribal, semi-tribal and non-tribal peoples occupying the triangle of Iraq between Mosul, Ramadi and Baghdad. This collection of non-religious, mainly nationalist Arabs is the social base of the Ba'thist oppressive machinery, with its monopolization of absolute power. Opposition to the Ba'thist regime is at its weakest in this region, and almost all Sunni Arab anti-Saddam activists are abroad. They enjoy less popular support than the Shi'is or Kurds and inside Iraq they are virtually unheard-of.

Among the Sunni Arab political organizations, there are many extreme pan-Arab nationalists who stress Iraq's Arab identity and its role as a potential leader of the 'Arab national liberation movement'. Groups such as former Ba'thists and the current pro-Syrian Ba'th Party not only insist on a firmly integrated Iraq and think that democracy will dismember it, but also see the expansion of Iraq and the formation with Syria of a giant United Arab Republic as a dream ticket. These 'leftist Ba'thists' count on Saddam's Ba'th Party as their organizational base in Iraq, hoping that Saddam's downfall will allow the exiled Ba'thists to fill his vacant post and continue Ba'thist domination.

The rest of the Sunni Arab opposition (i.e. the majority) consists of moderate democratic groups which are genuinely interested in establishing a constitution based on a Western-style democracy. They have long accepted that without this, the disintegration of Iraq is inevitable. Some have gone so far as to suggest a federal system (with a federal Kurdish state) for Iraq. It is important, however, that most of the organizations which have been arbitrarily labelled 'Sunni Arab organizations' are not founded on the basis of such an ethnic/religious identity. They all have a wide spectrum of membership, including Shi'is, Kurds and Christians.

## Shi'is

The terms 'Shi'i organizations' and 'Shi'i opposition' have been incorrectly used to describe Shi'i political/religious organizations or the people of southern Iraq. Apart from the purely clerical organizations, which recruit on the basis of Shi'i-Islamic religious commitment, the rest are largely party-political organizations driven by the plight of the people of the South. Shi'is in Iraq suffered from persecution under the Ba'thists simply because of their religious identity, just as the Kurds were persecuted because of their ethnic identity. However, it is important to stress that not all Shi'is in Iraq support the Shi'i clergy or the Shi'i political/ religious organizations, and not all Shi'is wish to see an 'Islamic state' in Iraq. All the various political viewpoints and affiliations can be found in the Shi'i community, developed according to personal ideologies and interests. Nevertheless, the way that the Iraqi regime has insulted the spiritual symbols of Shi'is and denied them their human rights has increased support for the clerical leadership abroad.

Such support is split between party-political organizations, like the Da'wa Party and the more religious pro-Iran clerical groups led by al-Hakim. Al-Hakim is the son of one who epitomizes the Shi'i religion for many Shi'is and is regarded by many as a symbol of their struggle against Saddam. More importantly, al-Hakim is now the head of the Tehran-based Supreme Council of the Islamic Revolution in Iraq (SCIRI), the umbrella organization of all Iraqi Shi'i groups. It is interesting to note that there is no unanimity within SCIRI on Iraq's future. Some have no problem with a modern Western-style democracy and accept the open market economy in principle. Others would accept nothing short of a pure Islamic state with a Shi'i-clergy dictatorship. During the Gulf War, members of SCIRI prayed for an Iranian victory which would carry them to power in Baghdad.

The end of the Iran-Iraq War and the changed circumstances it brought about helped lend a new dimension to Iraqi Shi'i thinking. More importantly, years of bitter experience in opposition have eventually enabled Shi'i organizations to understand the rules of the game of modern international politics. Whether they play by these rules is another matter; they ignored them for years and only recently have they given some indications of abiding by them. Nowadays, moderate Shi'i personalities are given a higher profile in international lobbying than the mainstream radicals of SCIRI. They have openly endorsed a Western-style democracy and are actively keen to be seen as truly modern statesmen. It is important to note that most Shi'i organizations no longer style themselves as the 'only' alternatives to Saddam Husain. Behind the scenes, however, a great majority of SCIRI members have not thoroughly digested the above rules, or the notion of a Western-style democracy in Iraq, let alone the rights of ethnic and religious minorities or the notion of a federal system.

The obvious dependence of the Iraqi Shi'i organizations, particularly the SCIRI leadership, on Iran, has had tragic consequences for the Iraqi opposition and the spring 1991 *intifada*, as it has masked the fundamental differences and genuine disagreements between the Iranian clergy and the Iraqi Shi'i party political leaders. There are innumerable religious and political differences between the two sides. For a start, the Iraqi Shi'i organizations do not believe in the same *wilayat al-faqih*, in which ultimate power is concentrated in the person of *al-faqih*. Such differences are deep rooted and go back centuries. More importantly, the Iraqi Shi'is strongly resent Iranian interference in their internal affairs and in Iraqi opposition affairs. On a private level, Iraqi Shi'i leaders do complain about this interference. Publicly, however, they would not put down their 'religious brothers' as the Western media do, because this would not serve their purposes. Also, they see no reason for giving up a 'brother', especially as they still await a gesture of good will from the West or its allies in the Arab world. It is unfortunate that the notion of Iran's Islamic state or Shi'i fundamentalism has been generalized to include all Iraq's Shi'i population in the South. Iranian attempts to export the Shi'i revolution to Iraq, Sa'udi Arabia, Afghanistan, the Lebanon and the former USSR made East and West unite in opposition.

It is tragic that the Iraqi Shi'i organizations have underestimated the power and danger of an unrivalled superpower. But the bigger tragedy lies in the illiteracy of this superpower which is yet to demonstrate skill and logic in manipulating the world. The only logic applied to US policies is 'protection of the US national interest', with no serious attempt to understand local politics and cultural values. Thus, the US administration has yet to demonstrate an understanding of the differences between Iraqi and Iranian Shi'i, and the very complex nature of their relations. In the same way as Shi'i organizations have realized that their only hope of participation in power is to accept Western-style democracy, the Americans should realize that without the participation of Shi'i political organizations in power there will be no stable, united and peaceful Iraq. Furthermore, as the Kurdish population of Iraqi Kurdistan will not settle for anything less than a federal state of Kurdistan within a federal Iraq, the Shi'is will not settle for anything less than full participation in any future governing institution. Unless the rights of these two long-suppressed groups are secured, and unless the West starts winning the good will of these people, there will be no guarantees for a stable market in Iraq or secure business with future governments.

The time for dictatorial rules in Iraq is over, and the time for democracy is now long overdue. The only system capable of saving Iraq's integrity is a genuinely democratic multi-party parliamentary system. Until recently, many believed that in an Islamic developing country of the Middle East it would be difficult to establish such a Western-style democratic system. These views, however, were put to the test in May 1992 in Iraqi Kurdistan, with the first historical opportunity to establish a parliamentary system in part of Iraq.

## The Kurdish federal state as a model for Iraq

Kurdish internal politics has many similarities with that of Iraq as a whole. It has comparable ingredients of conflict and bellicosity. Politically, there are the two main bitter rivals, the Kurdish Democratic Party (KDP) and the Patriotic Union of Kurdistan (PUK), in addition to the communists, right-wing nationalist parties, Islamic parties, Christian parties, and others. Ethnically, there are Kurds (Soranis, Bahdinis, Hawramis, *fa'ilis*), Turcomans, Assyrians, Armenians and Arabs. Religiously, there are Muslims (Sunnis and Shi'is), Christians and Yazidis. In fact, Kurdistan is more heterogeneous than any other part of Iraq. Nevertheless, it was possible to combine all these diverse groups under one legislative and executive system in which all parties (political, ethnic or religious) are represented. A few years ago, it would have been unthinkable to see leaders of the KDP and PUK even dine together; now they dine, travel and rule together. Both parties have realized the importance of the success of the experiment on which their own future and the future of their people depends. Their high level of collaboration and mutual compromise has provided security and reassurance for the people of Kurdistan.

This experience shows that irrespective of the ethnic and religious multiplicity, cultural diversity and geographical location of the nation, it is possible to establish a truly democratic system with a considerable degree of harmony. The actual constitution need not be an exact replica of that of any of the Western systems. In the same way as different Western countries have developed their own systems, Iraq can develop its own. The initial set-up of the current democratic system in Kurdistan was agreed before the election of 1992 by the different rival parties under the coalition of the Iraqi Kurdistan Front (IKF). The end result was the establishment of a unique parliamentary system which is well adapted to local politics and cultural values. Also, the rights of minorities like Christians have been secured through special mechanisms. As time goes by, the parliament will gradually develop the constitution and put down the roots of the system.

Despite the absence of any real income or external support, and despite the double imposition of sanctions, the democratic system in Kurdistan has managed to survive and grow in strength. The vast majority of its current problems are due to lack of funds and/or political security. How-

ever, there are a few problems which are purely local and require immediate attention. For instance, the problem of the supreme leader of the
Kurdish Federal State, locally named 'the head of the Kurdish Liberation
Movement' has proved difficult to resolve. In the circumstances, one could
argue that the people of Kurdistan were lucky that this issue was not resolved
in 1992, because not all parties were convinced of the necessity of such a
leader and they had not agreed on the extent of his or her executive power.
The whole concept of the election of such a leader was raised only days before
the 1992 election, and arguments about the powers of the post continued
until election day. Even now, the rival parties have not resolved the issue.

Failure to elect an outright leader in the first round of voting meant that
the two most powerful individuals in Kurdish politics – Jalal Talabani and
Mas'ud Barzani – remained outside the system of government in Kurdistan. Without them, the Kurdish parliament and the Kurdish government
remained relatively weak and financially poor. Throughout the past decade
and a half these two leaders have had the ultimate decision-making power
and they now jointly head the military coalition of the IKF. Even though
they have remained outside parliament and have not been given any state
positions, they constitute the ultimate authority behind the governing body
in Kurdistan. They have retained the power to appoint (or fire) a prime
minister, choose his cabinet and appoint (or fire) the speaker of the
parliament. Furthermore, on the international platform, they act on behalf
of the Kurdish parliament and its government. Their absence from government has been seen as a weakness, both in the internal authority and in
the international standing of that institution. Their inclusion in the legislative and/or executive bodies, in whatever capacity, is an absolute
necessity. The two leaders of the KDP and PUK have demonstrated their
genuine interest in supporting the elected bodies and demanded that the
*peshmerga* forces and the general population see them as their legitimate
rulers. Indeed, without the blessing of the two leaders, the whole experiment could have failed.

However, careful consideration clearly must be paid to the kind of
executive and legislative powers to be given to the sovereign leader.
His/her relation with the legislative and executive institutions must be
well defined before the election battle is conducted and such definition
has to be formulated in a way that leaves ultimate authority with the
parliament. There is no reason why a single leader cannot be elected by
the people of Iraq.

The experience in Kurdistan showed that the vast majority of Kurds
had not decided who they would vote for until near the election date, when
they were still examining manifestos to see who would protect their
interests best. The same thing should apply to the people of Iraq, including
those in the south. The people are sufficiently sophisticated politically to

think in terms of peace, justice, economic well-being and freedom rather than religious fundamentalism or Arab supremacy.

Currently, the Iraqi opposition has chosen a council of joint leaders consisting of a Kurd, a Shi'i and a Sunni, but the ultimate test for people's choice should be determined by a direct free election with nothing to stop any candidate becoming president, regardless of whether he/she is an Arab Sunni, a Kurd, a Shi'i, a Christian, a Turcoman, a Yazidi or a Communist. In Kurdistan the candidates for the leadership contest included representatives of four different parties, two of which were relatively small. One was an Islamic party represented by a Sunni clergyman, the other was socialist. One of the major candidates was a Bahdini Kurd while the others were all Soranis. Many Sunni clergymen and religious Kurds voted for agnostic political parties rather than the Islamic one, and many Sorani Kurds voted for the Bahdini candidate and vice versa.

## Conclusion

There remains a wide gulf between the Allies and the Iraqi opposition, and between different groups within the Iraqi opposition. The first has resulted from a lack of understanding between the two sides, caused by the ignorance and obsessive approach of Western governments (particularly the USA) towards the Iraqi opposition, and its fear of the unknown when it comes to alternatives to Saddam Husain's regime. On the other hand, some Iraqi groups (particularly the Shi'i organizations) have not yet learnt to play by the rules of modern politics under the supremacy of the USA. Each side, it seems, will have to begin to learn from the other. The Shi'i groups need to demonstrate true independence from Iran and the Allies need to demonstrate more skill and sophistication to help them achieve just that. Without winning the good will of the Iraqi people and the inclusion of Shi'is in the game, Iraq will neither be a stable country in the region, nor will it be a peaceful market for the West.

The gulfs between the Kurds, the Shi'is and the rest of the Iraqi oposition have largely been created by the stubborn demand of the pro-Iranian Shi'i groups for an Islamic State of Iraq, with a clerical dictatorship and the absolute denial of the aspirations of other ethnic and religious groups. Sunni Arab nationalists are just as undemocratic and stubborn. Both groups fear the disintegration of Iraq and resent the Kurdish movement and the declaration of a Federal State of Kurdistan. The Kurds have not yet fought for an independent state and have done their utmost to reassure all Iraqis, but further denial of their rights will undoubtedly fuel enthusiasm for such a fight. Iraqi opposition parties need closer ties and better understanding than ever before. Replacing one dictatorship with another is certainly no longer acceptable to Iraqis. Democracy is the only alternative to Saddam Husain that will secure stability and peace.

# Chronology

## 1990

| | |
|---|---|
| August 2 | Iraq invades Kuwait<br>UN imposes economic sanctions. |
| November | Demonstrations in Baghdad against the government, which retaliates by trying to forcibly evacuate two million people from the capital. Less than one million are evacuated. 600 Iraqi army officers are reported to have been executed. |
| December 27 | Seventeen mainstream Iraqi opposition organisations meet in Damascus to form the Joint Action Committee (JAC). They agree a common policy programme calling for the overthrow of Saddam Husain, an interim government of all parties and a solution for the Kurdish question. |

## 1991

| | |
|---|---|
| January 17 | US and Allies start air attacks on Iraq. |
| February 9-12 | A new (Western-oriented and Saudi-backed) opposition group is set up in London called the Free Iraq Council. |
| 23 | Ground offensive launched against Iraq. |
| 25 | Massacre of fleeing Iraqi soldiers at the Mutla Pass on the Kuwait-Basra highway. |
| 26 | Saddam Husain announces Iraq's withdrawal from Kuwait. |
| 28 | Formal ceasefire. *Intifada* sparked off in Zubair by soldiers returning from Kuwait. |
| March first week | Kurds meet the Turkish President Turgut Ozal who promises to support Kurdish autonomy within a united Iraq. |
| 1 | *Intifada* reaches Basra at three in the morning. |
| 4 | Najaf, Karbala' and Sulaimaniyya taken by rebels. |
| 5-6 | Damascus Declaration on security in the Gulf and Israel/Arab arena made by Syria, Egypt and the countries of the Gulf Co-operation Council (GCC). |
| 7 | Arbil taken by *intifada* rebels. |
| 7-8 | *Intifada* defeated by government forces in Basra. |
| 11-13 | Beirut Conference of Iraqi opposition. There are 350 delegates from more than twenty groups and many |

independents and personalities. They include tribal
leaders, ex-generals, dissident Ba'thists, Communists,
Democrats, Liberals, Islamists (SCIRI, Dawa Party,
Islamic Action Party), Kurds, Assyrians and Turcomen.
They identify three priorities: to unify and organize
themselves as a credible alternative to the Saddam Husain
regime, to increase support for the *intifada* and to seek
outside sympathy and backing for themselves and the
*intifada*.

| | |
|---|---|
| 16 | Najaf falls to the government. Karbala' soon after. |
| 17 | Dohuk taken by *intifada* rebels. |
| 20 | Kirkuk taken by *inifada* rebels. |
| | 106 relatives, staff and theology students of the Grand Ayatullah Abu al-Qassim al-Khoei are arrested and 'disappear'. |
| 28 | Battle to retake Kirkuk started by government forces. Dohuk retaken by government forces. |
| | The crushing by government forces of the *intifada* in the north precipitates the mass exodus of Kurds across the border into Turkey and Iran, which is filmed and seen on televisions throughout the world. |
| 29 | Samara retaken by government forces (last centre in the south to be retaken). |
| 31 | Arbil retaken by government forces. |
| Last week | A new prime minister, Sa'dun Hammadi, is appointed. He is a Shi'i and a relatively liberal figure who will argue publicly for economic liberalization and implementation by Iraq of UN resolutions. |
| April 2 | Zakho retaken by government forces. |
| 3 | Sulaimaniyya retaken by government forces (last centre in Kurdistan to be retaken). |
| 6 | UN adopts Security Council Resolution 688 on human rights in Iraq. |
| 8 | The European Community (EC) calls for a 'Kurdish enclave' to be set up. |
| | Memorandum of Understanding (MoU) signed by the UN and Iraq enabling the UN to establish humanitarian relief inside Iraq. |
| 14 | Jalal Talabani and Mas'ud Barzani meet Saddam Husain in Baghdad to discuss autonomy arrangements for Iraqi Kurdistan. |
| 16 | President George Bush commits 7,000 American troops to join British, French and Dutch troops to secure and build refugee camps inside Iraq. |
| 24 | Security zone established in Zakho. |
| May 20-24 | US-led forces move into Dohuk and Iraqi soldiers and secret police move out. |
| June 7 | Security zone/safe haven in Iraqi Kurdistan is officially handed over by the Western allies to the UN. Allied |

|                    | troops start to withdraw. |
|--------------------|---------------------------|
| July 15            | Western allies withdraw last permanent forces from northern Iraq, leaving a 'residual force' from eight countries in southeast Turkey. This marks the end of Operation Provide Comfort initiated in April. |
| August 5           | Turkish forces attack Kurdish Workers Party (PKK) guerrillas in northern Iraq (southern Kurdistan). |
| 10                 | Last of allied troops involved in Operation Provide Comfort leave Turkey. Planes from Turkey, however, continue to fly regularly over northern Iraq, north of the 32nd parallel, policing the no-fly zone designated by the UN in Operation Poised Hammer |
| Sept. first week   | Fighting between Iraqi government troops and Iraqi Kurdish *peshmergas* in Kirkuk and Arbil areas. |
| 13                 | Iraqi Prime Minister Sa'dun Hammadi is dismissed and dropped from the Revolutionary Command Council (RCC). He is replaced by Muhammad Zubaidi, another Shi'i and a political lightweight. |
| October 5          | Fighting between Kurdish guerillas and Iraqi soldiers in Kifri and later Kala, Arbat and Sulaimaniyya, |
| 11-13              | Bombing raids by Turkey, napalming and strafing runs and ground attacks on Kurdish villages, possibly to seal border (mines planted at the same time). |
| 24                 | Raid into Turkey by PKK guerrillas based in northern Iraq. |
| 25                 | Turkish reprisal raids against PKK positions in northern Iraq. |
| Last week          | Baghdad withdraws troops and Arab officials from Kurdish areas and halts salary payments to Kurdish officials. Also imposes an internal blockade stopping food and fuel crossing the de facto border. |
| November, early    | Defence Minister Husain Kamil Hasan, Saddam Husain's son-in-law. is replaced by Ali Hasan al-Majid, Saddam Husain's cousin, who is known as the 'Butcher of the Kurds'. |
| 12                 | Kurdish leaders agree to withdraw *peshmergas* from Kurdish cities if government lifts internal blockade. Blockade is not lifted. |
| Dec. first week    | Boutros Boutros-Ghali takes up post as UN Secretary General. |
| 28                 | Iraqi opposition groups meet in Damascus, without the Iraqi Kurdistan Front (IKF). |
| 30                 | Car bomb explodes in Baghdad. |
| Late December      | Iraqi Prime Minister orders army generals to wipe out three specific marsh tribes, including the Jawaber. It is not known how far these orders have been carried out. |

# 1992

| | |
|---|---|
| January 1 | Renewal of mandate for coalition forces based in Turkey. |
| First week | Jeffrey Archer visits Kurdish areas. |
| 6-7 | Meeting in Vienna, on oil sales, between UN and Iraqi government officials. |
| 14 | UN weapons inspectors annouce that Iraq admits to nuclear weapons programme. |
| 15 | IKF meeting in in Khalifan decides to withdraw from negotiations with the government and to call for elections to establish a Kurdish parliament. |
| 16 | An IKF delegation meets with other opposition forces in Damascus. |
| February 4 | Iraqi government officials withdraw from second round of talks on oil sales. |
| 6 | Renewal of sanctions (60-day Security Council review). |
| 11 | UK-Kuwait defence pact signed, similar to one signed in September 1991. |
| 20 | UK Foreign Secretary threatens coalition action on Kurdish blockade. |
| 23 | Iraqi opposition leaders meet in Riyadh. They include Ayatollah Muhamad Baqir al-Hakim, head of the Supreme Council for the Islamic Revolution in Iraq (SCIRI). This is the first time that Sa'udi Arabia has associated itself with Shi'i opposition groups from Iraq. |
| 20-27 | Security Council orders Iraq to destroy missile stocks. |
| 27 | Mas'ud Barzani, leader of the Kurdish Democratic Party (KDP), meets UK Prime Minister John Major in London. |
| March 6 | Bomb explodes in Sulaimaniyya. |
| 11-13 | Iraqi Deputy Prime Minister Tariq 'Aziz at UN. |
| 12 | King Hussein of Jordan meets President Bush for the first time since the Gulf War. |
| 16 | Bomb explodes in Arbil. |
| Mid-March | IKF delegation visits Iran. |
| 25 | Turkish air force bomb PKK bases in northern Iraq. Iraqi shelling in Kalak area; 40,000 evacuated. |
| 26 | Talks on oil sales between Iraq and the UN resume in Vienna. |
| April 1 | UN Under-Secretary General Jan Eliasson takes up post as Emergency Relief Coordinator. |
| 5 | Iranian air raid on Majahedin Khalq base near Baghdad. |
| 11 | State Security court trials re-open in Kuwait. |
| Some time in April | The 'rubber-stamp' Iraqi National Assembly in Baghdad approves measures to encourage people to leave the marsh hamlets of southern Iraq and settle on dry land in larger villages. |
| 14 | UN warns Iraq on missiles north of 36th parallel. |
| Late April | UN Iraq/Kuwait Boundary Demarcation Commission |

reports.

KDP sets up liaison office in Diyarbakir, south-east Turkey.

| | |
|---|---|
| May 19 | Kurdish Elections take place and are assessed as free and fair by more than fifty oberservers from more than a dozen countries. |
| 31 | Deadline for non-Kuwaitis to obtain resident permits to stay in Kuwait. |
| June | Muhamad Baqir al-Hakim, head of SCIRI, visits Sa'udi Arabia. |
| 16-19 | Iraqi opposition conference in Vienna inaugurates the Iraqi National Congress (INC). SCIRI and Damascus-based groups including the Iraqi Communist Party (ICP) do not attend. |
| 19-23 | Oil sales talks resume in Vienna, without success. |
| 19 | Turkish parliament renews allied air base agreement for flights over Kurdish-administered northern Iraq. |
| 30 | UN/Iraq Memorandum of Understanding (MoU) officially expires. |
| July | Intensification of attacks on the people of the southern marshes begins. |
| 6 | Bomb attack on Danielle Mitterrand during her visit to Iraqi Kurdistan. |
| 9 | Security Council warns Iraq on security of UN personnel. |
| 5-26 | UN weapons inspectors barred from Iraqi Ministry of Agriculture. |
| 22 | PKK closes Turkish/Iraq border. |
| 26 | In Baghdad twenty merchants are reportedly executed and 500 imprisoned for alleged profiteering. |
| 29 | Jalal Talabani and Mas'ud Barzani lead Iraqi opposition delegation to meet US Secretary of State James Baker in Washington. |
| 30 | Turkish warplanes bomb a village near Zakho in northern Iraq, reportedly killing three KDP guerrillas. |
| | Turkish land forces close the border and take up positions inside Iraq. |
| 31 | PKK forces in Iraq cut main road from Turkey into Iraq (Khaŀbur bridge crossing). This is in retaliation for KDP attacks on PKK positions inside Iraq and for an Iraqi Kurdish promise to Turkey to stop the region being used for cross-border raids into Turkey by PKK. |
| August 8 | Death of Grand Ayatollah Abolqassem al-Khoei, who was under house arrest in Iraq. |
| 10 | Security Council discusses report on southern Iraq. |
| 17 | UN Under-Secretary Eliasson begins talks in Baghdad. |
| 18 | Franco/Kuwaiti military pact. |
| 19 | Turkish/Iraqi border reopened. |
| 27 | Air exclusion ('no-fly') zone imposed in southern Iraq, south of the 32nd parallel, covering Basra, Nasiriyya, |

|            | Amara, Samawa, Najaf and marsh area. |
|------------|--------------------------------------|
| 27         | Kuwait election set for 5 October. |
| Sept. 23-27 | Meeting of opposition groups in Salah al-Din, Iraqi Kurdistan, to prepare for second INC conference. |
| October 4  | Iraqi Kurdish *pershmergas* begin attacking PKK bases in northern Iraq/Iraqi Kurdistan. |
| 24-27      | Conference of expanded INC in Salah al-Din. 20,000 Turkish troops enter northern Iraq in Turkey/Iran/Iraq border area to attack the PKK. Iraqi civilians are reported among the casualties. |
| November 14 | Turkish, Iranian and Syrian officials meet in Ankara to discuss the situation in northern Iraq. They strongly favour preserving Iraq's territorial integrity. |
| 16         | PKK lifts embargo on trucks going from Turkey to Iraqi Kurdistan after political agreement with PUK and KDP. |
| December 7 | 'Saddam Husain' (Third River) Project of draining southern marshes reaches completion. |
| 27         | US planes shoot down Iraqi MiG over southern no-fly zone. |

## 1993

| | |
|------------|--------------------------------------|
| First week | Allies report Iraqis moving surface-to-air missiles into the southern no-fly zone. |
| 3          | US and Allies' warplanes attack targets in southern Iraq in retaliation for Iraq's refusal to remove anti-aircraft missile batteries from the no-fly zone. Nineteen reported killed mostly when buildings in Basra were hit by mistake. |
| 5          | Kuwaitis report a clash with Iraqi soldiers in border zone. Turkey sends charge d'affaires to Baghdad. |
| 6          | US, UK and French UN ambassadors send a note to Iraq's ambassador demanding the removal of the missiles from the no-fly zone within 48 hours. |
| 7          | Stuart Cameron, working for Care International, murdered in Iraqi Kurdistan, near Chamchamal. |
| 8          | Hours before the ultimatum expires, the US reports that the Iraqi missiles have been moved. |
| 9          | UN weapons inspectors are refused permission to fly to Baghdad from Bahrain. Iraqis say they should use Iraqi planes. Security Council warns Iraq of the 'serious consequences' of this 'material breach of UN resolutions.' |
| 10-13      | Series of Iraqi incursions into the demilitarised Iraq/Kuwait border area to collect equipment. Security Council warns of 'serious consequences'. |
| 13         | Iraqis say they will stop moving equipment and allow UN inspectors to fly. 114 US, French and British planes bomb sites at Amara, Nasiriyya, Basra and Najaf. Only about half the targets are hit. |

| | |
|---|---|
| 14 | US demands that Iraq remove police posts in border area due to be handed to Kuwait on 15 January. |
| 15 | 1,200 US troops arrive in Kuwait. Iraq says it will guarantee the safety of UN weapons inspectors' flight 'except when hostile actions are being carried out against Iraq'. |
| 17 | Raid by 40 US Tomahawk missiles destroys a factory alleged to be part of the nuclear programme. |
| | Rashid Hotel in central Baghdad is hit and badly damaged, two women killed. Iraq removes its police posts on the Kuwait border. |
| 18 | 75 US, UK and French aircraft hit four sites south of the 32nd parallel. Iraqis report 21 people killed. |
| 17-19 | Clashes in the northern no-fly zone. |
| 19 | Iraqis announce a unilateral ceasefire from 20 January to coincide with US presidential inauguration. |
| 21-25 | Further clashes in both no-fly zones. |
| March 10 | Egypt sends senior diplomat to Iraq. |
| 12 | Massacre at Awaina village near Arbil in Iraqi Kurdistan, apparently by Arab tribes with Iraqi government backing. |
| 13 | Iranian air force attacks Iranian Kurdish opposition targets in Iraqi Kurdistan. At least six people killed. |
| 17 | Kurdish Prime Minister Fuad Ma'sum resigns. |
| | PKK announces unilateral ceasefire until 15 April. |
| 18 | UN Boundary Commission announces demarcation of Iraq-Kuwait maritime boundary. |
| 19 | Jalal Talabani visits Kuwait to try to enlist support. |
| 22 | Vincent Tollet, Handicap International's programme director is murdered in Iraqi Kurdistan near Dokhan. |
| 29 | Security Council renews sanctions in 60-day review. |
| 31 | Six-month Memorandum of Understanding expires. |
| April 9 | US planes bomb Iraqi positions in northern no-fly zone. |
| 11 | Abdullah Rasul ('Kosrat') appointed Kurdish Prime Minister. |
| 16 | PKK extends its unilateral ceasefire. |
| 18 | US planes bomb Iraqi positions in the northern no-fly zone. |
| 22-29 | INC delegation in Washington. |
| May 4-10 | Iraq withdraws the 25 dinar note and closes the de factor border with Iraqi Kurdistan. |
| 7 | Iranian assault on Iranian Kurdish position inside Iraq, reportedly hitting eight villages, but with no casualties. |
| 9-20 | First ever UK tourist package tour of Iraqi Kurdistan, under auspices of Kurdish Minister for Tourism, Mrs Kafia Sulaiman. |
| 24 | INC delegation visits Saudi Arabia. |
| 25 | Iranian air force bomb Majahadin Khalq bases north-east of Baghdad. |
| 27 | Security Council approves Iraq-Kuwait boundary |

|  | demarcation. |
| --- | --- |
| June 1 | Iranian artilliery attacks on villages in Iraq. Extensive damage but no reported casualties. |
| 7 | Turkish, Syrian and Iranian foreign ministers meet to discuss northern Iraq. |
| 8 | End of PKK ceasefire. |
| 9 | US government says it will recognise and give support to the INC. |
| 27 | US warships fire cruise missiles at Baghdad, reportedly killing six civilians, because of 'compelling evidence' that Iraq had plotted to kill George Bush. |
| July | Purge of Saddam Husain's 'inner circle', including Tikritis, is reported. |
| 22 & 23 | Iranian ground troops enter Iraqi Kurdistan, targetting Iranian Kurdish Democratic Party and Komala (Iranian Kurdish Communist Party). |
| August 19 | US planes attack an air defence battery near Mosul. |
| 24 | Two Iraqi ambassadors announce their defection in London. |
| 31 | Talks resume between Iraq and the UN in New York. |
| September 1 | Tariq Aziz and Boutros Ghali meet in Geneva. |
| 5 | Saddam Husain apppoints a new prime minister. |
| 20 | Sanctions renewed at 60-day review. |
| 22 | Two Swedes released from Iraqi prisons. |
| 26 & 29 | Chemical attacks reported on Marsh Arab villages, Hawr Allawi and Abu al-Zargi. |
| 28 | Kurds begin blockade of Faida checkpoint. |
| Oct. first week | Turkey stages cross border raids into northern Iraq. |
| 1 | Rolf Ekeus arrives in Baghdad for weapons talks. |
| 3 | Turkey attacks two villages in Iraqi Kurdistan using air and artilliery power. Nine killed. |
| 6 | Iraqi Foreign Minister meets Boutros Ghali in New York. |
| 18 | Talks between Iranian and Iraqi officials begin in Baghdad. |
| November 14 | UN inspectors arrrive in Iran to investigate allegations of chemical attacks against Marsh Arabs in sourthern Iraq. |
| 15 | US citizen Kenneth Beaty realeased from Iraqi prison. |
| 18 | Sanctions renewed at 60-day review. Weapons inspectors arrive in Iraq to investigate reports of chemical attacks. |
| 22 | Tariq Aziz and Boutros Ghali discuss sanctions in New York. |
| 23 | Special Rapporteur on human rights in Iraq reports to the UN General Assembly. |
| 26 | Iraq accepts Security Council Resolution 715. |
| 29 | UNIKOM reinforcements arrive on Iraq/Kuwait border. |
| 30 Nov to mid-Dec | Turkish raids against PKK in northern Iraq. |
| December 9 | Three Britons released from Iraqi prisons after Edward Heath visits Baghdad. |
| 10 & 11 | Fighting between KDP and breakaway Socialist Party |

|  | faction. |
| 18 | Kurdish Presidential Council formed. |
| 20 | Fighting begins between PUK and Islamic Movement (IMIK) |

# 1994

| January 4 | Permanent Four members of Security Council present demarche on human rights to Iraqi ambassador. Lord Archer arrives in northern Iraq. |
| 13 | French delegation holds talks in Baghdad. |
| 23 | Iraqi regime closes international exchange area after failing to manipulate money market following further collapse of Iraqi dinar. |
| 28 | Turkish raid against PKK in Zaleh area of northern Iraq. |
| February 2 | Rolf Ekeus, chief UNSCOM, arrives in Baghdad for talks. |
| 5 | Foreign Ministers of Turkey, Iran and Syria end talks in Istanbul. |
| 11 | Husain Kamil al-Majid, son-in-law of Saddam Husain and highly influential member of the ruling clique, is reported in hospital in Jordan with a brain tumour. |
| 17 | Iraqi Foreign Ministry delegation arrives in Iran. Peace agreement signed between PUK and IMIK. |
| February-March | Several reports of bomb attacks and clashes between opponents of the regime and its security forces in Baghdad. |
| March first week | Iraqi oil ministry delegation visits Paris. |
| 16 | Tariq Aziz holds discussions in New York with UN officials. |
| 18 | Security Council renews sanctions. |
| 20 | Iraq seals de facto border with Kurdish-administered northern Iraq. |
| April 3 | Assassination of German journalist Lizzy Schmidt and her bodyguard in Iraqi Kurdistan, by Iraqi government agents. |
| 5 | Two UN guards injured in an ambush on UN convoy near the city of Arbil in northern Iraq. This brings to 13 the number of attacks against foreigners in Iraqi Kurdistan in 1994, resulting in one death and seven casualties. Saddam Husain has reportedly ordered Iraqi security forces to attack foreigners in Iraq, offering a reward of US$10,000 for any foreigner killed. |
| 8 | Reports of further explosions in Baghdad indicating a deteriorating security situation. |
| May 1 | INC reports air drop of thousands of opposition leaflets over Baghdad. |

# Further Reading

## 1. On modern Middle Eastern history

Cleveland, William L., *A History of the Modern Middle East*, Boulder and Oxford, 1994

Hourani, Albert, *A History of the Arab Peoples*, London, 1991

Lapidus, Ira, *A History of Islamic Societies*, London 1988

## 2. On modern Iraq

Baram, Amatzia, *Culture, History and Ideology in the Formation of Ba'thist Iraq 1969-1989*, London 1989

Baram, Amatzia and Rubin, Barry (eds.), *Iraq's Road to War: Domestic Politics, Economics and Foreign Relations*, London 1994

Batatu, Hanna, *The Old Social Classes and the Revolutionary Movements of Iraq: a Study of Iraq's Old Landed and Commercial Classes and of its Communists, Ba'thists and Free Officers*, Princeton, 1978

Chaliand, Gerard, (ed), *People without a Country: the Kurds and Kurdistan*, London,1980

Farouk-Sluglett, Marion and Sluglett, Peter, *Iraq since 1958:from Revolution to Dictatorship*, London 1987, 1990

Fernea, Robert A., and Louis, Wm. Roger (eds), *The Iraqi Revolution of 1958: the Old Social Classes Revisited*, London 1991

Hiro, Dilip, *The Longest War: the Iran-Iraq Military Conflict*, London 1989,1990

Hiro, Dilip, *Desert Shield to Desert Storm:the Second Gulf War*, London and New York, 1992

Al-Khalil, Samir (Kanan Makiya), *Republic of Fear: Saddam's Iraq*, Berkeley and London, 1989, 1990

Makiya, Kanan, *Cruelty and Silence*, London 1993

McDowall, David, *The Kurds: a nation denied*, London 1992

# Index

Abdul-Aziz, Shaikh Othman, 127
Abdulrahman, Ameen, 123
abortion, 65
'Aflaq, Michel, 17, 32, 34, 37, 47, 162
Afram, 'Abd al-Ahad, 124
Agha, Qassim, 109
*al-Ahali* newspaper, 169
Ahmad, Corporal, 103
Ahmad, Ibrahim, 165
Ahmad, Salih, 124
Alaq, Ja'far, 17
'Alawi, Hasan, 13
Algiers accord, 165
'Ali, Imam, 135
'Ali, M., 103
al-'Ali, Salah 'Umar, 9, 13
Allison, Dorothy, 191
AMAR appeal, 145
'Ammash, Salih Mahdi, 33
Amnesty International, 60, 144
Anfal campaign, 131, 134, 164, 165, 183,
    191, 197, 202
anti-semitism, 190, 194, 198
*Aqlam* magazine, 16
Arab Emergency Summit Conference, 77
Arab nationalism *see* pan-Arabism
Arab Socialist Action Party, 32
Arab Socialist Movement, 32
'Arif, 'Abd al-Rahman, 33, 40, 49
'Arif, 'Abd al-Salam, 36, 49
army: disintegration of, 106; exhaustion
    of, 102-5
al-'Arsuzi, Zaki, 34
Artists' Union, 10
al-Asifi, Shaikh Muhammad Mahdi, 159
assassination, 12, 36, 41, 113, 153, 226
Assyrian Democratic Movement (ADM),
    118, 123
Assyrians, 119, 155, 166, 176, 179, 190,
    214, 241
'Aziz, Qadir, 124
'Aziz, Tariq, 10, 13, 29, 158, 184

Ba'th Party, 10, 11, 20, 21, 22, 28, 46, 55,
    63, 73, 74, 102, 106, 113, 134, 139, 156,
    161, 162, 163, 164, 170, 172, 174, 175,
    185, 190, 211, 224, 225, 226, 232, 238,
    239; 8th congress, 38, 39, 40, 43, 48;
    9th congress, 43, 46, 48; 10th congress,
    114; cultural policy of, 13-19;
    pro-Syrian, 111, 112, 162, 238;
    relations with youth, 41; voluntarism
    in, 47-9
Ba'thism, 7, 8, 9, 17, 32-51, 157, 167, 216;
    degeneration of, 1
*Babil* newspaper, 30, 64
Bafri, Hasan Husain, 122
al-Bakr, Ahmad Hasan, 13, 32, 33, 39, 42,
    43, 107, 113, 157, 162, 180
Bakri, Sulaiman, 13, 16
banking system, in Kurdistan, 126
Barzani tribe, 66
Barzani, Mas'ud, 105, 127, 167, 173, 242
Barzani, Mulla Mustafa, 130, 164, 165
al-Basri, 'Abd al-Jabbar 'Abbas, 16
al-Bayati, 'Abd al-Wahhab, 8
al-Bazzaz, 'Abd al-Rahman, 8
Bekass, Sherko, 123
betrayal, concept of, 201
birth-rate, increasing, 64-5
Bitar, Salah al-Din, 34
al-Bitar, Midhet, 34
Black September, 38, 39
blaming, language of, 197
bombing: of Iraq, 79, 81, 178, 179; of
    religious sanctuaries, 188
brain-drain, Iraqi, 180
Brifcany, Ma'mun, 124
Brittain, Victoria, 68
burglaries, official, 138-9
Bush, George, 105, 221, 233

Camp David accords, 47
canal-building in Iraq, 143-4
censorship, 8, 9, 10

Central Intelligence Agency (CIA) (US), 221, 236
Chadirchi, Kamil, 8, 169
Charter 91, 4, 205-10
chemical weapons, use of, 182, 235
children, sale of, 138
Christians, 29, 30, 119, 134, 181, 214, 218, 219, 237, 241
Comittee for National Coordination, 174
conscription, resistance to, 101
conspiracy theories, 179, 180
contraception, 65
corruption, 21, 24, 138, 148, 234
cost of living, in Iraq, 81
cruelty, Arab, 197, 199, 204, 205
cultural festivals, 14
culture, and politics, 7-11

al-Daini, 'Abd al-Wahhab, 18
al-Da'ud, 'Abd al-Rahman, 33, 35
al-Da'wa party, 99, 111, 158-60, 172, 173, 174, 215, 239
Dalu, Salah, 124
death penalty, 40
death toll of wars, 79
debt, 2, 73, 77, 78, 83, 84, 101, 154, 228
democracy, 3, 5, 7, 30, 44, 54, 99, 113, 114, 115, 119, 120, 125, 139-40, 155, 161, 169-71, 173, 189, 209, 212, 214, 215, 218, 219, 236, 238, 239, 240; liberal, 215-17; parliamentary, 4, 208, 241
Democratic Front for the Liberation of Palestine, 32
Democratic Independent Party of Kurdistan, 67
democratic movement, 169-71
demonstrations, 102, 105, 110, 158
deportations, 158, 160, 164, 224, 225
deserters, 103, 109, 235
disappearances, 65, 67, 138, 164, 187
divorce, 63, 64, 67
dress, regulation of women's, 70
al-Dulaimi, Naziha, 65
al-Duri, 'Izzat, 42

economic crisis, 76-7, 101
education, 60, 138, 186
Egypt, 47, 189
Elf Aquitaine company, 146
embargo *see* sanctions against Iraq
embargo, on Kurdistan, 131
emigration, 181, 188
equal pay of women, 60
executions, 44, 60, 103, 113, 135, 136, 138, 139, 144, 183, 225, 227; mass, 139
exile of Iraqis, 3, 11, 135, 153, 154, 160, 162, 175, 187, 201

Faisal I, King, 46, 226
Faisal II, King, 174
*falaqa* torture, 11
family: breakdown of, 138; law, 67; nuclear, 62-3, 224; risks to, 226; rule by, 114, 115
Farman, Sha'ib Tu'uma, 8
Fattah, Azad, 124
fear, freedom from, 4, 207
federalism, 4, 129, 159, 176, 211-22, 238, 241-2; problems of, 218-20
feminism, 185
fertility drugs, administering of, 65
Fine Arts Society, 10
food prices in Iraq, 90
food rations, composition of, 91
foreign trade of Iraq, 75
foreign travel, restrictions on, 30
France, 149, 166
Freedom Monument, 17

gas attacks on villages, 154
General Federation of Iraqi Women (GFIW), 61, 65-6
General Union of Students in the Iraqi Republic (GUSIR), 40
genocide, 197, 211, 224, 227-8, 238
Germany, 34
Ghafur, Nasih, 123
Ghaidan, Sa'dun, 35
Gorbachev, Mikhail, coup against, 180
gross domestic product of Iraq, 77-8, 82, 88
guerrilla tactics, 175
Gulf War, 1, 2, 3, 14, 18, 59, 68, 97, 98, 100, 120, 137, 154, 155, 165, 171, 202, 217; death toll in, 80
gun control, 126

Hadi, Idris, 123
Hadid, Muhammad, 169
al-Haalithi, Khalaf, 110
Hafidh, Salah al-Din, 124
Haigh, Frank, 141
Haija, Nawaf Abul, 17
al-Hakim, Sayyid Muhammad Baqir, 98, 104, 108, 159, 160, 161, 239
al-Hakim, Sayyid Muhsin, 158
Halabja, gassing of, 101, 131, 154, 165
Hama, destruction of, 195
Hammadi, Sa'dun, 101
Hammas movement, 104
Hammudi, Basim Jamil, 13, 16
Hammudi, Shaikh Human, 143
Hasan, Saddam Kamil, 25, 29

Hasan, 'Uthman, 124
health care, 137; breakdown of, 80
Helms, Christine, 41, 48
*hijab*, wearing of, 70
Hikmet, Ghani, 16
al-Hinnawi, Sami, 35
Hitler, Adolf, 34
honour, 60-71
Horwitz, Tony, 191
al-Huda, Bint, 65, 158
human rights, 148-52, 179, 206, 235, 237;
    abuses of, 144-5
Husain, Hala, 43
Husain, Qusayy Saddam, 29, 114
Husain, Rana, 43
Husain, Saddam, 10, 11-13, 32, 33, 37, 39,
    41, 42-6, 48, 63, 64, 74, 75, 77, 82, 100,
    101, 106, 109, 112, 113, 130, 134, 135,
    137, 141, 142, 147, 148, 149, 154, 156,
    162, 165, 167, 171, 178, 179, 180, 182,
    183, 184, 185, 189, 199, 212, 214, 217,
    221, 224, 226, 227, 228, 230, 233, 238,
    243; and Kurds, 191; and
    pseudo-religious ceremony, 45; as
    hero, 52; as leader symbol, 46-7;
    criticism of, 1, 18, 110, 225; death of
    mother, 26; glorification of, 17;
    Palestinian sympathies for, 182
al-Husain, Sharif 'Ali ibn, 174
Husain, 'Uday Saddam, 29, 30, 43, 114

Ibrahim, Sab'aui, 29, 43, 114
Ibrahim, Watban, 29, 30, 43, 114
identity, 200-4
imports of Iraq, 78, 88, 101
imprisonment, 1, 8, 9, 60, 135, 158
inflation, 75, 81
informers, 27, 63, 190
inheritance, law, 68
intellectuals: Arab, 199, 202, 203, 204,
    213; as functionaries, 18
international support, 230
*intifada*, 2, 23, 24, 25, 28, 29, 30, 46, 66,
    72, 105-8, 120, 134, 137, 139, 142-3,
    150, 154, 166, 172, 179, 183, 186, 187,
    188, 189, 190, 209, 212, 224, 233, 235,
    237; failure of, 97-117
intolerance, 194-204
Iran, 37, 99, 100, 102, 120, 125, 142, 153,
    158, 159, 160, 164, 165, 167, 171, 175,
    180, 217, 220, 225, 228, 234, 236, 239,
    240
Iran-Iraq war, 2, 15, 17, 26, 45, 61, 69, 77,
    78, 80, 82, 84, 97, 100, 102, 105, 135,
    153, 154, 155, 164, 165, 179, 183, 196,
    219, 235, 239; and opposition, 98-9;
    impact on Iraqi economy, 72-4

Iraq Petroleum Company (IPC), 72
*Iraq* newspaper, 45
Iraqi Broadcasting Corporation, 174
Iraqi Communist Party (ICP), 9, 10, 11,
    22, 36, 40, 65, 98, 99, 100, 105, 110,
    111, 118, 123, 157, 163, 165, 167-9,
    172, 173, 174, 176
Iraqi Democratic Party, 170
Iraqi Kurdistan Front (IKF), 3, 105, 118,
    119, 120, 121, 127, 128, 131, 165, 166,
    241, 242
'Iraqi man', 15, 26, 185
Iraqi National Congress (INC), 3, 4, 69,
    151, 172, 173, 174, 175, 176, 184, 186,
    216, 221, 224, 229-30
Iraqi Women's League (IWL), 65
Iraqi Writers' Union, 14
Iskandar, Amir, 12, 47
Islam, 70, 98, 99, 104, 108, 109, 111, 112,
    121, 134, 153, 158-60, 173, 180, 188,
    232
Islamic Action Organzation (IAO), 99,
    161
Islamic Masses Movement (IMM), 99
Islamic movements, 156-8, 160-1, 175, 215
Ismael, Jacqueline, 62
Israel, 53, 56, 102, 105, 175, 182, 186, 189,
    190, 197, 198, 200, 202, 204, 221, 225,
    234, 236; war with Arabs, 4, 8, 39, 157,
    170, 198
*Al-Istikhbarat al-Askariya*, 20, 23, 27
Izzat, Akram, 124

al-Jabbar, 'Adil 'Abd, 12
Jabir-Amin, Tayyib, 123
Jabr, Sa'd Salih, 216
Jadid, Salah, 33
*jash*, as derogatory term, 27, 109
al-Jasim, Latif Nisayyif, 14, 15
al-Jawahiri, Muhammad Mahdi, 8
*al-Jihad* newspaper, 160
*Jihaz al-Himaya al-Khas*, 20, 23, 24-6, 29,
    114
*Jihaz al-Mukhabarat al-Amma*, 20, 23, 110
*Jihaz Hanin*, 36
Joint Action Committee (JAC), 171, 172
Jordan, 33, 37, 102, 220
Joseph, Suad, 62
journalists, 12, 14
Journalists' Union, 10
judiciary, subservience of, 225
Juwaibar, Khalil, 107

*al-Kalima* magazine, 9
al-Kamali, Shafiq, 13
Kamil, Husain, 114
Kamil, Saddam, 12, 43

Kanibi, Hasan, 122
*Khabat* newspaper, 129
Khairullah, 'Adnan, 43
Khalaf, Ahmad, 18
al-Khalil, Samir, 62, 200, 203
al-Khayyat, Sana, 62
al-Khazraji, 102
Khudayyir, Muwaffaq, 14
Khumaini, Ayatullah, 99
*khuzuk* torture, 11
Kifah, 21
Kirkuki, Kamal, 123
al-Kubaisi, Tarrad, 11, 13
Kurdish Democratic Party (KDP), 9, 36,
   67, 105, 110, 118, 119, 122, 124, 128,
   164, 165, 166, 167, 168, 172, 173, 241,
   242
Kurdish Muslim Ulama Union, 121
Kurdish Parliament, 118-33
Kurdish Red Crescent, 127
Kurdish Toilers' Party (KTP), 118
Kurdish Writers' Union, 10, 14
Kurdistan, 153, 165, 167, 168, 181, 212,
   219, 237, 243; Iraqi, 4, 28, 46, 66-8, 97,
   110, 115, 118, 131, 155, 166, 171, 173,
   176, 185, 214, 232, 240; population of,
   121
Kurdistan Popular Democratic Party
   (KPDP), 118
Kurds, 2, 3, 23, 27, 28, 30, 36, 46, 65, 97,
   98, 99, 100, 101, 102, 103, 107, 109,
   110, 111, 119, 131, 134, 135, 140, 144,
   150, 153, 156, 159, 164-7, 168, 171,
   172, 174, 175, 176, 179, 186, 190, 191,
   197, 202, 203, 213, 214-15, 218, 221,
   224, 226, 228, 232, 233, 234, 235, 236,
   237-8; autonomy of, 238; negotiation
   with Saddam Husain, 191; relations
   with Arabs, 4; special status for, 3
Kuwait, 73, 149, 173, 196; invasion of, 53,
   56, 72, 76-7, 80, 81, 83, 102, 104, 147,
   153, 162, 179, 182, 184, 198, 220, 228,
   233 (economic consequences of, 77-9)

Lausanne, Treaty of, 130
law, rule of, 223-31
Lebanon, 198
Leonard, John, 189
literature, 10, 12; function of, 16
loans, from Kuwait, 77

Ma'sum, Fu'ad, 123, 125
Mahdi, Sami, 17
Mahmud, Shaikh, 130
Majid, 'Ayad Hajji Namiq, 122
al-Majid, 'Ali Hasan, 29, 114, 227
Major, John, 233

Makiya, Kanan, 216
*Maktab al-Amn al-Qawmi*, 21
Mamand, Sarkis Aghajan, 122
marriage, 63, 70, 189, 219; reform of law,
   67
Marsh Arabs, 135-6, 141-6, 224, 235
marshes of Southern Iraq, 15, 80, 155,
   160; army cordon around, 144;
   draining of, 3, 135, 137, 141-6, 219,
   235; people of, 29, 108
Marx, Karl, 52
Marxism, 7, 8, 32, 39, 40, 48, 54, 168
mass culture, 7
Matba'i, Hamid, 9
Mawlud, Amin, 123
medical supplies, 145, 229
military service, 14
military spending of Iraq, 89
Ministry of Agriculture building,
   inspection of, 181
Mofid, Kamran, 73
mortality, child, 68, 137
Mott MacDonald company, 141
Msayar, Kamil, 22
Mu'alla, 'Abd al-Amir, 12
*mu'taman*, figure of, 21, 22
al-Mudarris, Fahmi, 8
*Mudiriyat al-Amn al-Amma*, 21, 23, 24,
   26, 27, 29
Mufti, Kamal, 124
Muhammad, Mughdid, 22
Muhsin, 'Abd al-Jabbar, 13
Muslim Brotherhood, 104
Mutla pass, bombing of, 2, 105, 106

Namiq, Jawher, 129
napalm, use of, 144
Nasser, Jamal 'Abd al, 32, 37, 46
Nasserism, 161, 162, 163
Nassir, 'Ali, 196
National Action Charter, 36
National Democratic Party (NDP), 169,
   170
National Front, 168
National Peace Council (NPC), 187
nationalism, 115, 189, 221; popular, 100;
   state, 100
al-Nayif, 'Abd al-Razzaq, 33, 35
newspapers, 8, 11, 45, 127, 187
Nicholson, Emma, 145
no-fly zones, 4, 125, 136, 137, 144, 147,
   166, 180, 223, 228, 229, 230, 236

oil, 76-7, 104, 140, 146, 148, 165, 236;
   boom, 38, 136; income from, 75;
   nationalization of, 43; over-supply of,
   229; prices of, 2, 7, 72, 73, 77;

production of, 223; revenues from, 82-3, 89, 114, 151; sale of, 85, 147, 235

Operation Provide Comfort, 234
opposition, Iraqi, 3, 30, 69, 97, 104, 105, 106, 149, 153-77, 186, 212, 213, 223, 226, 236, 238, 243; conference of, 171
Organization of Lebanese Socialists, 32
Organization of Petroleum Exporting Countries (OPEC), 76, 83
Othman, Mahmood, 127
Ottoman Empire, 205, 212, 225, 232

Pakistan, 189
Palestinians, 3, 17, 37, 38, 104, 178, 180, 182, 183, 196, 197, 198, 199, 201, 237
pan-Arabism, 37-8, 98, 99, 153, 161-4, 174, 176, 216, 226
Patriotic Front, 36, 40-2
Patriotic Union of Kurdistan (PUK), 22, 67, 110, 118, 119, 122, 124, 128, 165, 166, 167, 168, 172, 241, 242
People's Party of Kurdistan, 67
Personal Status legislation (1978), 62
*peshmerga* guerrillas, 109, 110, 123, 126, 167, 168, 242
poetry, 13, 15, 19
poisoning: of marshes, 144; of waters, 235; with thallium, 11
politics, degradation of, 20-31
polygamy, 64, 70
Popular Front for the Liberation of Palestine, 32
privatization, 2; failure of policies, 74-6
prostitution, 138, 148; forced, 68

Qadir, Muhammad Mulla, 124
*Qadissiya*, 17
Qasim, 'Abd al-Karim, 8, 12, 33, 49, 130, 167, 169
al-Qasim, Muhammad, 29
Qattan, Colonel, 113

Ra'uf, Ma'ruf, 124
Rafiq, Faridun, 123
Rahhal, Khalid, 16
al-Rahhal, Husain, 8
rape, 11, 21, 68, 131; official, 66
Rashid, Arshad Yasin, 29
Rashid, Fawzi, 17
Rassam, Amal, 62
rations, sale of, 148
Realistic school of literature, 16
refugees, 2, 80, 97, 100, 136, 144, 145, 165, 185, 233, 234
religion, finding of, 188
Revolutionary Command Council

(RCC), 14, 26, 35, 36, 38, 39, 40, 43, 64, 65, 103, 162, 180, 225
Rhodes, Tom, 145
al-Ruba'i, Muwaffaq, 109
al-Rumi, Ghadah Jalal al-Din, 45
Rushbayani, Yu'nis, 124
Rushdie, Salman, 199
Russia, 149

Sèvres, Treaty of, 129, 131
Sa'id, Hamid, 17
Sa'udi Arabia, 73, 76, 83, 149, 171, 173, 220, 229, 236
al-Sabah, Su'ad, 18
sabotage, 144, 166
Sadat, Anwar, 46
al-Sadr, Amina, 65
al-Sadr, Sayyid Muhammad Baqir, 158, 159
safe havens, 2, 66, 147, 166, 229, 233-5
al-Sahhaf, Muhammad Sa'id, 9
Salar, Ahmad, 123
Salih, Muhammad, 124
Salih, Tawfiq, 12
Salim, Jawad, 17
Salman, Sabah, 13
al-Samarai, 'Abdullah Sallum, 9, 13
sanctions against Iraq, 2, 3, 72, 78, 79, 81, 84-5, 90, 104, 114, 125, 131, 146, 148-52, 179, 223
al-Sayigh, Yusuf, 19
al-Sayyab, Badr Shakir, 8
al-Shabacha, 'Abd, 108
al-Shawk, Ali, 11
science, 185
sectarianism, 190, 191
security forces, 138-9, 163
sewage treatment, 85
*Sha'r 1969* magazine, 9
Shakir, Kamal, 124
Shakir, Sa'dun, 43
shame, 60-71
Shammar, Shaikh of, 28
Shanshal, Jabbar, 102
*shari'a* law, 30, 67
Sharif, Ahmad, 124
Shatt al-'Arab waterway, 100
Shawais, Rosch, 123
Shi'ism, 2
Shi'ites, 3, 4, 24, 28, 29, 37, 40, 65, 97, 98, 99, 102, 108, 111, 112, 113, 142, 156, 157, 158, 160, 168, 170, 173, 174, 176, 180, 182, 186, 190, 191, 197, 202, 212, 213, 215, 217, 218, 219, 224, 226, 232, 233, 236, 237, 239-41, 243; suppression of, 134-60
Shishkali, Adib, 35

short stories, 16
Shukr, Ibrahim Salih, 8
silence of Arabs, 213
Simpson, John, 112
Sinjari, Husain Taha, 124
socialism, 74, 162, 168
Socialist Party of Iraqi Kurdish (SPIK), 118
Socialist Party of Kurdistan (PASOK), 67, 118
*Songs of Trees, The*, 16
Southern Iraq, 235-6
sovereignty of Iraq, 148-52
state, Iraqi, 53, 54
state terror, 20-31, 206
Sudan, 104
Sulaiman, Kafia, 124
Sunnis, 4, 26, 29, 112, 134, 156, 173, 186, 190, 191, 197, 212, 213, 214, 215, 216, 218, 221, 232, 236, 237, 238-9, 243
Supreme Council of the Islamic Revolution in Iraq (SCIRI), 98, 104, 108, 143, 145, 160, 172, 173, 239, 240
al-Surchi, Husain, 28
Switzerland, money transfers to, 228
Syria, 32, 35, 37, 38, 125, 153, 162, 167, 171, 172, 174, 195, 196, 203, 220, 234, 236

*Taakhi* newspaper, 9, 11
Taimour, 203
Takriti clan, 113, 114
al-Takriti, Barzan, 228
al-Takriti, Fito, 66
al-Takriti, Hammed Shiheb, 35
al-Takriti, Hardan, 33, 35
Talabani, Jalal, 22, 111, 127, 165, 167, 242
*al-tasattur* regulation, 63
Tawfiq, Muhammad, 123
taxation policy, 73
television, 11, 127
Thatcher, Margaret, 233
*al-Thawra* newspaper, 26, 29, 45
theatre, 17
theft: by Saddam Husain, 228; increase of, 138
toleration, principle of, 4, 207, 208
torture, 1, 10, 11, 19, 131, 138, 139, 144, 158, 182, 187, 190, 195
Total company, 146
totalitarianism, definition of, 227
Tulfa, Adnan Khairullah, 113
Turcoman population, 155, 176, 190, 214, 219, 241
Turkey, 102, 110, 120, 125, 147, 149, 165, 166, 167, 220, 230, 236; closure of borders, 234

United Nations (UN), 3, 78, 79, 84-5, 125, 143, 145, 148-52, 173, 181, 183, 184, 223, 228-9, 230, 235; flour, 137; human rights monitors, 151
UN Charter, 130, 131, 227
UN Compensation Fund, 84, 85
UN Declaration of Human Rights, 207, 227
UN Security Council, 72, 85, 166, 228; Resolutions: *242*, 37; *338*, 38; *661*, 147; *666*, 147; *687*, 229, 230; *688*, 4, 120, 131, 145, 147, 148, 150, 166, 169, 236; *706*, 147, 229; *712*, 147, 148, 229; *715*, 147, 149; *773*, 184
unemployment, 2, 75, 81
Union of Soviet Socialist Republics (USSR), 61, 180; collapse of, 170, 216
United Kingdom (UK), 7, 149, 156, 166, 171, 172, 173, 226, 232, 233
United Patriotic Front, 35
United States of America (USA), 4, 18, 21, 29, 30, 79, 99, 109, 112, 113, 114, 148, 150, 165, 166, 171, 172, 179, 180, 183, 184, 185, 187, 189, 221, 231, 232, 233, 237, 240, 243; attitudes to, 178-81

van der Stoel, Max, 144
victim thinking, 197
Vienna conference, 132, 172, 173, 216
*vilayat* system, 176
villages, destruction of, 196
violence: against women, 69; political, 54-5
virginity, 64
Voltaire, 195, 197, 199
voluntarism, of Ba'ath party, 47-9, 52, 53, 54

wages, 82, 91, 92, 93
al-Wahid, 'Abd al-Razzaq 'Abd, 13, 15, 17
Wali, Muhammad Ibrahim, 107
war crimes of Saddam Husain, 3, 18, 231
water, supply of, 80, 85
weapons inspections by UN, 149
West Bank, occupation of, 203, 204
West, attitudes to, 178-92
women, 60-71; arrests of, 139; doing men's work, 69; in Kurdistan, 66-8; killed for honour, 64; participation in the workforce, 62; position in Iraq, 186; rights of, 61-2; status of, 2
workforce statistics of Iraq, 87
writers: imprisonment of, 8, 10; wealth of, 19

Yasin, A'ida, 65
Yasin, Sahib, 13

youth organizations, 41
Yusif, Yonadam, 123
Yusuf, Sa'di, 8, 11

al-Za'im, Husni, 35
Zibari, Hushiar, 103